I0132241

Delft
Blue to
Denim
Blue

Delft Blue to Denim Blue

Contemporary Dutch Fashion

edited by **Anneke Smelik**

I.B. TAURIS

LONDON · NEW YORK

Published in 2017 by

I.B.Tauris & Co. Ltd

London • New York

www.ibtauris.com

Copyright text © 2017 Anneke Smelik
The right of Anneke Smelik to be identified as the editor of this work has been asserted by the editor in accordance
with the Copyright, Designs and Patents Act 1988.

Copyright individual chapters © Daniëlle Bruggeman, Maaike Feitsma, Anja Köppchen, Michiel Scheffer, Anneke Smelik,
José Teunissen, Constantin von Maltzahn

All rights reserved. Except for brief quotations in a review, this book, or any part thereof, may not be reproduced, stored in
or introduced into a retrieval system, or transmitted, in any form or by any means, electronic, mechanical, photocopying,
recording or otherwise, without the prior written permission of the publisher.

Every attempt has been made to gain permission for the use of the images in this book. Any omissions will be rectified
in future editions.

References to websites were correct at the time of writing.

Dress Cultures

 ISBN: 978 1 78453 197 3
eISBN: 978 1 83860 834 7
 ePDF: 978 1 83860 835 4

A full CIP record for this book is available from the British Library

A full CIP record is available from the Library of Congress

Library of Congress Catalog Card Number: available

The publication of this book has been made possible by the financial support of NWO,
the Netherlands Organisation for Scientific Research.

Netherlands Organisation
for Scientific Research

Designed and typeset by Christopher Bromley

Contents

Part II: Dutch Firms and Designers

Acknowledgements

Delft Blue to Denim Blue: Contemporary Dutch Fashion is based on a five-year-long research project that took place from 2008 till 2013. It was part of a larger research programme entitled 'Cultural Dynamics', which was generously funded by the Netherlands Organisation for Scientific Research. We are grateful to the many parties that have financially supported this interdisciplinary research project; they enabled the first in-depth insight into the under-researched field of Dutch fashion. Apart from the Netherlands Organisation for Scientific Research, the project was also financially supported by the Radboud University Nijmegen, the University of Amsterdam, ArtEZ Institute of the Arts in Arnhem, and Saxion University of Applied Sciences in Enschede. The project was further co-financed by three private institutions: a fund for Dutch fashion, Meester Koetsier Foundation; the educational fund for the Dutch apparel industry (OOC-fund); and Premsela, the Netherlands Institute for Design and Fashion, which is now part of The New Institute in Rotterdam.

The authors are especially indebted to the late Dany Jacobs for his sharp mind and his unerring support for the research project; without his relentless flair for debate the project would have not advanced as far as it did. We are very sorry he did not live to see the final result of our joint research group.

The authors wish to thank the Dutch fashion designers and companies who were willing to cooperate with us and who opened their archives and histories for our research. Such cooperation was not always easily to be found in the field of Dutch fashion, but it was indispensable for acquiring the necessary data, information and insight. We thank the anonymous peer reviewers for their critical reviews of the manuscript, which have been invaluable for making it a better book. Philippa Brewster at I.B.Tauris receives a special thanks for her belief in this project and for her professional guidance in bringing the book to its publication.

The editor and publisher thank the many rights holders to reproduce copyright material for the images. We are particularly grateful to fashion photographer Peter Stigter, who allowed us access to his wonderful archive. Finally, a big thank you goes out to Roos Leeflang and Marieke Folkers for their dedicated preparation of the manuscript and diligent tracing of the copyrights of the many images in the book. Every effort has been made to trace rights holders, but if any have been inadvertently overlooked the publisher would be pleased to make the necessary arrangements at the first opportunity.

Front cover: Image used for the poster of the exhibition *Gone with the Wind* (2009), Zuiderzee Museum Enkhuizen.

1.

Introduction: The Paradoxes of Dutch Fashion

'[F]ashion lends itself to being an optimal synthetic indicator of a nation's position, amidst memory, mystification, and imaginary.'

—Simona Segre Reinach (2011: 271)

'Today's all-encompassing culture demands that you acquire the ability to change your identity [...] as often, as fast and as efficiently as you change your shirt or your socks.'

—Zygmunt Bauman (2011: 25)

Anneke Smelik

Fashion in the Netherlands includes conceptual designer duo Viktor&Rolf as well as the affordable retailer C&A; it ranges from romantic designer Jan Taminiau to the popular jeans brand G-Star, and from colourful clothes by The People of the Labyrinths to the modernist designs by Alexander van Slobbe. For a country with hardly an established tradition in fashion, Dutch fashion has recently, and perhaps paradoxically, been remarkably successful. An array of designers, brands and businesses, some with international acclaim, shows the fascinating diversity of present-day Dutch fashion. A prominent designer like Iris van Herpen presents her shows in Paris, while Michael van der Ham shows in London and Lucas Ossendrijver works in Paris as the head designer for Lanvin's men's collection.

Delft Blue to Denim Blue: Contemporary Dutch Fashion maps the landscape of Dutch fashion in all its rich variety and dense complexity, both in its successes and its failures. The book is part and parcel of a recent interest in up-and-coming minor countries in the fashion world. The Netherlands is quite a small country that features several successful women's brands, including Supertrash, Just B., Sandwich, Turnover, Claudia Sträter, ˉCoraKemperman and Vanilia, and some luxury men's fashion designers such as Francisco van Benthum, Sjaak Hullekes, and Hans Ubbink. We could not study them all but have carefully selected case studies that we deemed the most relevant for the recent history of Dutch fashion. The case studies do not only feature success stories, but also contain failures and bankruptcies, including recent ones that happened after our research was finished, such as Mexx in December 2014 and ˉCoraKemperman in June 2016. Along with historical chapters and case studies of brands and designers, the present book also discusses the success of jeans in the Netherlands as well as the success of Dutch fashion photographers like Inez Van Lamsweerde and Erwin Olaf. The last chapter takes a peek into the future, by discussing the vanguard of wearable technology with the likes of designers Pauline van Dongen and Bart Hess.

Delft Blue to Denim Blue: Contemporary Dutch Fashion is the result of a large research project that the authors conducted together over five years from 2008 till 2013, financed by an extensive research programme on 'Cultural Dynamics' of the Netherlands Organization for Scientific Research.¹ The aim of the multidisciplinary programme was to study the dynamic role of cultural heritage and the interaction between culture and society past and present, with a strong focus on the issue of 'identity' in times of social and economic crisis. For our project it involved the study of recent Dutch fashion and its relation to national identity, for example in the use of cultural heritage in fashion design. We chose to focus not only on the popular culture of fashion, but also on the cultural dynamics in fashion production and consumption. The present book brings together the results of our joint research.

The underlying idea of *Delft Blue to Denim Blue: Contemporary Dutch Fashion* is that the creative industry of fashion in the Netherlands has increasingly been able to capitalise on a unique mix of playful individualism, organisational innovation and a creative relation to cultural heritage. Because fashion is embedded in cultural values, the volume aims to understand the cultural roots of Dutch fashion in a globalised context. We approach Dutch fashion as a dynamic process that changes over time and as full of contradictions and paradoxes. We use the word 'fashion' in the broad sense of the term, as referring to dress, appearance and style. More specifically, we understand 'style' as something 'that is accepted by a large group at a given time' (Solomon and Rabolt, 2004: 6). The concept of style refers to a way of expressing oneself, which is characteristic for an individual, a period, a 'school', an identifiable group, and possibly even a nation. A style may be a more or less explicit dress code, but mostly we take stylistic codes as a tacit element of a particular culture (Rubinstein, 2001: 14-15).

We have researched Dutch fashion as material culture and as a symbolic system (cf. Kawamura, 2005), but also as a clothes and textile industry. The field of fashion is so interesting because it is part of a commercial industry producing and selling material commodities, while it also entails an intangible system of signification. A dress always has a material quality, whether it is designed by Viktor&Rolf or by C&A. In the first case it may be made of expensive cashmere and embroidered by hand, while an inexpensively bought T-shirt at an international retailer is likely to be made of a cheap mix of fibres. Whether *haute couture* or mass-produced, the dress will have a certain symbolic value in society depending on the age, class, gender or ethnicity of the consumers. Signs and meanings are more often than not created through representations in visual culture, for example in commercials on television or in glossies, or by fashion bloggers. Fashion is thus made of both material things and symbolic signs, produced by individual and collective agents, which all merge through practices of production, consumption, distribution and representation (cf. Rocamora and Smelik, 2016: 2). Our study of Dutch fashion therefore covers a wide terrain, ranging from production and consumption, to material culture, and systems of meaning and signification.

Its innovative contribution to fashion studies lies in opening up the under-researched field of Dutch fashion through the use of interdisciplinary perspectives and methodologies. The interdisciplinary research includes art history, cultural theory, sociology, social economics and human geography. In order to explore diverse styles and manifestations of Dutch fashion, the authors research Dutch fashion in its cultural and historical context, combining historical overviews and theoretical analyses with in-depth case studies. Some chapters

pursue the postwar tradition of Dutch design and fashion and the textile industry, or fashion as a performance of local, global and 'glocal' identity, while other chapters explore fashion as a co-creation between brands and consumers of, for example, ⁻CoraKemperman and Vanilia, or study the effects of globalisation on the organisation of the design and manufacture of fashion in the cases of Mexx and Van Gils.

With this book we hope to show that the Netherlands today creates genuine fashion, not just 'clothing'. The chapters together aim to trace the process of legitimisation of Dutch fashion as a culturally meaningful product. This process is due to changes in external factors, such as the globalisation of the fashion industry; changes of factors internal to the Dutch fashion industry, such as national subsidy or policy instruments, or the creation of national fashion fairs or fashion weeks; or to a changing discourse in verbal and visual representations, such as journals or blogs. Some chapters discuss changes external to the fashion world, for example issues of globalisation in chapter 3 on the Dutch fashion industry, chapter 6 on Dutch denim industry, chapter 7 on Van Gils, chapter 8 on Mexx, and chapter 9 on Mac&Maggie and ⁻CoraKemperman. Other chapters review changes internal to the Dutch clothing and fashion industry, such as chapter 2 on cultural heritage, chapter 10 on Vanilia, chapter 11 on Spijkers en Spijkers, and chapter 14 on wearable technology. Of course, many of those chapters in fact show a mix of external and internal factors, most notably the chapters on Van Gils and Mexx. Other chapters discuss the legitimating discourse that helped to create, develop and strengthen the view of Dutch fashion as 'real' fashion (Janssen, 2006; Van de Peer, 2014). This is particularly strong in chapter 4 on the fashion discourse in Dutch magazines, but can also be found in chapter 5 on global influences on the designs of Oilily, Mac&Maggie and ⁻CoraKemperman, chapter 12 on Dutch fashion photography and chapter 13 on the materialist aesthetics of Viktor&Rolf.

1. (opposite) Two royal dresses by Jan Taminiau for Queen Máxima at the inauguration of Willem-Alexander as King of the Netherlands, 30 April 2013 in Amsterdam.

The three levels – external and internal factors and fashion discourse – have helped the cultural recognition and legitimisation of the field of Dutch fashion (Janssen, 2006). For their research the authors have made use of a wide range of different methods of analysis: archival research of journals and magazines; analysis of clothes and designs in archives and museums; analysis of visual material; archives of firms and chamber of commerce; and extensive interviews with consumers, journalists, shopping assistants, stylists, buyers, designers, producers and managers.

Delft Blue to Denim Blue: Contemporary Dutch Fashion belongs to a wider movement of what Lise Skov and Marie Riegels Melchior describe as 'decentering the study of fashion' (Skov and Melchior, 2011: 133, a special issue of *Fashion Theory* on minor fashion countries). This entails moving attention away from the dominant centres of fashion such as Paris, Milan, London and New York. The present book is part of that development, 'by turning the gaze to small European countries, which, although unquestionably belonging to "the West", have historically been marginal to the centralised dynamics of fashion' (ibid.). José Teunissen argues that there has been an increased interest in different national fashion styles, which resulted in a proliferation of national fashion weeks and new fashion centres since the 1980s (Teunissen, 2005). As Lise Skov puts it, 'fashion production has been split between a globalised clothing industry, which tends towards extreme centralisation, and localised designer fashion sectors, acting as intermediaries between international suppliers and national events, media, and public' (Skov, 2011: 138). Due to globalisation, questions of individual, social or even national identity are increasingly urgent, and a small country like the Netherlands is no exception to this development.

The very concept of 'identity' is full of ambivalences and paradoxes. One of the paradoxes of our research lies in opening up the field of Dutch fashion, which assumes the possibility of the qualifier 'Dutch', while we

2. A billboard for G-Star at Waterloo Square in Amsterdam, 2006.

simultaneously do not believe in a given national style. By the term 'identity' we refer to an *idealised* construction of certain characteristics that change over time. Yet, in spite of, or perhaps because of, this definition, in our joint research project on Dutch fashion we have fiercely debated the complicated issue of a possible national identity in fashion. In discussing the particular characteristics of Dutch designers and firms, but also the question of a specific Dutch style in dressing, or in trading or retailing, we have come up against the difficulties of thinking through identity in all of its complexity. From an individual preference to collective trends, from the local to the global, and wavering between post-modern flexibility and sociological identification, we have sometimes embraced identity as a productive concept for understanding Dutch fashion, and at other times relegated it to the trash bin of modernity. This introduction traces some of the discussions on the complicated relation between identity and fashion.

Identity: A Dress Rehearsal

'Identity' is a slippery term. As Brubaker and Cooper put it: 'Identity [...] tends to mean too much [...], too little [...], or nothing at all' (2000: 1). One of the complications of the term is that it refers both to individual and collective identity, i.e. to self and group – as Georg Simmel pointed out for fashion as early as 1904. In our book we follow Stephanie Lawler's claim that 'identity needs to be understood not as belonging "within" the individual person, but as produced between persons and within social relations' (2008: 8). In other words, identity is always relational or 'networked' (Smelik, 2006: 155). The question of 'who I am' is never far removed from the question 'who we are'. Lawler emphasises the interdependence between individual identity and the social world: '"Without you I'm nothing": without a nexus of others, none of us could be "who we are"' (2008: 8). We will come back to this important insight when discussing the relation between the global and the local in more detail below.

As Lawler points out, there is a paradox at the heart of the concept of identity. The very etymology of the word identity – from Latin *idem* – suggests that it refers to 'sameness', in the way in which people experience how they are identical to themselves but also how they belong to the same group, ranging from the local choir or football club, a nation, or to a global subculture like hipsters, skaters or emos (Muggleton, 2000; Stahl, 2003). At the same time the term identity also refers to 'difference', that is, to the way in which people differ from each other. They are, or at least perceive themselves as, unique individuals. While this simultaneous

sameness and difference already comprises a paradox in itself, Zygmunt Bauman pushes the argument even further. He points to the paradox of contemporary 'liquid' modernity, where 'To be an individual means to be *like* everyone else in the crowd' (Bauman, 2005: 16, original emphasis). In other words, he refers to the contemporary phenomenon that sameness and difference are eroding in a globalised world.

As a result of social fragmentation and changing structures of modernity, identity is increasingly considered to be constructed, fluid and multiple, without an essential core (Sim, 1998: 367; Bauman, 2000: 82-83; Lipovetsky, 2005: 64). This take on identity as unstable and fluctuating has become quite dominant in social and cultural theory in the past decades. Brubaker and Cooper refer to this view of identity as 'weak' or 'soft', as opposed to the 'strong' or 'hard' view that preserves a 'common-sense meaning' of the term identity with an emphasis on sameness, homogeneity and group boundedness (2000: 10). Sociologists have tended to understand groups also in those 'weak' terms as temporary or virtual communities, by relating brand identities to concepts like 'neo-tribes' or 'communities lite' (Polhemus, 1994; Maffesoli, 1996; Duyvendak and Hurenkamp, 2004). In order to 'unbundle the thick tangle of meanings that have accumulated around the term "identity",' Brubaker and Cooper propose instead a 'processual, active term': identification (2000: 14). The advantage of the term 'identification' is that it implies agency, an act of forming connections with others, whether short-lived or more lasting. As we shall see below, the Dutch government has also introduced this term in order to produce a more open and inclusive understanding of identity.

Rather than pursuing theoretical debates on identity, in the context of the topic of this book we further explore the work of sociologists who have written on identity in relation to consumption and fashion (see Bruggeman, 2014 for a sustained discussion of this issue). In this book we understand the practice of fashion as one of the myriad ways of (re)producing individual as well as collective identity. Gilles Lipovetsky has argued that 'hypermodernity', as an extension of post-modernity, is a liberal society that is characterised by 'movement, fluidity and flexibility' and dominated by the logic of fashion and consumption (2005: 11-12). The dynamics of fashion provides autonomous and mobile individuals 'with fluctuating personality and tastes' (Lipovetsky, 1994: 148-49). Zygmunt Bauman has also put forward the focus on consumption as a way of constructing contemporary identity. In *Liquid Modernity* he discusses the ways in which individuals choose social roles through consumption instead of being '"born into" their identities' (2000: 32). As this development has led to an 'intrinsic volatility and unfixity of all or most identities' (Bauman, 2000: 83), he argues, like Lipovetsky, that consumption potentially offers an answer to the contemporary quest for identity. He mentions specifically fashion as providing material tools for shopping around in the mall or supermarket to put together one's 'liquid' identity (Bauman, 2000: 82-83).The famous art work *I shop therefore I am*, made by American conceptual artist Barbara Kruger in 1987, sums up the predicament of contemporary individuals: by smashing up Descartes' philosophical adage 'I think therefore I am' into a contemporary slogan she ironically unravels the importance of commercial consumption for forming and boosting our (post)modern identity. A few decades later, Bauman expands: 'Fullness of consumer enjoyment means fullness of life. I shop therefore I am.' (Bauman, 2013: 60).

Consuming, whether it is food, gadgets, technologies, accessories or clothes, allows people to construct and perform their liquid identity. Our identity, clothed in fashionable dress, can thus be compared to karaoke; it is borrowed, copied and pasted (Smelik, 2011: 81). Bauman criticises the way in which 'Today's all-encompassing culture demands that you acquire the ability to change your identity [...] as often, as fast and as efficiently as you change your shirt or your socks', to quote one of the mottos for this chapter (2000: 87). Whether it is an illusionary freedom that Bauman deplores, or a sign of a liberating process of democratisation that Lipovetsky welcomes, they share the idea that identities can be constructed through commodities. Consumption is indeed 'one of the most significant means through which [...] contemporary individualism is developed and articulated' (Hill, 2005: 67). Fashion plays a pivotal role in shaping both individual and collective identities within the social-cultural power structures of today's consumer society. While some fashion theorists refer to the active 'construction and articulation of our social identities' in terms of categories such as gender, sexuality, social status, or age (Davis, 1992: 16), others suggest that the consumption of 'cultural goods, such as fashionable clothing, performs an increasingly important role in the construction of personal identity' (Crane, 2000: 11).

Of course, there are many more ways of constructing an individual and social self, but within the context of fashion studies the focus has been on consumption and on the practice of dressing. Importantly, consumption is not necessarily passive nor should we understand people as mere dupes of consumer society. Judith Butler (1990) comprehends identity as an embodied practice that needs to be reinvented on a daily basis, even in its complex aspects such as gender or ethnicity. Every day again we perform who we are, shifting among different roles such as teacher, colleague, mother, friend, lover, and so on. As Daniëlle Bruggeman (2014) has argued, fashion's material tools and dressing the physical body are both essential to the performance of identity in its many facets. Entwistle and Wilson (2003) accentuate the role of human agency in the ways in which we construct our individual and social self through dressing. They claim that the body is not a submissive object to be draped in accordance with the dictates of the social or cultural field, but that dressing is an active embodied practice. The bodily practice of

3. Viktor&Rolf, couture collection (S/S 2015), inspired by Vincent van Gogh's paintings and made with VLISCO's fabrics.

dressing is thus a dynamic construction or performance of identity. To quote Laura Bovone, 'we dress our identity' (Bovone, 2012: 78). We can therefore perhaps best understand identity as a 'continuous dress rehearsal' (Smelik, 2011: 82).

In the next section we turn to the issue of national identity. One of the ways in which fashion can contribute to performing both an individual self and a social self is by expressing a particular cultural tradition or national heritage. As we will see below, the cultural past is one of the shops in the mall where we construct our national identity.

The Rise of Dutch Fashion

Viktor&Rolf's collection of Spring 2015 was inspired by two Dutch traditions: the paintings of Vincent van Gogh and the fabrics of Vlisco. The buoyant pastel colours of van Gogh found their way into the floral prints of the dresses that somehow moved into 3D with outrageous hemlines pointing in all directions. Vlisco is a global design house that introduced premium Dutch wax print design to West Africa. It was established in 1846 in the Dutch city of Helmond. Hand-printed textiles formed the basis for the initial production and sales of Vlisco fabrics in the Netherlands and Europe. Today Vlisco is the market leader in African prints designed and produced through a unique process combining Indonesian batik, Dutch design and African heritage. Viktor&Rolf's Spring collection of 2015 thus brings together contemporary Dutch design with an honoured heritage of Dutch painting and an age-old tradition of wax prints in a globalised context. The use of Dutch national cultural heritage in contemporary fashion is quite a new development and in our book we trace its manifold origins. To that end, we will here give a brief overview of Dutch fashion and its historical context in the past fifty years.

The postwar period in Dutch fashion history is closely related to the societal rebellion that started in the 1960s, after the smug security of the 1950s (Schuyt and Taverne, 2004). The Netherlands were particularly affected by the youth culture in the sixties of the last century, leading to a highly liberal reputation that it still enjoys today as a permissive country that allows soft drugs, regulates prostitution, was among the first to have liberalised abortion as well as euthanasia laws, and introduced gay marriage as early as in 1998. As Jos de Beus writes about the Netherlands: 'In the peaceful and prosperous years between 1945 and 1980 its self-image used to be self-evident, satisfied and relaxed, on the verge of post-national ethos' (De Beus, 1996: 182). In the Netherlands the cult of individualism seems particularly strong compared to neighbouring countries, which may be partly due to the effects of sustained secularisation and the consequent demise of the religious and political organisation of the country in the former 'pillars' of Protestants, Catholics and Socialists (Righart, 1995).

One of the questions here is whether Dutch fashion embraced the democratic ideal of street and youth culture because it fitted smoothly with its burgher roots of equality, soberness and informality, or that this period can rather be seen as an overthrowing of those typical Dutch qualities in a search for rebellion and spectacle. As we will see in chapter 6, on jeans, the earlier egalitarian ideals are still persistent in contemporary fashion, but as Daniëlle Bruggeman shows in her chapter on fashion photography there is also a post-modern play in the blurring borders between art and fashion. A key question is the continuing influence of Dutch modernism, which was the dominant style in the art academies for decades, on fashion design. As both José Teunissen and Maaike Feitsma argue in this book, some Dutch fashion designers maintain the modernist idea of conceptuality and abstraction. Other chapters, on the contrary, discuss designers who bring the modernist tradition into a post-modern play of pastiche and performance, as we see in the Spring collection of 2015 by Viktor&Rolf.

José Teunissen and Michiel Scheffer have researched the development of Dutch fashion and the apparel industry in the last fifty years, a period in which Dutch fashion design started to build an international reputation. In the sixties the Dutch fashion industry and retail was dominated by mostly Catholic (C&A, P&C, Kreijmborg, Hunkemöller, Van Gils) and Jewish firms (Bijenkorf, Bonneterie, Hollandia Kattenburg, McGregor). In the seventies the industry broadened its focus from families to youth (e.g. Clockhouse in C&A, Mac&Maggie owned by P&C, and for men's clothes Van Gils). Generally, fashion turnover became much faster. Influential fashion boutiques emerged (e.g. Fong Leng, Jan Jansen, Puck&Hans). In the eighties and early nineties brand firms like Oilily, Soap Studio, ⁻CoraKemperman and Mexx came into existence. The nineties also saw the international recognition of Dutch modernism with firms including G-sus and G-Star, and designers such as Marlies Dekkers, Viktor&Rolf, Spijkers en Spijkers and Alexander van Slobbe. In the first decade of this century new designers came to the fore, for example the afore-mentioned Iris van Herpen, Michael van der Ham, Lucas Ossendrijver and Jan Taminiau. This period of economic crisis saw the bankruptcy of several brands like Mexx and Miss Etam, but also saw the rising success of a woman's brand, Vanilia. A new development is eco-fashion, for example by Monique van Heist or Studio Jux, or the recycling business Texperium.

The construction of national identities has been a relatively new phenomenon, coinciding with the emergence of modernism at the end of the nineteenth century (Anderson, 2006 [1983]), but in fashion this phenomenon is even more recent. It is only since about two decades that anything like a discourse on Dutch fashion identity has emerged (Teunissen and van Zijl, 2000). For a long time fashion in the Netherlands was basically a French invention and monopoly, with the dominance of Paris as the capital of fashion lasting well into the sixties of the twentieth century. The fashion system then radically changed through what Lipovetsky calls 'the democratic revolution of ready-to-wear' (1994: 88 ff). Fashion moved from haute couture to popular culture, and back again, until the borders between those two previously separate realms were eroded. Fashion was no longer determined by the major French couturiers, because street cultures launched new fashions, resulting in diversity and freedom of styles. Fashion thus changed from a top-down to a bottom-up system. This development also allowed for the emergence of other fashion centres (McDowell, 2000; Teunissen, 2005; Beard, 2011) as well as the rise of small yet successful companies in northern European countries for example Scandinavia, Germany and the Netherlands.

Indeed, in recent years, several small countries that traditionally are not regarded as fashion centres have strived to develop a 'national' fashion identity. Lise Skov (2011) refers to this phenomenon as the 'fashion dream of small nations' (compare for example on Belgian fashion, Windels 2001, and Bernheim 2015; and on Scandinavian fashion, Gundtoft, 2013). Small nations like the Nether-lands also have such dreams, partly because fashion increasingly plays an important role in national policies to endorse the creative industries as a way of boosting an economy in crisis after the deindustrialisation of the 1970s and 1980s (cf. Melchior 2011 on a similar development for Danish fashion). To that end, the Netherlands has initiated a governmental innovation network for the creative industries in 2012, CLICK NL, for which José Teunissen chairs the network for fashion. Alison Goodrum (2005) has argued that the creative industries have indeed become active producers of national identity. The creative industries in general have been used as a branding tool for cities and countries (Hartley et al., 2012; Hesmond-halgh, 2013); compare slogans like 'I AMsterdam', which is positioned in giant letters in front of the Rijksmuseum in Amsterdam. According to Simona Segre Reinach fashion has played a particular role in producing a national position in the global exchange of goods: 'Fashion is not just making clothes, but also an attribute that nations no longer seem to be able to do without' (2011: 270). As fashion is both a material commodity and an immaterial product it can evoke 'fresh imaginaries' (ibid.: 271). Fashion can thus function as the 'ambassador of a country' (ibid.: 270). The branding of Amsterdam as the new denim city, as explored in chapter 6, shows how fashion plays a crucial role in creating the image not only of an individual person but also of a city or country.

4. Marlies Dekkers, 'So Dutch' (2007).

Of Clogs, Dykes, and Tulips: Dutch Cultural Heritage

Viktor&Rolf's dresses in Vlisco wax prints and floral van Gogh colours and designs are not the only example of employing Dutch cultural heritage in fashion. A few years before, Viktor&Rolf's collection of winter 2007 was inspired by Dutch traditional costume: fisherman's trousers, pleated skirts and clogs with high heels (see chapter 2). The clogs were painted in a Delft blue colour and with techniques from folk traditions, but were all printed with the V&R logo (fig. 11). In the same year lingerie designer Marlies Dekkers held a fashion show in Paris, called *So Dutch* (2007) for which the models were adorned with typical elements of Dutch national heritage, such as little clogs inscribed with the text 'Holland', miniature windmills, Delft Blue prints and folkloric crafted hats. Alexander van Slobbe designed porcelain 'pearls', inspired not only by *The Girl with a Pearl Earring* by the Dutch painter Johannes Vermeer, but also motivated and made by the oldest factory in Holland, Royal Tichelaar Makkum, producing earthenware objects since 1572 (fig. 16). These examples all show a rather tongue-in-cheek if not ironical approach to Dutch cultural heritage and thus confirm Lise Skov's remark that 'The new demand is that designers engage with their national culture and dress tradition, but in such a way that it can be attractive to outsiders' (Skov, 2011: 149).

In trying to grapple with 'the problem of defining national dress', Jennifer Craik has suggested the use of cultural heritage as a source of national identity (2009: 410). Another salient Dutch example is the fashion exhibition *Blown by the Wind* in 2009 that serves as the cover image for this book.[2] This exhibition was set up in the Zuiderzee Museum, which collects objects and costumes from Dutch heritage and is situated in a small fisherman's village. The Zuiderzee used to be a dangerous sea gnawing away at the land below sea-level, but has now become a lake tamed by a great dyke built in

5. A fashion picture in the style of Johannes Vermeer. Clothes by The People of the Labyrinths, collection 'The Golden Age' (A/W, 2005–6).

the 1930s. The exhibition plays heavily on the Dutch heritage of the struggle against the sea, mediating elements of tradition and folklore as an attractive spectacle. Objects, materials, silhouettes, and images refer to the wind, sea, dykes, the clouds in the Dutch sky and the straight lines of the Dutch landscape. There are also references to the harshness of Dutch Calvinism with its emphasis on black and sober clothes, to the colours used by Dutch modernist painters like van Gogh and Breitner, and to specific Dutch icons like Vermeer's *Girl with the Pearl Earring*.

Dutch designers were asked to design clothes based on folkloristic patterns, techniques, colours, clothes and jewellery from specific regions of the Netherlands. Some of these images from the past had already entered Dutch high fashion, such as the reuse of patterns and materials from Dutch traditional costumes in Viktor&Rolf's fashion collection of 2007, including the wooden clogs with high heels. Klavers van Engelen reworked the 'millstone' collar, traditionally made of folds of white fine lace and worn by Dutch rich burghers in the seventeenth century, by placing the folds in the middle of a dress or on top of a T-shirt. Francisco van Benthum and Alexander van Slobbe have used the shape of traditional wide fisherman's trousers or farmer's prints to create new silhouettes for men's wear.

Another example of using Dutch heritage as a source of inspiration is the winter collection 'The Golden

Age' (2005) by the designer duo De Rooij and Démoed of the colourful label The People of the Labyrinths (see the profile in chapter 9). They asked the famous Dutch photographer Erwin Olaf to photograph this collection. Both the designers and the photographer were inspired by the Dutch masters of the Golden Age in the seventeenth century, like Rembrandt van Rijn, Jan Steen, and as in this picture, by Johannes Vermeer. The influence of the paintings can be detected in the rich colours, prints and fabrics of the clothes, but also in the composition and especially the lighting of the picture. The image is a modern amalgam of several paintings that Vermeer made of his favourite subject: a pensive or concentrated woman standing in a rather empty space, with the light coming from the window on the left.

In referring back to Dutch heritage all these designers contribute to the idea that people share of the Netherlands and what it stands for. They thus actively participate in the ongoing project of the discursive production of what the Netherlands means, which partly comes into being through their designs, catwalk shows and in their visual imagery. Garments, then, are not merely clothing, but symbolise Dutch identity and traditions. Traditions are, however, not simply a given. As Sandra Niessen explains, 'tradition, by definition, is unchanging, immutable and faithful to some authentic past time, even though the needs of the times are always changing, and similarly the content of "tradition" is also changing' (1998: 129). The traditions may come from the past, but in fact refer to the constantly mutating reality of today. In other words, the use of cultural heritage in Dutch fashion points to the famous notion of an 'invention of tradition' that the historian Eric Hobsbawm introduced (Hobsbawm & Ranger, 1983), rather than to an immutable or faithful rendering of past techniques, materials or designs.

The Vexed Issue of National Fashion Identity

The use of objects, artefacts and symbols for shaping and expressing a certain idea or meaning of nationality, shows both the imaginary character of national identity (Anderson, 1983), but also the importance of what Michael Billig (1995) has called 'banal nationalism'; it is in the use of everyday objects, habits and rituals that a certain nationalism finds its expression. Billig defines it as follows: 'The term banal nationalism is introduced to cover the ideological habits which enable the established nations of the West to be reproduced. [...] Daily, the nation is indicated, or "flagged", in the lives of its citizenry' (1995: 6). There is thus a continual reminding of one's nationhood by means of everyday representations of the nation, which constructs an imagined sense of national solidarity. Billig notes that although today globalisation has overtaken nationalism, a reminder is still necessary in order to reproduce ideas and experiences of nationhood. Taking Billig's notion of banal nationalism to British fashion, together with Pierre Bourdieu's notion of 'habitus', Alice Goodrum understands national identity in relation to clothing as a 'habitualised form of national belonging' (Goodrum, 2005: 70). According to her, these 'banal' mechanisms not only mobilise versions of nationhood, but are also invested with the power to actually shape these identifications. Fashion design as well as clothing habits can thus function as a largely unacknowledged yet significant force to build and construct sentiments of nationality.

The interest in and focus on a specific national context in which Dutch fashion designers and brands operate is part of a broader development where nationalism flourishes alongside globalisation, or 'cosmopolitanism' as sociologist Ulrich Beck calls it. This indicates an era in which 'the distinctions between national and international, local and global, us and them, lose their sharp contours' (Beck 2007: 287). Yet, in spite of advancing globalisation or cosmopolitanism, or perhaps because of it, in recent years the issue of 'national identity' has become an important topic in academia as well as on the political agenda in the Netherlands. One of the paradoxes of Dutch national identity is that it was traditionally anchored in an open society with an international outlook and religious tolerance, things which became threatened by globalisation and European integration and have now become 'a thing of the past' (De Beus, 1996: 182). This has instigated a new search for 'who we are' in times of cosmopolitanism. The report *Identification with the Netherlands* from 2007 by the Dutch Scientific Council for Government Policy (WRR) shows that this search is related to several social-cultural developments such as the unification of Europe, globalisation, individualisation, and multiculturalism (WRR, 2007: 11). As the report demonstrates, the concept of national identity consists of many layers that move from spatial, territorial understandings to conceptions of national identity as a cultural, symbolic and imaginary construction (ibid.: 45). Although 'national identity' has become a popular, if not populist, notion, it is quite a complex term in itself. By using the term 'identification' the Council aims to open up identity as an active way of creating connections with others. National identity is one of the many connections that form a group identity. Identity is thus understood as a networked category that is always multiple and inclusive.

To come back to the example of the exhibition *Blown by the Wind*, we can see how Dutch fashion designs here call for identification with the Netherlands. They do so in material and immaterial ways. Cultural heritage belongs both to the realm of material objects and to imagery or imagination: Viktor&Rolf's Dutch clogs with high heels are a heavy, wooden token of Dutch tradition, but at the same time they conjure up ideological images of 'Dutchness'. Erwin Olaf's updated version of a painting by Johannes Vermeer in the series 'The Golden Age' refers to the venerable era of the Dutch masters in the history of painting. *Blown by the*

Wind not only evokes a heroic past of the Dutch struggle against the sea, but also plays into a heated debate about Dutch identity at a time when it is perceived to be under threat from globalisation and multiculturalism. The identification with Dutchness is evoked by iconic and quite stereotypical images or objects, but the fashion designs use those clichés to question the identification with the nation. The creative and commercial use of heritage in fashion can serve the political interests of the present. In this case, the manufacturing of fashion by way of cultural heritage evokes a certain nostalgia for a past and perhaps even an ideology like nationalism, but also playfully questions the notion of a stable Dutch identity, thus inviting critical self-reflection.

The point here is that fashion does not merely evoke a national past, but also engages cultural heritage as an image, performance or spectacle with relevant meanings for today's society. With regard to fashion, the understanding of national identity in terms of a construction of cultural imaginations is therefore quite productive. In this respect it is important, as Stuart Hall claims, 'to remember that the nation-state is both a political and territorial entity, *and* what Benedict Anderson has called "an imagined community"' (2002: 74, original emphasis). Hall stresses the discursive practice of the formation of a national identity, by reflecting on the crucial role that specific objects, symbols and representations play in that process. He continues: 'In fact, what the nation "means" is an ongoing project, under constant reconstruction. We come to know its meaning partly *through* the objects and artefacts which have been made to stand for and symbolise its essential values. Its meaning is constituted *within*, not above or outside representation' (2002: 74, original emphasis). Fashion is then one of the ways in which national identity is discursively produced and constantly reconstructed.

A cultural perspective of national identity opens up an understanding of the role that commodified objects of fashion as well as fashion images may play in relation to a national identity. In fashion studies, Alison Goodrum has defined national identity as follows: 'National identity may be conceived as a confection of selective memories' (2005: 62). Amy de la Haye adds the commercial aspect: 'national identity offers a route to product differentiation and makes good business sense' (1996: 11-12). Difference is indeed a crucial aspect today; it is, in the words of Goodrum, 'the watchword of the postmodern marketplace' (2005: 21). This aspect goes hand in hand with Goodrum's idea that national identity in fashion is 'a confection of selective memories' being recognisable not only for the local inhabitants but also for the international consumer market (2005: 62).

The question then is how a small country like the Netherlands positions itself in the global marketplace. Fashion may be '[t]ied to a "national fabric",' but 'fashion is always traveling and ultimately aims at a global market', as Paulicelli and Clark argue (2009: 2). In other words, the focus on the global is essential to fashion. Marie Riegels Melchior points out that 'in order to increase market share and sales figures in a highly competitive international market, the articulation of cultural distinctiveness has become a pivotal business strategy for many fashion brands and local fashion industries' (2010: 58). The Dutch fashion industry is no exception to this dynamics. In that respect, it may be helpful to turn to the term that Melchior, Skov and Csaba (2011) have introduced in relation to thinking through the concept of national identity, namely 'cosmopolitan nationalism'. This concept suggests that the nation functions as a resource that can be reinvented within a globalised world. Cosmopolitan nationalism involves an interpretation and transformation of cultural heritage rather than the use of it in its original form. Similarly, Melchior argues that it 'enables fashion designers to use their awareness of cultural heritage for creative inspiration, enabling openness towards others and the negotiation of contradictory cultural experiences'

(Melchior, 2010: 59). As we show in chapter 5 on Oilily and ¯CoraKemperman and chapter 8 on Mexx, in Dutch fashion, too, we can find such a negotiation of the contradictory relations between the local and the global, often resulting in 'glocal' designs embracing multiple cultural sources of inspiration.

Local, Global and 'Glocal'

Fashion is generally viewed as a Western phenomenon, but it operates in global flows of consumerist capitalism and thus commodifies objects from a wide variety of local traditions and cultures (Paulicelli and Clark, 2009). In *Global Fashion, Local Tradition*, José Teunissen claims that Western countries have been fascinated by non-Western items of clothing in different time periods, but that since the 1980s 'major companies and commercial brands have started to exploit their national identity' (Teunissen, 2005: 17). The multiplication of new fashion centres has been further enhanced by globalisation, the Internet and the emergence of the creative economy. The growth of creative industries is connected to the rising importance of design and style innovation in economies where most of the basic needs have been fulfilled. Economic competition therefore leads to increasing product differentiation, which in turn requires ever larger diversity (Lipovetsky, 1994; Jacobs 2013).

One way of achieving product differentiation is to tap into local clothing styles and crafts for inspiration. This trend is reinforced by a growing preoccupation with local roots in times of globalisation (Teunissen, 2005). In the field of creative design and innovation we therefore perceive at the supply level as well as the demand level a need for product differentiation in which local identities play an important role. Even when identities are idealised and temporary constructions, designers take local fashion as raw material for a reconstruction and deconstruction of styles. On the demand side styles are related to (sometimes transnational) group identities beyond the local culture. Most fashion firms try to address several of these other identities, while also referring to and profiting from local roots, thus establishing a look that is both global and local at the same time. Due to globalisation 'diverse and remote cultures have become accessible, as signs and commodities' (Barker, 2008: 159). As Daniëlle Bruggeman (2014) has argued, the current interest of Western countries in their own local, national roots due to globalisation, cannot be separated from a fascination for 'cultural otherness' and for 'other' local traditions. The global flows of capitalist modernity thus lead to a renewed interest in the local, i.e. local or national identity and traditions. Although globalisation has often been seen as a synonym for cultural imperialism where one nation's values are imposed onto others, Hesmondhalgh claims that globalisation generates heterogeneity rather than universal sameness (2013: 275). While consumerist global flows may, at the same time, cause a process of cultural homogenisation, 'mechanisms of fragmentation, heterogenisation and hybridity are also at work' (Barker, 2008: 164). To give an example: as we show in chapter 5, 'Vivid Colours', the brand Oilily takes ethnic motifs and patterns from colourful Dutch regional dress as well as from other countries far away, resulting in a hybrid mix of both global and local influences.

The sociologist Roland Robertson refers to this process as 'glocalisation', a concept that he popularised after adopting it from marketing and business discourse. He uses this term to articulate the dynamics in which the global and the local are reciprocally constituted as 'mutually "interpenetrating" principles' (Robertson, 1995: 30). This is evidently essential to the formation of local, national identities as their meanings are always constructed in relation to the global flows that introduce us to local 'otherness'. Here, we may recall Lawler's words 'Without you I'm nothing' (2008: 8). She stresses the importance of acknowledging the complex interdependency between self and other, which has usually

been suppressed in the Western view of the individual. As chapter 5 analyses in more detail, the interaction with 'other' local traditions, and a fascination for cultural 'otherness' is not only a phenomenon of contemporary processes of globalisation. Oilily may take motifs and patterns from Dutch regional dress, but what may seem 'typical' if not folkloric Dutch can in fact be traced back to the use of Indian chintz in colonial times, when Western trading companies were travelling around the world, importing products and non-Western clothing styles from the Orient (Niessen, 2005).

Glocalisation is fundamental to the formation of local identities, because the idea of the local is produced within and by globalising discourses (Barker, 2008: 164). Assimilating the global 'other' into the local is a crucial aspect for national identity as, according to Barker, it is 'unifying cultural diversity' (ibid.: 164; 260). Fashion partakes in the creation of this unifying process. Goodrum argues that 'the apparently straightforward and economically driven process to do with the globalisation of fashion is, in fact, a far more culturally nuanced and locally embedded encounter than has previously been suggested' (2005: 12). According to her, due to globalisation the national characteristics of fashion become increasingly questionable and questioned.

The paradox of globalisation gives rise to an increased interest in the local roots of Western (fashion) countries, while simultaneously offering objects, commodities and traditions from local cultures from elsewhere. As we show in our analysis of Oilily and ⁻CoraKemperman in chapter 5 and of Mexx in chapter 8, the global and the local are inextricably interconnected. Our 'own' local, national roots (a 'Dutch self') and our 'others' (other nations, cultures, traditions, symbols, commodities, fashions, etc.) are necessarily involved in a reciprocal interplay. For example, in the chapter on jeanswear, Maaike Feitsma and Anneke Smelik explain how an American icon has been appropriated in the Netherlands into something that is called 'Dutch denim'.

These examples show that it is imperative to take into account the complex relationship with globalisation when researching the ways in which Dutch fashion brands and designers operate within their particular national and international context.

Delft Blue to Denim Blue

The title of our book is inspired by Maaike Feitsma's and Anneke Smelik's chapter on 'Dutch Denim' and indicates our focus on contemporary changes and developments in Dutch fashion. The title also refers to the fact that we have encountered cultural 'otherness' at the very heart of Dutch culture. Dearly valued icons of Dutch culture, such as Delft blue earthenware, regional dress, and even the famous tulip fields, derive, in fact, from elsewhere. Delft Blue was adapted from Chinese porcelain, while the tulips flourishing in the sandy grounds of the Dutch dunes were imported from Turkey. These paradoxical cultural dynamics play a central part in contemporary Dutch fashion. From the discussion in this Introduction it follows that Dutch fashion by necessity entails a paradox, as it inevitably moves between the local and the global, or wavers between an embarrassed denial of national identity and an unabashed promotion of 'Dutchness'. Dutch fashion thus pertains simultaneously to a 'weak' and 'strong' under-standing of identity (Brubaker and Cooper, 2000).

Let us tease out some of the paradoxes that we found in Dutch fashion. In chapter 2, José Teunissen argues that the Dutch case is unique because of a certain perception of a national style that implies the projection of continuity in style from Calvinism to Modernism; a style that can be described as sober and austere. The strong influence of modernism in Dutch design, from classical artists like Mondrian and Rietveld to today's conceptual designers such as Droog Design, also had its impact on Dutch fashion, for example in the classical modernism of Frans Molenaar but also in

the conceptual fashion of Viktor&Rolf. This particular cultural outlook combined open-mindedness and a strong affinity for artistic experiment on the one hand, with a recurrent reserve towards French fashion and frivolity on the other hand. However, modernist rigour is matched by post-modern play in Dutch fashion. While José Teunissen argues that Viktor&Rolf are paragons of modernism, Anneke Smelik (2014) and Daniëlle Bruggeman (2014) situate the designer duo within a post-modern aesthetics of play, pastiche, and performance. Chapter 14 presents another example of post-modern forms by exploring the extravagance of contemporary designers including Iris van Herpen, Bart Hess, and Pauline van Dongen, who embrace technology as well as a return to craftsmanship. As Constantin von Maltzahn argues in chapter 11, the designs of the twin sisters Truus and Riet Spijkers take its cues from both realms. He shows how many of their products are inspired by modernist aesthetics on the one hand, especially when it comes to graphic composition, use of patterns and fields of colour. On the other hand, the vibrancy and edgy appearance of their collections evidences a more playful and experimental stance that is mainly driven by the way the Dutch fashion narrative is inflected by various cultural influences.

In following Maaike Feitsma's research (2014), the chapter 'Vivid Colours' nuances the cliché of Dutch Calvinist and modernist sobriety in digging up an alternative historical line in Dutch fashion that abounds in colourful clothes, continuing to the present day with designer firms like Oilily and ¯CoraKemperman, and baroque if not carnivalesque designers such as The People of the Labyrinths and Bas Kosters. In chapter 12 Daniëlle Bruggeman pursues the paradox of repre-senting identity in fashion photography, as simulta-neously freezing it into solid blocks of social identity and releasing it into flux and fluidity. Another kind of paradox is revealed by Anja Köppchen's research on geographical distance between design, which takes place

6. Spijkers en Spijkers, V-dress for beer brand Bavaria for the occasion of the UEFA European Championship (2012).

in the Netherlands, and manufacture, which takes place in Eastern Europe, North Africa and Asia. She claims that the geographical distance between design and production has resulted in a certain freedom of Dutch fashion design, while it also points to the interrelation between the local and the global.

In this book we argue that a Dutch national style is always shot through with cultural hybridity. Rather than pursuing a myth of a national fashion identity within an international market, we have explored a 'cosmopolitan nationalism' (Beck, 2007; Melchior, Skov and Csaba, 2011), that is, the relation between national and transnational connotations of fashion in times of globalisation. The results from our interdisciplinary research over the past years offer a rich, complex and dynamic picture of Dutch fashion.

To conclude the theoretical part of this Introduction, let us turn to the world of sports because nothing stirs the national imagination as much as football. In 2012 the design duo Spijkers en Spijkers created an orange (Orange being the name of the Dutch royal family) and blue dress, lined with the colours of the Dutch flag, red, white and blue, and with a deep V-neck – 'for Victory'. It was meant for female fans of the Dutch football team and was commissioned by the beer brand Bavaria for the European Cup. The dress sold for a mere €9.99 including six bottles of beer, and became an overnight success.

This happy liaison between fashion and football reveals the consumeristic approach to national identity in contemporary society. The combination of a bottle of Dutch beer, a dress in the colours of the nation, and support for the national football team, was overexposed in the media, passionately embraced, yet short-lived. Once the Dutch football team was out of the game, the identification with Dutchness quickly turned from 'strong' to 'weak' and the orange dresses could be put back in the closet.

The Contents of the Book

As mentioned above *Delft Blue to Denim Blue: Contemporary Dutch Fashion* is the joint result of a large research project that took place from 2008 to 2013. It was largely funded by The Netherlands Organisation for Scientific Research. The project entailed an interdisciplinary cooperation between scholars from different knowledge institutions, including Anneke Smelik at the Radboud University Nijmegen, the late Dany Jacobs at the University of Amsterdam, José Teunissen at the fashion department of ArtEZ Institute of the Arts in Arnhem, and Michiel Scheffer at the textile department of Saxion University of Applied Sciences in Enschede. The project was co-financed by a fund for Dutch fashion, Meester Koetsier Foundation; the educational fund for the Dutch confection industry (OOC-fund); and Premsela, the Netherlands Institute for Design and Fashion that is now part of The New Institute in Rotterdam. The project resulted in four dissertations by Daniëlle Bruggeman, Maaike Feitsma, Anja Köppchen and Constantin-Felix von Maltzahn.[3]

We have met regularly once or twice a month for five years, discussing and debating the results of our research on contemporary Dutch fashion. Because of this collective experience, the present book is conceived and written more like a monograph than an edited volume. All chapters have been read and commented upon by all authors and have been discussed in several group sessions. The book brings together the most salient results of our joint research project. The theoretical and methodological background is coherent and sustained throughout the different subjects and cases in the chapters. The volume is interdisciplinary in bringing together different approaches: from the myths and narratives of Dutch fashion, via fashion as a performance of identity, and fashion as a form of co-creation between brands and consumers, to the effects of globalisation on the organisation of the manufacture of fashion. Several co-authored chapters are based on jointly researched case studies. The book as a whole assesses the diversity and complexity of Dutch fashion designers, firms and brands in relation to their historical and cultural context.

Delft Blue to Denim Blue: Contemporary Dutch Fashion follows a loosely chronological line from the 1950s, after the Second World War, to the present. The first part of the book brings together different aspects of Dutch fashion culture. Part 1 starts with an overview of the recent history of Dutch fashion, and of the textile and clothing industry from the 1950s till now. The historical chapters are followed by three chapters that describe and analyse different discourses, narratives and myths of Dutch fashion. Part 2 of the book focuses on individual and detailed case studies of Dutch firms and designers, zooming in on aspects of consumption and production. Part 3 opens up new perspectives on Dutch fashion by exploring a more theoretical approach for understanding contemporary art and photography, couture designers Viktor&Rolf, and the fusion of fashion with technology. Throughout the book short vignettes, written by Lianne Toussaint, are dedicated to individual designers or firms to give a more complete view of the rich landscape of Dutch fashion.

The first part of the book, 'Dutch Fashion Culture', opens with the chapter, 'Clogs on High Heels: Dutch Cultural Heritage and Fashion', by José Teunissen in which she compares the recent history of fashion of the Netherlands and Belgium; two small neighbouring countries in the north of Europe. Like most European countries, the Netherlands and Belgium were influenced by French fashion through imitation and inspiration until deep into the twentieth century. The proximity to Paris connected the Belgian clothing and textile industry to French couture, whereas the Netherlands kept a keen eye on Paris for design and creation while maintaining a certain reservation towards its perceived excess and impractical elegance. Only in the last decades of the previous century did the Netherlands and Belgium start to develop a national fashion culture, often instigated

by government policies for supporting the creative industries. In the 1980s, the Belgian government took its first initiatives to support young fashion talent, which was followed by similar support on the part of the Dutch government in 1988. Whereas Belgium supported fashion designers through financial incentives for the struggling textile and clothing industry, the Netherlands no longer attempted to save this branch of the industry. Instead, it made fashion designers eligible to arts grants, thus firmly situating fashion in the realm of art and design. The focus on art and design enabled Dutch designers to delve into their cultural heritage, freely explore creativity, and experiment with innovations in production and technology. José Teunissen argues that Dutch fashion can be characterised as conceptual and modernist, with its roots in Dutch design and a centuries-long culture of democracy, solidarity and egalitarianism.

In chapter 3, 'Contours of the Dutch Fashion Industry', Michiel Scheffer sketches the history of the textile and clothing industry in the Netherlands from the 1950s till now. The story of the Dutch textile and clothing industry is a rather classical one of growth, decline and renewal. Scheffer characterises this period of almost seventy years as containing three emancipation processes. The first one is the emancipation from the fashion of Paris. The second one is the adoption of an American production model and then the emancipation from it. The third emancipation is one of women workers, who were first recruited, then laid off, but now form the backbone of its middle management. This threefold emancipation signifies by no means a positive evolution: between 1958 and now the industry lost more than eighty per cent of its employment and over fifty per cent of companies. The Dutch clothing industry was locked in a model based on supplying large retailers with standardised fashion copied from Paris and made in large-scale factories. This industrial model was evidently hard to overcome when the circumstances started to change dramatically from 1960 onwards. The orientation towards low-cost fashion for large retailers finally disappeared in the period between 1980 and 2014, together with the companies that had adopted this model. Scheffer argues that the demise of domestic manufacturing enabled designers and brands to tap into a global sourcing base with factories oriented to a wider range of skills and product specialisations. Only after that painful transformation could a new model emerge; a model of the creative industry of fashion.

In chapter 4, 'Don't Dress to Impress: Fashion Discourse in Dutch Magazines', Maaike Feitsma investigates two dominant narratives on Dutch fashion. A discourse analysis of the Dutch fashion magazines *Elegance* and *Avenue* and of the woman's magazine *Margriet* over the last fifty years, reveals the first narrative of a post-war Dutch fashion mentality that is characterised by an aversion to ostentation and a preference for austerity, pragmatism, functionality and moderation. 'Please, don't dress to impress' is the message to Dutch women in the 1950s and 1960s. Only in the 1970s and 1980s does this conservatism give way to a cosmopolitan embrace of luxury. The second narrative pertains to the emergence of Dutch fashion design from the 1980s onwards when it emancipates itself from the dictates of Paris and is appreciated in its own right. Yet, in the visual and textual rhetoric of the 1990s, Dutch fashion hardly features in the fashion or woman's magazines. Although Dutch identity is (re) constructed through the use of stereotypical icons like tulips, wooden shoes and windmills, or by a venerable Dutch cultural heritage going back to illustrious painters like Rembrandt and Vermeer, Dutch fashion itself is not yet seen as an expression of a Dutch style or identity. It is not until the international breakthrough of several Dutch fashion designers in Paris in the mid 1990s that a narrative evolves around a distinct style of Dutch fashion. Feitsma argues that the emerging discourse of Dutch modernism seamlessly fits into the older myth of Dutch fashion mentality, because they are both characterised by austerity, functionality and rationality.

In chapter 5, 'Vivid Colours: From the Local to the Global and Back Again' Anneke Smelik explores with Daniëlle Bruggeman and Maaike Feitsma the use of vibrant colours in Dutch fashion designs. The chapter examines designs by the firms Oilily, Mac&Maggie and ⁻CoraKemperman, which have played a considerable role in the Dutch fashion industry and are known for their dashing colours, daring patterns, florid folds, and bold cuts. The chapter focuses on the style of the clothes in their cultural and historical context, by first analysing how a colourful tradition can be detected in Dutch regional wear belying the age-old Calvinist convention of black clothes. The authors then explore the foreign roots and exotic fascination underlying the tradition of colourful Dutch fashion. The case studies suggest an alternative narrative to the more dominant discourse of Dutch fashion as one of modesty and sobriety. In tracing the historical roots of this alternative line in Dutch fashion, we encounter cultural 'otherness' at the very heart of Dutch folklore. The case studies of Oilily, Mac&Maggie and ⁻CoraKemperman show the contradictory dynamics of the ways in which fashion incorporates both colourful indigenous and non-Western clothing styles as part of the Dutch fashion industry. The global dynamics of fashion produce 'glocal' Dutch fashion brands, contributing to a visual and discursive reproduction of 'Dutchness' that includes 'otherness'. For example, the vicissitudes of Indian chintz – first imported from India and integrated into Dutch regional wear, then reintegrated as an icon of 'Dutchness' into Oilily's designs – demonstrate the way in which fashion expresses and underwrites the cultural hybridity of the Netherlands. The inextricable interconnectedness of the global and the local undermines any idea of a homogeneous unity of a national identity. As such, the vivid colours of Dutch fashion signify the colourfulness of hybridity.

In chapter 6, 'Denim Goes Dutch: A Myth-in-the-Making', Maaike Feitsma and Anneke Smelik trace a new narrative of Dutch fashion: the Netherlands as a denim country with Amsterdam as its denim capital. With the assistance and support of trade organisations, design institutes, Amsterdam's municipal services, and brand stories, the media have facilitated a new fashion narrative to promote nation and city branding. Its constant repetition in the media has anchored the new fashion myth in the collective imagination. The initial motives for this new myth of Dutch denim are no doubt commercial, but the authors argue that it is not simply an instance of marketing blarney plucked out of thin air, because it is firmly rooted in prevailing myths about Dutch fashion culture as sober, functional, informal and egalitarian. This allowed the new narrative to take off so swiftly and smoothly. Yet, the ideology of this myth could only settle down because its commercial motives are denied, its original American roots glossed over, and reliable statistics on the density of denim companies and the number of denim jeans per head of the Dutch population are unavailable. The new fashion myth of 'Dutch denim' is so successful because of its mythical elements, tapping into prevailing perceptions of Dutch fashion identity. As the media uncritically present this myth as self-evident, it gets ever more firmly anchored in the Dutch imaginary. It may even end up replacing the tourist cliché of Delft blue with a new stereotype of Dutch denim blue.

Part 2 of the book is dedicated to in-depth studies of Dutch firms and designers. As the clothing industry was subjected to a very early phase of globalisation from the 1960s onwards, it allowed Dutch fashion designers freedom in the designing process and stimulated fashion firms to develop a conceptual approach to routines in the production process. Fashion firms have been struggling with what they see as the increasing volatility and unpredictability of their customers. We analyse the interactive way in which fashion firms increasingly co-create the collective identities of their audiences, appealing to the cultural values their consumers foster.

In chapter 7, 'Van Gils: Between Designing a Lifestyle and Making Suits', Anja Köppchen takes on the interesting case of Van Gils as a menswear firm that was highly successful, yet went bankrupt in the early 1990s and reinvented itself all over again. By addressing the question of Dutch fashion from a supplier's perspective, this chapter illustrates how globalisation can lead to a widening gap between the knowledge and skills of designers on the one hand and the capabilities of manufacturers on the other. The organisational development of Van Gils as a brand involves the gradual separation of the brand from its manufacturing roots. Creative practices have thus become distanced from their origin – i.e. the Van Gils family and their manufacturing heritage – but also in organisational terms from the manufacturing business as such. The case of Van Gils explains how design and manufacturing practices relate to each other and how this relation is challenged by increasing spatial and organisational distance. Köppchen argues that the tension between branding and manufacturing is a paradoxical one, as aesthetics and technical construction of formal menswear appear inextricably linked and highly interdependent. In the age of globalisation the main challenge for brands without manufacturing competences is to find organisational practices that allow for mutual engagement between brand and manufacturer. This would involve an understanding of design as a joint accomplishment rather than a clear-cut separation between design and manufacturing. Köppchen therefore concludes that designing a lifestyle and making suits are two sides of the same coin that define Van Gils as a brand.

In chapter 8, 'Mexx: a Dutch Brand with Global Reach', Anja Köppchen looks at the specific case of Mexx, a highly successful middle-range brand on the high street for over thirty years, but that went bankrupt in 2014 and was taken over by the Turkish company Eroğlu

Holding in 2015. She discusses the development of this global brand that was established by Indian immigrants in the Netherlands and had its main production centre in Hong Kong for over a decade. Considering its global complexity on the one hand, and its significance for the Dutch fashion industry on the other, the case of Mexx illustrates the ambiguity of national fashion boundaries. It also explains how the global orientation of its founders has enabled the brand to manage the connection between design and production at a distance. Mexx understood relatively early that fashion is both global and local. The Dutch fashion industry evolved with the globalisation of clothing production. Mexx is a highly significant case because it illustrates the ways in which design and manufacturing depend on and influence each other even at a large geographical distance. The case study of Mexx thus shows that we have to take into account the industry's global dimension in order to understand how Dutch fashion is made.

In chapter 9, 'From Mac&Maggie to ‾CoraKemperman: Successful Co-Creation in Production and Consumption', Anneke Smelik argues with Anja Köppchen and Constantin von Maltzahn that designer Cora Kemperman's unique style was the result of 'co-creation', that is, of the specific way in which production and consumption were organised by the brand ‾CoraKemperman. She worked first as a buyer for Mac&Maggie (1976–94), before she started her own brand in 1995, stylised as ‾CoraKemperman, which went bankrupt in 2016 as this book went to press. Kemperman's wilful choice to remain a small business was based on her desire to entertain close relations with her suppliers as well as her consumers. The small scale of her enterprise allowed for co-creation by combining buying and designing in the field of production, and for a particular relation in the field of consumption that created a strong emotional bond with the brand. This chapter takes a close look at the organisation of the production and consumption of Mac&Maggie and

‾CoraKemperman, arguing that Kemperman was a particular kind of fashion designer who drew together the different roles of designing, buying, styling, as well as retailing. The research shows how ‾CoraKemperman had developed two forms of co-creation that were based on reciprocity: on the one hand the firm had established an intense cooperation between buyer, manufacturer and retailer, resulting in garments that were co-created in interaction between the buyer Cora Kemperman and her suppliers. On the other hand the firm had capitalised on patronage and long-term relations with consumers, creating a high level of emotional involvement with the brand. The authors argue that this unique two-pronged approach to co-creation made for the success of the Dutch brand ‾CoraKemperman.

In chapter 10, 'Vanilia: High-Street the Dutch Way', Constantin von Maltzahn explores the Dutch high-street market with an analysis of Vanilia, erstwhile a supplier of business and formal wear that has recently switched gears to reinvent its business and product identity. He explores how, in the face of growing competition, a mid-sized, independent firm defines its market position by carving out a niche in the Dutch fashion market. The move from business attire to up-to-the-minute fashion clothing not only heralded a new product proposition, but also a change in marketing communication and corporate branding. Von Maltzahn traces that development and analyses the firm's coming of age as a contemporary fashion house on the Dutch high street. After sketching the firm's development at business level, he zooms in on the behaviour of consumers by taking a closer look at the value connections governing the relationship allowed between Vanilia and its audience group. The chapter explains the relays between supply and demand, and how brand and product involvement are driven by a variety of factors. The core of the company's success lies in the balanced and adaptable collections that continue to develop the brand profile across different demographics and sites of identification.

In chapter 11, 'Spijkers en Spijkers: A Cut Above', Constantin von Maltzahn details the development of the Dutch luxury fashion firm Spijkers en Spijkers, since its establishment in 2001 by identical twin sisters Riet and Truus Spijkers. With a hard-edged and distinct design identity, the firm was quick to successfully establish its business at product level. Working with an international outlook and no financial backer, however, they found the entrepreneurial side of things did not come quite as easily. Attuning the offerings to a diverse clientele required the two designers behind the company to develop business acumen and a specific repertoire to balance their upscale ambitions with clever sales tactics. This chapter presents a comprehensive sketch of Spijkers en Spijkers' coming of age as a brand – as well as of the designers as self-taught entrepreneurs – and identifies the tools necessary to develop a business identity and secure a steadier and more permanent market position. As the analysis shows, collaborations with high-street brands have helped increasing brand recognition in the more popular market segments while brand extensions have provided the necessary basis for growth in Spijkers en Spijkers' home market as well as abroad. Von Maltzahn zooms in on the respective steps the company has undertaken throughout the years to adapt to changes in the market and retain a competitive edge.

Part 3, 'Novel Perspectives', moves to the realm of photography, art, high fashion and wearable technology. The authors explore artistic, imaginary and futuristic fields of fashion. The chapters also introduce theoretical perspectives to understand recent developments in Dutch fashion.

In chapter 12, 'Dutch Fashion Photography: Liquid Bodies and Fluid Faces', Daniëlle Bruggeman explores the virtual realm of fashion imagery in which Dutch fashion photographers experiment with the porous boundaries between the body, clothes, and identity. Fashion photography has increasingly gained significance in the fashion system as well as in contemporary culture. The Netherlands has a strong tradition in photography and also in fashion photography, with many renowned names operating internationally, such as Inez Van Lamsweerde and Vinoodh Matadin, Anton Corbijn, Erwin Olaf, Freudenthal/Verhagen, Viviane Sassen, and Anuschka Blommers & Niels Schumm. On the one hand, fashion images may categorise, label and commodify individuals, suggesting that we can purchase this kind of appearance and identity. On the other hand, contemporary fashion photographers may also play with the flexibility of (clothed) bodies and identities. Fashion photography thus points out a paradoxical double dynamics of identity. Bruggeman focuses on a selection of Dutch fashion photographers whose editorial and artistic work questions, subverts and mobilises dominant representations of men and women. In transgressing boundaries and transforming bodies and identities, the photographers facilitate a reimagination of the self. The virtual space in which Dutch fashion photographers operate, Bruggeman argues, allows for an opening up to the flux and fluidity of subjectivity.

In chapter 13, 'Fashion as a New Materialist Aesthetics: The Case of Viktor&Rolf', Daniëlle Bruggeman proposes a fresh approach to the work of this internationally well-known duo. She mobilises an alternative reading of fashion by moving beyond fashion as a system of signification and representation that communicates identity. Based on analyses of the fashion shows of Dutch designers Viktor&Rolf, this more theoretical chapter argues for the importance of highlighting fashion's matter and materiality, i.e. not only the objects of fashion but also the matter of the human body. Although fashion obviously is an immaterial realm of codes, signs and meanings, this understanding at the same time fails to take into account the physicality of the body and the materiality of clothing. According to Bruggeman, there is an urgent requirement to bring back the body – the embodied subject – and materiality into fashion discourse, and vice versa. Therefore, it is important to develop an alternative, and more material, reading of fashion. Viktor&Rolf's work inspires to do so. Whereas Viktor&Rolf are typically regarded as conceptual designers, Bruggeman foregrounds their experimentation with the materiality of fashion by drawing upon the philosophy of Gilles Deleuze and Félix Guattari and on the theoretical discourse of 'new materialism'. Such an approach to fashion allows taking into account living bodies, embodied subjects, and the actual materiality of fashion objects. Viktor&Rolf's exploration of the possibilities of the medium itself, their play with materiality and immateriality, and with embodiment and disembodiment, requires rethinking the aesthetic power and the dynamics of fashion in a more material sense.

In the last chapter, 'Cybercouture: The Fashionable Technology of Pauline van Dongen, Iris van Herpen and Bart Hess', Anneke Smelik illuminates the new field of fashionable technology or 'wearables'. Wiring complex systems of microprocessors, motors, sensors, solar panels, (O)LEDs or interactive interfaces into the fabric, textile or clothing turns them into smart garments that have a certain agency of their own. Dutch designers such as Pauline van Dongen, Iris van Herpen, Bart Hess, Marina Toeters, Karin Vlug and Anouk Wipprecht form the vanguard in the international field of fashionable

technology. In this chapter Smelik explores the 'cybercouture' of avant-garde designers Pauline van Dongen, Iris van Herpen and Bart Hess. Their designs share a futuristic outlook, pointing to a horizon beyond conventional fashion. Moving in between art, fashion and technology, they experiment with the ways in which bodies can be shaped and identities can be performed. In their shared fascination for stretching the boundaries of the human body, they tempt the viewer or wearer to put identity at play. The strange shapes, forms, textiles and materials invite a reflection on new forms of embodiment and human identity. As Smelik argues, this play with identity can be understood – following Deleuze and Guattari – as a process of 'becoming'. By reshaping the human body beyond its finite contours, cybercouture offers an encounter between fashion and technology, opening up to a future world where garments are merged with human skin, body and identity. The artistic designs by Pauline van Dongen, Iris van Herpen and Bart Hess create fusions between art, fashion and wearable technology, and embark on a transformative process of becoming. The book *Delft Blue to Denim Blue: Contemporary Dutch Fashion* thus ends with a peek into the future.

Notes

1. See for more information the website of NWO, although the programme has now been closed down: http://www.nwo.nl/en/research-and-results/programmes/gw/cultural-dynamics/index.html.

2. The formal English title of the exhibition was 'Gone with the Wind', but I am unhappy with the specific and inopportune connotations in American-English and therefore prefer a literal translation of the Dutch.

3. Bruggeman, D. (2014) 'More than Meets the Eye: Dutch Fashion, Identity and New Materialism', Nijmegen: Radboud University: http://repository.ubn.ru.nl/bitstream/handle/2066/132976/132976.pdf?sequence=1;

Feitsma, M. (2014) 'Nederlandse Mode: Een Verkenning van Mythevorming en Betekenissen' ['Dutch Fashion: an Exploration of Myths and Meanings'], Nijmegen: Radboud University: http://repository.ubn.ru.nl/bitstream/handle/2066/127127/127127.pdf?sequence=1;

Köppchen, A. (2014) 'Mind the Gap: Balancing Design and Global Manufacturing in Dutch Fashion', Nijmegen: Radboud University: http://repository.ubn.ru.nl/bitstream/handle/2066/129879/129879.pdf?sequence=1;

Von Maltzahn, C. (2013) 'Dutch Identity in Fashion: The Co-Evolution between Brands and Consumers', University of Amsterdam: http://dare.uva.nl/document/2/123753.

G-Star (1989–present)

Lianne Toussaint

'We don't even have a separate budget for research
and development, because that is what we're doing
all the time.'

—P. Kool interviewed in B. Lampe, 2014

One of the global brands that turned jeans into a true fashion item originates from the Netherlands. Founded in 1989 by Jos Van Tilburg, G-Star builds a distinct brand identity from the start. The company notes that hardly anything has changed in the denim market ever since Levi Straus developed the first proper jeans in 1853, the classic five-pocket model of indigo blue cotton – Levi's 501: the original! What once was a rebellious garment worn by role models like Marlon Brandon and James Dean, increasingly became 'the Mao suit of Western culture' (see chapter six).

G-Star, however, does not care for that tradition: it wants to move forward. The label continuously seeks innovation in the rough unwashed fabric, raw denim, and presents a new collection every season. In fact, the untreated denim has become such a distinct trait in the course of time that it is now integrated into the trade name: G-Star RAW. Firm fabrics, sturdy zippers and prominent stitching and prints form the basis for G-Star's functional clothing. Its designs can be characterised as rough and robust, breathing the atmosphere of life in the big city. The latter marks another difference between G-Star and classical jeans manufacturers. Whereas brands like Levi's and Lee appeal to the myth of the Wild West, G-Star is the brand of the 'urban cowboy' who has to survive in the urban jungle. The approximately 3,500 G-Star sellers and 16 G-Star stores in 40 different countries around the world prove that plenty of these cowboys and -girls enjoy its products (Arts, 2006: 80).

G-Star owes its international breakthrough to the 'Elwood', a model that has become a classic in itself. The Elwood was introduced in 1996 in collaboration with the French jeans designer Pierre Morisset, and is still in production today. Morisset based his design on the outfits worn by motorcycle riders, creating a ground-breaking new look with articulated kneepads and a reinforced bottom (Kuijpers, 2009: 24). Though it is proud of that Elwood success, G-Star prefers to focus on the future. The smoothly organised company constantly innovates on ideas, projects and collaborations. Creativity and out of the box thinking are highly valued. For that reason, the brand regularly collaborates with different kinds of companies, such as Leica (cameras), Land Rover (jeeps) and Prouvé (furniture). The most innovative of all collaborations, however, started when Pharrell Williams invited G-Star to work with Bionic Yarn, a company that transforms plastic waste into fibres and textiles. Together they launched 'RAW for the Oceans', a project that uses recycled ocean plastic to create a collection of fabrics, including two new sorts of denim. RAW for the Oceans is the crowning moment of twenty-five years of innovation. In February 2016 the news was launched that Pharrell Williams is now co-owner of G-star. As standing still means going backwards, G-Star rather looks ahead (Lampe, 2014).

7. G-Star catwalk show A/W 2007–08.

8. G-Star catwalk show A/W 2010.

10. G-Star catwalk show Summer 2011.

9. G-Star catwalk show Summer 2011.

Dutch Fashion
Culture

2.

Clogs on High Heels:
Dutch Cultural Heritage and Fashion

'There is a history, a tradition, a craftsmanship and a guiding principle in things, and here I see an abstract quality. It is a quality that I find striking. A Dutch way of thinking.'

—Alexander van Slobbe (in van der Berg, 2008: 106)

José Teunissen

Government Support for Dutch and Belgian Fashion

In the work of Viktor&Rolf the designs and the imaginary worlds they inhabit are inextricably linked. Since they started their own label in 1993 they have often used museums and galleries for their fashion presentations: 'We turn the phenomenon of fashion into its own subject matter. We have expressed and reflected just that position in various ways through various media, in an art context but also within the context of fashion,' explained Viktor&Rolf in *T Magazine* (2008). One might be inclined to regard this as a logical result of the unique Dutch policy in which Dutch designers were funded by art grants. It has often been suggested that these grants enabled Viktor&Rolf to adopt an experimental and artistic approach. However, research into Dutch cultural history and a comparison between the Dutch and the Belgian fashion successes shows that the matter is more complicated.[1]

In 1988, the Dutch government decided to support fashion designers by making them eligible for art grants. When Viktor&Rolf (as part of 'Le Cri Néerlandais') and orson + bodil (by Alexander van Slobbe) began to show their first collections in Paris in 1994, the Netherlands started playing a role of some consequence in the world of international fashion. The international fashion press

11. Viktor&Rolf , black clogs 'Romina', yellow clogs 'Anna Maria', brown clogs 'Heather' and blue/white clogs 'Raquel' (A/W 2007–8).

celebrated 'Le Cri Néerlandais' (Viktor&Rolf, Saskia van Drimmelen, Lucas Ossendrijver, Pascale Gatzen and Marcel Verheijen) and van Slobbe as the new identifiable fashion trend from a distinct country. The journalists followed up on the Japanese and the Belgian designers, treating the Dutch as a national 'school' that launched a new style and fresh views on fashion in Paris, inspired by a specific national character. During the 1990s more young Dutch designers like Klavers van Engelen and Spijkers en Spijkers started to build up an international label. At the time I was one of the journalists who dubbed their style 'Dutch Modernism' in the national quality newspaper *NRC* (Teunissen, 1994), because of their conceptual approach and development of clear shapes and forms. The term quickly stuck to the fashion designers, probably because of a robust Dutch modernist and conceptual tradition in graphic, architecture and interior design: 'The Netherlands like to think of themselves as a modernist culture in which dry, minimalist and conceptual design is a focal point of modern idealism' (Huygen, 2007: 429).

In the same period the Belgian government also took its first initiatives to promote young fashion talents through the so-called 'Textielplan' ('textile plan'), enabling six young designers to start their own labels. These were Walter van Beirendonck, Dries van Noten, Dirk van Saene, Dirk Bikkembergs, Ann Demeulemeester and Marina Yee, who all had graduated at the Fashion Department of the Royal Academy of Fine Arts in Antwerp in either 1980 or 1981. A government economic mission allowed them to visit Japan and to present their collections twice a year at the London fashion week from 1986 onwards. Their international breakthrough came when they presented their first group show in the Westway film studio in London in 1988. The international press and buyers quickly labelled them 'the Antwerp Six', described by talent scout and press agent Marysia Woroniecka as follows: 'What makes them special is that they are so fresh. Belgium had no tradition or history in fashion and that is why they are so original and open minded' (Es et al., 1989: 76). The image of freshness stuck to the Belgian designers, including the second generation that emerged in the 1990s, with Martin Margiela, A.F. Vandevorst, Veronique Branquinho, Haider Ackermann and Raf Simons. The deconstructionist style that was supposedly tying these creative avant-garde designers together captured a global trend at the time, shunning immediate cultural references.

Noticeably, the governments of these two neighbouring countries took quite different approaches to support the emerging designer fashion sector. The Dutch designers were funded by art grants and adopted a probing experimental approach, which was just as often directed at the art world as at fashion markets. The Belgian designers were backed by government and industry support and aimed for commercial success through brand building (Gimeno Martinez, 2006). The differing governmental ways of supporting fashion were a result of different industrial and cultural backgrounds, and marked out different trajectories for Dutch and Belgian fashion designers.

In this chapter I will explore the unique case of Dutch fashion first by a comparison with its Belgian counterpart and then by focusing more on the recent history of Dutch fashion itself. It might seem obvious that two small neighbouring countries on the northwestern coast of the European continent should share a contemporary fashion culture, given that they share a language (Dutch and Flemish are similar languages); have shared a long history; and were even a united kingdom for a short period in the nineteenth century. Yet, contrary to expectation, a closer look reveals that there are as many differences as similarities. Unlike their Belgian counterparts, Dutch fashion designers have increasingly turned to the cultural traditions and arts of the Netherlands, including the Calvinist style of the seventeenth century, regional dress and craft traditions. They have done so in order to sustain and develop a distinct Dutch fashion style. Different historical and industrial backgrounds, then, resulted in different ways for Dutch and Belgian designers to construct concepts of 'national identity' in fashion.

National Identity: 'A Confection of Selective Memories'

Since fashion works as a polycentric global fashion system, it is striking that designers and industries in small nations have taken part in national debates since the 1980s. As I have argued elsewhere, there has been a revival of interest in local heritage and craftsmanship in the past few years throughout the world (Teunissen, 2005). In the Introduction Anneke Smelik referred to Alison Goodrum in explaining the complexity of national identity; let me repeat and extend the quote here:

> National identity may be conceived as a confection of selective memories, generating traditions and rituals in order to reinforce ideas of permanence and longevity and also supplying the plebeian masses with a collection of codified emblems through which to foster national belonging and a sense of identification. (Goodrum, 2005: 62).

Goodrum illustrates her point with the examples of Paul Smith and Mulberry disseminating a British style throughout the world as a form of cultural imperialism of taste. Defining Britishness is relatively easy, since the English have played an important role in fashion history, especially in men's fashion. The traditional male fashion as well as the London street culture of the 1960s is recognised worldwide as part and parcel of English taste and style (Breward et al., 2002). Savile Row and Carnegie Street both have a rich iconographic heritage as a source for reusing, remaking and recycling contemporary fashion. In contrast, neither Belgium nor the Netherlands played an influential role in the history of fashion,

making it more difficult to market a national identity. Identifying a 'selective confection of memories' that can be turned into a piece of iconographic heritage is indeed a difficult task, which Dutch and Belgian designers have approached quite differently.

Jennifer Craik has tried to unravel a 'national identity' in the dressing style of Australia as another country with no history in fashion. She argues that a national sense of style or fashion is the expressive encapsulation of the cultural psyche or zeitgeist of a place (Craik, 2009: 413). A certain national style can be recognised when three realms come together: aesthetic distinctiveness, cultural practice and cultural articulation. Craik understands the 'aesthetic dimension' as the distinctiveness and recognisability of national clothing styles, including the choice and habitual preferences for certain motifs, particular cuts and compositions in the garment and the preference for certain fabrics and materials in the manufacture of clothes. It also refers to a distinctive way of wearing and combining clothes to create a particular 'look' (2009: 414). 'Cultural practice' refers to the uptake and consumption of clothing as either everyday wear in ways that express specific relations between the body and the cultural domain. While local adoption is crucial, this specificity must be recognisable to those from elsewhere who may, in certain cases, adopt this style to emulate 'localness' (2009: 414). 'Cultural articulation', finally, symbolises the point where internal and external perceptions of the essence of national stylistic identity overlap. Here, one is able to project a style to a point where it is 'taken for granted' and accepted as the 'natural' identity of a nation (2009: 314).

Not all fashion theorists are convinced by the force of a national style. In his study of 'the Antwerp Six' Javier Gimeno Martinez, for instance, argues that the success of Belgian fashion is primarily an outcome of the Textile Plan and its subsequent identification with the city of Antwerp, where political and economic circumstances functioned as catalysts for the identification of a creative practice. He does not believe in superimpositions of national identity on notions of style, in the world of today where communication and media erode those national boundaries (Gimeno Martinez, 2008: 52). Although I agree that the Belgian case illustrates that a notion of national style does not necessarily build up a national identity, I do think that a local or national cultural heritage and tradition in dress taste and style are traceable and identifiable within a dress culture. Let me first expound on the Belgian case, before zooming in on the story of Dutch fashion to support my argument.

The Story behind Belgian Fashion: Changing National Politics

As mentioned above, the Belgian government launched a so-called 'Textile Plan' in 1981, an ambitious project to revitalise the faltering textile industry. The government created a new Institute for Textile and Clothing of Belgium (ITCB), which started with an overall budget of 687 million euros divided into three parts. First, there was a financial component of 496 million euros for modernisations and the reorganisation of companies. Second, there was a 'service' component of 141 million euros for marketing, research and education, mainly used for large promotional campaigns. The ITCB launched a campaign 'This is Belgium' in 1983, meant to enhance the image of Belgian fashion. It included the inauguration of the Golden Spindle Award in 1983, a prize that gave young designers the opportunity to finance a collection. As a result of both the prize and the promotional campaign the young designers of 'the Antwerp Six' gained access to local manufacturers' production facilities in the Belgian industry, while they were also able to attract significant attention internationally. In this way they could slowly build up their own companies (Moons, 2008: 70). Finally, a third social component of 50 million euros was used to alleviate unavoidable lay-offs.

For all its ambition, the Textile Plan was not that successful. In the 1990s it became clear that the cooperation between the young designers and the Belgian manufacturers was not working out very well. Designers including Ann Demeulemeester and Dirk Bikkembergs were forced to search for producers outside Belgium. In the end, the majority of Belgian manufacturers and producers did not survive and went bankrupt, because they could not compete with outsourcing in other parts of the world. In retrospect, the service component turned out to be the only successful part of the Textile Plan. The research and development measures, as well as the stimulating and coordinating role of the ITCB with regard to training, education, management and networking, were responsible for a dynamic new approach in the sector.

The complex political situation of Belgium with its Flemish (Dutch-speaking) and Walloon (French-speaking) regions resulted in a federalisation in 1993, meaning in fact that the government was split into two parts. The service component of the Textile Plan was then abruptly split into a Flemish and a Walloon part. The Flemish government took the initiative to start the Flanders Fashion Institute (FFI) a few years later, in 1998. The FFI has two tasks: to stimulate the entrepreneurship of the Flemish fashion industry by providing business training, and to promote Flemish designers in Belgium and abroad.

The Belgian nation headed into an unfortunate legitimacy crisis in the early 2000s, which shows that co-branding with a nation can have a most negative side effect when politics turn sour. Political circumstances in general and federalisation in particular played an important role in modifying the meaning of Belgian fashion. The Flemish part soon developed an infrastructure, with the MoMu Antwerp (2002) and Flanders Fashion Institute (FFI) helping to promote Flemish design abroad. Gradually, the term 'Belgian fashion' became geographically reduced to Antwerp fashion (Gimeno Martinez, 2008: 64).

CLOGS ON HIGH HEELS

Promotional efforts transformed the city of Antwerp into a fashion hotspot. Linda Loppa, then director of the Fashion Department of the Royal Academy of the Fine Arts, and Geert Brulot, a shopkeeper who was actively involved in promoting the Antwerp Six, both played an important role in the realisation of the fashion museum MoMu in 2002, focusing primarily on Belgian and more specifically on Antwerp fashion. The museum is located in the so-called 'Fashion Nation' building, which also houses the renowned Fashion Department of the Royal Academy of the Fine Arts, as well as the Flanders Fashion Institute. Moreover, the designers Dries van Noten, Ann Demeulemeester and Walter van Beirendonck have (or had) their flagship store in the same neighbourhood. Such a fashion hotspot turns Antwerp into a dynamic fashion city attracting many tourists every year. In this way, Antwerp has put Belgium on the map as a fashion country.

The Belgian case illustrates that it is possible to construct a national identity in fashion without referring to a specific cultural heritage. Rather than a shared heritage, the promotional institutions in Belgium were the defining agents in the creation of both the concept of 'Belgian fashion' as well as the later concept of 'Antwerp fashion': the first was the outcome of the Textile Plan of the 1980s, and the second of a complicated process where political and economic circumstances acted as catalysts (Gimeno Martinez, 2008: 64).

The Dutch Way to Success: Funding and Subsidies for Design

The situation in the Netherlands was and still is quite different. The field of fashion in the Netherlands became gradually more sophisticated in the 1980s in a country without much of a fashion history. New developments in Paris were followed with interest. Especially, the Japanese designers Yohji Yamamoto and Comme des Garçons made an impression in the Dutch field of fashion, with their conceptual designs in which they investigated

and 'deconstructed' the form and meaning of clothing. New stores appeared in the Netherlands specialising in such designer clothes (Teunissen, 2006). Dutch fashion students could relate to the abstract ideas and well thought-out concepts of Japanese fashion designers. They also felt inspired by the deconstructive approach of 'the Antwerp Six' and especially by their courage to present themselves as young and independent designers between the top designers of Paris, London and Milan.

Dutch fashion designers did not receive the same fundamental support from the government as the Belgians, but they could apply for a newly established art grant from the Fund for Visual Art, Design and Architecture (BKVB). This national organisation was established in 1988 to support the careers of talented artists and designers with an incentive subsidy. The sum of money supported them with an income for a year and enabled them to buy materials. The fund BKVB started with an overall budget of 23 million euros for 1988 and 1989, out of which fashion designers received around 700,000 euros. Compared to the Textile Plan investment of Belgium that delivered 141 million euros for marketing and education in fashion in 1981, this was quite a small amount of money.

By 1990 a number of small labels were established with help of the BKVB fund and managed to build up an international reputation and clientele, following a joint presentation in London, as did 'the Antwerp Six' before. They called themselves the GILL group (an amalgamation of Gletcher, Lawina, Illustrious Imps and the shoe label Lola Pagola) and had their collections photographed by the then young photographer Inez van Lamsweerde (she is now one of the world famous duo of fashion photographers, together with her husband Vinoodh Matadin; see chapter 12). However, none of them succeeded in making their designer labels commercially viable in the long run. The main reason was that they were not supported by any investors and that it was difficult to find small-scale production facilities near home. A year later, in 1991, the BKVB fund shut off the supply of government subsidies for these specific fashion brands, because the funding was meant as a start-up for designers or brands and they were expected to be able to stand on their own feet by then.

In 1994, 'le Cri Néerlandais' and orson + bodil, the second generation of designers who had been funded by BKVB, held their first show in Paris. The designer Alexander van Slobbe had started orson + bodil in 1988 together with Nanet van der Kleijn. Both had worked for labels in the Dutch clothing industry, which was already completely outsourced since the early 1970s (see chapter 3 for a more detailed history of the Dutch fashion industry). Van Slobbe and van der Kleijn were unhappy with the cheap and simple clothes this system produced. They dedicated their label orson + bodil to handicraft and conceptual design, driven by an intrinsic love for clothing, form, material and make. In the first years they earned their money with freelance commissions for the industry, while the grants from BKVB enabled them to develop orson + bodil as entrepreneurs.

Meanwhile, the designers of 'Le Cri Néerlandais', Viktor&Rolf, Saskia van Drimmelen, Lucas Ossendrijver, Pascale Gatzen and Marcel Verheijen, had graduated from the renowned Fashion Department of the ArtEZ Institute of the Arts in Arnhem in 1992. Funds from the BKVB provided them with a grant that enabled them to develop a first collection. They decided to present their collection – which was financially quite hard to produce – in Paris as 'the New Dutch Six', with a nudge and a wink to 'the Antwerp Six'. Perhaps to their own surprise, their launch was an instant media success. The international press took over the label 'Dutch modernists' immediately (Van den Berg, 2008: 102). They did indeed position themselves self-consciously within the solid Dutch design tradition of the twentieth century with its reputation for austere, clear-cut modernist design, mostly in the field of graphic design, interior design and architecture (Huygen, 2007). In several press articles and in

exhibitions that followed, the fashion designers were associated with 'Droog Design' (literally 'Dry Design'), the famous Dutch product design label that made a successful appearance on the international scene in the early 1990s (Teunissen and Van Zijl, 2000). Differently from the Belgian designers, who built their reputation mainly by marketing, branding and business plans, the Dutch designers presented themselves foremost as artist-designers who were part of a modernist heritage in the Netherlands dating all the way back to Mondrian and De Stijl.

The consequences of the financial support system in the Netherlands can be illustrated with the careers of Viktor&Rolf and Alexander van Slobbe. From the start in 1994 up to 2000 Viktor&Rolf made only artistic designs and presentations without being able to create a wearable collection for retail. Since they lacked the financial back-up to build a professional fashion business, they preferred to concentrate on presenting concepts and ideas on fashion with grants from the fund BKVB. Only when a Japanese investor gave them financial backing in 2000 were they finally able to start a commercial ready-to-wear line for women, quickly followed by a men's line. The Viktor&Rolf range has since grown to include shoes, accessories, eyewear and perfumes. With the desire to expand, in 2008 Viktor&Rolf entered into a partnership with Italian clothing magnate Renzo Rosso of Only the Brave (OTB), allowing the company to develop new product ranges, extend distribution and open boutiques. In 2013 they started to develop haute couture collections again. In 2015 they decided to stop their ready-to-wear line and to focus only on their successes: perfume and haute couture.

In 1993 Alexander van Slobbe (see the profile in chapter 11) was invited by the Dutch investor van Veldhoven to start a menswear collection, 'SO', which turned into quite a successful label on the Japanese market. However, van Slobbe was forced to stop the woman's collection orson + bodil in 1995 because he could not find a financial backer for it. In 2003 van Slobbe sold SO because he did no longer enjoy the scale and the commercial way of working, and relaunched orson + bodil to be able to concentrate again on handicraft and couture. Both the labels of Viktor&Rolf and of Alexander van Slobbe could only become successful because they were lucky to have found investors on the international market helping them to commercialise their labels.

Dutch Fashion in a Historical Perspective

The specific historical and industrial background of Dutch fashion culture also contributed to a particular concept of national identity in style. It is widely accepted that French haute couture was dominant in European fashion until the 1960s (Lipovetsky, 1994). In the Netherlands French fashion served as a basis until after World War II, whether this concerned inexpensive, ready-made garments or haute couture (Teunissen, 2008). In 1928 Joan Praetorius was the first Dutch couturier to establish a fashion house in his name. His debut show was favourably reviewed in the press with praise for its international appeal as well as its personal style. Rather than adopting the Parisian garçonne style, Praetorius emphasised women's curves with loose flowing lines. This aspect was particularly appreciated by both the Dutch press and the consumers, because it supposedly better suited the plump built of Dutch women (Teunissen, 2006: 172).

In the 1950s Dutch designers emerged with a new generation, represented by Max Heymans (see the profile in this chapter), Ferry Offerman and Cargelli. They still closely followed Parisian fashions (Teunissen, 2006: 8), often working with patterns purchased at the shows of Coco Chanel, and later Christian Dior, which they were licensed to copy. The Dutch couturiers translated French fashions to suit Dutch taste. In practice, this meant that they simplified the styles, making them more sober and practical, which fitted both the taste of Dutch women and the northern climate. Hence, when they visited Paris they chose patterns of rather practical designs over more frivolous creations. For most of the twentieth century the Dutch were pragmatic followers of the Paris fashion style, and the Dutch fashion industry as a whole expressed a certain cultural aloofness from Paris fashion. Magazines and newspapers articulated reservations about the frivolity of French fashion by presenting a practical, no-nonsense Dutch woman as the cultural opposite of the elegant and fashionable '*Parisienne*' (see also chapter 4).

From the 1960s on, French haute couture lost its monopoly and avant-garde status (Lipovetsky, 1994). The emergence of ready-to-wear and of youth culture made fashion accessible for everyone. Moreover, for the first time it became possible for designers not to copy Paris fashion but to develop a creative style and a brand with a distinct signature. Marijke Koger and Josje Leeger were the first Dutch designers to open a boutique in the Jordaan district of Amsterdam in 1965, which was – and still is – a favoured part of town for hipsters (Teunissen, 2006: 136). Koger and Leeger were not only connected with Dutch pop culture, but also designed clothes and record sleeves for the Beatles. Smaller-scale shops followed, featuring special designs and unique styles, such as the shoe shop of Jan Jansen, still successful today. For the first time in the Netherlands, ready-to-wear lines appeared with a personal signature responding to the zeitgeist of the times. Marieke Olsthoorn started in 1963, incorporating traditional fabrics from regional dress into colourful children's clothes under the brand name Oilily, which grew to become one of the most successful ready-to-wear labels at the time (Teunissen, 2006: 132; see also chapter 5). During the 1970s retail chains began to be receptive to young talent. The era of small-scale boutiques was superseded by chains like Mac&Maggie (1976) and Fooks, which stocked various

Dutch ready-to-wear labels such as Soap Studio (1979), Nico Verhey (1978) and Sandwich (Henriëtte Daniels, 1979). All these labels conquered an international market. Particularly noteworthy is the international success of a number of new women's labels aimed at the modern working woman with practical and comfortable designs. This is the philosophy behind Turnover (1988), Sandwich, Humanoid and Stills; labels that have remained successful into the twenty-first century.

In the 1960s the Netherlands was one of the first countries to move textile and clothing production to Portugal and later to the Far East (see chapter 3). The fact that production industry has left the country does not mean that the creative industry of fashion is not successful. In 2013 the fashion industries in the Netherlands reached a total turnover of eight billion euros. Another sign of success is a small group of well-known designers that circulate at the top of the international fashion world, such as Viktor&Rolf, Alexander van Slobbe, Spijkers en Spijkers, Iris van Herpen and People of the Labyrinth. In addition, there are a number of designers who present themselves on the national and international scene, though most do not have a commercial collection to sell.

The commercial trade in the Netherlands, and the number of large commercial fashion brands, is quite large. Some popular middle-market to premium brands did well in the market till recently, such as G-Star, Mexx, Turnover, Stills, Sandwich, Claudia Sträter, Oilily and ¯CoraKemperman, some of which we discuss more extensively elsewhere in this book. They have built up a successful fashion industry with labels such as Stills, Turnover, Scotch & Soda and Sandwich serving the Scandinavian and German market with fashionable clothes for the practical, informally dressed Nordic woman, while jeans brand G-Star and lingerie by Marlies Dekkers sell their products worldwide.

A significant new development in the field of fashion has been the hundreds of fashion weeks that have appeared on the scene in the last fifteen years all over the world. National fashion weeks are primarily oriented towards promoting the designers' own country and culture, more often than not by means of producing a 'local fashion' inspired by local crafts (Teunissen, 2005). While Amsterdam did start its own fashion week, remarkably, Antwerp did not: the Belgian designers still use Paris as the platform for their presentations and sales. Located one hour from Paris, and financially supported by its government for promotion, Belgium perhaps does not need a fashion week to market a national design.

Since 2004, Amsterdam hosts a fashion week twice a year where young Dutch talent is presented: the Amsterdam International Fashion Week (AIFW). However, more established designers such as Viktor&Rolf, Iris van Herpen, and Spijkers en Spijkers continue to present their shows outside the Netherlands. This means that the AIFW is above all a platform for young talented designers and not a place where buyers and traders purchase collections. In an effort of city branding and of cleaning up the (in)famous Red Light District, the Amsterdam municipality started the Red Light Fashion project in 2008, offering sixteen young designers the space of former brothels to use as a studio and showcase with the intention to help them professionalise their business. While only the odd designer actually sells anything in the studios, the project has attracted and still attracts a great deal of international fashion interest.

In addition to Amsterdam, the city of Arnhem has also been active, hosting the famed Fashion Department within the Institute of the Arts, ArtEZ, since 1953. The city municipality established a Fashion Biennale in 2005 in cooperation with the Fashion Department of ArtEZ, exhibiting fashion as a wider cultural phenomenon. In 2007, the council also set up the project 100% Fashion, where young designers can rent cheap studios and shops in the city's Klarendal district. In contrast with the Red

12. Frits Klaarenbeek
Soap Studio
Amsterdam for
Mac&Maggie
(A/W 1987).

13. Turnover: image from lookbook, 2006.

Light Fashion project in Amsterdam, designers are only eligible for space if they can present a convincing business plan and if they actually open a shop. Arnhem further aims to strengthen the fashion infrastructure by opening a sample studio where starting designers can carry out small productions close to home.

Whereas in Belgium Antwerp has been successfully transformed into a commercial and tourist fashion hotspot, the Dutch still maintain their focus on fashion as art, highlighting interesting designs and concepts by Dutch designers. The Red Light Fashion project in Amsterdam and the Fashion Biennale in Arnhem both explore fashion in the first place as an artistic and cultural phenomenon. This particular perspective has opened up new ways in which Dutch designers explore their national identity by delving into sartorial heritage in craftsmanship as well as cultural heritage in Dutch art and design (Teunissen, 2005). Dutch designers have thus explored local traditions as well as national heritage since the 1990s. In particular, they have engaged with two elements in Dutch history: the bourgeois fashions of the seventeenth century, i.e. the Dutch Golden Age; and regional dress. In the remainder of this chapter, I will explore those two aspects of cultural heritage within contemporary Dutch fashion.

Calvinism: From the Golden Age to Modernism

The Dutch dress of The Golden Age, when the Netherlands was a world power in the seventeenth century, is acknowledged as the only moment where the country appears in fashion history. While dignitaries at the French and English courts wore colourful and extravagant clothing, the Dutch regents dressed in austere black garments, decorated with white lace and starched collars (Laver, 1985: 108). They thus underscored a Calvinist approach to life of soberness and austerity without an ostentatious display of wealth,

although the fabrics and trimmings were in fact quite expensive. In contrast to the kingdom of France with its court culture, the Netherlands was an egalitarian and more or less democratic republic. Simon Schama explains the Dutch attitude of 'an embarrassment of riches' as the outcome of an uneasy and ambiguous relationship between the Protestant regents and their newly acquired wealth and power (Schama, 1987). The Dutch burghers did not delight in a flamboyant show of affluence, but preferred a sober, black, yet refined outfit, not only to give subtle expression to their taste but also to illustrate civil ideals of equality.

We will come back more extensively to the effects of the Golden Age on Dutch fashion in chapter 5, but here I want to explore its link to contemporary modernism. If we look beyond the surface of the seventeenth century clothes themselves, we see that today little has changed in Dutch attitudes toward dress and fashion. The fact that modernism found such a fertile breeding ground in the Netherlands some three centuries later is, in my view, closely related to the same mentality. In modernism, the concept of sobriety is perhaps less founded in religion, but the main idea remains that a good design should be protected from superfluous decoration or frivolous ornamentation. The strict lines, forms, shapes and restricted choice of colours in Mondrian's paintings and the designs of the artists of the De Stijl group pertain to a similar ideology as Calvinism in the seventeenth century. It is an ideology of equality, functionalism and rationality that is of essential importance in modernistic, or modernism-based, design.

'Form follows function' is the famous principle of the modernists. The design should always follow from an abstract idea or lofty concept. I want to argue that such conceptualism is visible in the work of all Dutch designers, which is the main reason why I advocated the label of 'Dutch Modernism' (Teunissen, 1994). Even the work of Viktor&Rolf, which is sometimes experienced as baroque, can be relayed back to a single central idea.

Take for example the 'Flowerbomb' collection (2005), which appears to be rather exuberant, but is in fact entirely based on the relatively simple principle of the bow (Smelik, 2014).

The austere fashions of the Dutch Golden Age, the strict and sober lines of Dutch modernist design and the conceptualism of contemporary fashion design together show that the Netherlands were never afraid of assuming its own idiosyncratic attitude to fashion. Founded on a clear and egalitarian vision of culture and certain ideals of sobriety, a characteristic notion of dress and fashion arose during the seventeenth century that is still valid today.

Dutch Fashion and Regional Dress

Since the new millennium Dutch fashion designers have shown a remarkable interest in Dutch folklore, regional dress and its related local crafts and techniques. Alexander van Slobbe, for example, started to use horizontal folds, amongst other techniques, for his 'Re-wind' menswear collection in 2001. The principle of horizontal folds was used in the province of Zeeland to fold clothes up as compactly as possible so as to be easily transported in the case of flooding by the sea if the dykes broke. In his own collection of menswear entitled 'Hope' (2008), Francisco van Benthum also plays with traditional elements of local costume, such as the use of buttons, pom-poms and old-fashioned baggy trousers. In their collection entitled 'Fashion Show' (A/W 2007–8) Viktor&Rolf applied dots and spots as conventionally used in the village of Staphorst, combined with traditional red coral, Zeeland buttons and various folding techniques employed in regional costume. This is also the show that prominently featured the ironic Dutch clogs on high heels (Teunissen, 2009).

The aim of the designers was not to evoke a romantic picture of bygone times, but rather to use form and technique as an inspiration to achieve a lucid,

modern design. This paradox is quite remarkable: how can modernist and conceptual Dutch designers also be devoted to traditional crafts and techniques and to regional costume? An explanation lies in the fact that although the Netherlands did not have an iconographic fashion heritage, the country did have a strikingly diverse culture of traditional costume (see Feitsma 2014 for a full exploration of this point). If there is such a thing as a dress tradition in the Netherlands, it can be found in regional dress. In old fishing villages such as Urk, Marken, Volendam or Spakenburg, regional dress is still worn, albeit to a limited degree and only by a hard core of devotees. It is moreover fully exploited for tourist purposes. Dutch citizens – and most tourists – are familiar with the folklore of clogs, tulips, windmills and Delft Blue, but hardly anyone knows that, in contrast to many other countries, the Dutch explicitly cultivated regional dress in the nineteenth century to escape from modernisation, urbanisation, consumerism and other urban whims (De Jong, 1998).

Dutch sociologists and ethnologists claim that regional dress fulfilled an important function in the realisation of the political ideals of the country in this period. In the early nineteenth century, the Netherlands had again become an assorted collection of provinces, just as in the seventeenth century (De Jong, 1998). After the secession of Belgium in 1830, the Netherlands became a kingdom. The monarchy and traditional customs were responsible for providing the necessary unity. The provinces were therefore allowed to cultivate their own mores, customs and traditions as long as everyone was prepared to fall in line with the national government.

According to Dutch historian Herman Pleij, this diversity can also be explained by the fact that since the late Middle Ages the Dutch had a culture primarily based on solidarity rather than on nationalism (Pleij, 1991). For centuries the Dutch could only survive if they collaborated in conquering the sea by building dykes and maintaining

14. Viktor&Rolf, 'Fashion Show' (A/W 2007–8).

them. Therefore, they worked together within a refined system that was primarily driven on cooperation, solidarity and equality (Prak and Van Zanden, 2013). The tolerance towards diversity in cultural origins and dress as well as the tolerance towards religion also fit in this typical Dutch culture where one tries to collaborate in a more or less democratic way, instead of obeying the rules that a nation dictates or prescribes. In such a perspective, solidarity is the opposite of nationalism.

After the heyday of the Golden Age, the country fell slightly behind the times in the following centuries. With the rise of industrialisation, newspapers, mobility and cosmopolitan city life in the course of the nineteenth century, French fashion became attractive for many European countries and cities (Steele, 1988). However, the Dutch were deterred from participating in the upcoming French fashion in the nineteenth century, because for them it was nothing more than an anonymous urban culture, while most people in the Netherlands still lived in villages or small towns. Afraid of losing their own identity and culture, the Dutch nostalgically preferred to sustain a traditional rural life, which they regarded as pure and uncontaminated by modern times (Rooijakkers, 1998: 175).

What did and does regional dress offer the Dutch that cosmopolitan – that is, Paris – fashion cannot? Regional costume is generally regarded as a style that is not subject to change, in contrast to the fast-changing trends of fashion (Lipovetsky, 1994: 21). Regional costume is based on fixed codes and certain meanings in clothing. The colours, ribbons or buttons on display show the social status of people, what religion they embrace, or their civil status. In short, it is a dress system that offers society various guidelines, certainties and a sense of belonging. In contrast, fashion is a self-reflective system: it constantly changes in form and meaning, and primarily refers to itself – just like autonomous art. To become familiar with the ever-changing fashion codes, one has to move in the right circles and be in the know. Fashion and

regional dress identify people in different ways – fashion mostly through class and regional dress mostly through origin. In a sense, this makes fashion more democratic than regional dress. Fashion is accessible to everyone (provided one has enough money), whereas regional dress is a question of birthright. As Georg Simmel (1919) already pointed out at the beginning of the twentieth century, fashion offers the wearer the opportunity to fit in with the group but also creates scope to emphasise one's own individuality. This means that fashion was ideal for meeting the needs of the modern masses of bourgeois citizens that arose as a result of the Enlightenment, urbanisation and modernisation in the nineteenth

15. Regional costumes in the Netherlands in the eighteenth century: farmer and wife from Gelderland, a province in the east of the Netherlands.

century. People acquired the freedom to indicate to which group they wished to belong by means of dress, while they retained the freedom to position themselves as individuals within that group (Lipovetsky, 1994: 82-83).

In regional dress there are strict social rules: people had to dress according to their social standing, gender, profession and civil status. Nevertheless, there was some leeway for individual variation. People could give the waistcoat, shawl or other parts of the costume a unique and personal look with handmade work, embroidery and variations in fabric. It was often a question of who could make the most attractive waistcoat, which others would then follow. As a result, Dutch regional dress culture developed an extensive culture of handmade work and treating textiles in which people could express their creativity. Yet, after the Second World War, regional dress quickly fell into disregard and is now relegated mostly to some mostly elderly devotees or to nostalgic fairs and tourist attractions.

In the last decade Dutch fashion designers have shown a remarkable interest in Dutch regional dress and they have started to cooperate with small-scale manufacturers and local craftsmen who are producing for the villages where regional dress is still worn. While the traditional crafts and manual techniques exude an atmosphere of traditional quality and lend 'authenticity' to a product, the Dutch designers regard them mainly as a rich source of inspiration for developing new and fresh designs. An interesting cooperation is an excellent example of this practice: fashion designer van Slobbe worked together with the oldest porcelain factory in the Netherlands, Royal Tichelaar Makkum, to create ceramic pearls in the spirit of the seventeenth century painter Johannes Vermeer. The porcelain 'pearls' are not only beautiful, but acquire an extra dimension with their reference to Dutch history and especially to Vermeer's famous painting *The Girl with a Pearl Earring*. Moreover, the design expresses a deep love of fine craftsmanship, making it into a valuable artistic object.

Along the same lines, Viktor&Rolf regularly take Dutch heritage as a starting point for their designs. For instance, they studied Dutch lace for their 'Bedtime Story' collection (A/W 2005–6), and created the collection 'Silver' (A/W 2006–7) on the traditional Dutch custom of silver-plating baby shoes. The duo centred the 'Fashion Show' collection (A/W 2007–8) on various styles of regional costume, including Dutch wooden clogs with high heels. In addition to regional dress, this collection also covered the fashion show as a social phenomenon. Each model wore a ready-made installation of sound and light, where the installation itself influenced the design. In such a way, both cultural heritage and a conceptual approach came together in the fashion show.

To come back to the concepts that Jennifer Craik (2009) introduced for recognising a national style in a country without much fashion history, we can now see that the first term of 'aesthetic distinctiveness' can be found in Dutch fashion based on local craftsmanship and certain techniques of folding and pleating and the preference for fabrics as wool and cotton. The second term, 'cultural practice', expresses the mixing together of cultural heritage with the conceptual approach of modernism, as we have seen in the examples of appropriating aspects from regional dress and craftsmanship into modern designs. And finally, the third term, 'cultural articulation', refers to the specific attitude of soberness, austerity and democratic equality dating back to the seventeenth century, and enhanced by the conceptualism of modernism in the late nineteenth and early twentieth century. This is the point in Dutch fashion where internal and external perceptions of the essence of national stylistic identity overlap. Here, we can project continuity in style from Calvinism to Modernism, which in the Dutch context is 'taken for granted' and accepted as the 'natural' style of the nation. This has resulted in a particular Dutch cultural outlook towards fashion of solidarity and open-mindedness with a strong affinity

16. Porcelain 'pearl' designed by Alexander van Slobbe and made by Royal Tichelaar Makkum (2006).

JOSÉ TEUNISSEN

for artistic experiment on the one hand, and a recurrent reserve towards French fashion and frivolity combined with a strong preference for modernist rigour on the other hand.

Conclusion

Starting from a comparable historical background, the fashion cultures of the two neighbouring countries of Belgium and the Netherlands have gone different ways since the 1980s. They developed dissimilar approaches to 'national identity' as a strategy to promote their fashion designers. Where Alison Goodrum (2005) describes national identity in British fashion as 'a confection of selective memories' recognisable both to the local inhabitants as well as to an international consumer market, this only held true for the Dutch designers and not for the Belgian ones. As we have seen, many Dutch designers actively mine their cultural heritage for novel designs. In promoting SO by Alexander van Slobbe in Japan during the 1990s, the Japanese kept emphasising the importance of enhancing the product's Dutch identity. Van Slobbe managed to convince the Japanese market with press material telling the story of the long history of Dutch modernism in abstract and formal design (van den Berg, 2008). The Belgian designers were equally successful in Japan, but none of them referred to their Belgian roots. Internationally, they were seen as 'creative' and 'original'

designers having managed to transform Belgium and Antwerp into a fashion hotspot. Their success was first driven by an ingenious marketing and business strategy for young Belgian designers by the national government, and then followed by a convincing city branding of Antwerp by the Flanders federal government.

The Dutch designers were on the contrary less supported by government or industry, but were instead marginally subsidised by artistic funds. They developed a more artistic and experimental approach to design, referring back to the clear lines and forms of both Dutch Modernism of the early twentieth century and Calvinism of the seventeenth century. The conceptual approach fitted in with a general cultural outlook in the Netherlands based on democracy, solidarity and egalitarianism, combined with a persistent reserve towards the frivolities of high fashion. While this particular expression of cultural identity can partly be explained as a compensation for the lack of an industry network, I have argued in this chapter that Dutch Modernism in fashion is part and parcel of a robust and vivid Dutch design tradition and cultural mentality.

Notes

1. An earlier and quite different version of this article has been published in *Fashion Theory*, 15 (2), 2011: 157-76. The article has been extensively rewritten for the context of the present book, including updates of the data and other factual information.

Max Heymans (Arnhem 1918–Amsterdam 1997)

Lianne Toussaint

> My style never changes. Sometimes even I
> don't know any more from what year a particular
> garment dates.
> —Max Heymans, 1997

The fifties and sixties were the highlights in the career of this doyen of Dutch fashion, but Max Heymans remained active until well into the nineties and always stayed true to his classical style. Labelled as an 'unbusinesslike, chaotic, colourful bohemian,' Heymans considered Parisian couture his shining example (Van der Meyden quoted in G. Koning, 2010: 108). Adopting as well as wearing Parisian womenswear with vigour, Heymans soon earned the nickname 'Madame Chanel'. His salon presentations, with golden chairs, a lady speaker providing comments and mannequins holding numbered plates, were a close imitation of the classic Parisian salon style. Heymans frankly admitted this by frequently and willingly citing the words of his mother, the most beloved person in his life: 'everyone lives by copying and imitating. That's why everything is always exactly the same, yet also always completely different' (Koning, 2010: 108).

During the fifty years of his career in couture, the flamboyant designer presented over 8,000 creations. Being anything but business-minded and always short of money, Heymans still managed to present a collection twice every year. His final shows were said to pass by 'like a sluggish train with a broken motor'; the pace was slow and several garments still contained visible pins and tacking cotton (De Baan, 2006: 86). Yet, up until the very end of his career Heymans was praised for his elegant ensembles, capturing the essence of Parisian fashion, or, as he liked to describe them himself: 'dead chic'. He did not master the couture profession technically, but thought of himself as 'a top dog in pinning': 'I am a producer rather than a couturier. I make the drawings and the seamstresses do the rest' (Ibid.).

An autodidact, Heymans started his career at a very young age. As a teenager he was a window dresser at two Jewish enterprises: fashion house Gerzon in The Hague and the prestigious department store Hirsch in Amsterdam. In 1938 he opened his own hat salon, but being a Jewish 'guy with a considerable nose', he immediately went into hiding when the war started (Kromer, 2012). For lack of material during the war, he sometimes coloured tricot underwear with tea and then turned it into lovely headgear. Heymans survived the war, but his cherished mother was killed just before the liberation.

At the beginning of the fifties Heymans designed garments to go with his hats and gradually created a position for himself as fashion designer. His elegant evening dresses and tight-fitting tailored women suits were in great demand in the art and theatre world. Renowned Dutch actresses, dancers and singers belonged to his loyal clientele. By the time the sixties started, Heymans was a famous couturier who was asked to design a series of hats for then crown princess Beatrix. In the 1980s a biennial lifetime achievement award was named after the eccentric fashion designer: the Max Heymans ring. After his death, his archive was entrusted to the Gemeentemuseum (Municipal Museum) in The Hague, where Heymans is still treasured as the paragon of veritable old school couture.

3.

Contours of the Dutch Fashion Industry

Michiel Scheffer

Introduction

This chapter gives an overview of the evolution of the clothing and fashion industry in the Netherlands over the period 1946–2015. A sketch of the contours of the Dutch industry involves two stories: one of a fashion industry with a focus on the creation of cultural and symbolic value (as mostly told by José Teunissen in the previous chapter) and one of a clothing industry with the focus on factors of production and the creation and appropriation of economic and financial value. The clothing industry can be defined as an industry that makes textile materials into finished products through sewing operations. The concept of 'fashion industry' is more difficult to use, since it has no fixed definition nor does it translate into statistical classification, but I take it here as a post-industrial phenomenon that focuses on the design activities within a fashion cycle.

This chapter discusses changes in the Dutch clothing and fashion industry due to external factors as well as internal factors, such as are discussed in the Introduction to this book. In tracing the history of the Dutch clothing and fashion industry, the focus in the postwar period until 1980 lies more on the industrial side of the story, while after 1980 the fashion dimension is foregrounded. The transition from material value creation (through manufacturing) to immaterial value creation (through design and branding) is a paradigm change that summarises the key challenge of the overall period. This transition is, I shall explain, also visible in the discourse on the industry in annual reports of the industry and policy reports. Such a shift meant overcoming barriers that Grabher (2003) has called 'lock-in' factors. The evolution of clothing manufacturing into a fashion industry requires new skills and the ability to overcome cognitive and institutional lock-ins. It involves deindustrialisation, a reorientation of assets and the handling of functional lock-ins. The paradigm shift also requires a different institutional environment in terms of policies, industrial organisation and industrial relations.

In the postwar story of the Dutch clothing industry I shall focus on three emancipation processes. The first one is the emancipation of Dutch fashion from the dominance of Paris as a fashion metropolis towards a creative sector in a global context. The second process is the adoption of and then emancipation from the American Taylorist production mode. The third process culminates in the massive involvement of women as workers in the clothing industry, but also their emancipation in the work process and in the industry at large. As will become clear in this chapter, these processes are neither linear nor unproblematic.

Three historical stages can be distinguished in the evolution of the Dutch clothing industry. Between 1946 and 1958 the sector evolves from a tailoring craft to an industry, largely inspired by American production methods and fuelled by a rapid growth of consumption. Between 1958 and 1988 the clothing industry restructures and downsizes by off-shoring production. This period is also characterised by attempts to shape a national fashion identity. From 1988 onwards, the clothing industry is revived by a change into a fashion industry, inspired by a post-industrial fashion paradigm. While the turning points are somewhat arbitrary, they do coincide with the founding of the European Economic Community in 1958 and the start of negotiations on multilateral trade liberalisation in 1988. Before turning to the period after the Second World War, I will first describe the beginnings of the clothing industry in the Netherlands.

Inception of the Dutch Clothing Industry

The clothing industry is rather a young industry in the Netherlands. In Amsterdam and Groningen most factories before 1920 were large tailor shops, except in the lingerie industry. Clothing manufacturers were often merchants in fabrics, with cutting rooms and a network of home tailors and seamstresses. In larger

21. Queen Wilhelmina pays a visit to the Hollandia clothing factory with managing director Jacques Kattenburg (1936).

cities family-owned sweatshops competed for work from these merchants. Many of those tailors were Jewish immigrants. In the 1920s Amsterdam emerged as the centre of the clothing industry. It was the hub of ladieswear and in Europe a leader in ladies' coats (Grijpma, 2001). The pioneer in clothing-making in the Netherlands was Berghaus. This firm made women's coats in a labyrinth of workshops on the Prinsengracht in Amsterdam. In the east, Twente's clothing industry was cotton-based and a spin-off of the local textile industry, while in the south Tilburg specialised in woollen trousers and coats, and in the north Groningen was the leading city for men's suits.

In the 1930s the Dutch clothing industry received a stimulus from political events in Germany. As Gerard Van Dalen, former Chairman of the industry association NEVEC, expressed it: 'we hosted the Jewish ladieswear industry from Berlin' (Scheffer, 1990). The Second World War signified a dramatic interruption of the development of the Dutch clothing industry. Although the clothing industry would recover rapidly after 1945, the anti-Jewish policies of the German occupiers decimated the entrepreneurship and skills base of the industry. Most Jewish workers and clerks in the clothing industry were deported and killed in the extermination camps. The story of Hollandia-Kattenburg was typical of larger Jewish firms (see the profile in this chapter). Factories were hardly affected by bombing, while most firms were substantially engaged for military production. The production of uniforms, tents and tank covers was a rather basic routine production that deskilled workers and did not foster a high quality attitude. The loss of skilled workers would have a profound and long-term effect on the industry's competitiveness, especially its ability to upgrade in quality and flexibility. The German occupation also created the basis for a corporatist model, with the introduction of a collective wage convention. The office responsible for allocating army orders formed the basis for the postwar industrial organisation.

1946–58: Dynamic Growth

The period 1946–58 was a period of dynamic growth for the clothing industry and for the Dutch textile industry in its slipstream. The ingredients for this success were simple. Demand for clothing recovered in Europe from 1947 onwards. The Netherlands had the production capacities and infrastructure to meet this demand, unlike the German industry. Germany would only reach pre-war production in clothing in 1960. The United Kingdom had shifted its labour base to military production. Wages were lower in the Netherlands than in surrounding countries such as Belgium. At the time, the Netherlands had relatively higher import duties for textiles and clothing compared to other European countries. The Netherlands could thus become the ladies' coats supplier of postwar Europe, with the town of Tilburg in the south, which now hosts the Dutch Textile Museum, producing the coarse woollen fabrics.

The clothing industry developed along a paradigm of large-scale industrialisation. Recovery of the economy fuelled mainly demand for mass production. Trends were set in Paris, but the skill of the Dutch industry was to simplify the designs in order to be able to make them in an industrial mode. Rising labour participation

also fostered the replacement of domestic needlework by industrial prêt-à-porter, while the rise of a large-scale retail formula fostered concentration of buying power. Large clothing chains like C&A (see profile in chapter 7), V&D, P&C, and Kreymborg sold medium-quality fashion for the entire family, in a rather conformist style.[1] The industry in this period can be seen mainly as a provider of affordable and conventional clothing – following more or less the Paris fashion trends.

Marshall Aid and study trips to the United States helped to adopt modern factory equipment and Taylorist production methods such as modern factory outlay, conveyor belts, and time and motion studies. The factories were organised towards a maximum division of labour. This was made possible by a focus on large production orders and limited variety in designs. It made possible the recruitment of workers without prior qualifications, who could obtain high productivity with little training. Substantial investments were done in cutting equipment and in fast sewing machines. The clothing industry was much more inclined than the textile industry to invest in labour-saving equipment as the fast-growing demand could not be matched by labour supply (Scheffer, 2009).

The Dutch clothing industry organised its work around a typical female labour participation pattern. Dutch women joined the industry after secondary school at sixteen years of age and worked for five to eight years until marriage or pregnancy. Female incomes helped to establish a household, as male incomes were deemed sufficient to run a family. Dutch manufacturers chose to (re)locate factories in places with a high birth rate and a high propensity of young women to take up factory work, which was a typical feature of Catholic communities in an otherwise predominantly Protestant country. These were, for instance, Catholic villages around Amsterdam, such as the fishing village of Volendam (now a tourist attraction), and especially the Catholic south and east of the Netherlands. In Limburg the State Mining Company (now DSM) set up clothing workshops to offer employment for the daughters of mining workers. New factories had a reputation of being well laid out with ample light, good canteens and good sanitary conditions. However, management was paternalistic, organisation was rigid and workers were drilled to be efficient in a small number of operations. As labour turnover was high, upgrading quality and flexibility remained difficult. The industry is mainly seen as a paternalistic employer providing incomes and good working conditions for young women before their marriage, without, however, having a vision for the emancipation of women.

Growth of the industry was enabled by a corporatist organisation structure. Its foundation was laid in the 1930s, but was expanded by the German occupation. The office for allocation of German army orders was transformed into the industry association NEVEC. Its first director Herman Koetsier set up the clothing engineering school in Amsterdam that would bear his name from 1948 until the 1990s (now AMFI, the Amsterdam Fashion Institute). The framework of collective bargaining agreements was further developed. Relationships with unions followed a pacification model, because the high demand for clothing did not tolerate labour unrest. Since unionisation was high amongst male workers, rapid increases in wages were negotiated for male jobs, but much less so for female jobs.

The economic interests of the clothing industry were well covered. NEVEC initiated a range of activities such as market information services and export promotion. The Amsterdam Fashion Week was the first European postwar trade fair, set up in 1947. Its biannual occurrence, including a sea cruise with fresh herring, proved a highlight in the buyers' season. In this period marketing was in the process of becoming a discipline, and the clothing and textile schools took up marketing in their curriculum from 1954 onwards. But marketing still meant simply selling: the marketing practice is one

of advertising and sales training, while NEVEC merely collected market information and followed trends. Developing a design narrative or brand identities was not yet on the agenda.

In the 1950s, Amsterdam developed as the unrivalled capital of the European coat and rainwear industry. Kattenburg re-emerged after the war with factories across the Netherlands with almost 7,000 workers. When Macintosh took over Kattenburg in the 1960s it became the largest clothing manufacturer in Europe. The menswear industry thrived in northern Groningen (Brothers Levie) and flourished in the south in Brabant (Van Gils; see chapter 7).

While the pre-war industry could boast a wide variety of industrialisation models, from retailers with own manufacturing units to tailoring sweatshops, postwar industrialisation featured only two dominant models. The first model consisted of manufacturing integrated with design and wholesaling functions. The companies organised according to this model had a headquarters, or at least a showroom, in Amsterdam, first along the canals in the city centre and later in a special centre for the textile industry in the western outskirts of the city. The second model consisted of manufacturing integrated in retailing. Especially from 1950 to 1970 large retailers wanted to secure access to manufacturing, and C&A set up a factory in Amsterdam with subsidiaries near to Eindhoven in the south, while Peek & Cloppenburg had factories in and around Rotterdam.

Two other clothing industry models did not make it after the war. One, the model of designers operating independently with their own brand, did not develop in the Netherlands. And while Paris fashions had a notable influence, its business model failed to be taken up. Well-known designers such as Max Heymans (see profile in chapter 2) and Frans Molenaar (see profile in chapter 4) remained tailoring boutiques for a limited audience without ever developing an industrial approach.

22. Textile factory Mi-Lock with female workers in Hulst, Zeeland (c.1956).

This is quite unlike the situation in Paris, where for instance Christian Dior was backed by textile manufacturer Boussac, and Pierre Cardin developed a system of licensing. The established industry in the Netherlands showed little interest for designers until 1970. Designers lacked access to international markets or to finance and missed an industrial backbone of subcontractors to make quality products. This was partly due to the fact that subcontractors working for industrial clients had disappeared in the war. Unlike Paris the Netherlands lacked the flexibility of a large network of subcontractors until 1980.

1958–88: European Unification and Industrial Decline

The formation of the European Economic Community in 1958 was a decisive moment for the Dutch clothing industry. Till 1958 the Netherlands had benefited from a rapid recovery of demand and production and an easy entry to the German and Belgian markets. The Dutch market was protected because of import duties; Italian imports in particular were discouraged. Moreover, the Dutch industry benefited from cost advantages because the law allowed uneven pay between men and women. Women's wages in the Netherlands were lower than in the other five founders of the single market of the EEC. Most of these benefits were to be lost in the 1960s.

23. In spite of this merry and colourful advertisement, business was not going so well for Hollandia (date unknown).

By 1960, Germany's clothing industry had recovered its pre-war level. Germany chose a different industrialisation path: the surplus of single women after the war prompted the industry to offer women long-term employment and multi-skilling of workers, while it also adopted more flexible labour methods and a more participatory management style. This German system was reinforced by a dual education system, combining formal education and in-company apprenticeship. With rising demand the German industry developed into a higher market segment. The German textile industry, unlike its Dutch equivalent, modernised its equipment, assisted by a strong machine-building sector. Hence the German industry had access to more competitive fabrics than the Dutch. In menswear the German industry was far more skilled in processing fine woollen fabrics than the Dutch industry.

Italy also emerged after 1958 as a leader in fashionable products. This was born out of scarcity. Since Italy had had difficult access to world markets from the 1920s, it had become highly skilled in making fashionable synthetics, wool blends and fabrics from regenerated wool. Besides a price advantage Italy offered a broader variety of styles than the Dutch industry. In the 1960s, with the advent of Valentino and Gucci, the Italians developed an industrial approach to luxury fashion that surpassed even the French. By the mid 1960s the German and Italian

MICHIEL SCHEFFER

industries had a firm foothold in the middle and upper part of the fashion market.

It is, then, not surprising that the Dutch textile industry went into crisis from 1958 onwards, while the clothing industry was to follow from 1967 onwards. The Dutch textile industry had generally not used the growth years of the 1950s to modernise in product-mix or equipment (Scheffer, 2009; Hesselink, 2010). German, French and Italian weavers had the benefits of economies of scale of a large home market. Germany had developed a price advantage and both Germans and Italians maintained higher-quality standards. Unlike in those countries, the Dutch textile and clothing industry had not developed a value chain approach. Textile 'barons' (as they were called in the Netherlands) had a condescending view of Dutch clothing firms (called 'boeren' or farmers), which they considered merely as a captive outlet. Dutch clothing makers took benefit of the single market to source fabrics in other European countries. The Tilburg weavers were the first to suffer from competition from Biella and Prato in Italy.

While brands from other European countries got a good footing in the Dutch market through independent retailers and upmarket department stores such as De Bijenkorf, the lower end was pressured by cheaper imports. The first liberalisation of international trade from 1958 incited large retailers such as C&A to start sourcing lower-cost products abroad. They did this partly in Europe, especially in Italy and in Portugal. In the same period Hong Kong, Taiwan, Singapore and South Korea emerged as textile and clothing suppliers. The typical pattern of the 1960s for the Dutch industry was to be squeezed between a middle and upper market with an upcoming European competition and a low end covered by imports. This means that in the middle of the market large retailers had a dominant market share and a strong bargaining position towards manufacturers, squeezing their profit margins.

In the first half of the 1960s the growth rates of the industry dropped, and with growing productivity employment started to stabilise. In the second half of the 1960s production started to decline, leading to a fast drop in employment. The initial response of the Dutch industry was price competition. It was necessary to reduce costs as large retailers pressured selling prices and profit margins were squeezed. Cost reduction was, however, much hampered by rapidly rising labour costs due to two developments in Dutch society: the introduction of wage equality between men and women in 1964 and the introduction of the minimum wage in 1968. Attempts to increase productivity by improving factory layout, work methods and modernising equipment were largely squashed by rising wages.

The Dutch clothing industry thus started to move production out of the Netherlands in the 1960s. This happened first for reasons of labour market shortages and later due to labour costs. The main beneficiary of the delocalisation of production in the 1960s was initially the neighbouring country, Belgium. Production in Southern Europe and in Northern Africa started later, around 1970. Subcontracting of production to Eastern Europe, mainly Yugoslavia and Hungary, started around 1967. The Dutch clothing industry adopted few other strategies to counter decline. Upgrading in quality or market position rarely occurred, with any attempts ending in failure. Levie Brothers in Groningen tried from 1960 onwards to target a higher quality level in suits, but failed to master the interlining techniques required to process fine woollen fabrics. It therefore lost market share to German competitors. From 1968 onwards the Dutch industry failed to respond to more casual dress styles. Jeans production started around 1971, while denim production was only picked up in a joint venture by Ten Cate in Greece as late as in 1974. The Dutch textile industry also ignored the emergence of synthetic fibres. The demand for synthetic products was covered by imported fabrics (e.g. for women's blouses) or imported products (e.g. anoraks).

From 1967 the story of the Dutch clothing industry was characterised by closure and reorganisation of production, and bankruptcies of firms. The bankruptcy of the large Haarlem-based Konesmann group in 1967 came as quite a shock to the industry. When Hollandia-Kattenburg came into trouble, it was taken over by Macintosh. However, consolidation of the industry did not avoid restructuring of production: Macintosh continued to close factories and shifted production to Portugal and Tunisia. Some clothing companies were taken over by textile suppliers that wanted to secure sales, but this only postponed the necessary restructuring.

Towards Globalised Production

The 1970s was a period of ongoing restructuring but also of a change in strategies, with new business models emerging. By the beginning of the 1980s these had mostly converged, with companies only engaged in design and commercialisation. Production was by then almost entirely subcontracted or delocalised offshore. This convergence was a combination of different strategies. Berghaus, the second largest manufacturer, chose for a 'big bang' and closed all its Dutch factories in 1976. Van Gils opted for a gradual shift, closing production in the Netherlands, moving them first to Belgium, and later to North Africa, Greece and Mexico, until ultimately by 1980 only two factories in Morocco remained. Vilenzo also shifted all manufacturing from the Netherlands to North Africa, Sri Lanka, Mauritius and Pakistan.

Other companies followed a different strategy, solely engaging in design and marketing, with all production subcontracted. The Velthoven Group as well as the founding group of G-Star emerged in the 1970s as designers, importers and marketers of casual clothing. They relied on subcontracting in Eastern Europe and sourcing in Asia. The founder of Mexx, Rattan Chadha, started his successful (import) business (see chapter

8). Established retailers set up retail formulas aiming at a younger audience and therefore integrated design teams with subcontracted production; Peek & Cloppenburg, for instance, started Mac&Maggie with designer Cora Kemperman (see chapters 5 and 9). In these years, designers such as Frans Molenaar (see profile in chapter 4) emerged, who had a licensing agreement with menswear firm Van Kollem. But designers produced on a small scale, mainly for a small clientele.

More design-oriented fashion brands emerged in the 1970s, of which only a few had an industrial background. Van Gils, for example, was a manufacturer successful in developing a younger, more colourful approach to men's fashion, that also learned to master the techniques for lighter jacket structures (see chapter 7). Claudia Sträter, a retailer born of a merger between two family companies, set up its own brand for the affluent middle classes supported with subcontracted production in the Netherlands (see profile in chapter 8). Examples of brands that worked with subcontractors in the Netherlands are Marielle Bolier, who started a new approach to swimwear, and childrenswear Oilily. Gloria Kok initiated a factory mainly to support small designer brands emerging in the 1970s. Interestingly, it was former managers or employees of large firms, who, after being made redundant, started their own company, who made these initiatives possible.

In those years the importance of design was recognised, although it was still viewed as rather problematic. A policy report made in 1972 for the Ministry of Economic Affairs highlighted the transition of the clothing industry from a manufacturing sector to a creative and commercial sector (KWW, 1972). As José Teunissen writes in the previous chapter, the 'dictate' of Paris was no longer dominant due to a number of influences, including street fashion. Fashion was understood as a vector of differentiation and competition, but also as a risk factor leading to clearance sales and unsold inventory, and hence to lower profits. In the 1970s design was still largely defined as rapidly picking up and translating trends. The industry set up, with government support, the Dutch Fashion Institute with the aim of forecasting trends, which would operate from 1972 until 2000. The importance of design as a function for revamping the industry was recognised and assistance was offered to ailing industrial firms. Designer Dick Holthaus, for example, brought his modernist industrial design approach to the Groningen menswear sector. Colour and polyester fibres were introduced – with little success – in the traditional tailoring sector.

The attempts in the Netherlands of saving the clothing industry were not as systematic and enduring as the approaches set up by Scandinavian countries or by Italy: while Denmark and Finland engaged in defining a Scandinavian fashion identity, the Italians set up a strong coalition of design, industry and government. The Italian design strategy was thus largely export-oriented and based on a competitive industrial base.

Government intervention became a salient feature in the Netherlands in the seventies, but it was erratic in its implementation. The benchmark of policy was to stay ahead of low-cost competition and partly accept it, because delocalisation of production seemed inevitable. Strategies and policies did not deliver the necessary analysis – that the Dutch industry was not competitive in the middle-to-upper segments of the market and that comprehensive upgrading was needed. Consequently, investment in modern production equipment was largely geared towards increasing productivity, and not to increasing quality or flexibility. Instruments fostering (financial) restructuring were mainly oriented towards ailing firms with demotivated management. Design actions were more oriented towards styling and less towards developing a singular identity. Marketing was merely defined as a push strategy of identifying target groups and mobilising advertising, but not as a branding strategy. Most firms failed in developing a clear design identity and brand narrative.

24. An ad in black and white in the magazine *Panorama* in the early 1960s for the Stijlgroep Groningen to promote 'the summer feel of wool'. The heading reads: 'Summer suits by Stijlgroep Groningen, nicely cool'.

There were some attempts to slow down the closure of production in the 1970s, mostly in places with strong unionisation, such as Groningen. Public policy remained split. On the one hand, there was a feeling of inevitability of a new international division of labour in which there was no longer a place for a textile and clothing industry in the Netherlands. On the other hand, social democratic parties were sensitive to the social impact of closures in Groningen in the north (menswear), in Enschede in the east (textiles), and Breda in the south (fibres). In all of these cities, restructuring gave rise to workers' unrest and strikes. Moreover, strategies to turn the tide were not successful. The main approach was to bundle unprofitable companies in cooperatives, such as the

Stijlgroep ('style group') in Groningen. However, these concentrations were invariably based on overestimated sales targets and were soon followed by yet another round of downsizing.

The consulting firm Kurt Salmon Associates (KSA, 1982) presented a rather sombre analysis of the Dutch clothing industry in 1982. By 1980 the industry had already lost two-thirds of its employment compared to 1967 and employed little over 20,000 workers. High labour costs were not considered to be matched by a high level productivity, skills and technical organisation. While KSA considered production equipment to be good, the management of workers and organisation was found weak. The paternalistic management style and the inability of motivating staff to reach a higher skills base was a constant factor in the decline of the industry. The KSA report confirmed that investments were purely motivated by higher productivity, not quality and flexibility.

Moreover, it underlined the biased gender policies of the Dutch clothing industry. In 1982 the majority of workers in the clothing industry, 60 per cent, was female and below 27 years of age. KSA noted the high labour turnover and sickness leaves. This confirmed a constant pattern after the war of recruiting young and unskilled female workers. The low share of workers employed for more than twelve years (20 per cent compared to 35 per cent in other EU countries), compounded the lack of skills needed to make quality products. The industrial organisation of Dutch firms relegated them to the lower market segments, which hindered a consistent product quality and restrained designers in their creativity. KSA reported a lack of interest in improving the factories, since management concentrated its efforts in foreign production and subcontracting.

KSA also stressed that the cost disadvantage of the industry was not matched by a better product policy or marketing. Product quality, styling and branding scored significantly lower than the European competition in

all product groups. The dominance of large retailers, the weakness of brand identity and the lack of focus in product range led to collections that were too broad and manufacturing orders that were too small. Companies were mainly sales-driven, trying to keep large retailers as clients at all costs. The industry may have become skilled in picking up the trends, but it was certainly not trendsetting. Brands lacked a clear identity with a deep narrative, while branding policies were not consistent and publicity budgets and policies were erratic. Sales expenditures were high compared to European competitors; although Dutch firms were active on fairs and had large sales staffs, their effectiveness was limited by poor marketing.

While the Kurt Salmon Associates report sketched a rather devastating image of the Dutch clothing and textile industry, the 1980s were a period of further decline but also of transformation (Scheffer, 1990). The decline mainly concerned established firms, while the transformation was largely the result of newcomers into the industry. As mentioned above, many of the new firms and brands were spin-offs of defunct companies like Macintosh and Berghaus. In contrast to the decade before, companies started to develop a styling identity and branding strategies. The 1980s witnessed the growth of Mexx (chapter 8) and Mac&Maggie (chapters 5 and 9), but also of smaller brands like Sandwich and Turnover. The 1980s also witnessed the success years of Van Gils (chapter 7) and Oilily (chapter 5) as well as the start of G-Star (see profile in chapter 1) and Vanilia (chapter 10).

The 1980s saw the advent of fast fashion (Scheffer, 1994a). This created a new class of wholesalers and was supported by an emerging group of immigrant entrepreneurs, often with a Turkish background. The sweatshops they set up were geared to fast fashion, but their closeness to Amsterdam also provided production facilities for starting designers (Tap, 1986). Around the mid-1980s there were hopes that the growing demand for better products, faster fashion and customisation, combined with automation of manufacturing, would fuel a revival of production in the Netherlands. This did not happen, as the majority of companies had adjusted to global competition by outsourcing production.

1988–Present: Towards a Creative Industry

As we have assessed, by the 1990s clothing production in the Netherlands had disappeared almost completely (Scheffer, 1992). Industrial employment had gradually declined in the 1980s from over 20,000 to little over 10,000 people. Most of the employees were still female, but the majority no longer worked in the factory (c. 35 per cent) but in design, marketing and clerical functions. My PhD research was the next comprehensive study of the Dutch clothing industry after the KSA report in 1982 (Scheffer, 1992). By 1992 the problems of industrial organisations were largely solved. Most factories in the Netherlands were now closed; in the menswear sector, for example, only four out of more than thirty factories in 1980 remained. Surviving factories often served as product development units for small-scale production and for quick response to reorders of retailers. Restructuring often meant that staff had to be made redundant on the basis of a fair representation of all age groups. Although skilled workers had been retained, the lack of younger workers now put a constraint on the future of firms. Between 1989 and 1994 most of the remaining manufacturing units in the Netherlands closed (Scheffer, 1994b).

Unlike in previous restructurings the overall employment impact was small, as the decline in production jobs was compensated by growth in non-manufacturing jobs. Moreover, immigrant Turkish entrepreneurs set up a large sweatshop sector in Amsterdam and other cities (Tap, 1986; Raes, 2000). The Turkish clothing workshops provided Amsterdam, like Paris and London, with a flexible production capacity. The combined action of public authorities and the established industry first curtailed and then eliminated this segment in the 1990s. Suspected reliance on illegal immigrants and substantial evasion of taxation and social charges were reasons to severely constrain this sector, which also out-competed the established subcontractors in the south of the Netherlands.

The commercial approach of the industry looked far more positive in 1992 than in 1982. This is merely an effect of the composition of the industry. Firms with weak brands and styling had disappeared and firms with a clear lifestyle brand had survived or developed. Manufacturers only servicing large retailers also survived. They achieved this by combining large-scale production in Eastern Europe with reorders and quick response enabled by a flexible Turkish sweatshop sector.

From the 1990s onwards, the clothing industry defined itself as a fashion industry or even – timidly and too early – as a creative industry. The industry association (now called FENECON), co-funded by the Ministry of Economic Affairs, set up a Holland Fashion programme with the aim of promoting export. This policy highlighted a new generation of designers amongst international buyers: Soap Studio, orson + bodil and Marlies Dekkers were championed as the Dutch novelties. Together with the success of 'Le Cri Néerlandais' in the middle of the 1990s, described by José Teunissen in the previous chapter, such 'enfants terribles' served to change the image of Dutch fashion, giving it a much more unorthodox profile in line with the progressive image of the country. From the point of view of the industry, their role was merely to help sell more conventional brands, because the economic significance of high-end fashion brands remained small, covering less than 5% of the industry's total turnover.

The major step towards a creative industry came rather from the demise after 2000 of those large companies that served organised retailers without a clear design identity. The companies that had survived the 1970s and 1980s had largely done so by off-shoring and outsourcing all production, and by combining sales to large retailers (so-called private label) with own brands. These brands had been repositioned towards the upper-middle segment and had become more successful with a clearer branding story. After the devaluation of the dollar in 2001–2 and further liberalisation of international trade, this mixed model was no longer tenable (IFM/Saxion, 2006). The mixed model, adopted by SECON, the group owning the G-Star and Turnover brands, but also by Vilenzo and Berghaus, had the benefit of combining economies of scale through the volumes for large retailers and higher margin because of own brands. Most companies had indeed acknowledged that a profitable survival would come from brands alone, preferably supported by their own retail outlets. The strategy of for instance Vilenzo, like many others, was to gradually move out of their private label and shift to a portfolio of brands. Large retailers could not enable this gradual transition, but speeded up their direct sourcing, also because of fierce competition of H&M and Zara, that combined a fashionable offer, a fast turnover of collections and directly controlled sourcing. Many Dutch firms started to develop their own brands too late and were hit by declining buying orders from large retailers. Interface Fashion, a spun-off of the C&A factories, went bust in 2004; Modens, the successor of Hertzberger, the factory of Peek & Cloppenburg, went bankrupt in 2002; Berghaus, the oldest remaining Dutch manufacturer went bust twice, and Vilenzo went bankrupt in 2007. Yet, looking back on sixty years of rise, decline and transformation, it is remarkable that the Dutch clothing industry has maintained its turnover. After 1990 overall employment has remained stable, with a shift from manufacturing to design and trading activities (Scheffer, 2012).

Moreover, there are some new developments. From 1990 onwards the Netherlands became a base for many European headquarters of foreign firms because of tax benefits. This – now criticised – trend started in the sportswear-industry when NIKE set up European headquarters in Hilversum, near Amsterdam. NIKE became the largest employer of textile and clothing graduates in the 1990s. The jeans industry was to follow, with Pepe relocating its design department from Manchester to Amsterdam. Pepe's presence in Amsterdam was short-lived, but its takeover by Tommy Hilfiger made Amsterdam into the global headquarter of one of the biggest global fashion companies.

By 2010 Amsterdam started calling itself the jeans capital of the world, as evidenced by chapter 6. This is a slight exaggeration, demonstrating the end of the dominance of Levi's and the transformation of the jeans business into a multipolar world (Scheffer, 2008). However, with Tommy Hilfiger, Dockers, G-Star, Blue Blood and many smaller brands, Amsterdam has a sizeable concentration of design, marketing and financing functions in denim. The combination of advantageous tax policies, excellent logistical infra-structures and a large design school capacity, makes the Netherlands an interesting location.

The design cluster has also been strengthened from 2005 onwards by a policy of creating more economic value out of artistic or creative activities. The industry has already promoted its creative dimension in the Holland Fashion programme from the 1980s onwards. An attempt to position the fashion industry as a design-led sector failed in 1996 (Scheffer, 2009). However, a government strategy document of 2004 recognised fashion as a creative industry. In 2006, the creative industries were recognised as a so-called 'top sector' by the national government and consequently enjoy support and investment. The fashion sector puts forward the commercial dynamism of Amsterdam, combined with the artistic flair of Arnhem.

The recent branding of the Netherlands as a fashion country is well adopted by the media, politics and international buyers. However, except for the jeans cluster, the Dutch creative fashion industry remains small. It simply lacks the financial backing that Bernard Arnault and Francois Pinault can provide to the French luxury industry. It has no strong industrial connection, as is still present in Italy. Political support is more superficial than that given in the United Kingdom. Nevertheless, the Netherlands has become a niche player, with a major role only in the jeans sector (Saxion, 2012).

Since 2000 the industrial dimension of the industry has almost vanished. Between 1990 and 2000 the sweatshops tarnished the industry's image. From 1995 onwards the general public came to be seen as increasingly sensitive about the labour conditions in clothing production in developing countries. This has led to the establishment of the Fairwear Foundation and to an increased awareness to improve labour standards. As labelling in products now shows the origin of production more often (largely because brands export outside the EU), consumers are better aware of where clothing is made. From 2012 there has been more debate on reshoring, bringing production back to the Netherlands. This trend has been well covered in the media with focus on initiatives such as I-Did and 'Mode met een Missie' ('fashion with a mission') and designers' workshops, but the trend is largely discursive with marginal economic impact.

Three Forms of Emancipation

In the introduction to this chapter I characterised the period since the war as containing three emancipation processes. The first one is the emancipation from the fashion of Paris. The second one is the adoption of an American production model and then the emancipation from it. The third emancipation is one of women workers, who were first recruited, then laid off, but now form the backbone of its middle management. This threefold emancipation signifies by no means a positive

evolution: between 1958 and now the industry lost more than 80 per cent of its employment and over 50 per cent of companies. In fact, by 2014 none of the clothing firms that were established in the period 1945 to 1958 still existed in their present form.

The first emancipation started at the end of the 1960s, when influence and inspiration from Paris waned as the era of formal dress styles ended. In my view, the emancipation from Paris set off three trends. The first is the development of an internationally multipolar set of influences on fashion, with London emerging as an inspiration for youth culture, Italian materials and production methods offering new styles, and casual styles from the USA creating a jeans industry. The second trend is the recognition of styling as a profession, even though styling is sometimes considered as a clever forecasting and combination of styles. The third trend is the emergence of brand identities with an authentic design signature.

While these three trends helped Dutch designers and brands to establish themselves, the emancipation from the Paris fashion dominance was also much hampered by several phenomena in the Netherlands. First, many large lower-middle retailers sought a cheap derivate of high-end fashion from their suppliers, making it difficult for Dutch brands to create their own story and style. Second, the orientation to European markets was, until the 1970s, obtained by 'international collections' forming the backbone of a middle-market retail store, again hampering Dutch brands' ability to foster an idiosyncratic narrative. Third, until the 1990s the industry and the fashion design community formed two distinct worlds, with their own objectives and values. This impeded the industrialisation of design, so its high prices made it less accessible to a larger public.

The second emancipation was a very different one: it implied liberation from an American Taylorist production model. This proved to be a painful process. With the decimation of skilled Jewish workers in the Second World War and the rapid growth of demand for cheap garments, the adoption of a Taylorist production model initially presented a good business case. But this model, especially with its reliance on young women workers and the little attention paid to developing technical skills for the middle management, meant that the industry was ill-equipped to upgrade in quality in the 1960s when consumers demanded better products. The lack of competitiveness in the European unifying market in the 1960s has rarely been put forward, but I think it is a factor of paramount importance in the decline of the Dutch clothing industry. While the competition with low-cost countries was seen as the culprit, the massive delocalisation of production in the 1970s in fact enabled the industry to keep on reproducing the Taylorist production method and continue to service large retailers with cheap fashion. It postponed the inevitable upgrade in design and quality until the second half of the 1980s. When Dutch brands upgraded, and when a creative industry developed after 2000 in the Netherlands, it occurred largely without a manufacturing base. While most European countries, even smaller ones like Belgium, still have a small luxury or craft manufacturing sector, the Netherlands neither retained nor developed such a niche. This contrasts with the Dutch furniture industry and product design industry, which were able to combine domestic manufacturing with quality, design and branding.

The third emancipation pertains to female workers. In the 1950s the clothing industry employed close to 100,000 women, most of them with little training, and only for a short period of their lives, after leaving school and before getting married. Over the last sixty years the clothing industry has probably employed over half a million women. The paternalistic labour conditions have left a trace in the Dutch collective memory. For many women the clothing factory was the first experience with the workplace, structured work processes and the mastering of time and motion. It was socialisation, but not emancipation. Today, the industry still predominantly employs women, but now in design, marketing and sourcing functions. Fashion has become an attractive career, combining artistic and entrepreneurial skills for women.

Discussion: Overcoming Lock-ins

Looking back on an evolution in the Dutch clothing industry of almost sixty years, the story is a rather classical one of growth, decline and renewal. What is perhaps most striking is the difficulty of adjusting to changing economic conditions. The Dutch clothing industry was locked in a model based on supplying large retailers with standardised fashion copied from Paris and made in large-scale factories. This industrial model was evidently hard to overcome when the circumstances started to change dramatically from 1960 onwards.

In order to explain this lock-in to a specific industrial or commercial model, Grabher (2003) has put forward some interesting concepts. He argues that lock-ins signify functional, cognitive and/or institutional barriers to change. Functional lock-ins are related to the equipment of firms (e.g. the Taylorist factory model). Cognitive lock-ins relate to the knowledge base and skills of management and workers (e.g. the focus on private label production). Institutional lock-ins are related to policies and arrangements between employers and unions.

Functional lock-ins were not very dominant in the Dutch clothing industry, because capital investment was low and technological equipment was rarely specialised to a specific operation before 1970. In other words, neither capital nor equipment presented major barriers to differentiation and diversification. Of course, diversification demands some retooling while upgrading in quality demands re-engineering of the workshop layout, but the costs would not have been prohibitive. Yet the industry often pointed towards functional lock-ins as an argument for failure (KSA, 1982).

In my view, such a discourse in fact hid cognitive lock-ins. Upgrading in quality is clearly related to cognitive lock-ins. Setting-up a design culture also requires cognitive lock-ins to be overcome. KWW (1972) and KSA (1982) and later Scheffer (1992) point to the internal knowledge barriers that companies had to deal with in establishing a design culture in face of a dominant industrial paradigm focused on economies of scale and cost control. It is important to stress that in the Netherlands manufacturing and creativity are considered as antagonistic concepts, something which was reinforced by the gender gap in worker recruitment and the female labour participation model focused on young, low-skilled workers until the 1970s. This was further reinforced by institutions, most notably collective wage agreements and the corporatist model in industry organisation.

The Dutch clothing industry hung on to a model from the 1950s for too long. The combination of functional, but mostly cognitive and institutional lock-ins, resulted in too slow an adaptation to changing circumstances. The orientation towards low-cost fashion for large retailers finally disappeared in the period between 1980 and 2015, together with the companies that had adopted this model. The transformation was largely one of creative destruction, as most of today's dominant companies in the Dutch fashion industry did not exist twenty years ago, and none of the dominant firms from twenty years ago still exists. Only after that painful transformation could a new model emerge, the model of the creative fashion industry. As Anja Köppchen argues in her chapters in this book, it was the demise of domestic manufacturing that enabled designers and brands to tap into a global sourcing base with factories oriented to a wider range of skills and product specialisations. Scheffer and Duineveld (2004) stress that by 2005 the industry had largely shifted to a model of flexible sourcing enabling manufacturing to be done in those factories best suited for the style of the year. In other words, globalisation of production freed creativity from the constraints of the in-house industrial base.

Notes

1. The letters refer to the first or second names of the generations who started the shops at the beginning of the twentieth century: C&A indicates the first names of the brothers Clemens and August Brenninkmeijer; V&D stands for Willem Vroom and Anton Dreesmann; P&C stands for the Germans Johann Peek and Heinrich Cloppenborg, while Kreymborg refers to the German Anton Kreymborg. V&D went bankrupt at the very beginning of 2016.

Hollandia-Kattenburg (1911–1969)

Lianne Toussaint

> The raincoat that always used to be a grey or beige gabardine has disappeared. People now wear them as fashionable shelter in an endless variation of fabrics, with cheerful designs in every colour of the rainbow.
>
> —**Kattenburg and Verdenius, 1959**

Each year, on 11 November, a memorial service is held at IJ Square in Amsterdam to commemorate one of the most tragic events in the history of the Dutch textile industry. On that day in 1942, vans of the German Sicherheitsdienst (SD) pulled up in front of the Hollandia-Kattenburg garment factory in Amsterdam North and arrested all Jewish employees, along with their families, for alleged sabotage. Of the over 820 people that were deported on the so-called 'Hollandia-Kattenburg transport' to Germany, only eight survived the concentration camps.

Jacques Kattenburg (Amsterdam 1877–1947), descendant of a Jewish textile family with Alsatian roots, established the Hollandia-Kattenburg garment factory in 1911 in Amsterdam. Undoubtedly, no one knew as much about raincoats as Jacques Kattenburg. Under his capable guidance, the company quickly expanded and specialised in waterproof raincoats made of a rubber-coated fabric imported from England: 'gummi'.

Kattenburg had introduced the gummi raincoat in the Netherlands in 1909, first as an importer and two years later as a manufacturer. And he did so with great success. Kattenburg set up a factory in Manchester in 1927, and decided to start another one as a joint venture in Amsterdam a few years later. Following the English manufacturing procedure, the coats produced by the 'NV Hollandsche Gummifabrieken Weesp' were treated with a thin, waterproof layer of rubber on the inside. Originally, the gummi coats and gabardines had a functional and sober design, but after a designer from Berlin was attracted in 1937, Hollandia-Kattenburg started to produce

25. 'Falcon' coat (date unknown). Hollandia-Kattenburg Amsterdam.

26. 'Big Ben' coat (date unknown). Hollandia-Kattenburg Amsterdam.

the colourful and houndstooth pattern raincoats that the brand is still known for. The collections of Parisian fashion houses brought inspiration, but the designs were fully adapted to the Dutch climate. Soon Kattenburg's 'Big Ben' and 'Falcon' raincoats became household names worldwide.

After that disastrous afternoon in November 1942, Kattenburg was transported to the Dutch transit camp Westerbork. He miraculously survived the war, while his factories had persisted under the management of Johannes Scheffer, producing coats and tents for the German Army. On his 70th birthday Jacques Kattenburg passed the leadership on to his son Fred. Shortly after, in November 1947, he died suddenly (Micheels, 2009).

Now led by Fred Kattenburg and his brother-in-law Sven Meyer, Hollandia-Kattenburg expanded to Volendam, Tilburg and Nijmegen. It implemented American production methods and schooled many engineers in the industry. As Michiel Scheffer explains in chapter 3, the tide turned in the 1960s: the firm was taken over by Macintosh in 1969 and closed down a few years later. The historical raincoat company and its characteristic collections of colourful and elegant raincoats have now long disappeared, but the Falcon brand still lives on as a casual sportswear label.

4.

Don't Dress to Impress:
Fashion Discourse in Dutch Magazines

'Since the Dutch woman was more moderate, and highly critical of too much ostentation, she restrained from any excess in her clothes. Her serene mind kept family, marriage and religion in a much better balance than the French woman, who sought stimulating influences from the outside world, and wanted to radically express her changed state of mind and mentality through a fitting dress. The Dutch woman thus never followed [...] fashion to a great extent.'

—Description of an 18th-century Dutchwoman by Christine Frowein in 1941 (2008: 54; translation M.F.)

Maaike Feitsma

Introduction

In 2012 Dutch bookshops prominently displayed a Dutch translation of *La Parisienne* by celebrity model Inès de La Fressange, a style guide to dressing with the same chic and elegance as that personification of French fashion: the Parisian woman. This book is only one of many French style guides, with recent titles including *Paris Street Style: A Guide to Effortless Chic* (Thomas and Veysset, 2013); *Lessons from Madame Chic: 20 Stylish Secrets I Learned While Living in Paris* (Scott, 2012); *How to Dress Like a French Woman: The Beginner's Guide to Dressing Classic, Chic, Sexy and Elegant Just Like the French* (Montagne, 2011), et cetera. This is not necessarily a recent phenomenon either; there are older titles like *French Chic: How to Dress Like a Frenchwoman* (Sommers, 1988). These books – and there are many – all describe a French aesthetic and distinct clothing behaviour that are seen as typically French and even typical of the metropolis Paris. The authors construct fashion as an expression of some kind of unchangeable essence of the 'Parisienne'. This image is internationally recognised; few would dispute the perceived elegance of French women in general or of Parisian women in particular.[1]

The fact that similar titles about a Dutch fashion style do not exist, shows that the image of Dutch women is not one of fashionability or elegance, nor that there is a clear image of what a Dutch fashion style or aesthetic looks like. This raises the question how Dutch fashion culture is described and visualised in its own national fashion media. This chapter focuses on changes and developments in Dutch fashion discourse in three fashion and women's magazines over the last fifty years. By means of a discourse analysis of these magazines, I explore how a Dutch fashion discourse constructs myths and narratives about a Dutch fashion identity.

National Fashion Identities

The concepts of nation and national identity are social constructions that mostly exist in people's imagination; Benedict Anderson has called them 'imagined communities' (2006 [1983]). As we read in the Introduction to the present book, national identities are defined by a selection of memories, mythologies, traditions and rituals and a matching set of symbols, which gives a sense of national belonging and identification (Goodrum, 2005: 62). Although the selection of these elements is a relatively recent phenomenon – most nations were formed in the eighteenth and nineteenth century – the constructions portray the nation and national identity as something with ancient roots. In this context, Hobsbawm and Ranger speak of the 'invention of tradition' (1983: 1). By regularly repeating the memories, mythologies, traditions and rituals and symbols that make up the discourse on national identity, such a construction remains deeply embedded in the minds of the citizens inhabiting the nation.

This buttressing of the construct is usually associated with grand gestures like national holidays, national monuments and political campaigns. However, it also takes place unconsciously and unnoticed through a process that is referred to by Michael Billig as 'banal nationalism'; an everyday reminder of nation and national identity in ordinary objects, for example through the images on money and stamps (Billig, 1995: 8). This is an interesting notion for fashion, because, as Alice Goodrum (2005) observes, fashion can also play an important role in sustaining a national identity in such an unconscious manner. She argues that ideas about nationhood and ways in which fashion can signify a certain national identity are reproduced and commodified through brand stories and iconographies as well as through the textual and visual rhetoric of fashion magazines (Goodrum, 2005: 62).

By focusing on Dutch fashion discourse in three fashion and women's magazines over the last fifty years,

I unravel the ways in which they passively reproduce and actively shape ideas on Dutch fashion identity. The magazines inform their readers what is 'normal' and 'suitable' behaviour and how a woman is supposed to act and dress. The continuous repetition of ideas and idealised images shape the identity of their readership (Jensen, 2004: 7; Vegt, 2004: 39). My research is based on a discourse analysis of textual and visual references to 'Dutchness' and fashion in three Dutch magazines: the women's magazine *Margriet* (1938–present), the classical fashion magazine *Elegance* (1937–2013), and the avant-garde fashion magazine *Avenue* (1965–94). My selection of these three magazines is based on several criteria. First, the fact that they are Dutch, as none of the magazines are or were published under license of foreign publishers (unlike for example Dutch *Elle*, *Marie Claire*, *Cosmopolitan* or *Vogue*). This ensures that the 'foreign' format of the magazine does not influence the content or ideas about 'Dutchness'. Secondly, their availability and completeness; the magazines are publicly accessible in the Royal Library of The Hague and the volumes are (as good as) complete. Thirdly, their longevity, guaranteeing an overview of the second half of the twentieth century. Fourthly, the size of their circulation; for example *Margriet* had 800,000 subscribers in 1965 in a country of eleven million inhabitants (Hülsken, 2006: 94-95).

Margriet (1938–present) is a typical woman's magazine, focusing on practical information about housekeeping, bringing up children and clothing (Vegt, 2004: 42-43; Vegt, 2006: 92-93). Although it is not the oldest in the Netherlands, it had the largest circulation from the 1950s to the 1980s. *Margriet* is a magazine that is mostly read by Dutch women from the middle classes (Hülsken, 2006: 95-95; Kwant, 2006: 286).

Elegance (1937–2013) was selected because it is the oldest Dutch fashion magazine still in print at the time of my research. It is an upmarket magazine, with a stylish but refined overall appearance, aimed at a well-off readership of a social and cultural elite.

Elegance distinguishes itself by its emphasis on 'the good life'. By selecting these two magazines I covered both low and high ends of the middle class.

Avenue (1965–94) was selected because it was the first Dutch glossy. Its profile was different from that of its predecessors and it was marketed as a new kind of magazine for the modern woman. Its contributors were leading Dutch authors, photographers and illustrators (Hemels and Vegt, 1997a: 350-58; Teunissen, 2006: 28; Wishaupt, 2006: 124-25). In the editor's own words: 'a clear "no" to the boring patterns of living and thinking of the past' (*Avenue*, November 1965: 2).[2]

The discourse analysis of these magazines consisted of systematically collecting all visual and textual references to Dutch fashion, a Dutch style of dressing, Dutch fashion designers, Dutch textiles, et cetera. A whole year of a magazine was studied at five-year intervals; for example the entire 1965 run and then the entire 1970 run. I made a systematic analysis of the visuals and texts, looking for the connotations (Barthes, 1991 [1957]) of Dutchness whenever a connection was made between the Netherlands, the Dutch and fashion.[3] In this chapter I focus on the two most prevalent narratives that I discovered in the magazines: firstly, a specific Dutch attitude towards fashion, and secondly, the idea of a typical Dutch fashion. However contradictory and paradoxical in themselves, the two narratives construct a discourse on Dutch fashion culture as characteristic of Dutch identity. As we will see, the idea of what constitutes a Dutch fashion culture changes quite dramatically over the decades.

The 1950s: Paris Fashion within a Dutch Mind-Set

One of the key themes in both the fashion and women's magazines of the 1950s and early 1960s was the question how Dutch women should deal with Paris fashion.[4] Through a binary opposition between French taste (excessive, frivolous, flamboyant and impractical) and Dutch taste (sober and practical) texts and images create generalisations about the French and Dutch people.

Paris fashion was deemed far too eccentric, daring and expensive, even opulent, for Dutch standards of the postwar period (Teunissen, 1990: 90). The women's magazine *Margriet* put it as follows in a review from 1960: 'As always, among those hundreds and hundreds of new designs most are unwearable for mere mortals, or they showed an exceptional, wasteful or ugly opulence.' (*Margriet*, 1960, no. 36: 4-9; all translations from Dutch are mine). Dutch women were urged to take into account their own personality and the 'psychological and geographical climate' of the Netherlands (*Elegance*, October 1952: 44). Reliability, durability and frugality were touted as important qualities when selecting a wardrobe. In other words, a Dutch fashion mentality cautioned 'don't dress to impress'.

Dutch couturiers like Max Heymans (see profile in Chapter 2), Dick Holthaus and Ferry Offerman were considered to be the professional intermediaries who could adapt and translate Paris fashion into something wearable for the Dutch women, creating what fashion magazine *Elegance* refers to as 'the famous Dutch concepts'. The magazine does not expand on these concepts, which allows us to assume that this was unnecessary because it was self-evident to the reader. In the following excerpt from 1952, the readers of the magazine were expected to be familiar with the narrative of the Dutch fashion mentality of those days:

The Dutch couturiers and fashion houses will help you to achieve this [the adaptation of Paris fashion]. They form a kind of bridge between you and '*La Grande Mode*'. On the one hand they focus on the instructions and inventions of great foreign eminences, and on the other hand they take into account the famous Dutch concepts. From these two elements they distil, especially for us, Dutch women, a concoction that is fashionable, flattering and wearable. (*Elegance*, October 1952: 44)

Although women from the Netherlands were advised to preserve their critical attitude towards Paris fashion, the sources that I have researched also show that the Dutch felt inferior to the French in relation to fashion. The Dutch were convinced that 'Paris is simply the birthplace of every new fashion' (*Elegance*, April 1954: 46). The following quote shows this somewhat contradictory attitude towards fashion: 'In our country this coat would be highly impractical, but this should not prevent us from admiring the way in which the sleeves and collar are incorporated and constructed' (*Margriet*, 1960, no. 17: 10-11). Admiration for Paris was combined with an independent, if not emancipated, attitude based on usefulness in the climate of the Netherlands. Practicality and functionality were thus one of the central themes in the discussions of fashion in this period.

Another recurrent rhetorical device is the unfavourable comparison of the graceful Paris mannequins with the body shape of Dutch women, in which the latter are regularly described as being too plump for elegant Parisian silhouettes.

With these models a bit of self-criticism is not a superfluous luxury either; as elegant as such a model may look on a slender mannequin, for the Dutch woman in general it has a big disadvantage. The fact of the matter is that our bosoms are too small (or too large) and our hips are often too wide to be able to wear such a design flawlessly. (*Margriet*, 1960, no. 21: 10-11)

27. Collage *Margriet* in the 1960s, by Nouchka Huijg (2014).

My analysis shows that one of the key themes in the fashion and women's magazines of the 1950s is a process of adaptation to the Paris fashion dictate within the boundaries of a Dutch fashion mentality. Although women from the Netherlands adopted many items from French fashion during the postwar period, the magazines urged them time and again to retain a critical attitude towards anything new, unusual, let alone flamboyant. Never should the women lose or deny their own 'essential' Dutch character. The journalists founded their assessment of the suitability of Paris fashion for Dutch women on three main requirements that can be distilled from the magazines: wearability, the Dutch climate, and the body shape of Dutch women. These ideas mainly centre on practicality and functionality. This is then the typical Dutch fashion culture, which is articulated in the pages of women's and fashion magazines of the 1950s and early 1960s.[5]

The 1960s: A Change of Tone

As is well known within the history of fashion, the youth revolution of the 1960s provoked a change in the fashion system (Lipovetsky, 1994). With the shift to a youth-oriented consumer culture, the Parisian couturiers' 'dictate' lost its strength. From then on, the streets became an important originator of fashion (Polhemus, 1994).

With the disappearance of the dominance of the couturiers in Paris, the rhetoric of the Dutch women's and fashion magazines also changed. While in the 1950s the magazines read more like a manual with strict guidelines to be followed, from the second half of the 1960s onwards the rhetoric gradually became less authoritarian. While the critical stance of the Dutch woman towards international fashion could still be found in the pages of established magazines like *Elegance* and *Margriet*, the tone was less prescriptive and authoritarian. One of the linguistic techniques used in their pages

was the recurrent question: 'Can you imagine yourself wearing this?' (*Elegance*, June 1970: 28). This was clearly a rhetorical question, because the prevailing idea was still that the new fashions were not suitable for the Dutch woman or for the wet and windy climate of the Netherlands. Another frequent technique was to describe the new trends as 'mad pranks'. These wild fashions could only be fully embraced by the younger generation and might be suitable for them as some kind of youthful error (*Margriet*, 1960, no. 26: 29-31). The critique of the early 1960s thus gave way to a mild form of ridicule.

The articles in *Margriet* and *Elegance* show an image of women who are quite bewildered by the choice of many different and contradicting fashions, as there is no longer one fashion that must be followed. The magazines try to take the confusion away by reassuring their readers that it is really not compulsory to dress in the excessive designs modelled on the Parisian catwalks, as we can read in a later passage:

It need not be that extreme, it need not be that loose-fitting and it need not be that wide! Just remember that the extreme and extravagant part of what Paris shows, is to a large extent based on the need to receive as much free publicity as possible. (*Elegance*, May 1975: 52-53)

The disapproving tone of the early 1960s, and the slight bewilderment and ridicule of the second half of the decade, was slowly replaced during the 1970s by a reluctant acceptance of short-lived fashion fads. Consider *Elegance*'s ambivalent advice for dealing with these fast-changing trends:

Quickly evaporating fashion whims, irrelevant variations on and excesses of the gradual development of the fashion in clothes, already get enough attention. Far too much even. For those who wish to take part in it – and that might be amusing for a change, as long as it is done without the annoying emphatic attitude of 'this is fashion and should therefore be worn' – it is wise to choose from the cheaper collections. Those who sensibly build up their own wardrobe should mainly look at the top quality collections. (*Elegance*, 1975 September: 46)

While a more moderate tone slowly replaced the disdainful tone of the postwar period, the discourse remained basically the same. *Elegance* and *Margriet* still urged their readers to maintain a moderate Dutch attitude towards extravagant Paris fashion, i.e. to choose the functional over the fashionable.

The 1970s: The Emancipation of Fashion

As a result of the individualisation as a general trend in society (Lipovetsky, 1994), from the 1970s onwards references to 'the' taste of 'the Dutch woman' disappear from the pages of *Elegance* and *Margriet*. Instead, the focus shifts towards 'finding one's own individual style'. However, the fashion mentality that is propagated remains largely the same: a rejection of extravagance and a preference for practical, wearable and functional clothing. The difference is that this mentality is no longer explicitly described as 'Dutch'. This does not mean that the narrative of the Dutch fashion mentality goes underground; surprisingly enough it is picked up by the new fashion glossy *Avenue*.

Avenue was launched in 1965. Its look was glossy, its tone revolutionary, and its contents arty. The magazine promised a clear break with the past, as the editorial of the first issue explains:

Before you lies the first issue of a new type of magazine for the new type of woman. *Avenue* is a compliment to your good taste, a confirmation of your modern style, a clear 'no' to the boring patterns of living and thinking of the past. (*Avenue*, November 1965: 2)

From the start, *Avenue* assertively positioned itself in the market as different from its predecessors. Its format was aimed at a new generation; those that were the first to cast off the yoke of the Parisian fashion dictate, and who sympathised with the women's liberation movement of the time. Traditionally, fashion magazines were based on the female realm of domestic matters such as house-keeping, needlework, parenting and, of course, fashion. With the women's emancipation of the 1960s and 1970s, these traditional topics become too limited for the new and broadened horizon of younger readers.

Avenue's format fitted in with the new social status of women. Next to the usual themes of fashion and interior design, it also addressed contemporary social issues and taboos and changing social and religious conventions. Not only was the content new and different, the magazine also emphasised innovative graphic design, with a central role for artistic photography, while it was printed on high-quality paper. *Avenue*, then, was an upmarket novelty, something completely new to the Dutch media landscape (Brands, 2006). It had a distinctly avant-garde feel to it.

The question is whether *Avenue* – in its attempt to be different – left behind the Dutch notions of soberness, modesty and functionality. My analysis of the descriptions that accompany the fashion spreads, shows that *Avenue* indeed often rebelled against the rigid and strict society of the previous years, emphasising instead the 'good life'. The break with the past, however, was not as clear as all that. For example, *Avenue* at first maintained the usual DIY knitting and sewing patterns – quite surprisingly, to the modern eye. It also retained some of the familiar rhetoric on the Dutch climate:

In this country of wind and rain vinyl clothes are of course an ideal garb. But do not just think of their usefulness ... This is also the fashion for winter sports, for lounging sumptuously and fashionably in Kitzbühel or Gstaad. (*Avenue*, December 1965: 28-29)

JONG MET ALLURE
creaties van Nederlandse mode-ontwerpers

GLORIE

MODE VAN NEDERLANDSE BODEM

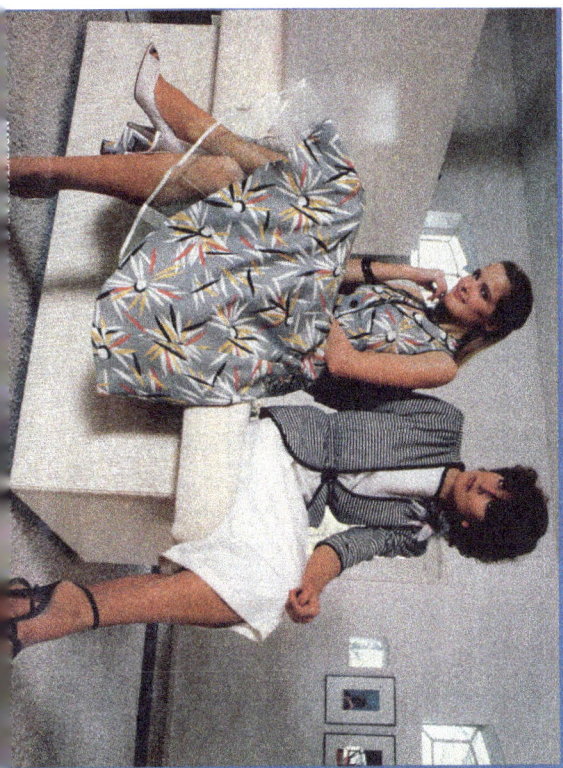

... land spreekt een aar-
lig woordje mee in de
magische modewereld. En
lat is best te begrijpen:
vanneer we deze fijne,
fragebre mode bekijken:
is allemaal Nederlands
abrikaat! Toch, als we de kranten mogen geloven,
aat het niet zo best met onze confectie. Allerlei bedrijf-
en sluiten hun poorten en vele fabrieken moeten alles
op alles zetten om hun zaak draaiende te houden. On-
lands deze negatieve berichten zijn er confectiebedrij-
ven die heel succesvol zijn. En dat zijn juist degene
vaarvan de ontwerpers een opvallende, eigen mode

zendsnel komen ze met
verfrissende ideeën en
nieuwe trends. Uiteinde-
lijk begrijpen deze Neder-
landers beter dan wie dan
ook wat Nederlandse
vrouwen willen dragen. Zes van deze ondernemende
ontwerpers, ieder met een eigen stijl, laten een glimp
zien van wat zij deze zomer brengen. Of eigenlijk ze-
ven, want ook Jan des Bouvrie is een bekende Nederlandse ontwerper, niet van mode, maar van stijlvolle
moderne meubels. Wij fotografeerden in zijn studio,
waar veel van zijn ontwerpen te kijk staan.

LOTUS:
JURKEN VOOR MODEBEWUSTE VROUWEN

Lotus. Achter deze bloemennaam
schuilt een oer-Hollands bedrijf: de firma
Postuma. De ontwerpster voor deze fabri-
kant, Babette Kloeker, is van Italiaanse origine.
Babette probeert zo goed mogelijk de huidige
mode-tendens te vertalen voor de Nederlandse vrouw. Ze let erop, dat haar kleren
voor veel vrouwen draagbaar zijn. Goede
kwaliteit en afwerking staan een haar
lijst. Dat ze het klappen van de zweep kent,
komt niet alleen door haar praktijk-erva-
ring, maar ook door een gedegen mode-oplei-
ding in Duitsland. Over haar manier van
werken zegt ze: "Als ik iets ontwerpen heb,
kruip ik eerst achter de naaimachine om
te kijken of het allemaal wel klopt, wat ik op
papier heb uitgedokterd. Want op papier is
het wel even anders dan in de praktijk.

Deze zomer ben ik eigenlijk uitgegaan
van twee lijnen: de vrouwelijke, filmster-
achtige jurken met smalle bovenlijfjes en su-
perwijde rokken, en de eenvoudige rechte
jurken met een wat sportieve chic, vaak met
een bijpassend jasje erbij. Ideaal voor onze
Nederlandse zomers." Het valt ons op dat zij
onze zomers zegt. Ze kijkt ons verbaasd aan
en zegt dan lachend: "Ik veel me ook bijna
Nederlands en soms vergeet ik helemaal dat
ik uit Duitsland kom."

Voor de foto links kozen wij uit de col-
lectie een paarsprijze doorknoopjurk met ge-
sifleerde bloemmotieven, ± f 160, en een tricot pak, recht van lijn, die nog extra bena-
drukt wordt door het contrast van zwart en
wit, ± f 190.

NICO VERHEY:
DE NIEUWSTE TRENDS VOOR BETAALBARE PRIJZEN

Nico Verhey, Amsterdam. Heel wat kleding-
stukken dragen het etiket met zijn naam.
Want die kleren die deze ontwerper maakt,
zijn populair, zowel in Nederland als in
Frankrijk, Spanje en Italië. Hij begon als as-
sistent van de ontwerpster Sophie van Kleef
en werkt nu al weer negen jaar voor de Gebr.
Rutgers. "Het is een kleine firma, wat ik heel
prettig vind, omdat je gemakkelijk betrok-
ken wordt bij allerlei zaken die misschien
niet direct op je terrein liggen. Ik heb een
grote vrijheid in dit bedrijf om te maken wat

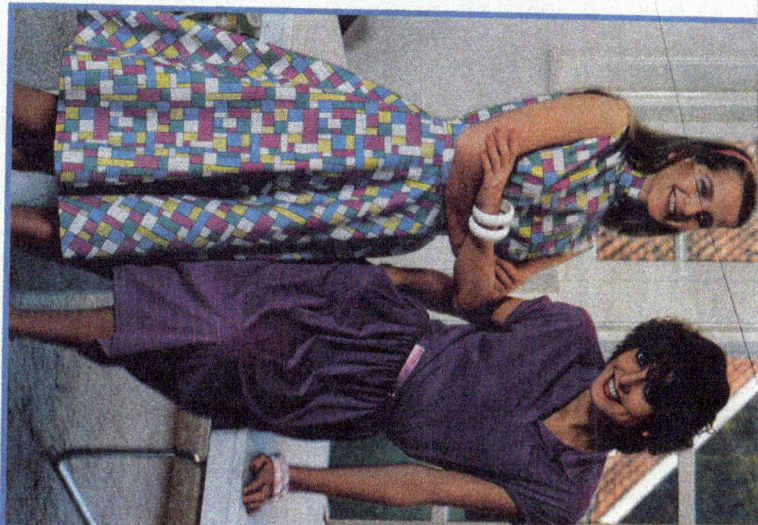

zijn bij het begin van een nieuw seizoen."
Naast extravagante modellen voor de enke-
ling (zoals mini-jurkjes in felle motiefkleuren)
maakt Nico ook mode die niet zo karakteris-
tiek van stijl is, maar wel nodig en solide, zoals
op de foto rechts is te zien.

Wat is het geheim van zijn succes? [...]
Samen met Nico kozen we een vrolijke
seersucker jurk in een kleurig dessin met een
wijde kinderok en een modieuze halterlijn, ±
f 185. Daarnaast een tweedelig, sportieve, ±

28. Collage *Elegance* in the 1980s, by Nouchka Huijg (2014).

Functionality is here combined with a new image of luxury. *Avenue* embraced luxury and extravagance – and this was surely a break with the cliché of Dutch soberness and aversion to extravagance. According to *Avenue* luxury was something to display.

Avenue therefore gave its readers quite different advice from more traditional magazines like *Elegance* and *Margriet*. Instead of advising its readers to be frugal and modest, it celebrated the excesses of fashion. The readers of *Avenue* were portrayed as self-assured and critical individuals with good taste, who do not need guidance but information about what is new. *Avenue* thus gave relatively factual reports on what was to be seen on the international catwalks, rather than moralistic rules on what to wear or not wear.

The lack of guidelines led to fewer references to Dutch fashion mentality. This does not mean that the traditional narrative disappeared altogether. During the 1980s and 1990s *Avenue* ran a regular feature called 'Modezaken' ('fashion affairs'), which in Dutch can refer to both fashion stores and to matters of fashion. The column was an advertorial in which the leading Dutch fashion shops and their customers were discussed. Interestingly, *Avenue* set up an opposition between its readers and the cliché of 'the average Dutchman'. This stereotype was described as someone who only started to follow a fashion fad when everyone else was already wearing it (*Avenue*, November 1990: 54). The average Dutch person was conservative in his or her fashion choices and, of course, thrifty: 'The average Dutchman is not willing to spend money on things you do not see. And since shoes mostly remain under the table, they are of little importance' (*Avenue*, April 1990: 84). *Avenue* thus portrayed the Dutch people as still adhering 'to the virtues of reliability, durability and frugality'. This stereotype, however, was at the same time deconstructed by *Avenue* and replaced by the new cosmopolitan, more fashionable, Dutch man or woman. The Dutch fashion narrative and its characteristics that were portrayed by

the more classical *Elegance* and *Margriet*, turned into a negative stereotype in the 1960s. The new glossy *Avenue* both fought the old norms and values and set up new standards of fashionability and cosmopolitanism.

1980s: A New Generation of Designers

In this section I turn to Dutch fashion itself, rather than the Dutch fashion mentality. Recall how the Dutch nurtured a feeling of inferiority with regard to Paris fashion in the postwar period; a self-image that would only start to gradually change towards the 1980s. Until then, Dutch couturiers took their main inspiration from Paris. Dutch women's and fashion magazines therefore presented them as intermediaries rather than as trend-setters. Generally, journalists and consumers regarded the clothes by French designers as superior to the designs by the Dutch themselves. Consider the following quote from the May 1960 issue of *Margriet*:

We Dutch people unfortunately still have the strange inclination to consider anything from abroad as better, more beautiful or of higher quality. For a gown made in Amsterdam with a label in the French language we readily pay many guilders more. Shoes with the magic word Italia in the label 'fit' better, even if they were made in Brabant. Woollen fabrics from Tilburg sell more quickly if they are marketed as British. And many countless examples like this could be mentioned. (*Margriet*, 1960, no. 23: 10-11)

In combining images of fashion from different European countries, this quote shows how areas of superiority are established: the French for their fashion designs, the Italians for their shoes, and the British for their tweeds. Dutch fashion magazines thus maintained national fashion identities of both themselves and others through a process of what Billig has called 'banal nationalism' (1995; see also the Introduction). In the same article *Margriet* also advanced a more emancipated image of Dutch fashion, by disapproving of the preference for foreign goods and the Dutch nation's insecurity about its own local products. The article's main theme was to advertise the qualities of the Dutch cotton industry, by means of a collection designed by the renowned Dutch couturier Dick Holthaus. The fabrics were said to be of an 'international fashion level', giving one's wardrobe 'unique chic' – when processed in a modest way. This was one of the first steps in the magazines towards a new image of Dutch fashion as unique and as able to meet international standards, while maintaining traditional traits of modesty, soberness and functionality.

During the 1960s and 1970s the magazines consider the work of the traditional couturiers that largely followed the Paris trends – such as Holthaus, Edgar Vos, Frans Molenaar and Frank Govers – on an international par. Yet this value judgement remained rather ambivalent. Although the Dutch couturiers received positive reviews in the magazines, the prevalent image was that 'Dutch couturiers go to Paris to jumpstart or replenish their inspiration is a normal state of affairs' (*Elegance*, December 1975: 10). Generally, the focus on international fashion shows in the magazines indicates that the public still preferred to read about couture from abroad.

As we read in chapter 2, the 1980s saw the rise of a new generation of Dutch fashion designers and brands. They no longer merely translated Paris fashion, but created new fashion themselves. It was this younger generation that stood at the cradle of Dutch fashion as we know it today. *Avenue* is enthusiastic about this new development:

The new generation of designers turn the Nether-lands more and more into a fashion country. Their creativity, coupled with realism, puts an end to the traditional, bourgeois mentality that used to nip every fashion development in the bud. The very absence of a strong fashion tradition now makes the climate highly favourable to innovations. The individualism of a growing number of people, who prefer to distinguish themselves from the masses instead of disappearing into them, is an extra incentive for these fashion designers. (*Avenue*, May 1984: 32-33)

Avenue paid regular attention to Dutch fashion design as well as stores specialising in fashion from the Netherlands, in particular to the avant-garde. They portray the average Dutch customer, however, as still a bit reluctant towards Dutch fashion:

The collection [of the stores] is definitely daring: creative, unorthodox designs of a quality that we, with Dutch understatement, like to refer to as 'un-Dutch'. 'The average Dutchman will only wake up if you casually mention that Illustrious Imps is doing so well in Japan, or that Georgette Koning of Pearls Before Swans is going to design bags for Mugler,' says Tonny [the shop owner] [...] The Dutch designs often occupy the middle ground between French and English fashion: a classic shape is the basis, to which an ironical twist is subsequently added. (*Avenue*, November 1990: 197)

My analysis of the magazines shows how in the 1970s and 1980s the fashion discourse has changed. The stereotype of the Dutch woman embodying soberness, functionality, unpretentiousness and austerity slowly disappeared from the pages of the magazines; she is now allowed some display of luxury and to 'dress to impress'. At the same time, the magazines gradually made room for a cautious appreciation of Dutch fashion design.

Vóór 'De Nachtwacht'
(gedateerd 1642) in een
witte batisten blouse
met volumineuze kraag
(Frank Govers), een zwart
gilet met glitters en een
oversized blazer van
zwarte zijde met pailletten
(beide Callaghan).
Zwart stretchbroekje
(Puck & Hans), witte
manchetten van broderie
('t Kantenpandje), zwarte
leren lieslaarsen
(Stephane Kélian). Het
Rembrandteske beeld
wordt gecompleteerd door
een doorgestikte
baret van changeant velours
(Frank Govers).

Brienenoordbrug Marineblauw broekpak met bijpassende blouse van gebreid nylon van Helmut Lang, gouden sandalen van Stephane Kélian.

Lisse Zijden pak in bree

Hollands Glo

Zomermode die zich voegt naar de achtergrond van
bloeiende boomgaarden. Een decor dat de naam van

indrukwekkende brugge
ons land in de hele were

29. Collage *Dutch national icons* in the 1990s, by Nouchka Huijg (2014).

The 1990s: Dutch Cultural Heritage

Not only did the textual rhetoric concerning the quality of Dutch fashion change, the visual rhetoric changed too. In studying the connotations of the images that were used in the fashion shoots of the 1990s, I was quite struck by the rather sudden use of icons from Dutch cultural heritage, for example windmills, wooden shoes and regional dress. This trend is perhaps a result of the ever-increasing globalisation of fashion, as well as the international breakthrough of foreign fashion designers such as the Japanese Deconstructionists and the Antwerp Six, which prompted a focus on national identity in fashion (see the Introduction and chapter 2). My research shows that whereas in the past international themes and settings like Russia and India were favoured, from the 1990s onwards Dutch heritage became a fashionable theme in Dutch magazines. As my analysis was informed by the semiotics of Barthes (1991 [1957]), I became aware of the ambiguities of the relation between text, images and fashion. National identity was clearly an issue in the decade of the 1990s, but its visual rhetoric functioned much more as backdrop to the fashion shoots than as a meaningful source of inspiration for the fashion itself. In other words, the visual rhetoric may have reinforced cultural identity, but Dutch fashion as such was not understood as expressing a national identity.

Let me discuss some examples. In 1990 *Elegance* dedicated its July/August issue to the Netherlands: the travel section discussed travelling in the Netherlands, while the literary section featured fourteen well-known authors with stories about the Netherlands. The magazine clearly wanted to investigate what makes the Dutch different from the rest of the world's populations, because the issue also contained an essay about the characteristics and peculiarities of the Dutch people. The fashion section consisted of two fashion shoots. One was called 'Holland's Pride', depicting clothes against a background of typical Dutch landscapes such as tulip fields, bridges over canals,

a girl on a bike in front of a windmill. The second shoot is called 'Going Dutch' (in English!), portraying a young couple in a vintage convertible decorated with a floral garland from the famous spring garden 'Keukenhof', on their way to visit a Dutch sea resort. The couple is then shown at the beach, in a typical Dutch pub, and the girl sitting on top of two gigantic wooden shoes. In both photo shoots, the images are all 'typically Dutch', which is underscored by the captions and titles, but only a few of the fashion items are made by Dutch designers. Apparently, in the 1990s 'Dutchness' can be portrayed by tourist icons such as tulips, wooden shoes, windmills, bikes, but not by fashion designs.

Much the same goes for *Avenue*. In October 1990 *Avenue* for example features a fashion shoot, called 'Fietsbelles', a pun signifying both bicycle bells and 'belles' (pretty girls) on a bike. Young women cycling along the canals of Amsterdam are dressed in designer clothes from both international and national brands. One of the spreads is captioned 'Dutch Ride', and shows a girl in an evening gown on the back of a bike, with a young man in a suit riding it (*Avenue,* October 1990: 108-109). Although the title and the scenery remind the reader of what it means to be Dutch, the clothes themselves do not play an explicit role in the rhetoric of Dutch identity.

A year later, in 1991, *Avenue* featured a fashion shoot inspired by the traditional dress of the province of Zeeland; the images are still famous today and are often used and reused in the field of fashion (Feitsma, 2014: 81). The introduction reads:

Did you ever see a contemporary variation on Dutch breeches or neckerchiefs? Designers prefer to draw their inspiration from Indian saris, Chinese Mao jackets and Turkish zouave trousers. Or is traditional Dutch dress just not suitable as a fashion muse? *Avenue*'s fashion director Frans Ankoné thinks it is. With fashion from the new international winter collections he composed outfits based on the traditional Zeeland clothes, crowning them with caps that were also inspired by this dress. Maarten Schets [the photographer] immortalised the result in a series of seascapes. (*Avenue*, September 1991: 44-55)

The setting and composition of the images refer to traditional Dutch seascapes, while the models are modelled on paintings of fishermen's wives waiting on the beach or on the docks for their husband and sons to return home. These are characterised by a worried expression on their faces, as the wind blows through their hair and fluttering skirts and shawls. International fashion by Romeo Gigli, Yves Saint Laurent and Chloé is adapted to this Dutch visual tradition, in a way that is reminiscent of the predominantly black clothes of nineteenth-century Dutch regional wear, as well as those of the seventeenth-century Dutch regents. The photos make the international clothes look 'authentically' Dutch. There is thus a post-modern play of authenticity and identity (Smelik, 2011), with the ambiguous message that Dutch imagery and clothing traditions can be a source of inspiration while the fashion that is shown is still not made by Dutch designers.

The same goes for the Old Masters of Dutch painting. In the same year *Avenue* dedicated the styling of one of its fashion shoots to the Dutch artist Rembrandt, entitled 'In the light of Rembrandt'. The introduction reads:

Outside, in front of the Amsterdam Rijksmuseum, you see jogging suits, faded jeans and down-at-heel sneakers. But inside, on the walls of this building, where the spectacular Rembrandt exhibition will open soon, one beholds delicate lace, glowing velvet and sparkling brocade. And these are precisely the materials from which the new fashion is made. A resplendent report rendered in chiaroscuro worthy of Rembrandt. (*Avenue*, October 1991: 79-89)

Avenue here explicitly connects Dutch national heritage and contemporary fashion. The clothing is staged in Dutch heritage sites that are linked to the life of the artist, such as the Rijksmuseum, in front of Rembrandt's *Night Watch*, and in the fifteenth-century Nieuwe Kerk (New Church), in Amsterdam. The captions not only inform us about the clothes, but also tell us about the painter's life.

What emerges from these examples is that Dutch identity is constructed in the pages of women's and fashion magazines through the repetitive use of Dutch imagery. However, national icons are merely used as a backdrop for international clothing. Dutch fashion design itself does not feature as a symbol of national identity.

Conclusion

In this chapter I have argued that Dutch women's and fashion magazines – *Margriet* (1938–present), *Elegance* (1937–2013), and *Avenue* (1965–94) – construct two narratives on fashion. The first tells the story of a postwar Dutch fashion mentality that is characterised by an aversion to ostentation and a preference for austerity, functionality and moderation. 'Please, don't dress to impress' is the message to Dutch women in the 1950s and 1960s. Only in the 1970s and 1980s does this conservatism give way to a cosmopolitan embrace of luxury.

The second narrative pertains to the emergence of Dutch fashion design from the 1980s onwards. Dutch fashion emancipates itself from the dictate of Paris and is appreciated in its own right. Yet, in the visual and textual rhetoric on national identity of the 1990s, Dutch fashion hardly features at all. Although Dutch identity is (re)constructed in fashion magazines through the use of stereotypical icons like tulips, wooden shoes and windmills, or by a venerable Dutch cultural heritage going back to illustrious painters such as Rembrandt and Vermeer, Dutch fashion itself is not yet seen as an expression of this perceived typical Dutch identity.

DON'T DRESS TO IMPRESS

It is not until the international breakthrough of several Dutch fashion designers in Paris in the mid 1990s that Dutch fashion gradually evolves from something that is seen as 'merely made in the Netherlands' to 'something distinctly Dutch'. In the 1990s, the 'Dutch' in Dutch fashion does not merely signify a typically Dutch attitude towards fashion, but the highly minimalist designs themselves are used to express national identity. The emerging myth of typical Dutch design seamlessly fits into the older myth of Dutch fashion mentality, because they are both characterised by austerity, functionality and rationality.

Around the turn of the century several Dutch avant-garde designers start using their cultural heritage as a source of inspiration, referring to Dutch icons like clogs, vividly coloured regional dress or Delft blue earthenware. This results not just in a new – less modernist and more decorative – style, but also in a shift of the gravitational centre of what is 'Dutch' in Dutch fashion culture. The next chapter explores such a different fashion narrative of vivid colours, while other chapters delve into the wonderful world of Dutch high fashion. Then we will see that the mantra 'don't dress to impress' is not necessarily the only one in Dutch fashion discourse.

Notes

1. An earlier version of this article has been published in 2011 in J. Foltyn (ed), *Fashions: Exploring Fashion through Culture*, Oxford: The Inter-Disciplinary Press.

2. References to *Margriet, Elegance* and *Avenue* are not included in the bibliography, as it makes for a long list of titles in Dutch. The references can be found in my PhD (in Dutch): Feitsma, 2014.

3. For a more detailed report on my methodologies and findings, I refer to my PhD (Feitsma, 2014).

4. Empirical research by Susanne Jansen (2006) confirms the international importance of the French high fashion world from 1955 till well into the 1990s, in her comparison between quality newspapers of France, Germany and the Netherlands.

5. Recent research by Aurélie van de Peer (2015) has shown that the same discourse was used in high-end American newspapers such as *New York Times and International Herald Tribune* in the same period of the 1950s and early 1960s. Fashion journalists targeted the American women (living both abroad and in the States) who bought their clothing in Paris. Even this group was urged to review the collections on the criteria of functionality and elegance – interpreted as soberness. I maintain that the Dutch discourse stands out for its emphasis on frugality in connection to sustained references to body shape and climate. Moreover, the discourse of functionality and soberness in relation to fashion is still around in the Netherlands today, although it takes different shapes, e.g. in terms of casual or under-dressing (see also chapter 6). Of course, it would be interesting to make a comparison in future research of the discourses on fashion in different countries.

Frans Molenaar (Amsterdam 1940–2015)

Lianne Toussaint

Clothes predominantly have to underline the
personality. One should not be thinking: 'Nice dress,
but who wore it again?'

—Frans Molenaar, quoted in Carvalho, 1996: 3

Without any shade of irony Frans Molenaar loved to call himself the Dutch king of fashion (Van Rossum, 2015: 2). He started an haute couture showroom to display his minimalist designs in 1967 and was active in Dutch fashion for the rest of his life. Whatever trend the fashion world prescribed, Molenaar always stayed true to his sophisticated style and signature. A typical Frans Molenaar design has clear lines, bright and plain coloured fabric, and contrasting piping or a geometrical pattern.

At age nineteen Molenaar went to Paris, where he spent eight years working for Guy Laroche and Nina Ricci. Inspired by the modern, revolutionary chic of Yves Saint Laurent and the futuristic, youthful fashion of André Courrèges, he created his own, rather architectural, approach to fashion. Back in the Netherlands he was the first Dutch designer to develop a personal and distinct design vision, rather than unthinkingly follow Parisian couture. Based on a deep-felt connection to the geometric abstractionists of the sixties, Molenaar started to design fashion with clean geometrical shapes and architectural lines.

Molenaar's eye for style was not only noticed by the fashion press; the world of art and design soon welcomed him as a fully-fledged artist. Yet it is the neat women's suit with a knee-length skirt and a tailored jacket that became his trademark: decent, flattering and representative. In 1970 he was asked to design suits for the hostesses of the Dutch pavilion at the World Exhibition in Osaka. In 1972 he created new overalls for The Hague's garbage collectors. Over the years he has dressed the personnel of Dutch companies like Akzo Nobel, Albert Heijn, Heineken and the Rabobank, to name just a few (Teunissen, 2006: 148). Nowadays a corporatewear market without the designs of Molenaar seems unthinkable. Yet, Molenaar's creativity did not limit itself to fashion and clothing. He also designed glass vases, scarves, bicycles, car interiors, shavers, curtains and carpets, which allowed him to express his geometrical and architectural forms in many different ways.

As versatile as the objects of Molenaar's design are, couture continued to be the source and basis of his work. To emphasise the importance of that vanishing profession and sustain the couture tradition in the Netherlands, he established the Frans Molenaar Prize in 1996. The annual prize is intended to stimulate young Dutch fashion designers in building a career in couture and while he was alive provided them with all the possible support from the great master himself (Sponselee, 2005).

The consistency of Molenaar's style may not have made him the most fashionable or innovative designer, but is surely the key to his enduring success. Molenaar is still known and valued for his 'Molenaar suits', sober A-line dresses, use of classic fabrics and techniques, and basic geometrical forms. Till the very end of his life his formula remained the same as it was in 1967: beauty lies in simplicity. He suddenly died in January 2015; after having presented 99 shows in total, Frans Molenaar could unfortunately just not make it to the grand finale of his 100th show.

32. Frans Molenaar, for fashion show Summer 2013 (95th show); two dresses and cape, inspired by Molenaar's collection 1976.

5.

Vivid Colours:
From the Local to the Global and Back Again: Oilily, Mac&Maggie and ‾CoraKemperman

'For the last 400 years, Western fashion has flirted with Orientalism as a source of reference and "inspiration" for a diversity of designs.'

—Hazel Clark (2009: 177)

Anneke Smelik, Daniëlle Bruggeman and Maaike Feitsma

Introduction

In this chapter we look at a possible alternative narrative in Dutch fashion that is quite different from the one Maaike Feitsma sketched in the previous chapter. This is a story of dashing colours, daring patterns, florid folds and bold cuts. Firms like Oilily, Mac&Maggie and ‾CoraKemperman, or designers such as The People of the Labyrinths, Viktor&Rolf, Iris van Herpen, Fong Leng, Bas Kosters, or Jan Taminiau – to name a few – show a range of audacious colours, patterns and shapes that contradict the reigning myth of Dutch soberness. In tracing the historical roots of this alternative line in Dutch fashion, we encounter

33. Colourful clothes designed by Cora Kemperman (A/W 2005).

cultural 'otherness' at the very heart of Dutch folklore. Dearly valued icons of Dutch culture, such as Delft blue earthenware, regional dress, and even the tulip fields, derive, in fact, from elsewhere. These paradoxical cultural dynamics play a central part in contemporary Dutch fashion. In this chapter we argue how a Dutch national style is always shot through with cultural hybridity.

In order to add more layers to the history of Dutch fashion, we take as case studies: (1) the children's and women's label Oilily (1968–present); and (2) the brands Mac&Maggie (1976–1996) and ‾CoraKemperman (1995–2016).[1] The latter serve as one case study because of their joint history and shared buyer and designer, Cora Kemperman. (To distinguish between Cora Kemperman as a person, and ‾CoraKemperman as a business, we refer to the latter by their distinctive brand name.) The firms have played a considerable role in the Dutch fashion industry, and have been awarded with a Grand Seigneur award. This is annually given to people, companies or institutions that have significantly contributed to the fashion industry in the Netherlands over a longer period of time.[2] Cora Kemperman won the award in 1987, and the couple Marieke and Willem Olsthoorn, the founders of Oilily, in 1989. In chapter 9 we will analyse Mac&Maggie's and ‾CoraKemperman's production and consumption in more detail; here we will focus on the style of the clothes in its cultural and historical context. As the designs of all three brands are known for their bright and vivid colours, we will first analyse how a colourful tradition can be detected in Dutch regional wear, belying the Calvinist convention of black clothes. We will even claim that the use of bold and bright colours fits into an alternative narrative of Dutch culture. In the second part of the chapter we explore the foreign roots and exotic fascination underlying the tradition of colourful Dutch fashion. An intermezzo on chintz connects the two parts.[3]

Part I: An Alternative Narrative of Colourful Clothes

Sober and Sombre Calvinism

The Netherlands have only recently built up a fashion culture. The one historical period in which the country is considered to have featured a distinct 'fashion' was during the Golden Age when the Dutch Regents wore rich black clothes in combination with crisp white linen trimmings, well known from their depictions on portraits by Rembrandt, Hals and other famous Dutch painters (Laver, 1996 [1969]; Boucher, 1987 [1965]; De Winkel, 2006). The influence of a fairly democratic bourgeois culture was typical of the Dutch republic, expressing burgher values of religious faith, ardent work and social responsibility through dark clothes that did not immediately betray their wealth (Schama, 1988), although they showed it clearly enough to their peer group (Groeneweg, 1995).

As José Teunissen argued in chapter 2, the stark modernist tradition of foregrounding functionality and rationality in Dutch design and later in Dutch fashion prolonged and reinforced the use of sober colours and restrained shapes. The dominant tradition in Dutch fashion is one of strict modernism; or at least such is its image. At the same time, some of the most successful commercial brands like Oilily, Mac&Maggie and ¯CoraKemperman are characterised by a vivid palette of bright and bold colours, wild patterns and flowing shapes. This leaves us with the question as to whether Dutch fashion is really as 'black and white' as its image suggests.

The austere look of seventeenth-century Dutch clothes is often taken as the spirit of a Dutch tradition with its roots in the soberness, if not sombreness, of Calvinism. The Dutch fashion historian Irene Groeneweg (1995) argues that while black clothing was considered an expression of religious faith, and colourful clothing was associated with vanity and shallowness,

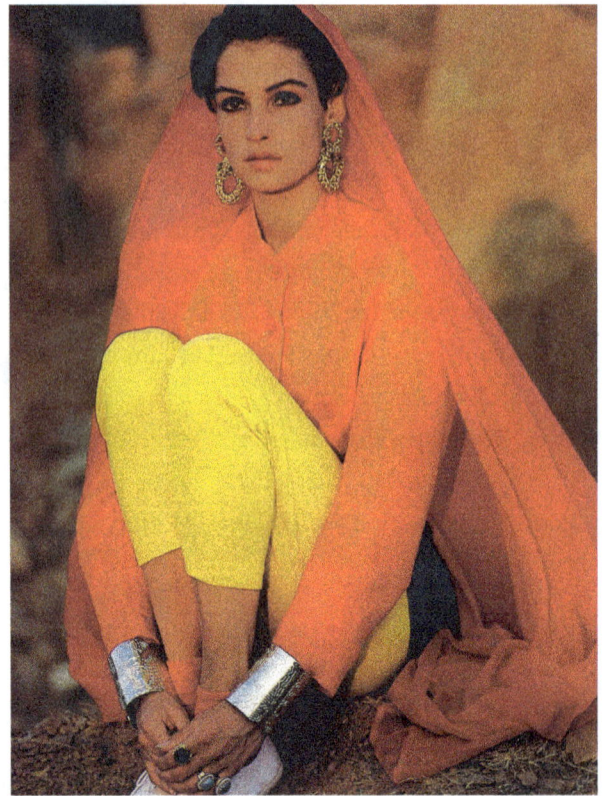

34. Bold colours for Mac&Maggie (Summer 1986).

dressing in black was mostly a matter of etiquette rather than Calvinism. The Dutch court, nobility and wealthy Dutch citizens followed the etiquette of French elite in wearing black clothes for formal occasions from around 1625 until the end of the century (Groeneweg, 1995: 233). For informal occasions, however, at home women wore colourful clothing made of chintz imported from India. Because of their status in society men did not have the same freedom in dress and mostly wore black, except soldiers and young men (ibid.: 238). The widespread image – and misconception – of Dutch clothes as exclusively black is mostly derived from the celebrated Dutch paintings, on which people are depicted in formal attire because portraits were meant to express the subject's status and wealth (ibid.: 226). Against this prevalent image, however, we have traced an alternative tradition of colourful Dutch clothes.

ANNEKE SMELIK, DANIËLLE BRUGGEMAN AND MAAIKE FEITSMA

Bright and Bold Colours: Another Tradition

Shocking pink, hard blue, fierce turquoise, curry yellow, olive green, crimson red: such are the colours used by contemporary high street brands like Oilily, Mac&Maggie and ˉCoraKemperman. There are two main sources of inspiration for such colours: Dutch regional wear and Asia, especially India. We will come back to these (post) colonial influences in the second part of this chapter and will first concentrate on Dutch regional wear. Today Dutch regional dress is mostly reduced to folkloristic use, but it has influenced Oilily's choice of colours as well as patterns and shapes. Oilily clothes freely mix and match costumes of fishing or farming villages such as Marken, Volendam, Staphorst, Hindeloopen and Spakenburg. Some of those villages are tourist attractions today, like

Marken and Volendam close to Amsterdam, while other villages keep to their religious faith and reject tourism. An Oilily knitted sweater, for example, is based on the upper part of the costume of the women from Marken, mimicking the striped sleeves of the traditional smock, the laced bodice, the top part of the skirt, and the square flowered piece of textile covering the chest of the original regional costume (Olsthoorn-Roosen and Michielsen, 1992: 112-13).

Such an example shows a connection between contemporary colourful clothing and Dutch regional dress. Dutch society did not favour one official style or national dress, but is characterised by regional diversity: each community had its own style of dress. Dutch historian Eveline Koolhaas-Grosfeld (2010)

35. Oilily: colourful children's clothes (1986).

36. Inspiration for Oilily's designer Marieke Olsthoorn: women dressed in the colourful regional dress of the fishermen's village Marken in the North of Holland (no year).

recently argued that regional diversity became an important feature in discourses on Dutch identity in the eighteenth century. In the course of the nineteenth century, regional dress paradoxically played a double role as both a symbol of local and of national culture (De Jong: 1998, 2001).

In the countryside women and men both wore clothes in flamboyant colours, combined with jewellery, contrary to the sober sartorial customs of men in cities where such pageantry was deemed unmanly (De Leeuw, 1991: 65; De Leeuw, 1998: 15). It is relatively unknown, but of pivotal importance for our analysis, that during the late nineteenth century the use of colours in regional dress was toned down drastically (Feitsma, 2012). While regional dress is now characterised by a black backdrop with details in vivid colours, before 1880 most regional dress distinguished itself by its colourfulness

(De Leeuw, 1991: 64-65). These colourful costumes are recorded in a book of prints with the title *Images of Clothes, Customs and Traditions in the Batavian Republic* by the Dutch publisher Evert Maaskamp between 1803 and 1807. While at first sight the colours may seem a bit washed out, the colouring in the prints – being over two hundred years old – has probably faded (fig. 38).

Koolhaas-Grosfeld (2010) argues that the prints were published with the intention of advancing Dutch national awareness. Significantly, at least to the contemporary eye, Maaskamp chose images of regional dress over the familiar seventeenth century portraits of Dutch regents in his attempt to fabricate a national Dutch identity. Koolhaas-Grosfeld carefully traces the source of the idea of regional diversity as the backbone of Dutch identity back to the four-volume *Natural History of Holland* (1769–1811) by the Dutch physicist and writer Johannes Le Francq Berkheij. Berkheij recounts the founding myth of an ancient tribe in pre-Roman times, the Batavians, from whom the Dutch supposedly descended: 'with their golden hair, their blue eyes, their strong build, their short, multicoloured clothing, their enduring disposition and their freedom-loving character' (in Koolhaas-Grosfeld, 2010: 109). Within eighteenth century ideology, it follows that for Berkheij 'true Dutchness' is expressed through a line of undeviating continuity with the virtues of the Batavians. In Berkheij's view farmers, fishermen and petit bourgeois embodied such unswerving continuity, because they were the least corrupted by time and consequently most resembled

37. Oilily is still colourful today: women's collection presented at the Amsterdam Fashion Week (A/W 2008).

their ancient forefathers (Koolhaas-Grosfeld, 2010: 390).

Berkheij discusses clothing in the third volume of his 'Natural History of Holland'. He contrasts the Batavian style of dress, characterised as close-fitting, decorated and colourful, to the wide, white and pleaded robes of the Romans (Koolhaas-Grosfeld: 97-98). Regional dress at the time of his writing (between 1773 and 1776) showed the desired link with Batavian dress. Especially, the costumes of fishing villages around the Zuiderzee (then the 'South Sea', now reduced by reclaimed land to a lake, the IJsselmeer), such as picturesque Marken, Volendam and Enkhuizen, were a showcase for 'true Dutchness' (Koolhaas-Grosfeld: 148). Berkheij argues that historical continuity can be found especially in the colourfulness of the clothes, which he considers one of the 'original' characteristics of the Batavian style of dress.

From the eighteenth-century prints and books we can learn two things. First, there is indeed a strong tradition of colourful regional dress in the Netherlands throughout the centuries. Second, since the eighteenth century, regional dress has become part of an ideology of national identity. Against the prevalent image of sober and black clothes dating back to the Golden Age of the Dutch Republic, we have thus not only found an alternative tradition of colourful clothes in both history and in contemporary fashion, but we also traced an alternative ideological narrative of Dutch identity.

Cultural Memory, Regional Dress and the Myths of Dutch Culture

We have dug up forgotten stories and traditions from cultural memory, which shows an unexpected continuity – of striking colours – from Dutch regional dress in previous centuries to trendy designs by Oilily, Mac&Maggie and ⁻CoraKemperman today. Revealing these different stories and traditions raises the question why they had been forgotten. Cultural memory can be defined as the 'what' and 'how' a culture remembers, but equally as the what and how a culture *forgets* (Plate and Smelik, 2009: 1). By understanding cultural memory as a continuous process, as an act 'in the making' (ibid.: 2), we can look at the way in which historical narratives are constructed.

Jan Assmann (1992) argues that cultural memory is focused on myth rather than on facts, or, more precisely, that it changes historical fact into myth. In Assmann's definition, cultural memory has normative and formative powers, since it serves to actively construct the identity of a social group or of an individual. At the time of Berkheij's publication (1773–6) the Batavian founding myth was actually the dominant narrative concerning a collective Dutch identity. The myth of the seventeenth-century

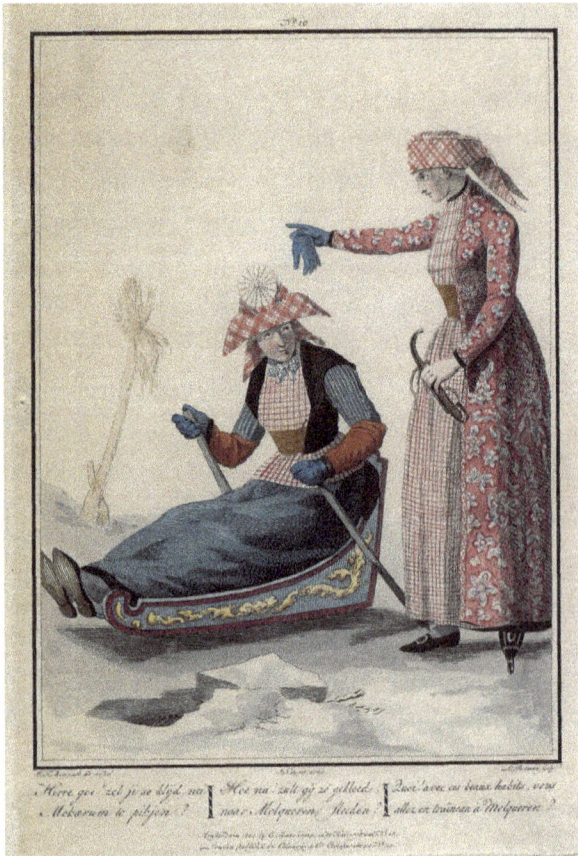

38. Regional costumes in the Netherlands in the eighteenth century: a woman and girl from West-Friesland, a province in the north of Holland, coloured engraving made by L. Portman after C.F. Bounach and J. Kuyper.

Golden Age of the Dutch Republic as the bedrock of contemporary Dutch society was still to be constructed. It was not until the early nineteenth century that this era of economic and cultural flourishing became the touchstone for modern Dutch society (De Jong, 2001: 30). It still is today, although contemporary historians are not only lyrical about its positive effects (democracy, urban planning, social welfare, painting, religious tolerance, reclaiming land against the sea), but offer a more critical view of its downsides (slavery, colonial violence and the beginning of ruthless capitalism in the example of speculation in the tulip trade) (Emmer, 2006; Berger Hochstrasser, 2007; Goldgar, 2007).[4]

The political and financial powers of the seventeenth century were for the most part situated in the provinces of North and South Holland, which is now the urbanised area of the metropolises of Amsterdam, The Hague and Rotterdam. Thus, this part of the country played an important role in the creation of a national identification for the entire Dutch nation. At the end of the eighteenth century, Berkheij and Maaskamp resisted such cultural dominance and strived for a different sense of national unity by advocating cultural diversity. Regional dress could then become a symbol for national identity. The cultural uniformity that was later wilfully effectuated by the nineteenth-century nation-state dispersed and weakened regional diversity and undid its symbolic function as a signifier for national identity.

Towards the end of the eighteenth century processes of modernisation, industrialisation and urbanisation caused regional cultures, including regional costumes, to lose their distinctive functions and meanings. Regional culture lost its authenticity, was deemed old-fashioned, and turned into folklore, relegated to the world of fairs, exhibitions or festivals. Regional dress itself became more subdued in its appearance in the course of the late nineteenth century (De Leeuw, 1991: 65). The fading out of colour was a result of both religion and of fashion. The second half of the nineteenth century witnessed a double revival of religious belief: the emancipation of Catholics on the one hand, and two major schisms in the Dutch Protestant church on the other. Renewed religious fervour provoked a greater sobriety in dress, replacing the bright colours of regional dress with more sober shades of brown, dark blue and black (De Leeuw, 1991: 65). During the second half of the nineteenth century black becomes a fashionable colour (Meij, 2000: 9; De Jonge, 2010: 89-99). New fashionable elements that were incorporated into regional dress tended therefore to be black as well. The colourfulness of regional wear was partly subdued in the nineteenth century and was partly forgotten in the cultural memory of the twentieth century. It was consequently repressed from the dominant idea and myths of Dutch culture.

In this part of the chapter we have shown that a historical continuity can be found between colourful clothing in Dutch regional wear and fashion today. Oilily's, Mac&Maggie's, and ̄CoraKemperman's shocking pink, hard blue, fierce turquoise, curry yellow, olive green, and crimson red are then not the exception in an otherwise bleak landscape of sober and sombre Dutch fashion. The alternative narrative of a colourful tradition in Dutch dress shows that cultural memory is not cast and settled forever in a certain form but, on the contrary, is continually subject to negotiation and renegotiation. As we saw above, this recalling and recollecting is always memory for something – a remembering in the interests of a particular group of people, a particular ideology, or a particular notion of the individual or collective self (Plate and Smelik, 2009: 2). By changing over time, memory may unsettle received ideas of the past. Neither the Batavian myth nor the narrative of the Golden Age tells the full story of Dutch identity. Rather, sober black-and-white versus vibrant colours are two parallel stories of Dutch habits of dressing. Stories that sometimes contrast, sometimes complement, and at other times cross or intersect. Stories that are variously

foregrounded or pushed backwards; remembered or forgotten. In our view, the vivid palette in Dutch fashion should not only be acknowledged, but also nuance or even change the dominant narrative of a Dutch sober and 'colourless' fashion style dating back to the seventeenth century. Perhaps bold and bright colours are even more typical for Dutch fashion than a sober palette of dark hues. Renowned stylist Frans Ankoné, who worked for both Mac&Maggie and ̄CoraKemperman, suggested that much in an interview with us in 2012. In his view, northern countries such as the Netherlands and Scandinavia use bold and bright colours because of the particular quality of the northern light.[5] But maybe this is just another myth in the making …

Intermezzo: The Glocal Connections of Chintz

In this 'Intermezzo' we focus on the example of chintz in order to further unravel the myth of Dutch identity related to Dutch regional wear. Both Mac&Maggie's and ̄CoraKemperman's designs have important roots in India, which, as we will argue, also holds true for Oilily due to its link to Dutch regional wear.

Designer Cora Kemperman and stylist Frans Ankoné have been essential to the development of a recognisable style of the brand ̄CoraKemperman, as they had also been to Mac&Maggie in the late 1970s through to the 1990s. India was – and still is – an important source of inspiration for Kemperman and Ankoné, which affected their abundant use of colour. ̄CoraKemperman regularly plays with references to other countries, cultural traditions and folklore, which are translated into the design of the clothes (Bruggeman, 2014). The brand's collection 'Jump Around the World' (Spring 2010) (fig. 39), for example, illustrates how different countries, cultures and traditions encounter each other in Kemperman's designs.

As explained on an information sheet that was sent to the loyal consumers of the brand, the collection is inspired by traditional kimonos from Tokyo, the

39. Cora Kemperman designed colourful clothes for the collection 'Jump Around the World' (A/W 2010).

glamorous city Paris, eccentric London, and by headgear worn by men in Jaipur and Udaipur, India. In addition, the warm and intense colours are supposed to remind us of the colourful markets in Goa, India and Zanzibar.

While ⁻CoraKemperman is inspired by India for its use of bold colours, we have seen above that Oilily is inspired by Dutch regional wear. Yet, this may not be such an opposition as appears at first sight. If we take a closer look, interesting links emerge between the different sources for the use of bold colours. In relation to Dutch regional dress the late Marieke Olsthoorn, then designer of Oilily, claims that chintz caught her attention because of its designs and colours (Olsthoorn-Roosen and Michielsen, 1992: 31). The hand-drawn and dyed cotton fabric was brought to the Netherlands in the seventeenth century by Dutch traders of the Dutch East India Company (Crill, 2008; Hartkamp-Jonxis, 1987), a controversial trading company that also engaged in colonialisation, slavery and violence. In the third quarter of the seventeenth century chintz became fashionable in the Netherlands, especially as home wear for women, and was frequently worn in the northern part of the country near the coasts of the North Sea and Zuiderzee (Van Zuthem, 1987; Arts, 2010). Since the seventeenth century, but especially in the eighteenth century, chintz was used in any type of clothing, such as children's clothes, gowns, skirts, jackets, handkerchiefs and capes.

The popularity of chintz was a result of the country's prosperity during the Dutch Golden Age, when the textile trade of the colonial Dutch East India Company reached its peak (Breukink-Peeze, 2000). Chintz was popular in different social classes in society, from the urban elite to farmers and fishermen, and increasingly became part of Dutch regional dress styles (Van Zuthem, 1987). After the fashionable chintz mostly disappeared towards the end of the eighteenth century, it was still used for folkloric and traditional regional dress purposes (Arts, 2010). Although chintz was originally an exotic textile, its bright colours and richly decorated

motifs were soon integrated into Dutch regional wear, which is nowadays viewed as an icon of Dutch folklore. Equally, Oilily's link to Dutch regional wear is often perceived as an important part of the 'Dutchness' of the brand, while Marieke Olsthoorn transposed the motifs and colours of chintz into Oilily's collections.

Paradoxically, then, the designs of 'Dutch' traditional costume have been greatly influenced by Indian chintz from colonial times. There are more icons of 'Dutchness' dating from the Golden Age with roots in foreign countries: Delft Blue earthenware was adapted from Chinese porcelain, while the tulips flourishing in the sandy grounds of the Dutch dunes were imported from Turkey. In this way, an interesting dialogue has

40. A family wearing chintz: regional wear from fishermen's village Marken near Amsterdam. Gouache made by Jan Duyvetter, 1948.

ANNEKE SMELIK, DANIÈLLE BRUGGEMAN AND MAAIKE FEITSMA

been created between 'cultural otherness' (objects, fabrics, motifs, and colours from other countries and cultural traditions) and narratives of 'Dutchness'. Fashion epitomises these cultural dynamics as it operates in global flows of consumerist capitalism, while commodifying objects from a wide variety of local traditions and cultures. José Teunissen reflects on these dynamics, arguing that fashion 'has always sought inspiration in other cultures, starting with the importing of silk from China and later cotton and cashmere from India' (2005: 13). In the use of bold colours, patterns and motifs, and fabrics by Oilily, Mac&Maggie and ⁻CoraKemperman we recognise the complex dynamics of the ways in which the 'other' – for example chintz from India – is incorporated into the 'self' on a national level. Chintz has become part of the objects and representations that create shared imaginations of what 'Dutchness' means, which has subsequently become part of contemporary Dutch fashion.

As we have already argued in the Introduction, the current interest of Dutch fashion designers or more generally of Western countries in their own local, national roots due to globalisation cannot be separated from a fascination for 'cultural otherness' and for foreign local traditions. Moreover, it is because of globalisation that 'diverse and remote cultures have become accessible, as signs and commodities' (Barker, 2012: 159). The global flows of capitalist modernity thus lead to a renewed interest in the 'local' – 'national identity' as well as 'other' local traditions. Roland Robertson refers to this as a process of 'glocalisation' (1992: 173-74), a concept that he popularised after adopting it from marketing and business discourse. He uses this term to articulate the dynamics in which the global and the local are reciprocally constitutive as 'mutually "interpenetrating" principles' (Robertson, 1995: 30). This is evidently essential to the formation of local, national 'identities' as their meanings are always constructed in relation to the global flows that introduce

us to local 'otherness'. The interaction with 'other' local traditions, and a fascination for cultural 'otherness' is not only a phenomenon of contemporary processes of globalisation. It can be traced back to colonial times in which Western trading companies like the Dutch East India Company were travelling around the world, importing products and non-Western clothing styles from the Orient. As Sandra Niessen argues, fashion's 'ethnic novelties generate a false sense that the global, multicultural nature of fashion is unprecedented' (2005: 157).

When researching the ways in which Dutch fashion brands and designers operate within their particular national context, it is thus imperative to take into account their multifarious relationship to 'others'. An intricate dynamics is at play in which 'otherness' has become part of a certain idea of Dutchness. By analysing visual material of Oilily, Mac&Maggie and ⁻CoraKemperman, we will show how these brands eclectically incorporate cultural 'otherness' into Dutch brands.

Part II: Cultural Hybridity

Oilily: Rooted in 'Dutchness'?

Oilily put down the importance of colour in an 'Oilily principle' in the very first *Oilily* magazine: 'The most striking aspect is the colourfulness of our clothes. We use bright and cheerful colours, which children find attractive. A loud variety of pink and turquoise are found in all of our collections' (*Oilily* magazine, 1984: 4-5). Graphic designer and initiator of the *Oilily* magazines, Jean Philipse, connects Oilily's aesthetic signature – its particular use of striking colour and unusual combinations – to its 'origin' in Dutch folkloric costumes. While Olsthoorn acknowledges the presence of 'typically Dutch elements' in Oilily's designs, she was also inspired by a wide variety of other clothing traditions, such as the 'dazzling colour combinations of women in the pink desert of Rajasthan as well as the wonderful multi-coloured clothes in South America' (Olsthoorn-Roosen and Michielsen, 1992: 7, our translation). This points to a complex relationship between Oilily's strong connection with traditional Dutch costume and its explorations of 'other' local dress styles that are also incorporated into Oilily's designs and promotional images.

In Oilily's magazines from 1984 until the mid 2000s, Oilily's clothes are frequently worn by children and women from various ethnicities, photographed in different countries, cultures and traditions. For instance, on one of the covers of Oilily's childrenswear magazine in 1993–4, a small Bolivian girl sits on piled rocks, presumably in front of her home in La Paz, wearing a colourful dress (fig. 41). In the accompanying text of the magazine, the resemblance between Oilily's clothes and traditional Bolivian dress is

emphasised: 'In Bolivia you still see a lot of traditional clothing worn by people of a particular family, village or district. Some of it is just as colourful as Oilily clothing' (*Oilily* magazine, A/W 1993–4: 39).

Oilily's clothes are frequently presented within the context of other local traditions, different cultures, and native people. Each magazine from 1987 until 1996, with only a few exceptions, is photographed in a different country, region or city. Specific motifs and colours of Oilily's collections are regularly positioned in such a way that they foreground the remarkable similarities to the motifs and colours inherent to that particular cultural setting. Oilily's motifs resemble the motifs in, for instance, wallpaper, blankets, tablecloths or carpets in other countries, suggesting links between Oilily's and foreign patterns in the most unexpected places.

We want to argue, that, not unlike Benetton at the same time, Oilily's magazines intended to connect children all over the world through its specific colours, functioning as a universal visual language that appeals to every child. Jean Philipse claims that, even before Benetton introduced its slogan, a text on one of Oilily's first bags read: 'United Colours of Oilily'. The links that the photographs in the magazines suggest between Oilily and the motifs and colours of other cultures emphasise the idea that Oilily's aesthetic signature has a universal quality. For instance, in the magazine photographed in Guatemala (1991), a Caucasian model, dressed in a richly decorated sweater with different colourful motifs by Oilily, sits next to native men wearing traditional Guatemalan dress. The woman in the photograph is positioned in such a way that she accentuates the resemblance between Oilily's designs and the native dress style with similar elaborately decorated and multicoloured stripes. Another example can be found in the magazine photographed in Slovakia (1995), in which numerous Slovakian children, whose names are explicitly mentioned, wear Oilily's clothes. Even when the photographs for the magazines are not taken in specific

41. Cover of *Oilily* magazine (A/W 1993–4).

other countries, children with different ethnicities are regularly brought together in a playful way, comparable to Benetton's way of celebrating cultural difference in the 1980s. Yet, Benetton's advertising has also been criticised for its paradoxical presentation of diversity 'within a wider unifying articulation' (Giroux, 1994: 9). Post-colonial theory has rejected this claim for unifying universality, which suggests that Benetton's and Oilily's 'universal' visual language must be understood as a Western or perhaps Eurocentric phenomenon.

The idea that Oilily's colourful designs appeal to all the children in the world is supported by specific texts accompanying the photographs in the magazines, such as 'Oilily, a language they all understand'; 'Colours and comfort for all characters'; 'Oilily, a colourful look on life'; 'Your colours speak for themselves. Oilily, fluent in all languages'; 'It's a world of colour'; and 'Students of Oilily; the colourful university'. These texts suggest that the colours of Oilily speak a universal visual language that all children are able to understand, maybe even uniting all children worldwide, regardless of nationality, ethnicity, gender or class. Yet, in some cases it can be quite estranging to see, for instance, native Bolivian children wearing clothes with the logo of the Dutch brand Oilily. As logos have become central to a politics of identity, and are used to connect individual identities (Giroux, 1994: 13), the *Oilily* magazines express the idea that children's identities are connected, as they are all labelled with the Oilily logo. When children from a wide variety of different countries and ethnicities are dressed in Oilily's clothes, they are simultaneously fashioned with the meanings attached to Oilily's commodified vision of what a child is. Although it seems a noble purpose to unite all children through Oilily's colourful clothes, this strategy is certainly also reductive of their cultural differences as it presents an idealised homogenisation of cultures through colours and patterns.

Oilily's focus on travelling around the world and their representations of different cultures can be understood as a 'fascination for "otherness"' (Hall, 1997: 225) to which popular representation is so frequently drawn. As Hall explains, these representations of 'otherness' can easily slip into a stereotypical image reinforcing the exotic 'other' as subordinate to the dominant West. There is a fine line between portraying different ethnicities in a stereotypical way, confirming deep-seated hierarchical representations of the races rooted in colonial history, and using a more positive, effective strategy to break with these hierarchical oppositions. While Oilily's magazines show an interest in different cultures and cultural differences, these are assimilated into the Dutch brand and hence become part of the dynamics of Western fashion. Local 'others' are thus unified into Oilily as a Dutch brand, because Oilily is continuously creating 'narratives of unity', to borrow Barker's term (2012: 259), through its emphasis on the universality of its visual language of colour.

The interconnections with other cultures go seamlessly together with Oilily's use of Dutch regional wear. In her book *On Children's Clothes* (1992, our translation), Olsthoorn explains that traditional regional wear from Marken is her favourite dress style because of its colourfulness, which, as we saw above, is derived partly from Indian chintz. Although these traditional regional dress styles are highly codified, Olsthoorn takes the liberty to interpret these motifs in a more creative, cheerful and playful way (Arts, 2010). The importance of traditional Dutch costume to the creation of Oilily's designs suggests the Dutch origin of the brand. One of Oilily's magazines (1994–5) explicitly foregrounds the shared imaginations and meanings of Dutch culture (fig.42).

A little girl on the cover wears a lace hat, which traditionally stems from the old fishing village of Volendam, sitting in front of a painting of a woman wearing a similar traditional Dutch hat. This image is presented in the context of Delft Blue vases and tiles,

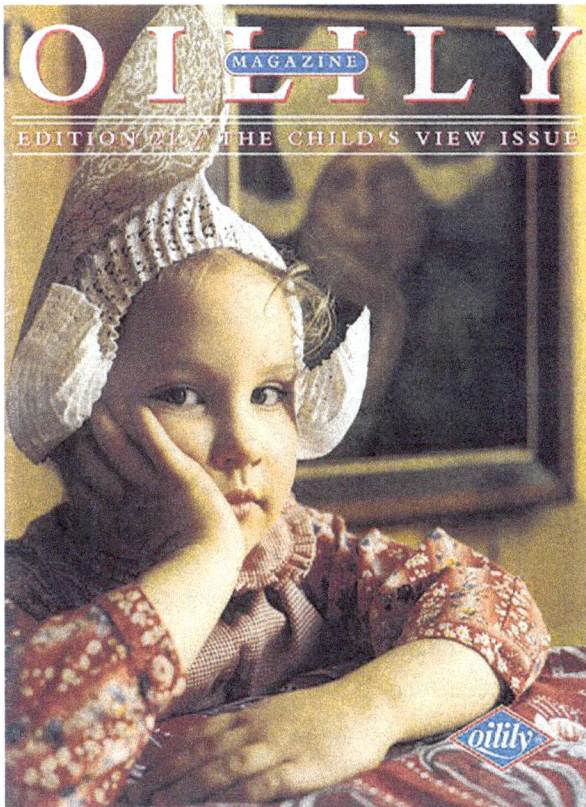

42. Cover of *Oilily* magazine (A/W 1994–5).

windmills, farmers and cows, the royal Dutch airline KLM, the Dutch national flag, and clogs – stereotypical objects and representations symbolising the shared idea of what the Netherlands stands for.

Oilily thus creates a dynamic, perhaps post-modern, interplay between cultural otherness and narratives of 'Dutchness'. The inextricable inter-connection between the 'global' and the 'local' shows that they are mutually constituting principles. Our 'own' local, national roots and our 'others' are thus necessarily involved in a reciprocal interplay, blurring the distinction between the two. As Stuart Hall argues, 'the "Other" is fundamental to the constitution of the self' (Hall, 1997: 237). This is also the case for Oilily, as it incorporates cultural otherness into itself as a Dutch brand. This pertains to both the material dimension of the fabrics and the representational dimension of the

fashion images in Oilily's magazines. The paradoxical process of assimilating the global 'other' into the local is fundamental to the dynamics of national identity, which is a way of 'unifying cultural diversity' (Barker, 2012: 260). Thus, fashion objects and representations can participate in the discursive reproduction of national 'narratives of unity' (Barker, 2012: 259). While Oilily is often perceived as a Dutch brand due to its connection to regional Dutch costume, we cannot dismiss the strong presence of 'otherness' – and its underlying colonial and political dimension – within the brand.

Mac&Maggie and ˜CoraKemperman: Fashion's Orientalism

A focus on travelling to faraway countries and a fascination for different cultures is a central theme for designer Cora Kemperman and stylist Frans Ankoné working for the Dutch brands Mac&Maggie (1976–96) and ˜CoraKemperman (1995–2016). Mac&Maggie was a trendy, young, Dutch fashion brand in sync with the new youth movements at the end of the 1970s and in the 1980s.

As Mac&Maggie grew to be a successful company and became more profitable, Kemperman and Ankoné could further develop their fascination for 'exotic' places, faraway countries and other cultures. The brochures and advertisements increasingly presented Mac&Maggie's clothes in different settings such as India, Arizona, Egypt, the Canary Islands or New York. Different countries, cultural traditions, or fashion designers were actively translated into Mac&Maggie's designs. There was the influence of Japanese designers, classical Chinese Mao suits and Indian ikats, uniforms, colours and turbans. Mac&Maggie's incorporation of non-Western clothing styles into its collections should be partly placed against the backdrop of youth and pop culture of the 1960s (Teunissen, 2005). The fascination for other cultures was also expressed by Mac&Maggie's choice for models from different ethnic backgrounds for their advertisements, which made it one of the first brands within the Dutch context to break with all-white modelling.

Different cultural traditions and folklore are continuously assembled in the promotional material and designs of both Mac&Maggie and ⁻CoraKemperman, exemplifying the ways in which cultural 'otherness' is eclectically incorporated into these Dutch brands. Other local clothing styles travel in tandem with global flows of capitalism, become part of Western fashion dynamics, and are subsequently integrated into glocal fashion brands. According to Paulicelli and Clark the focus on the global is inherent to fashion: 'Tied to a "national fabric", but also aimed to widen its remit, fashion is always traveling and ultimately aims at a global market' (2009: 2). Yet this explanation of fashion's global orientation is not sufficient with regard to ⁻CoraKemperman, a company that aimed to remain small and exclusive by only operating nine stores in the Netherlands and Belgium, with no need to expand its business. Polhemus offers another possible explanation by pointing to the contradictory ways in which Western fashion is often centred on non-Western clothing traditions, 'celebrating Peruvian peas and embroidery one season, capriciously discarding it as passé the next' (2005: 89). Such inherent contradictions suggest an orientalist perspective of fashion's interest in the 'exotic' – emphasising its 'otherness' – to confirm the power of Western fashion as the ultimate standard. As Edward Said famously argued, orientalism is a 'Western style for dominating, restructuring, and having authority over the Orient' (Said, 1979 [1978]: 3). This is intricately connected to deep-rooted colonial imaginations of the 'other'.

Said's book has been significant to postcolonial studies for understanding how the Orient, the 'other', was crucial in defining the West as well as reiterating Western hegemony. Said's argument helps to realise the ways in which the construction of Dutch national identity is dependent on its 'others'. As he points out,

this is manifest in contemporary culture, as 'a wide variety of hybrid representations of the Orient now roam the culture' (Said, 1979 [1978]: 285). Drawing upon the work of Said and Foucault, Stuart Hall reflects on these cultural dynamics in relation to representations, arguing that different practices of representation produce 'a form of racialised knowledge of the other (orientalism) deeply implicated in the operations of power (imperialism)' (Hall, 1997: 260). This opens up an understanding of the role that fashion – its material objects as well as fashion images – plays in the Western discursive production of its 'others', which is rooted in orientalism and imperialism.

The dynamics of orientalism are indispensable when trying to understand fashion's fascination for 'cultural otherness'. As Clark argues: 'For the last 400 years, Western fashion has flirted with Orientalism as a source of reference and "inspiration" for a diversity of designs' (2009: 177). It is often argued that the textile

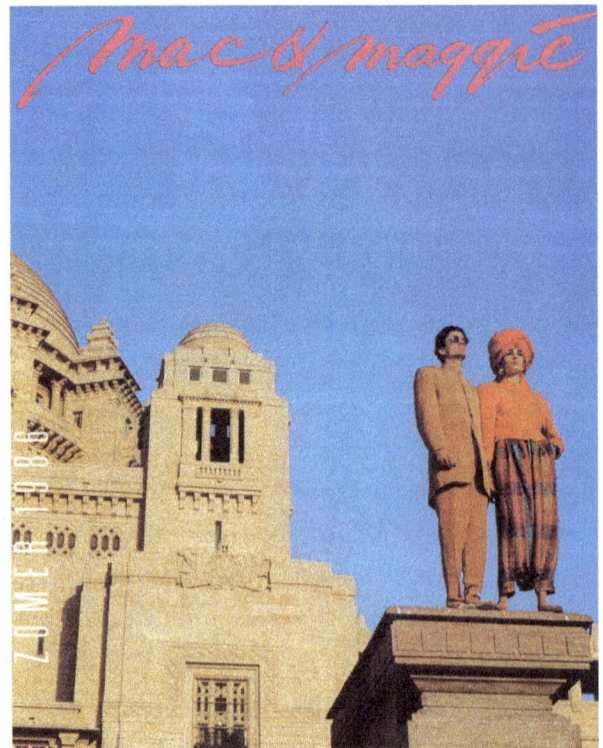

43. Cover of magazine *Mac&Maggie* (Summer 1986).

44. Image from the book *20 Seasons Mac&Maggie* (1986).

trade marks the beginning of 'a typically Western view of the world', emerging with Western industrial dominance (Niessen, 2005: 157). The textile industry was 'at the core of the social, political and economic transformations' as well as 'at the heart of colonialism; and central to the consequent struggle for independence from colonial empires, as in the case of India' (Paulicelli and Clark, 2009: 2). The interest in 'exotic' objects and the Western orientalist gaze are rooted in textile trade, and are still present, albeit often implicitly, in contemporary fashion.

The eclectic incorporation of elements of other cultures and faraway countries into the brands Mac&Maggie and ¯CoraKemperman cannot be separated from this colonial perspective. Especially in the images and designs of Mac&Maggie we can detect explicit references to colonial pasts. In the magazine

of the summer collection in 1986, a photograph of a couple wearing black and white pants and shirts, shot in India, is accompanied by the text: 'colonial black and white' (Plas 1986: 73). The text describing the summer collection of 1984 in the book *20 Seasons Mac&Maggie* explicitly refers to colonialism: 'Classical forms from other parts of the world are still more or less important. India, and the familiar Nehru suits and sarouels, but also with memories of the colonial uniform' (Plas 1986: 49, our translation). While this collection is also inspired by Japan, America and Russia, such explicit colonial references are remarkable. Memories of the uniforms of colonial pasts are present in these collections, which is an expression of the way in which fashion performs cultural memory by actively 'transferring and migrating visual motifs from the past to the present' (Smelik, 2011: 80). As Plate and Smelik argue: 'Memory is always re-call and re-collection [...] and consequently, it implies re-turn, re-vision, re-enactment, re-presentation; making experiences from the past present again in the form of narratives, images, sensations, performances' (2013: 6). In this case, cultural memories of colonial pasts are explicitly performed and thus remade and renegotiated in Mac&Maggie's collections. As such, fashion plays a pivotal role in the constant process of remaking cultural memories of the past.

In contrast to actual historical colonialism and its social, economic and political oppression and exploitation, in contemporary fashion we can find signifiers of the performance of colonial attitudes. As Mac&Maggie embraces clothing styles of the exotic 'other', while acknowledging the colonial legacy of these practices, the brand is part of the tradition of Western fashion that has 'flirted with Orientalism' (Clark, 2009: 177) by performing and commercialising colonial, neo-colonial and post-colonial tropes. Two decades later, ¯CoraKemperman integrated non-Western clothing traditions into its collections in a more playful and implicit way, as a continuous process of appropriating elements from diverse cultures, traditions and time periods. As 'other' cultural clothing styles were the core of the brand ¯CoraKemperman, its collections expressed a cultural dialogue comparable to other fashion designers who morph 'references and motifs from different periods and cultures into single fusions' (Evans, 2003: 29). Instead of participating in the Western discursive production of its global 'others' as notably different from the local 'self', ¯CoraKemperman playfully presented them as an integral part of its Dutch brand.

Conclusion

The case studies of Oilily, Mac&Maggie and ¯CoraKemperman show the contradictory dynamics of the ways in which fashion incorporates both colourful indigenous and non-Western clothing styles as part of the Dutch fashion industry. A variety of local and foreign cultural traditions become an intrinsic part of these brands, in some cases to the extent that the boundaries between them are blurred. The global dynamics of fashion produce 'glocal' Dutch fashion brands, contributing to a visual and discursive reproduction of 'Dutchness' that includes 'otherness'. The inextricable interconnectedness of global and local undermines any idea of a homogeneous unity of a national identity. Instead, at the heart of national identity we find cultural hybridity.

The changes in fortune of Indian chintz – first imported from India and integrated into Dutch regional wear, then reintegrated as an icon of 'Dutchness' into Oilily's designs – demonstrate the way in which fashion expresses and underwrites the cultural hybridity of the Netherlands. Although these dynamics may pertain to most post-colonial European countries, it is remarkable that Dutch fashion brands such as Oilily, Mac&Maggie, and ¯CoraKemperman show such a sustained interest in cultural 'otherness'. By doing so, they express the cultural hybridity of the national context in which they are rooted. Although 'the pendulum of Dutch politics had swung wildly' in the last decade, a dominant Dutch myth had it that the Netherlands is a 'multicultural haven of tolerance', as sociologist Frank Lechner asserts (2008: xv). The Netherlands was generally viewed as an open society: 'a progressive country, open to the world' (ibid.), which he traces back to the seventeenth century when the Dutch were sailing around the world, and when the scale of Amsterdam's city trade was unprecedented, something in which the colonial Dutch East India Company played a crucial role. Lechner claims that the 'local well-being of the Dutch depended on their global connections' (2008: 35). In this sense, the Netherlands became a 'diffusion country', where 'cultures made contact, products were exchanged and new things discovered' (Frijhoff and Spies, 2004: 56). Because of its growing wealth, the republic drew many migrants which further 'globalised' the society (Lechner, 2008: 36). At the time of the Golden Age, the Netherlands harboured a higher percentage of foreign citizens than it does now (Goedkoop and Zandvliet, 2012: 48). The high percentage of foreigners, together with a relative religious freedom for Catholics and Jews, and a relatively free press, created the myth of Dutch tolerance. It is this Dutch narrative, rooted in the Dutch Golden Age, which contributed to the myth of the Netherlands as an open, multicultural society with a strong interest in other countries and cultures. Like any myth, it downplays the dark sides of colonialism; for example the fact that the gold of the Golden Age was gained by suppressing colonised peoples and by upholding slavery until very late in the nineteenth century. The myth of Dutch tolerance has played and still plays an important role in Dutch cultural discourse, as part of shared imaginations of what the Netherlands stands for; much in the way that Benedict Anderson describes the nation as an imagined community (Anderson, 2006 [1983]: 6).

Although narratives of national unity have taken centre stage in the last decade, these cannot be separated from narratives of cultural diversity within the Netherlands, which have been an important part of cultural imaginations of Dutchness since the Golden Age. Expressions of a strong interest in cultural 'otherness' are thus part of dominant Dutch narratives. Since it is this hybrid cultural context in which Dutch fashion brands operate, it is hardly surprising that the cultural dynamics of hybridity resonate in fashion. By expressing an interest in cultural 'otherness', Oilily, Mac&Maggie and ¬CoraKemperman echo memories of (post)colonialism, while at the same time discursively reproducing hybrid narratives of Dutch national identity. As such, the vivid colours of Dutch fashion signify the colourfulness of hybridity. Dashing colours, daring patterns, florid folds and bold cuts have made it from the local to the global and back again in a 'glocal' mix of trendy fashion.

Notes

1. As this book went to press, the Dutch press unexpectedly announced ¬CoraKemperman's bankruptcy.

2. The Grand Seigneur award has been granted since 2001 by MODINT, the trade association for the Dutch clothing industry. Between 1984 and 1998 the price was awarded by MODAM, the Association of the Dutch Fashion Fair.

3. The research for this chapter was done by Daniëlle Bruggeman and Maaike Feitsma with a multi-method approach, from visual analysis and literature review to theoretical background. In 2010 the researchers conducted interviews with Cora Kemperman and Marieke and Willem Olsthoorn; graphic designer and initiator of the *Oilily* magazines,

Jean Philipse; and stylist Frans Ankoné at Mac&Maggie and ¬CoraKemperman. They performed archival research into fashion and women's magazines, journals, newspaper articles and corporate documents, and studied clothes in the archives of the Central Museum in Utrecht. They made a visual analysis of promotional material of Oilily, Mac&Maggie and ¬CoraKemperman, including magazines, advertisements, fashion editorials, promotional picture postcards, the websites and online archives of image material. The rich data and methodological details can be found in the dissertations of the co-authors (Bruggeman, 2014; Feitsma, 2014). This chapter brings the results of the research together in a synthetic interpretation.

4. The story of the Golden Age is still popular with the Dutch audience; for example public television recently broadcast a well-received and much viewed historical series in 13 episodes on the seventeenth century by historian Hans Goedkoop (NTR and VPRO, 2012–13). The series was accompanied by a book, also available in English: Hans Goedkoop and Kees Zandvliet, *The Dutch Golden Age*, Walburg Pers, 2012.

5. Compare the documentary *Dutch Light* by Pieter-Rim De Kroon and Maarten De Kroon (2003) on the question whether Dutch light is a myth or not (The Netherlands, 91 mins). The film received many national and international awards.

Jan Taminiau (b. Goirle 1975)

Lianne Toussaint

As a designer my goal is to make the ultimate dress,
every single time, over and over again.

—www.jantaminiau.com

Undoubtedly, the eventful year 2013 turned Jan Taminiau into one of the best known and most celebrated fashion designers in the Netherlands and beyond. He designed two much-discussed dresses for Queen Máxima's inauguration that year and has been flying high ever since (fig. 1). With the majestic 'royal blue' dress and incredibly detailed aubergine-coloured evening gown, Taminiau permanently established his name and fame as couturier. It led to a boom of media attention, new assignments, requests and collaborations for his atelier: 'I find it very special that my work now somehow belongs to national history' (Taminiau, 2013: 18).

Prior to his successful career as a couturier, Taminiau developed a firm educational basis. He started at the European School for Antiquarians in Antwerp, then continued to study at the The Academy of Art and Design St. Joost in Breda and finally signed up for the master's programme at the ArtEZ Institute of the Arts in Arnhem, where his graduation project earned him the prestigious Roos Gesink Award for the most talented student of 2001. After various traineeships with corsetier Hubert Barrere and lacemaker Hurel in Paris he launched his own label, JANTAMINIAU, in 2004.

Taminiau's work is characterised by romantic and elegant, yet vigorous designs that bear witness to his partiality for delicate materials, artisan techniques and nostalgic fabrics. Coming from a family of antiquarians, decorators and interior designers, Taminiau's couture embodies the modern revival of tradition and craftsmanship. In his continuous

45. JANTAMINIAU, Mailbag jacket (2009).

46. JANTAMINIAU, Couture Collection (S/S 2013).

47. JANTAMINIAU, Couture Collection (S/S 2014).

quest for the perfect form, he combines the unconventional and innovative with the traditional and romantic (Ferwerda, 2006: 210). Ranging from the use of old priest's gowns, antique Chinese fabric and recycled mailbags to delicate tulle, pearls and crystal ornamentation, Taminiau's work is pervaded by a love for traditional production techniques, original materials and feminine aesthetics: 'All to give women back the art of showing themselves, thus proving that romance, attraction, elegance and style still have an important role to play in today's fashion.' (www.jantaminiau.com/discover/about-us/, last accessed 11 May 2016).

From 2007 onwards Taminiau has shown his couture collections twice a year during the Paris Fashion Week. Pop stars including Lady Gaga, Beyoncé and Björk wear his designs. In the Netherlands he is well known for the recycled mailbag jacket (fig. 45) that the then princess Máxima wore to the opening of the Arnhem Fashion Biennale in 2009. More recently, Taminiau has been working on different kinds of projects, such as the design of staff outfits for hotel Waldorf Astoria Amsterdam and costumes for the movie *The Hunger Games* and the Dutch theatre version of the film *Gone with the Wind*. Just when it seemed things could not get any better, Taminiau was awarded a Fashion stipend by the Prins Bernhard Cultuurfonds in December 2013 and a Grand Seigneur Fashion Award in 2014. As rewarding as the past ten years may have been, Taminiau has many more dreams for the years to come: 'I am hoping to become very old, so that I can do as much as possible and expand the Jan Taminiau universe' (Schriemer, 2013: 4). And who knows, national couture hero Taminiau may even take the step from royal robe to prêt-à-porter again in the future.

6.

Denim Goes Dutch:
A Myth-in-the-Making

'When we talk proudly about Holland when we are abroad, it's usually about tulips, cheese and football. If it's in polite, cultured company we may talk about the Rijksmuseum or the Stedelijk Museum of Modern Art; in less politically correct circles we talk about hash and whores. [...] Oddly, we generally overlook another ultra-Dutch speciality, an important export product we should be proud of: *denim*.'

—Cécile Narinx (2014)

Maaike Feitsma and Anneke Smelik

Introduction

On reading the above statement by fashion editor Cécile Narinx in the *ELLE Denim Bible* of Summer 2014, there may well have been quite a few readers, both in the Netherlands and abroad, who raised their eyebrows in mild surprise. Denim jeans are probably one of the most popular garments in the entire world; can denim therefore really be mentioned in the same breath as such treasured icons of Dutch culture as tulips and cheese? What's more, jeans are generally regarded as an icon of American culture, while the spread of this garment across the whole world since the 1960s is often understood as part and parcel of global Americanisation

(Miller, 1990; Conrads, 1992; Sullivan, 2006; Miller and Woodward, 2007). Random samples by the anthropologists Daniel Miller and Sophie Woodward suggest that everywhere in the world (apart from South Asia and China), on any given day, half of the population is wearing jeans (Miller and Woodward, 2007, 2012). Jeans are thus unquestionably an icon of globalisation. This raises the pressing question of how an object symbolising not only America, but also globalisation, can be associated with Dutch culture. In this chapter we return to the complex relation between the global and the local that we already addressed in the Introduction and in chapter 5, now focusing on the case study of denim.

48. The cover of a vinyl record of Dutch pop bands including Golden Earring from 1977, with a woman in regional costume wearing jeans, apparently produced by Levi's to celebrate ten years of Levi's in the Netherlands. The scene is situated in the tourist fishing village of Volendam.

The idea that jeans play a central role in Dutch fashion identity, and that the Dutch may actually be leaders within the denim industry, is a relatively recent one; it is a story 'in the making'. In order to answer the question why and how jeans have become associated with Dutch culture, we explore the relationship between the global and local meanings of jeans in this chapter. We will address two issues: first, how does an American or global garment like denim jeans acquire local meanings? And secondly, how are Dutch meanings attributed to denim jeans? As this particular case will show, Dutch denim is a national fashion myth-in-the-making that reveals how certain symbolic meanings are attributed to jeans. In this context, we use the notion of 'myth' as it was introduced by Roland Barthes (1991 [1957]) as a particular kind of culturally and historically specific – and thus ideological – myth that passes itself off as self-evident (Barthes, 1991: 10-11; Sturken and Cartwright, 2001: 19-20). Our research is based on a systematic analysis of newspaper and web articles and blogs over the last five years, and on interviews with key figures in the field. While the fashion myth of 'Dutchifying' denim is still relatively new, the speed with which it has been activated and accepted in the field of contemporary Dutch fashion suggests that this particular discourse is quickly regarded as becoming self-evident.

Jeans: Global and Local Meanings

The popularity of jeans is generally ascribed to their functional attributes: strong, comfortable, inexpensive and easy to wash. John Fiske, however, cautions that their functionality is only 'the precondition of their popularity, but does not explain it' (Fiske 1989: 1). He claims that the ability of jeans to cut across different social worlds – gender, religion, nation, class – can only be explained in cultural terms; that is to say, by the cultural meanings ascribed to them. Fiske therefore sees jeans as receptacles of meanings: 'they are a resource bank of potential meanings' (Fiske, 1989: 5). Jeans, and more broadly denim, indisputably signify characteristics of American national identity: 'strong, unpretentious, unadorned, informal, comfortable, classless, hard-working, reliable and consistent, improving with time' (Little, 1996: 11). Yet, because jeans derive their meaning from their context, they can be given a range of different – even contradictory – meanings within different cultures, as both Fiske (1989) and Iain Finlayson (1990) argue. Given the constraints of this chapter it is not possible to give an in-depth overview of the symbolism of jeans as an American icon; we have done so elsewhere (Feitsma, 2014; Smelik and Feitsma, 2015). We therefore take the 'Americanness' of jeans as a given and focus in this chapter on what happens to this particular American icon when jeans 'go global' and are worn in other cultures. In other words, what happens when consumers ascribe local meanings to jeans?

The 'Americanisation' that took place in large parts of the world, particularly following the liberation after the Second World War, is widely regarded as the reason for the original dissemination and worldwide popularity of denim (Miller, 1990: 103). In Europe, more than in the United States, jeans signified a new and modern world (Finlayson, 1990: 21). Miller and Woodward, leaders of the international *Global Denim* research project, argue that today 'Americanness' is no longer inextricably linked with jeans (Miller and Woodward, 2011: 18). According to them, 'people are wearing jeans simultaneously for global and local reasons' (Miller and Woodward, 2007: 337). This distinction between the different dimensions of meaning – from the global, through the national, to the local – opens avenues for alternative, non-American meanings for jeans, which leads us to the second and main issue of this chapter: jeans as an icon of Dutch culture. In our discussion we will address three questions: how are jeans and other denim garments linked to the myth of 'Dutch denim'? What arguments are being adduced to create this myth? And how is this myth rooted in Dutch fashion culture?

MAAIKE FEITSMA AND ANNEKE SMELIK

49. Jacket by Dutch jeans brand G-sus (A/W 2013–14).

50. Women's jeanswear by Dutch jeans brand Blue Blood (S/S 2009).

'Dutch Denim': A New Fashion Myth

In the past few years Dutch newspaper, magazine and web articles have asserted a connection between denim jeans and Dutch culture, as testified by headlines like 'Dutch Blue' (Van Rossum, 2012); 'Netherlands Blue' (De Baan, 2012); Netherlands, Country of Denim (Lampe, 2012); 'In the Land of Dung, Mist and Denim' (anon., *Trouw*, 2012) and 'Denim Jeans are the Dutch Mao-costume' (Van den Boom, 2012).[1] Coincidentally – or perhaps not so coincidentally – the same year saw a successful exhibition entitled *Blue Jeans* in an art museum, the Centraal Museum of Utrecht (24 November 2012 until 10 March 2013). Quite out of the blue then, there is this recent association of jeans with Dutch culture. Indeed, it looks like a myth-in-the-making.

What is perhaps even more remarkable is that international media put forward a similar fashion narrative. For instance, in a 2009 trend report the internationally-renowned trendspotting website WGSN called Amsterdam 'one of today's most exciting denim capitals' (Veld, 2009). Elsewhere, denim guru Adriano Goldschmied named four 'top denim-spotting' destinations, including the Netherlands – Amsterdam in particular – and northern European countries (McIlveen, 2003). *Sportswear International*, too, referred to Amsterdam as 'Denim City' (Dartmann, 2011: 50-54).

The new fashion myth has also been used by the Dutch brand Scotch & Soda, who in 2010 launched the denim line 'Amsterdams Blauw' ('Amsterdam Blue'). In the brand story on their website Scotch & Soda presents 'Amsterdams Blauw' as if it were a name derived from the colour of the pigment used during the Dutch Golden Age to decorate Delftware. 'Amsterdam Blue' thus links denim blue with a well-known icon of Dutch cultural heritage, blue Delftware. In attributing specific Dutch cultural meanings to the jeans we have moved from Delft Blue to Denim Blue. The mythical character of the denim story is further enhanced by references to the colour blue in the signs for street names in Amsterdam; as if other major cities didn't have blue signs for street names – Paris, for example.

So far, Scotch & Soda is the only Dutch denim brand that has profiled itself explicitly as a Dutch, even as an Amsterdam brand (interviews by Feitsma with James Veenhoff of 'House of Denim', 2011; and Mariette Hoitink of HTNK Fashion Recruitment and Consultancy, 2012).[2] The driving forces behind the depiction of the Netherlands as a leading denim country with Amsterdam as its jeans capital are thus not so much the brands themselves, but rather a number of organisations working hard to put Dutch fashion and the city of Amsterdam firmly on the map, such as the trade association MODINT, the fashion trade fair Modefabriek, the strategic internationalisation programme DutchDFA, the Fashion Cluster of the Amsterdam Metropolitan Area and the new platform for the Dutch denim industry, House of Denim, founded in 2009. The House of Denim is an ambitious project with a main focus on the development of craftsmanship and sustainability within the denim industry. While this platform does not have the ambition to take over production, it works together with the Dutch denim industry to realise several educational facilities – the combination of a school, archive, laboratory and a network of denim experts – to enable experimentation and stimulate innovation (Veenhoff, 2011: 34-35). The new fashion myth in which the Netherlands is a denim country and Amsterdam is a denim capital should therefore be understood, first and foremost, as an instance of 'national branding' or 'city branding'. The fashion myth is thus not so much shaped by the denim brands but rather by organisations that are fostering this image for policy reasons with the aim of promoting the local and national creative economy.

The original motives for the rise of this fashion myth are then quite commercial. Yet, as we will argue

51. House of Denim logo (Amsterdam Denim Days, first edition, 2014).

MAAIKE FEITSMA AND ANNEKE SMELIK

below, the myth could only be successful because it taps into specific characteristics of Dutch culture. Rather than featuring another instance of marketing blarney plucked out of thin air, the narrative of Dutch denim falls neatly in line with existing ideas about Dutch identity. This explains the rather smug self-evidence with which this particular fashion myth has been adopted by the media. In the following section we will explore the arguments that the media as well as the brands and organisations use for supporting the idea of a 'typically Dutch' relationship with jeans and denim. In other words, how is this new fashion narrative rooted in Dutch tradition?

The Netherlands, Country of Denim

The media put forward two main arguments for portraying the Netherlands as a distinctive denim jeans country and Amsterdam as a special capital of denim (Dartmann, 2011; Kops, 2010; Veld, 2009). The first, quantitative, argument is the fact that many jeans and jeans-related companies are located in the Netherlands, particularly in and around Amsterdam. The second argument is equally quantitative, but spills over into a cultural argument: the fact that the Dutch are particularly fond of wearing jeans. According to denim experts and the media, not only does the Netherlands offer the right business conditions for entrepreneurs, but the growth and success of the denim sector is also due to a 'typically Dutch' culture of informal dress. A link is therefore made between the industry's practical concerns that facilitate an attractive business climate and a general perception of Dutch fashion culture.

Denim Density

The national fashion myth of 'Dutch denim' entails that Amsterdam has the greatest density of denim companies in the world. (It should be noted that this claim refers not just to the city of Amsterdam, but to the larger metropolitan area of Amsterdam.) This includes or has included not only Dutch companies such as G-Star, Blue Blood, G-sus, Jason Denham, Kings of Indigo and Kuyichi, but also international brands like Pepe Jeans, Hilfiger Denim and even Levi's. Despite repeated attempts, we have been unable to obtain and verify any hard figures that substantiate this claim. For example, the Fashion Cluster of Amsterdam counted twenty-five denim companies in 2012 (Olde Monninkhof, 2012), while trade organisation MODINT counted fifty in the same year (Betlem, 2012). The problem lies partly in the vagueness of the criteria on what exactly makes a fashion company a denim company. There is also disagreement on the question whether Amsterdam should be seen as a denim capital on the basis of the number of companies per square metre, or on the basis of their combined turnover.

Be that as it may, the media have not hesitated to frequently and emphatically depict Amsterdam as a capital of denim and the Netherlands as an international centre of denim (e.g. Lampe, 2012; Stamkot, 2012; Betlem, 2012; anon., *Trouw*, 2012). One daily newspaper writes that 'the country is being swamped by denim' (Van den Boom, 2012), while another claims that the Netherlands plays 'no small role in the denim world' (Baks, 2012), and yet another writes that the Netherlands 'has grown into a genuine jeans country' (Van Rossum, 2012). This growth is principally attributed to favourable business conditions and advantageous tax arrangements for international companies located in the Netherlands (interviews with Veenhoff, 2011 and Hoitink, 2012; Duineveld and Scheffer, 2004: 343; Scheffer, 2009).

As mentioned above, the denim industry has also been actively promoted by the trade association MODINT, the trade fair Modefabriek, the strategic internationalisation programme DutchDFA and the platform for the Dutch denim industry House of Denim, amongst others.

The growing media interest in 'Dutch denim' and the manifest way in which the Netherlands, and specifically Amsterdam, is being portrayed as a leading international denim centre, demonstrate that it was indeed quite easy to tap into a general perception of a 'typically Dutch' fashion culture that easily accommodates and embraces denim. According to denim professionals the 'open-mindedness' of the Netherlands, and of Amsterdam in particular, makes it an ideal place to live for denim designers (interviews with Veenhoff, 2011 and Hoitink, 2012; Dartmann, 2011: 51). Alongside the general characteristics of Dutch culture, which are probably attractive to workers in all creative disciplines, journalists and fashion professionals have claimed a unique relationship between Amsterdam (or the Netherlands) and denim. For instance Karl-Heinz Müller, the general manager of Bread & Butter, the most important denim trade fair in Europe, has said that 'an extreme denim culture holds sway here,' which he and his team find so stimulating that they have opened an office in Amsterdam even though their trade fair is held in Berlin (Dartmann, 2011: 51). Dieter De Cock, the head designer of Cold Method, has described the city as 'jeans-centric' (Dartmann, 2011: 51). British-born Jason Denham, who made the move to Amsterdam with his then employer Pepe Jeans in the 1990s, goes a step further. In a 2010 interview he says:

Immediately on arriving it dawned on me that this, finally, was the real denim capital of the world. Amsterdam is the personification of everything jeans represent. Unyielding, slightly rebellious, adventurous, firmly opinionated, never afraid to make a statement and always uniquely individual. From the very first day, I felt like I had come home. So I think it makes sense that many of the major modern denim brands are getting their start in Amsterdam or are moving here. This is the modern heart of the international denim industry. (Kops, 2010: 10)

According to the media, the recent success of the denim industry in the Netherlands, and in Amsterdam in particular, is therefore attributed not just to practical aspects such as an attractive business climate but also to a lively 'denim culture' that fits in with the rebellious youth culture of Amsterdam. The first, quantitative, argument of a high density of jeans-related companies in the Netherlands is thus part and parcel of the second, cultural, argument that the Dutch are particularly fond of wearing jeans. In the next section, we will take a closer look at the relationship between Dutch people and their jeans.

The Most Jeans per Head of the Population?

As we saw above, the national fashion myth of 'Dutch denim' claims that the Netherlands is a leading jeans country because of its favourable business climate and a certain denim culture that inspires jeans designers. This jeans culture is first and foremost put in quantitative terms: Dutch people buy a lot of jeans and wear them often and on all occasions. This is the argument that the media most often use for regarding the Netherlands as a jeans country. In Dutch newspapers we can read, for instance, that 'Dutch people are the biggest jeans fans in the world' (Wouters, 2012); that 'No population is so addicted to wearing jeans as the Dutch' (anon., *Haarlems Dagblad*, 2012); that 'Nowhere else do you see so many blue jeans on the street' (De Baan, 2012); and that the number of jeans per head of the population is higher in the Netherlands than anywhere else in the world (Van den Boom, 2012; Hol, 2013; Baks, 2012; anon., *Haarlems Dagblad*, 2012; Wouters, 2012; Stamkot, 2012; anon., *Trouw*, 2012; anon., *De Gelderlander*, 2012).

52. Interior Exhibition *Blue Jeans*, 24 November 2012–10 March 2013.

Interestingly, most of these articles appeared in response to the exhibition *Blue Jeans* in Utrecht's Centraal Museum in 2012. The journalists all took their information from the catalogue, which they uncritically used as source material, losing much of the nuance in the process. In the exhibition catalogue curator Ninke Bloemberg argues that 'jeans determine the identity of Dutch fashion to a significant degree' and that 'the seed of this success [...] possibly [lies] in our own country' (Bloemberg, 2012: 1). She refers to the great popularity of denim jeans in the Netherlands: 'we take the first place when it comes to purchases of this garment' (Bloemberg, 2012: 1). Importantly, the curator draws on a recent report from the market research bureau GfK ('Growth from Knowledge'), which investigated the sales of jeans only in Europe, and not worldwide. However, a variety of newspapers imply that the Dutch are global leaders. Also, when we do not look at *sales* but at *ownership* within a global context, it is quite questionable whether the Dutch own the highest number of jeans per person. Research carried out by Ruigrok Netpanel in 2008 indicated that the average Dutch person owned 5.4 pairs of jeans, while research by Cotton Incorporated in 2005 showed that the average American owned 8.3 pairs (Miller and Woodward, 2007: 337).

Whether or not the Dutch actually do own the highest number of pairs of jeans per head of the population worldwide, it is striking that the media have uncritically, even eagerly, embraced this idea. Evidently it fits readily into existing perceptions of Dutch fashion culture. It is interesting to note here that both arguments for the narrative of 'Dutch denim' are at first quantitative, but at second sight appear cultural. The first, the large number of jeans and jeans-related companies in the metropolitan area of Amsterdam, is explained by its 'denim culture'. The second, that Dutch consumers own the largest number of jeans and wear jeans exceptionally often, is related to Dutch fashion culture. Both claims then have their origins in a perceived 'typically Dutch'

attitude to fashion, producing a seamless fit between jeans culture and Dutch fashion sensibilities.

Dutch Fashion Culture

Miller and Woodward argue that the 'rise of a particular variant of denim' within a given region is the most convincing argument for a unique local relationship with denim (Miller and Woodward, 2007: 339). The fashion media in the Netherlands, however, make very little mention of a link between the 'Dutchness' of Dutch denim and any specific aesthetic. In the Dutch context the new fashion myth is principally about a certain, typically Dutch fashion mentality. Maaike Feitsma described this attitude towards fashion in chapter 4 as characterised by an aversion to ostentation and a preference for sobriety, functionality and moderation: dressing down rather than 'dressing to impress'. Denim in general and jeans in particular symbolise precisely such an unpretentious, comfortable and informal way of dressing. It also signifies egalitarianism, which is often seen as another defining characteristic of Dutch society (Pleij, 2010). In the new myth of Dutch denim we can thus recognise an uninterrupted link with an older, already naturalised, myth about Dutch fashion culture. In our view this goes a long way towards explaining the ease with which this national fashion myth in the making has been so quickly and uncritically espoused by the media, and has been so widely accepted by readers. Let us explore in more detail the way such a construction comes about in the rhetorical practice of newspapers and fashion magazines.

In 2012 the cover of a weekend magazine of the renowned national newspaper *De Volkskrant* showed the back pocket of a pair of denim jeans, with the title: 'Blue Blood: The Netherlands Is the Most Important Jeans Country in the World'. The choice of the phrase 'blue blood' is significant: while it refers to a jeans brand, it also indicates that the success of denim jeans in the Netherlands is not just because of a favourable business climate but because the 'denim culture' is as it were in Dutch people's veins. In the article the fashion journalist writes 'that jeans brands do particularly well here because jeans are such a good fit with the Dutch fashion mentality, which is remarkably casual' (Lampe, 2012). A fashion journalist of the quality newspaper *NRC Handelsblad* similarly writes: 'But the [success] must also be seen as part of our practical, casual fashion culture. Evidently we do it so well, wearing jeans, that others are inspired' (van Rossum, 2012). Journalists thus explicitly refer to the informal and relaxed clothing culture in the Netherlands as one of the reasons for the success of 'Dutch denim'.

This particular aspect of Dutch fashion culture is also mentioned by denim professionals such as Mariette Hoitink of HTNK Fashion Recruitment and Consultancy, James Veenhoff of House of Denim, and Harry Bijl of the trade association Mitex (interviews by Feitsma with Veenhoff, 2011, Hoitink, 2012 and Bijl, 2012). In an interview with the free daily *Spits*, Veenhoff says 'We have an informal style, even at work. We have little hierarchy, so you see people in jeans at the office and at weddings; even mayors [wear jeans]' (Stamkot, 2012). In another interview with *Spits*, Veenhoff says: 'In our culture a homeless person under a bridge might be wearing jeans, but so might the Prime Minister' (Hol, 2013). Veenhoff also mentions that an informal dress culture leads to jeans being worn on all occasions. We can read similar comments in other media, for instance: 'In the Netherlands we've reached the point where jeans are as likely to be worn in the theatre box as in the retirement home' (Geuze, 2012). And: 'In the anti-authoritarian 1970s [...] denim permeated everywhere; now nobody thinks it's a problem to wear jeans to the Royal Concert Hall' (Jensen, 2012). Stylist Bastiaan Van Schaijk refers to denim jeans as 'easy, democratic clothing. Call it our Dutch Mao-costume' (Van den Boom, 2012). Veenhoff and other denim

or fashion professionals thus present the popularity of denim jeans as an immediate consequence of the country's informal clothing culture.

There may be a longer tradition of the Netherlands' leading position in denim jeans. According to costume historian De Leeuw they have characterised Dutch streetwear since the early 1970s (De Leeuw, 2000a, 2000b). Again, this is being picked up in the media. A recent article in *Sportswear International*, for instance, paints a picture of denim fans who made 'pilgrimages to Holland' in the early 1970s, where jeans were popular, especially in the hippie Eldorado of Amsterdam. According to the author, this was a uniquely Dutch situation: 'when compared to Amsterdam other European countries were nearly denim-less' (Dartmann, 2011: 51).

The Dutch then appear to be a people who wear jeans to work and even to more formal occasions such as the opera or weddings, and have done so since the sixties. It is questionable, however, whether this informal dress culture can be claimed as 'typically Dutch'. The informal clothing style – pullovers, jeans, weekend shirts, and trousers or shorts (also for women) – that more and more people started adopting in the Netherlands since the late 1950s, comes originally from America, where this style had been popular since the 1940s (De Leeuw, 2000b). An American influence is therefore at work, which makes the picture a bit more complicated. The American informal clothing style was perhaps accepted more quickly in the Netherlands than in other European countries, because it was in keeping with Dutch fashion sensibilities of egalitarianism and dressing down. Despite any such historical nuance, the dominant theme in the media is that 'Everyone wears [jeans] everywhere' (Lampe, 2012).

The media have advanced some other reasons for the success of 'Dutch denim', but they all remain within the same discourse of aversion to ostentation and preference for functionality and sobriety. The

53. Streetwear during the Amsterdam Denim Days (second edition, 2015).

quality newspaper *Trouw*, for instance, suggests that 'perhaps the fabric itself, in all its bland sobriety, gives expression to our individualism; it adapts to the wearer even as it wears out' (anon., *Trouw*, 2012). Dutch thriftiness is also part of the discourse: a fashion journalist of *De Volkskrant* contends for example that jeans are worth their money, because they are hard-wearing and you can wash them yourself instead of having to take them to the dry cleaners 'which just costs more money' (Lampe, 2012). Moreover, jeans are practical as you can easily ride a bike in them. In fact, these kinds of arguments seamlessly fit the discourse of a 'typically Dutch fashion mentality' that Feitsma analysed in chapter 4. According to both denim professionals and fashion journalists, jeans are particularly popular amongst the Dutch because they are egalitarian, practical,

long-lasting and affordable (Lampe, 2012; Van Den Boom, 2012). In other words, jeans not only meet the attributes of the country's informal dress culture, but they also perfectly fit the prevailing image of the Dutch as frugal and egalitarian.

The discourse analysis of the print media and the interviews with stakeholders reveal how the national fashion myth of 'Dutch denim' taps into pre-existing and widely accepted ideas of Dutch fashion culture. Denim jeans – originally an American garment – can thus be given a particular local, Dutch, meaning. This is all the more fascinating, because the characteristics that are ascribed to jeans in the Netherlands – informal, cheap, egalitarian, functional and sober – are very much the same as in the United States, where they are believed to symbolise the American character (Little, 1996; Sullivan,

54. G-Star shop in Amsterdam (2014).

MAAIKE FEITSMA AND ANNEKE SMELIK

2006). In other words, what is typically American in one part of the world counts as typically Dutch in another part of the world! By collapsing both myths into one, the non-typical characteristics which would otherwise have projected an American image are now 'Dutchified' and merged into a prevailing national narrative of Dutch fashion culture.

The shifting process of meaning in different contexts reveals the mythical, that is, ideological, character of the new fashion myth of 'Dutch denim'. This can be explained with recourse to theories of fashion (Rocamora and Smelik, 2016). We know from the semiotician Roland Barthes (1991 [1957]) that things and objects, such as jeans, seldom have just one clear-cut meaning but carry many, often ambivalent, connotations. Barthes argued in *The Fashion System* (1990 [1967]) that clothing – for example the jeans that we wear in our everyday existence – derives its meaning from the ways in which it is articulated in the verbal and visual rhetoric of media. Fashion is first and foremost a sign system where meaning is encoded and can therefore be decoded. Such meanings are fundamentally unstable and forever shifting. Jean Baudrillard took this idea one step further in arguing that fashion is particularly adept at playing a game of free-floating signifiers (Baudrillard, 1993 [1976]). The parallel meaning of jeans in the United States and in the Netherlands as characteristic of either an American or Dutch culture reveals the importance of ideology. Ideology is here taken as a dominant myth rather than as a coherent system of thought (Sturken and Cartwright, 2001). For Roland Barthes popular culture, like fashion, naturalises ideology; a myth is then a sign or meaning that comes across as natural and self-evident. The fact that the narrative of Dutch denim has been adopted wholesale by the media and eagerly accepted by consumers signifies that the myth has been able to hide its ideological agenda. This is possible because deeply rooted ideas of Dutch national identity form a perfect match with well-established connotations associated

with denim. The link that is created between a perceived unchanging Dutch national identity and the narrative of the Netherlands as a denim country, and Amsterdam as a denim capital, veils the fact that it is a construction that was only recently put in place by the fashion industry and city councils. As we saw above, the notion of Dutch denim is also a question of city branding and of nation branding, which is aimed to improve the creative industry of fashion in the Netherlands.

Conclusion

The establishment of the House of Denim in Amsterdam in 2009; the exhibition *Blue Jeans* in the Centraal Museum in Utrecht in 2012; the publication of the *ELLE Denim Bible* in 2014, all testify to the myth-in-the-making of Dutch denim, 'the blue pride of the Netherlands' (Narinx, 2014: 8). In this chapter we have unravelled how an icon of American culture, Americanisation and globalisation has come to express Dutch fashion culture and even Dutch identity.

With the assistance and support of trade organisations, design institutes, Amsterdam's municipal services and brand stories, the media have facilitated a new fashion myth to promote nation branding – the Netherlands as a denim country – and city branding – Amsterdam as a denim capital. The initial motives for this new myth of Dutch denim are no doubt commercial, but nevertheless it is more than advertisers' sweet talk. It could only take off so swiftly and smoothly because it is firmly rooted in prevailing narratives about Dutch fashion culture as sober, functional, informal and egalitarian. Its constant repetition has anchored the new national fashion myth in the collective imagination.

The myth-in-the-making of Dutch denim suggests an image of the Netherlands as an egalitarian country where everyone wears jeans, from the Prime Minister to a homeless person, on many occasions; on a relaxing day at home, to the office or even to the opera. Yet, the ideology of this myth could only settle in because its commercial motives are unacknowledged, its original American roots are forgotten, reliable statistics on the density of denim companies remain absent and the number of denim jeans per head of the Dutch population is not always correctly interpreted. The literal meaning of 'denim jeans' – 'trousers made of denim strengthened with rivets' – gradually gets obscured, while a new culture-specific meaning – 'typically Dutch trousers' – becomes increasingly embraced. The new fashion myth of 'Dutch denim' is so successful because of its mythical elements, tapping into prevailing perceptions of Dutch fashion identity. As the media uncritically present this myth as self-evident and constantly repeat it from year to year, the myth gets ever more firmly anchored in the Dutch mind. By the time the myth-forming process has been completed, few will be surprised to find blue jeans among the Dutch tourist clichés of cheese, clogs and tulips. By then, the new fashion myth has successfully replaced Delft blue with denim blue.

Notes

1.   For reasons of readibility we have translated all titles from Dutch.

2.   The methodology of this research is multidisciplinary, consisting of a discourse analysis of print media; interviews with stakeholders in the field; and figures and data from institutions like the Chamber of Commerce. More information on the methodology can be found in Feitsma's dissertation (2014).

Francisco van Benthum (b. Boxmeer 1972)

Lianne Toussaint

When I started, men's fashion hardly existed in the
Netherlands. There was only one male mannequin in
the entire Academy.

—Francisco van Benthum, quoted in N. Wouters, 2012

Before launching his men's label FRANCISCO VAN BENTHUM in 2003, Francisco van Benthum never thought his designs would end up in stores, let alone that customers would actually be buying them. Van Benthum started his career in the late 1990s, running an avant-garde couture label with Michiel Keuper under the name KEUPR/vanBENTM. Both Keuper and van Benthum graduated from the ArtEZ Institute of the Arts in Arnhem and strongly identify with each other's conceptual design approach. The collections they presented biannually in Paris between 1996 and 2001 primarily evolved around ideas of seduction, illusion, surprise and caricature (Van den Berg, 2006: 112). Well-known elements are exaggerated or minimised into sheer absurdity. Their most famous design is 'The Stallion': a pink coat with a life-size horse's head on the shoulder. Conventional shapes of coats, dresses or trousers are turned into new hybrid creations that incorporate all previous functions in one. 'We only cared about creativity and experiment', van Benthum explains (Ibid.). The experimental designs did not sell at all, but thanks to the support of several funds KEUPR/vanBENTM existed until 2001.

Although van Benthum has left the conceptual style of those early days behind, the experimental approach definitely shaped his vision as the menswear designer that he is today. Out of exploring and stretching the boundaries of traditional men's fashion, playing with its codes and restrictions, van Benthum developed his own trademark. His high-end label gives a contemporary twist to the classical menswear silhouette by reinterpreting and recomposing traditional elements. Upon closer inspection van Benthum's classical designs always appear to have some kind of surprising and unconventional detail. An unexpectedly placed breast pocket, a hidden buttonhole, a hem that is slightly wider than usual, or a jacket that is just a few inches longer. Often, van Benthum uses masculine stereotypes – the construction worker, the cowboy, the sailor – as inspiration for his designs and combines them with feminine elements like transparent fabric or lace (Van Rossum, 2008: 40).

Alongside developing the FRANCISCO VAN BENTHUM brand and business, van Benthum has been involved in external design projects, assignments and collaborations with other designers. Over the past few years he launched three special lines of spectacle frames for optician Specsavers; an ongoing collaboration that perfectly aligns with his intention to reach out to a wider public. His most recent collaborative project is the label VAN SLOBBE VAN BENTHUM that he founded with fashion designer Alexander van Slobbe (see profile in chapter 11). Critically questioning and challenging the growing power of fast-fashion chains at the cost of independent designers, the label infiltrates and 'hacks' their mighty production system. Now mostly working on the basis of projects rather than collections, van Benthum continuously rethinks and reinvents his own design practice: 'a fashion system in which one collection funds the production of the next has become obsolete, that's just not how things work anymore' (Van Benthum quoted in Van Loon, 2014).

55. Wolf/van Benthum (S/S 2008).

56. Francisco van Benthum, 'Marlin' (S/S 2014).

57. Francisco van Benthum, 'Marlin' (S/S 2014).

58. Francisco van Benthum (A/W 2014).

Dutch Firms and Designers

7.

Van Gils:
Between Designing a Lifestyle and Making Suits

'I'm not sure whether we will continue to say "It's all about the suit."
Maybe we'll say "It's all about Van Gils."'

—Rob van Bilsen (in Van Slooten, 2009: 121, translation A.K.)

Anja Köppchen

Introduction

This chapter addresses the paradoxical relationships between brands and manufacturers in the world of tailored garments. It tells the story of Van Gils: a Dutch menswear brand that emerged from a product-driven manufacturing firm run by the Van Gils family in the 1970s and 1980s, and became detached from its manufacturing legacy in the 1990s. After its bankruptcy in 1992, brand and manufacturer went separate ways. The brand gradually withdrew from manufacturing as much as possible, while the Van Gils family returned to their roots of 'making suits'.

The separation of brand and manufacturer in the case of Van Gils illustrates a widespread phenomenon in Dutch fashion: an increasing distance between design and manufacturing, between aesthetic and industrial practices, and between immaterial and material value creation. Dutch fashion is a relatively recent phenomenon that coincided with the massive breakdown of Dutch clothing manufacturing since the 1960s, as recorded by Michiel Scheffer in chapter 3. Dutch fashion firms were among the first to delve into foreign sourcing and specialise in design, marketing and sales, indicating an early shift from material to immaterial value creation.

The 1980s were the period in which branding became an important marketing strategy among fashion firms and retailers (Teunissen, 2006). Brands such as Van Gils and Oilily were set up and gained international recognition in this period. Other successful brands included Soap Studio, Nico Verhey, Mexx, Turnover, Sandwich and The People of the Labyrinths (see profile in chapter 9) in the 1980s and Marlies Dekkers (profile in chapter 10), G-Star (profile in Chapter 1), and G-sus in the 1990s. Based on well-thought-out designs combined with smart business sense, these brands succeeded in building flourishing international businesses with their own distinctive styles. Through branding, marketing and styling, the Dutch clothing industry changed into an internationally oriented fashion industry.

However, due to the industry's increasing relocation and outsourcing of manufacturing functions, the site of fashion design has become *spatially* separated from the site of clothing manufacture. This gap raises the questions how Dutch fashion relates to its manufacturing heritage, and how Dutch fashion design may be affected by its detachment from the manufacturing industries. After all, the majority of Dutch fashion is being designed in the Netherlands, yet manufactured abroad.

By analysing the concurrent developments of both brand and manufacturer in the case of Van Gils, I aim to reveal how design and manufacturing practices relate to each other and how this relationship is challenged by increasing spatial and organisational distance. The research for this chapter draws on semi-structured interviews with managers and (former) employees of Van Gils, observation of working methods at a factory in Tangier, and analyses of secondary sources such as newspaper articles and corporate documents, all of which I conducted between 2010 and 2012 as part of my PhD research (Köppchen, 2014).[1]

The chapter is structured as follows. The first two sections describe Van Gils' transformation from manufacturer to brand, and the separation of brand and manufacturer since 1992. In sections three and four I analyse how brand and manufacturer deal with the resulting distance between design and manufacturing. In the last part I conclude by arguing that increasing distance between design and manufacturing can lead to a widening gap between the knowledge and skills of designers on the one hand and the capabilities of manufacturers on the other. As I will demonstrate in this chapter, such a gap can be problematic as the aesthetics and the construction of a suit are highly intertwined. The case of Van Gils serves to unravel such mutual dependencies.

Van Gils
STRICTLY FOR MEN

EAU DE TOILETTE
AFTER SHAVE

59. Van Gils
Strictly for Men
advertisement
(1990).

The Story of Van Gils: Strictly for Men

Van Gils is a Dutch menswear brand focusing mainly on formal wear and suits.[2] The brand name Van Gils was launched in 1980, but its origin goes back to 1937, when Adrianus van Gils established a tailor's business in a small town in the southern part of the Netherlands. Shortly after the Second World War his sons Miel and Janus van Gils turned from tailoring to clothing manufacturing.

Whereas the postwar period was marked by scarcity, from the 1960s onwards Miel van Gils noticed that clothing supply increasingly exceeded demand. This development required a different approach to clothing manufacturing, based on distinctiveness. As early as the 1960s, Miel van Gils was one of the first to understand the importance of thinking in terms of target groups. He decided to focus on a younger generation of men, who no longer wished to dress like their fathers (Joosten, 2004). He understood that fashion was made on the street and – inspired by his frequent visits to European capitals – he made affordable suits with innovative fabrics and designs that appealed to young men.

During the 1960s and 1970s, Van Gils set up a considerable number of manufacturing plants in the Netherlands and abroad in Belgium, Malta, Greece, Portugal, Morocco and Mexico. The company's southern location already gave Van Gils a competitive advantage, because labour costs were lower in the Dutch periphery, and Van Gils could offer better prices than established companies in Amsterdam and Groningen. These northern firms considered the up-and-coming Van Gils as a threat to their own businesses and made a deal with Dutch fabric suppliers that resulted in a boycott of Van Gils. As a consequence, Van Gils was forced to go abroad and found more fashionable and even better-priced fabrics in Prato, Italy.

Up until the 1970s, the company's development was primarily driven by international growth and manufacturing. But the end of the decade heralded a new era for Van Gils, marked by reorganisations in terms of manufacturing and a reorientation in terms of brand strategy. Van Gils sent his three sons Alwin, Jacques and Ben to the Fashion Institute of Technology in New York to learn the business. They gradually took over the company and developed Van Gils as a lifestyle brand.

The third Van Gils generation further developed their father's successful strategy by focusing on marketing and branding. Whereas Miel van Gils thought mainly in terms of product quality, his sons invested in establishing Van Gils as a brand. Van Gils no longer was the only company that made fashionable suits. By gaining distinction, brands enabled retailers to communicate the difference between product A and product B to their consumers. Born out of a defensive strategy to compete with other brands specialising in formal menswear such as Hugo Boss, the new Van Gils generation therefore added emotional content to their brand.

Jacques van Gils, the creative mind of the three brothers, is considered to be one of the founders of the 'lifestyle' concept in the Netherlands. Early on, he realised that men's fashion needed to be more than just a suit, a jacket, or a pair of trousers. Following the advice of marketing expert Giep Franzen, Van Gils developed advertisements that no longer focused on the product, but rather featured experiences, a lifestyle, and the environment in which Van Gils suits could be worn. This was a unique and innovative approach to men's fashion at the time in the Netherlands, and was further developed by the launch of the Van Gils fragrance for men in 1985.

The marketing of Van Gils was not directed at a particular consumer group in terms of income and age, but rather in terms of mentality and aspirations. The witty Van Gils Strictly for Men campaigns that play on changing gender relations illustrate the new branding strategy (fig. 59). Van Gils became known for its formal wear with an informal appeal, which Jacques van Gils has termed 'disciplined nonchalance' (Joosten, 2004).

It promotes a somewhat 'laid-back dress behaviour', explicitly positioning itself against the 'power dressing' of Hugo Boss.

Van Gils became a renowned brand for fashionable formal wear with points of sales in the Netherlands, Belgium, United Kingdom, Sweden, Denmark, France and Germany (Kuitenbrouwer, 1985; Van Grinsven, 1988). Marked by increasing brand recognition, the 1980s can be considered Van Gils' heyday. Jacques van Gils was rewarded for this success with a Grand Seigneur in 1986; an annual award established in 1984 by the Association for the Dutch Fashion Fair, which is considered the highest award for the fashion industry in the Netherlands (Costin and Grotenhuis, 1989).

The new strategy of branding and marketing required a different organisational approach than the focus on manufacturing. As a manufacturer, Van Gils had always produced for others. As a brand, Van Gils needed to refocus further downstream in the value chain. This resulted in a constant identity struggle; as one interviewee said: 'Do we produce what we can sell or do we sell what we can produce?'

Van Gils had transformed from a manufacturer into a brand with its own manufacturing plants. This means that the company had full control over the manufacturing process. At the same time it complicated the organisation, because running an efficient factory can conflict with developing marketable collections that are increasingly subject to seasonal fluctuations. As a brand, Van Gils needed most of its products to be delivered twice a year, to present its new collections at the beginning of the season. As a manufacturer, however, it preferred more constant flows of production throughout the year. To keep the factories going, Van Gils therefore combined production for its own brand with making collections for other (private) labels.

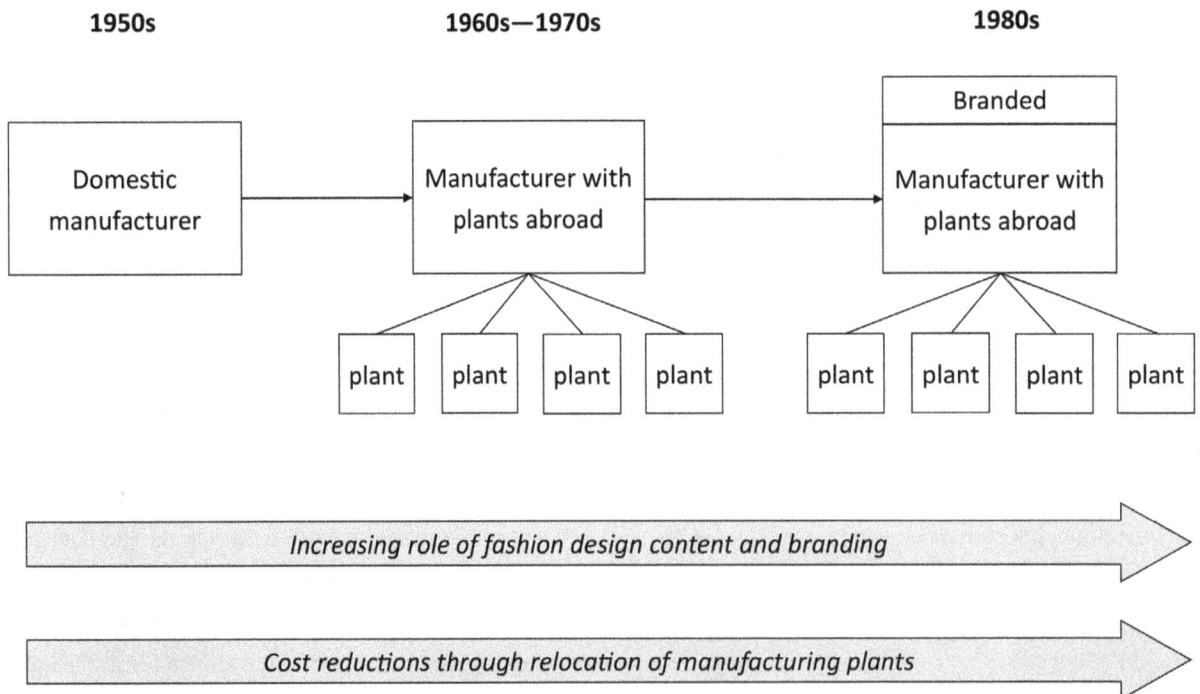

60. Development of production network Van Gils, 1950s–80s.

ANJA KÖPPCHEN

Although the 1980s can be considered Van Gils' heyday, they were also marked by a number of reorganisations that involved the closure of most of its factories. While the brand flourished, and production costs had been cut down considerably by concentrating manufacturing in Morocco, the Van Gils family says it was primarily financial mismanagement that caused the company's bankruptcy in 1992.

Van Gils' organisational development from the 1950s to the 1980s is illustrated in figure 60. It shows the company's transformation from a domestic manufacturer, to a manufacturing firm with factories abroad, to a branded manufacturer with its own manufacturing plants. This transformation involved an increasing role for design and branding and a reduction of manufacturing costs through relocation – but not outsourcing. Design and manufacturing were geographically separated, but brand and manufacturer were still part of one and the same company. This would change after its bankruptcy.

The Story Continues: Brand and Manufacturer Go Separate Ways

After the bankruptcy, the brand was taken over consecutively by three companies that differed in terms of branding and sourcing strategies. What they all had in common is that none of these companies continued to produce Van Gils products using in-house manufacturing plants. From 1992 onward, the main focus was on design, marketing, and sales, while manufacturing was outsourced to different (types of) suppliers.

Jacques van Gils – together with Van Gils' former marketing manager Ronald de Vree – searched for a financial partner to relaunch the brand. Such a partner was found in Centaur Clothes, a wholly owned subsidiary of London-based holding company William Baird. Manufacturing was primarily subcontracted to Icomail, Van Gils' production unit in Casablanca that was led by Alwin van Gils. While the 'new' Van

Gils brand could still draw on its former creative management and production facilities, it no longer owned any manufacturing plants.

In 2001, Dutch holding company Vilenzo International acquired Van Gils as part of its multi-brand growth strategy. However, for various reasons, Vilenzo was unable to bring Van Gils back to its former glory. Manufacturing was relocated from Morocco to manufacturers in Eastern European countries including Serbia, Croatia, Slovenia, and Bulgaria. These manufacturers were selected primarily with the aim of cost reductions and changed several times throughout the years. According to one of Vilenzo's former production managers, these changes were problematic; whereas the Moroccan supplier understood the requirements of a Van Gils suit, it took a few seasons for a new supplier to become acquainted with the brand and deliver the right quality. The company was unable to find the right balance between cost reduction, consistent quality, and brand strategy. Vilenzo's overall performance rapidly deteriorated from 2002 onward, leading to the company's bankruptcy in 2004.

The reasons for this failure are manifold and to understand the complexity of Vilenzo's bankruptcy would require a research project of its own that goes beyond the scope of this chapter (cf. Fermont, 2009). After Vilenzo's bankruptcy, another Dutch company acquired most of Vilenzo's children's and menswear brands, including Van Gils. Apparently, despite its ups and downs, Van Gils was still an appealing brand in which to invest. Waalwear Men, a subsidiary of Dutch holding company WE International, acquired Van Gils in the same year. In 2010, Waalwear Men changed its name to Van Gils Fashion, as Van Gils had become the most important brand of the company.

Van Gils Fashion has outsourced the entire manufacturing process to Bulgaria and China, except for fabric sourcing, block pattern making, and quality control, while retaining a close relationship with its suppliers based on mutual trust and long-term commitments. Furthermore, Van Gils Fashion provides technical support to its suppliers by employing its own on-site quality controllers and technical managers who pay regular visits to the factories. Today, Van Gils Fashion combines manufacturing in the Far East with European products in order to offer more luxurious signature suits, made with Italian fabrics, alongside more affordable suits made in China. The brand still sources its own fabrics, determines where its suppliers should purchase which materials, and maintains relatively strong control over the production process through its quality control and technical support.

Van Gils' organisational development has eventually resulted in a brand that has become organisationally detached from its original manufacturing legacy. The focus has shifted from 'how to brand a manufactured product' to 'how to organise manufacturing behind the brand'. This implies that the relationship between the creative side of the brand and the technological side of manufacturing its products has changed as well, because certain knowledge and skills related to manufacturing are no longer 'owned' by the brand.

Ever since its bankruptcy in 1992, Van Gils has been marketed with varying success by different CEOs, who have put substantial effort into (re)defining the brand's 'DNA' (Bosman, 2012). Although the company's current organisation is no longer related to the Van Gils family who had established the brand in the 1980s, both Van Gils Fashion's current CEO Robert Meijer and his predecessors explicitly refer to the brand's heritage (Mirande, 2008). Meijer defines this heritage as the craftsmanship that goes into constructing a high quality suit:

> We want to restore the brand's strength. We reload its history of craftsmanship, tailoring, and style in a contemporary way. In the last years, Van Gils has become too Scandinavian and clean. With the new collection we have taken a step back towards the original Van Gils. This also means an important role for quality again. The designs again evoke many experiences: we convey male luxury with crossed buttonhole stitches, multicoloured linings, the comeback of the tongue pocket and many more beautiful details. ('We Willen het Merk', 2010, my translation);

and the rebellious image of Van Gils' advertisements in the 1980s:

> I believe in evolution, not in revolution. The core of the brand, the DNA, is something you should not tinker with. Instead, you must further develop its strengths. For example, one of our brand values is 'never too serious'. The brand has always been a little bit rebellious. Think of the old advertisements in which a woman stands urinating next to a couple of men in a public lavatory and the accompanying slogan 'Strictly for Gentlemen'. That is Van Gils. (Bosman, 2012: 6, my translation).

Likewise, one of Van Gils' latest slogans, 'No Stitch no Story', is part of a manifesto that describes the mentality of the 'Van Gils man'. At the same time it refers to how a suit is 'made'. The tangible and technical elements of suits play an important role in defining the brand's identity, which is why Van Gils continues to communicate its manufacturing legacy of craftsmanship. However, telling a story of craftsmanship involves more than just marketing jargon. The design and aesthetic elements of tailored garments are highly connected to their actual manufacturing, as I will demonstrate in the next sections. Before further exploring this relationship between design and manufacturing in tailored garments, it is important to take into account how the Van Gils family proceeded after 'losing their brand'.

After Van Gils' bankruptcy in 1992, the Van Gils brothers Alwin, Jacques and Ben reconsidered their business and decided to continue manufacturing of formal menswear. They founded The Makers, 'a network of business units that produce top quality tailored clothing' (The Makers, 2012). Trojaco and Icomail, the two most important production units of the Van Gils brand until 1992, were (until 2011) also part of The Makers. In 2004, The Makers started manufacturing in China as well. Through this network, The Makers specialises in producing formal wear for different types of customers, ranging from high fashion designers to mid-market chain stores.

In 2011, Icomail did not survive the departure of one of its main clients – Marks and Spencer – and went bankrupt. Trojaco in Tangier started with private label production but gradually specialised in customer-oriented flexibility and quality. As of 2011 Trojaco has become the primary manufacturing unit of The Makers.

The concurrent organisational developments of the Van Gils brand on the one hand, and the manufacturing organisation of The Makers on the other, indicate an increasing organisational distance between design and manufacturing. Brand and manufacturer have gone separate ways, leading to organisationally detached creative and industrial practices, illustrated in fig. 62. While this distance is common practice for most

61. Van Gils 'No Stitch No Story' (Van Gils A/W 2014 campaign).

of contemporary Dutch fashion firms, it comes with certain challenges regarding the translation of aesthetic design ideas into physical garments. In the following two sections I address the ways in which both brand and manufacturer deal with this distance, thus revealing their mutual dependencies.

The Brand's Perspective: Creating Van Gils ...

As we have seen from the previous section, Van Gils Fashion aims to focus on brand management and collection development, while outsourcing the manufacturing process as much as possible. At the same time the company encounters the boundaries of outsourcing. Van Gils Fashion explicitly strives for long-term partnerships with only a small number of suppliers.

Formal wear apparently involves a specific type of product that needs a consistent quality and fit that would not benefit from frequent change. While Van Gils Fashion no longer owns any production facilities, it has invested in a stable manufacturing base through these long-term commitments. Moreover, the company has not withdrawn from manufacturing entirely – at least, not yet. In order to maintain the expertise to develop a unique product, the roles of purchasing fabrics and trims, developing basic block patterns, and maintaining on-site quality control and technical support are kept in-house; they are considered too important for Van Gils' signature and fit to outsource.

To understand what outsourcing means for Van Gils Fashion, it is helpful to consider the differences between manufacturing in China and manufacturing in Eastern Europe. Manufacturing in China is more driven

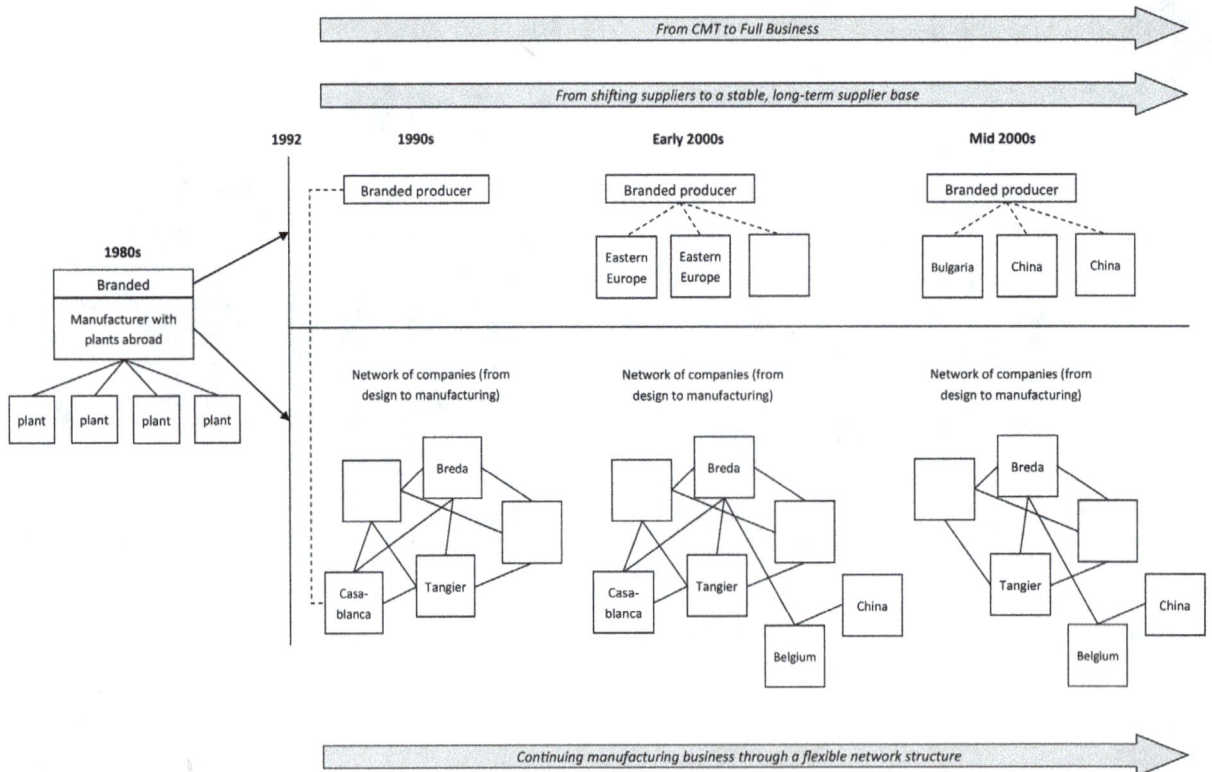

62. Developments of production networks, Van Gils (upper half) and The Makers (lower half), 1990s–2000s.

by costs, as suppliers are required to manoeuvre within a fixed-price target. In Bulgaria, it works the other way around: the process starts with fabrics, styles, and raw materials driven by quality, after which Van Gils' product managers visit the manufacturer to discuss the styles and their price.

In terms of face-to-face contact, Van Gils Fashion visits China only once to negotiate price targets, while Bulgaria is also visited during the sampling process to discuss product development. To some extent, these different approaches can be explained by Eastern Europe's relative geographical proximity. It is obviously easier and less time-consuming to travel from the Netherlands to Bulgaria than to China. Furthermore, most Eastern European factories are not used to offering full-product manufacturing, due to the strong presence of German fashion firms outsourcing to these countries. As several researchers have demonstrated, among German fashion firms, CMT (cut, make and trim) manufacturing is more pronounced than full-product outsourcing [1] (Lane and Probert, 2006). As a result, Eastern Europe's industrial culture is primarily built on subcontracting relationships, highly driven by the expertise of Western European lead fashion firms.

The company's decision to keep in-house technical designers in charge of developing basic block patterns and providing technical support to the factories is also related to the different ways of organising production in Bulgaria and China. In principle, Chinese suppliers are used to developing patterns on the basis of their clients' so-called size specifications – technical drawings and measurement details. More and more European brands outsource the costly pattern making process, as Chinese suppliers have acquired this expertise. Yet, as one of Van Gils' product managers explains, there is more than one way to develop patterns from one and the same size specification, resulting in different fits. Outsourcing the development of basic block patterns therefore involves the risk of losing control over the translation of size specifications

into patterns. This could eventually lead to a change of fit, without knowing exactly what has changed in the process. Particularly in formal wear, it is important to maintain a consistent fit and to guarantee that the fit of Bulgarian style A does not differ from the fit of Chinese style A. This is one of the reasons why Van Gils Fashion retains (costly) in-house technical designers. As one of Van Gils' (product) managers explains in an interview:

For me – I consider it the basic building blocks of the product. And if you lack a decent foundation, the rest just will collapse like a house of cards. I thus prefer more investment and effort at the start of the development process to make sure that the product is right, instead of finding out later at the production stage that the end product is not at all what you expected. Hence, it is a kind of quality warranty.

In all the interviews conducted for this study, the role of technical designers or pattern makers manifested itself in the great emphasis that respondents put on the importance of fit in formal wear and suits. Compared to, for instance, women's shirts and dresses, variations in men's suits are only marginal. Variations are found in details such as stitching, pockets, linings, buttons, buttonholes, and jacket lapels. Yet, the distinctive features of the design of a tailored garment are its fit and its fabric. Apart from branding and marketing, the fit is what distinguishes a Van Gils suit from, say, an Armani or Hugo Boss suit. Design, technical design and pattern making are closely related.

The central role of pattern making is further reflected in Van Gils Fashion's design practices. Generally speaking, the entire process from first idea to sampling and production is similar to other men's and womenswear fashion brands. It always starts with a phase of orientation in which designers draw inspiration from different media, fairs, shopping, and travelling, which is then translated into themes, colour palettes, and sketches, followed by phases of sampling, sales, and final production. In particular, three interrelated teams are involved within the creative process: designers, technical designers (i.e. block pattern making), and product managers (i.e. buying). Within this process, designers develop new styles based on their creativity, trends, the Van Gils 'DNA' and a commercial framework that defines the number of styles and their price categories. Technical designers are concerned with the actual construction of the suit and translate the styles into patterns. Product managers, then, are in charge of organising the sampling and production process, including price negotiations and purchasing materials.

Since fit is such an important element of formal wear, a crucial moment in the creative process described above is the translation of styles into patterns. In the past, pattern makers had an even more powerful position within the manufacturing of tailored garments, though their role changed with the influence of fashion. In the 1960s, Van Gils was one of the first to approach formal wear from a fashion point of view. The pattern maker remained important, but was no longer the only decisive factor in the process. Design became, and continues to be, the product of a discussion between a creative person – the designer or stylist – and a more technical person – the pattern maker. Furthermore, in the case of the 'old' Van Gils, the creative process was largely defined by a close collaboration between designer and fabric buyer (Van Grinsven, 1988, my translation). Fashion trips to New York were followed by visits to (primarily Italian) fabric suppliers to translate new trends and ideas directly into fabric designs, which further underlines the importance of fabrics in tailored garments. Van Gils' fabric buyer in the 1980s explained: 'Together, designer Jacques van Gils and I form a unity. He is more concerned with creating styles and I select fabrics and fabric designs. Yet, there is no clear boundary between our practices.' (Van Grinsven, 1988).

Considering these interconnections between design, fabric buying, and pattern making, I can conclude that

in the case of Van Gils design is very much a relational product of both creative/aesthetic and technological practices. The relations between design and manufacturing thus play an important role in the performance of the brand, which partly explains why Van Gils Fashion preserves a close relationship with its small selection of suppliers. In the next section, I will turn to the role of the manufacturer in this regard. Based on interviews with (former) managers of the 'old' Van Gils and The Makers, and observational fieldwork at Trojaco in Tangier, I will argue that distance between brands and manufacturers can also lead to a shift of creative practices in the direction of the manufacturer.

...or Making Suits?: The Manufacturer's Perspective

The separation of brand and manufacturer is not without problems. A recurrent theme in both interviews and observations is an apparently widening gap between designers and stylists on the one hand and manufacturers on the other hand. This gap is regarded as problematic to the degree that it complicates the translation of an abstract idea into a physical garment. According to one of The Makers' managers, the simultaneously interesting and difficult issue of making men's suits is that one has to work with at least three layers: (1) the three-dimensional, abstract idea of the designer, (2) two-dimensional patterns, and (3) 'living' materials, that move, shrink, or stretch during and after the manufacturing process. On top of that, manufacturers of tailored garments have to deal with manual labour and craftsmanship.

A successful translation, then, means that for one thing the manufacturer is able to perform the necessary processes, while for another that the end product corresponds to the designers' expectations in terms of style and price. Pattern makers are crucial in this practice of translation. Yet, due to fashion's deindustrialisation in the Netherlands, in combination with a decreasing number of Dutch fashion and textile students choosing to specialise in pattern making, and the consequent disappearance of knowledge and expertise in this field of work, brands increasingly depend on the knowledge and skills of (distant) manufacturers in this regard. As one of The Makers' directors explains, the main problem of deindustrialisation is that students no longer have opportunities to learn on site and gain first-hand experiences through internships. Eventually, with the disappearance of industry, knowledge and skills will probably disappear as well.

In the case of Trojaco and The Makers, the resulting lack of knowledge manifests itself in the ways in which certain customers approach the manufacturer. In particular, the type of information that customers present to the manufacturer indicates an increasing shift of knowledge, but also of responsibilities, to the manufacturer. Many fashion brands no longer provide their own patterns; they provide sketches and size specifications, or even just a picture, a bought sample, or an abstract idea that materialises in discussion with the manufacturer. The consequences of this shift are that customers, be they retailers, brands, buyers, or stylists, become increasingly dependent on the knowledge and expertise of their suppliers. For instance, in the Makers' experience, fewer and fewer customers understand the consequences of their design ideas for manufacturing.

This does not mean, of course, that Dutch fashion brands and designers would no longer be able to develop high-quality and innovative collections. When there is a close relationship with suppliers, such as for instance Van Gils Fashion strives for, in the discussion between designer or brand on the one hand and manufacturer on the other, knowledge can be shared, created, and translated at a distance (Allen, 2000; Amin and Cohendet, 2004). That is, *if* customers actually visit manufacturers and seek out a productive discussion with them. However, it seems to be a general tendency

within the fashion industry to travel less frequently despite increasing globalisation. On top of competitive pressures and financial crises, some fashion professionals attribute this reluctance to travel to the disaster of 9/11, others to the outbreak of SARS in 2002, as I further explore in the case of Mexx in the next chapter. Irrespective of the reasons, less face-to-face contact threatens to further weaken mutual understanding between designers and manufacturers, thereby complicating practices of translation.

Regarding the development of private label collections for retailers, The Makers responds to these developments by applying a proactive approach. This simply means that market research, fabric sourcing, and style development are done prior to the sales meetings with retailers' buyers. In this way, when a buyer approaches The Makers, the latter can somewhat steer the conversation by anticipating the retailer's profile and potential consumer groups. For example, they can show a pre-selection of fabrics and styles that match the customer's profile.

This way of working is quite remarkable, because it raises questions about where and how new designs actually originate. There is no clear boundary between the company that creates new designs and the company that executes its manufacturing. The designs develop through a mutual discussion and, in this case, are even highly influenced by the manufacturer. This means that the manufacturer has to be more than just a manufacturer, and should possess creative and commercial expertise as well.

Such an inclusive approach to design and manufacturing also means that designers, buyers, and retailers are able to develop innovative styles with virtually no knowledge of the garment's construction. What happens is that buyers are mostly capable of evaluating a certain garment and deciding that style B looks better than style A, while they often cannot deduce what exactly has been changed based on the garment alone. The Makers has to explain which parts have been lengthened, shortened, widened, etc. Many designers and buyers seem to lack an understanding of how certain technical changes of the product affect the aesthetics and overall design of the garment, and vice versa. It thus further increases the interdependencies between these designers and their manufacturers.

To understand what these interdependencies mean from a manufacturing perspective, we need to take a closer look at how Trojaco has responded to the changing demands of customers and how this manifests itself in the organisation of the manufacturing plant. As mentioned, The Makers countered this development by applying a proactive and customer-oriented approach. This customer-orientation was already reflected in Trojaco's reformulated mission shortly after Van Gils' 1992 bankruptcy: it aims to produce suits according to the customer's technical specifications, raw materials, and patterns. But since the majority of customers no longer provide these specifications, Trojaco and The Makers invested in these specific services to meet their clients' requirements.

As Tangier cannot compete with China in terms of price, Trojaco focuses on quality and flexibility. When designers and stylists present new ideas, Trojaco's employees' initial response is often: 'We cannot make that.' On a second thought, as one of Trojaco's managers explains, it often takes just a few adjustments in terms of price, fabric, methods, and machines to be able to make a style that the factory has never made before. This means that Trojaco's willingness to place flexibility and customer orientation above costs – in addition to the clients' willingness to pay the price – can thus lead to innovation and development on both sides. Such willing-ness is far from common among garment manufac-turers; one of Van Gils' current product managers describes the sampling process as 'giving headaches to manufacturers', because it disrupts the continuous flow of manufacturing processes.

It needs to be emphasised that although increasing lack of knowledge of designers and buyers is a general trend, it does not apply to all of The Makers' customers. The Makers serves a variety of customers ranging from cut, make and trim to full-business, and from high fashion designers to mass-customised orders. Moreover, while the issues concerning the detachment of design from manufacturing reflect developments in the fashion industry in general, they appear more prominent in formal menswear.

While relocation of manufacturing units is always driven by cost savings, such relocation turned out to be more difficult in the case of tailored garments, because of the craftsmanship, knowledge, and skills that are required to construct a suit. Men's fashion is less volatile and ephemeral than women's fashion and variations lie primarily in the details. But it is precisely this emphasis on detail that is reflected in more specific technologies – and a presumably greater focus on quality. Attention to technology, detail, and quality manifests itself at both ends of the value chain – in the ways designers and buyers talk about a suit, and in the way manufacturing plants are organised. Regarding the former, Jacques van Gils argues that 'to match the quality of his father's work, [...] you need to be able to talk at least half an hour about one single buttonhole' (Joosten, 2004: 203, my translation). Sales meetings with womenswear buyers appear to take only a fraction of the time a menswear buyer needs to discuss the new collection. According to The Makers, womenswear buyers focus primarily on the overall appearance in terms of colour and shape, while menswear buyers are more interested in details, construction, fabric, and quality (Joosten, 2004: 203).

Although designers' lack of knowledge can be frustrating for manufacturers, it has also led to a situation in which Trojaco generally prefers to take care of pattern making, because patterns provided by customers always need to be adjusted to Trojaco's own system. For example, customers may present paper patterns while Trojaco only works with digitised patterns. Or the submitted patterns are incomplete, either because the customer lacks the right expertise or because the patterns are taken (i.e. copied or stolen) from other manufacturers. Other clients send new patterns every season without marking what has changed from the previous season. It is thus more efficient and often qualitatively better for Trojaco to develop the patterns on the clients' behalf.

My analysis of Van Gils Fashion's design practices in the previous section showed that pattern making is considered a crucial part of tailored garments' aesthetic signatures. The manufacturer's perspective in the current section indicates a shift of pattern making toward the manufacturer. This development has produced certain tensions as it involves an increasing role of trust in the relationship between brand and manufacturer. Outsourcing pattern making not only means a heavy reliance on the manufacturer's capabilities, but also involves a bond of trust that these patterns will not be used for collections of other clients. Since 'copying' and 'stealing' are a widespread practice in the fashion business, many brands are reluctant to leave pattern making to the manufacturer. If pattern making is completely outsourced to the manufacturer, an important

63. Van Gils 'No Stitch No Story' (Van Gils A/W 2014 campaign).

part of the brand's identity will rely on the manufacturer's knowledge and expertise as well. Furthermore, manufacturers have an aesthetic signature of their own, which enables them to differentiate themselves from each other and further strengthen the relationship between brands/designers and suppliers.

Mind the Gap?

The organisational development of Van Gils as a brand involves the gradual separation of the brand from its manufacturing roots. Creative practices have thus become detached from their origin – i.e. the Van Gils family and their manufacturing heritage – but also in organisational terms from the manufacturing business as such. This separation of brand and manufacturer can be partly explained as two business models that require different types of expertise. According to the Van Gils family, the seasonal character of developing and marketing fashion collections is difficult to synchronise with the more efficiency-driven manufacturing business that demands continuous, regular orders:

Actually, those are two conflicting things – two businesses that might be incompatible. Because, if you look at brands, they focus on marketing, develop collections, run flagship stores. All their resources and attention go into these aspects. The fact that the product also needs to be made is of subordinate importance for those brands, because it requires a completely different way of thinking, [it is] a different discipline, completely different.

The Makers developed partly out of doubt whether brand and manufacturer were compatible businesses. Fashion brands are marked by seasonal fluctuations and diversity, while manufacturers focus on continuity and efficiency. In Van Gils' view, these conflicting aims thus indicate two business models that are hard to unite:

The reason why brand and manufacturer have gone separate ways is not only due to cost reductions, but is also a consequence of the fact that their [different ways of working] are no longer attuned to one another. If you let a factory decide, it will always make just one suit, one jacket, in one type of fabric […], because that is the most efficient.

The tension between fashion brands' and manufacturers' business orientations does, however, not mean that outsourcing the entire manufacturing part is a straightforward decision. Especially in formal wear, aesthetic and technological practices are highly intertwined, which complicates organisational separation. This results in a continuous re-evaluation of which aspects of the value chain are of such importance for the brand's identity that they need to be kept in-house, and which aspects can be managed from a distance without the control of ownership.

In the case of tailored garments in general and Van Gils in particular, distance between design and manufacturing is primarily the product of knowledge discrepancies and associated issues in terms of knowledge translation. The translation from abstract ideas into physical garments is not a straightforward process, which means that even when production is organised through arm's length relationships, manufacturing continues to play an important role in brands' signature aesthetics.

In the case of Van Gils, design is explained as the outcome of a discussion and interaction between designer, pattern maker, and manufacturer. The translation of a design into a garment thus relies on a combination of different types of knowledge pertaining to aesthetics and construction. Although most professionals working within the men's fashion business acknowledge that the construction of a garment is closely related to its aesthetics, for many designers – at least from the manufacturer's perspective – the manufacturing process has become a kind of 'black box' instead of being integrated within the creative process.

In the 1980s, the branded manufacturer Van Gils experienced a certain tension between branding and manufacturing. After its bankruptcy The Makers withdrew from branding, but due to its 'Van Gils heritage', this manufacturer understands both types of organising, that is, both branding and manufacturing. Through its customer-oriented and flexibility-driven approach, The Makers is now able to combine that knowledge in such a way that – although it problematises designers' lack of knowledge – it can bridge the gap between design and manufacturing itself. The branded producer Van Gils Fashion, in turn, now deals with this tension by building strong and durable relationships with its suppliers and not withdrawing from manufacturing entirely by maintaining in-house quality control and technical support.

Van Gils' experienced tension between branding and manufacturing is thus a paradoxical one, as aesthetics and technical construction of formal menswear appear inextricably linked and highly interdependent. Therefore, to overcome a widening gap between the knowledge and skills of designers on the one hand and the capabilities of manufacturers on the other, the main challenge for brands without manufacturing competencies is to find organisational practices that allow for mutual engagement between brand and manufacturer. This would involve an understanding of design as a joint accomplishment rather than a clear-cut separation between design and manufacturing. In other words, designing a lifestyle and making suits are both sides of the same coin that defines Van Gils as a brand.

Notes

1. For reasons of readability I do not refer to interview numbers in this chapter; more information on methodology can be found in my dissertation (Köppchen, 2014). Quotes without a reference have their source in the many interviews I conducted; all translations from the Dutch are mine.

2. The story of the early history of Van Gils is mainly based on the interviews that I conducted with Ben and Jacques van Gils; an anecdotal account written by the company's attorney Gaston Mens, Sr for the company's staff magazine and a number of Dutch newspaper articles.

3. CMT relationships rely on the brand or lead firm sending the whole package of fabrics, patterns, and haberdashery to the supplier, which then only needs to cut and assemble the garments. In a full-product relationship, purchasing of fabrics and trims and often pattern making is outsourced to the supplier.

C&A (1841–present)

Lianne Toussaint

For C&A, it's the people that make the clothes,
not the other way around.

—E. Ziegler quoted in De Feijter, 2014

If you ask the Dutch about C&A, most of them will immediately mention the brand's affordably priced and quotidian clothes. Yet, many are unaware of the age-old family history that lies behind those two capital letters. The story of C&A begins as early as the seventeenth century, when the German Brenninkmeyer family, the forebears of the later company founders, started to trade in linen and textiles from its hometown, Mettingen in Germany. Two centuries later, the brothers Clemens and August Brenninkmeyer whose initials still make up the company logo today, continued the ancient family tradition. In 1841, they established a company in Sneek in the North of the Netherlands. It marked the beginning of a long success story.

64. The original C&A shop in 1841 in Sneek, a town in Friesland.

Revolutionary as it was at the time, the business plan of the two founding brothers never went out of fashion: good quality, ready-to-wear and affordable clothing for the common people. Introducing standard sizes as well as the customer-friendly option of exchanging goods, the company set the benchmark in fashion retail. By the time Clemens and August retired, they left behind a flourishing business at the beginning of the twentieth century. Their heirs took over and decided to extend the successful model beyond the borders of the Netherlands. C&A began its international adventure with a store in Berlin in 1911, soon followed by several others in England and gradually spreading across Europe (Ferwerda, 2006: 36). What started off as a two-man operation in 1841 is now one of Europe's leading fashion companies, with more than 1,575 branches and over 37,500 employees in Europe and beyond.

C&A sells fashion for the whole family. The eleven dedicated sub-brands vary from hip and trendy, and classic and elegant, to sporty and casual, ensuring that all tastes are catered for. Since 2006 the family company has moreover been trying to take organic cotton out of the niche and

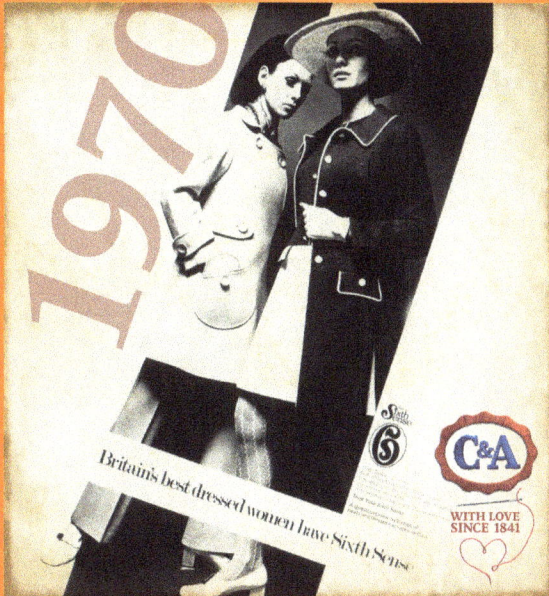
65. Advertisement for C&A in a newspaper from 1970.

66. Opening of C&A's flagship store in Amsterdam in October 2015.

67. Interior C&A shop in Amsterdam (2016).

68. Interior C&A shop in Amsterdam (2016).

into the mass market. At the moment, C&A is in fact the world's leading supplier of this ecological and sustainable fabric.

Although the brand's original formula has proven successful for over one and a half centuries C&A has increasingly been confronted with growing competition from large budget chains, even leading to the closure of all its UK stores in 2000. Forced to reposition and refresh the brand, the Brenninkmeyers recently launched a brand new retail strategy. Large, bright-lit window displays, glass sliding doors and a snow-white interior full of trendily dressed mannequins; the shopping concept may be new, but the product and prices remain the same. Part of the new strategy is the emphasis on e-retail. Each store now has a 'Click & Collect' service where online orders can be picked up, fitted, and returned. Some of the clothes hangers of C&A in Brazil show an even more striking novelty: thumbs-up signs that indicate how many Facebook 'likes' the item has received. How can a historical family business like C&A distinguish itself from other competitive retail chains? For C&A, it's the people that make the clothes, not the other way round (E. Ziegler quoted in De Feijter, 2014: 82).

8.

Mexx: A Dutch Brand with Global Reach

'Recognised as a truly international brand, based in the Netherlands, some people are surprised to discover that Mexx's founders are Indian. For me, and the friends with whom I started this company, the combination could not be more ideal. A truly global brand needs its leaders to be global thinkers. We've never considered ourselves to be strictly Indian, Dutch or English. We are citizens of the world, with an international perspective and a contemporary lifestyle. This is the DNA of our brand, and it was this attitude we aimed to convey when we set out to build this company from scratch.'

—Rattan Chadha (in Chadha, 2006: 19)

Anja Köppchen

Introduction

This is a chapter about one of the Dutch fashion industry's major success stories of the twentieth century, but it is a story with a twist: Mexx went bankrupt at the time of writing this chapter. Moreover, the company does not seem Dutch at all: Mexx never positioned itself as a Dutch brand as it strove for an international status right from the start. Still, the company's headquarters have always been situated in the Netherlands, the garments are designed in the Netherlands, and the brand can be considered part of the Dutch fashion landscape just as much as G-Star, Oilily or C&A. In this chapter, I put forward the case of Mexx to unravel the ambiguities of national fashion boundaries. By drawing attention to the organisation of production, I situate Dutch fashion in its globalised context. At the same time, this case illustrates how internationally operating fashion brands are partly embedded in national contexts. In the case of Mexx, global production even shows to be an essential attribute of Dutch fashion.

This chapter is based on my PhD research that involved over sixty in-depth interviews with Dutch fashion professionals conducted in 2010–12 (Köppchen, 2014).[1] I start this chapter by exploring Mexx's global dimension in terms of its brand heritage and commercial image. In the second part I demonstrate that the brand's global image corresponds with the global complexity of its production and sales organisation, albeit always anchored in the Netherlands. To understand the consequences of such global complexity for the production of a Dutch brand, in the third part I analyse Mexx's ability to manage design and manufacturing at a distance. It is important to take into account how the relationship between design and manufacturing works at a distance, because it illustrates how Dutch fashion is produced globally. In the last part of this chapter I return to the national context to argue that despite its global character, Mexx has both shaped and is being shaped by the Dutch fashion landscape. In other words, Mexx is – or rather was, considering its recent bankruptcy – a Dutch brand with global reach.

A Story of Entrepreneurship, Global Identity and Lifestyle Branding

The brand name 'Mexx' was launched in 1986, but the company's history dates back to the early 1970s when Rattan Chadha travelled from India to the Netherlands to set up his first fashion business:

> If my friends had lived in Iceland, I would have gone there. They were the only acquaintances I had in Europe. I had no choice. I would have preferred to go to Italy. Obviously, the Netherlands is not known as a fashion country. That is why I have always tried to strategically hide the origin of Mexx. (Rattan Chadha in Hooimeijer, 2001: 18, my translation)

Together with a couple of close friends, Chadha set up a company called Shäfferson Shads, importing and selling private label collections specially designed for, and carrying the label of, Dutch department stores such as V&D and C&A, and speciality chain stores like Foxy Fashion. The first collections were made in India, in the factory of Chadha's sister Prabha. By the late 1970s, Chadha had his own buying office in New Delhi and production was distributed among various factories in India and Sri Lanka. As it was the time of the hippie movement in the Netherlands, Shäfferson Shads thrived on the popularity of typical Indian styles and took advantage of the cheaper production opportunities that the Indian clothing industry had to offer.

In 1979 a combination of quality issues, changing fashions, late deliveries and order cancellations forced Chadha to liquidate his first business. In retrospect, this 'failure' turned out to be an important learning experience for Chadha that would largely shape the way he built his future fashion empire. In his own words:

> I have made all the mistakes that one can possibly make. But from each and every mistake I have learned

something. My first experience in the fashion business taught me how one should not go about setting up a successful organization. (Rattan Chadha in Bomers and Boudeguer, 1990: 6)

Two issues in particular are relevant to emphasise here. First of all, while Chadha understood that design and sales are important aspects of the fashion business, the problems he encountered in the mid 1970s made him realise that production is an essential factor as well. Although production costs in India were low, the company's Indian suppliers 'were not always prompt when it came to production schedules [and] garments were often late and had quality control issues' (Chadha, 2006: 33). Furthermore, Chadha and his partners realised that the specific styles of Indian garment manufacturers might limit the company's fashion sense once the hippie movement came to an end. In other words, the location of supplying manufacturers could affect the brand's design aesthetics.

Based on the lessons learnt from the failure of Shäfferson Shads, Rattan Chadha thoroughly rethought his business and established a different company in 1980, called Amex Fashion. To ensure a more reliable and flexible organisation, Chadha implemented new branding, sales and sourcing strategies that would alter the company's entire way of doing business in the next decades.

In 1980, Amex launched two brands: Emanuelle for women and Moustache for men. The collections offered what they called a 'total look': 'articles and accessories with matching colours, fabrics, styling and gimmicks which can be bought separately allowing the customer to "assemble" his/her own outfit' (Bomers and Boudeguer, 1990: 7). The collections consisted of 'fully coordinated, cheerful designs with bright primary colours and creative prints like polka dots and florals' (Chadha, 2006: 40). They appealed to young, fashion-minded people who were looking for 'clothing that was fun,

comfortable and affordable but also easy to understand and to combine' (Chadha, 2006: 45).

The concept was a successful approach to fashion in the 1980s. The company quickly expanded sales beyond the Benelux countries to include Sweden, Finland, Norway, Denmark, France, the United Kingdom, Switzerland, Greece and Canada (Chadha, 2006). This resulted in a rapid increase of turnover: from approximately 36 million euros in 1980 to over 200 million euros at the end of the 1990s (Boudeguer and Van Leeuwen, 1994; Dutch Chamber of Commerce). However, whereas in 1980 the company faced only two or three serious competitors within the mid-price segment – Esprit, InWear and Benetton – five years later there were over a hundred: 'Imitation had become rampant and it was more and more difficult to distinguish oneself' (Bomers and Boudeguer, 1990: 4).

Determined to turn Amex into a worldwide corporation, Chadha decided to build a lifestyle brand with a global image. In 1986, the company launched the new brand name of Mexx, marketed as a marriage between Moustache and Emanuelle, sealed with two kisses: 'We are not selling pieces of cloth any longer, we are selling a concept to customers who have a young, optimistic, modern, urban, international and self-assured approach to life.' (Rattan Chadha in Boudeguer and Van Leeuwen, 1994: 116).The brand concept was still based on the idea of a 'total coordinated look'; a 'casual coordinated design concept' (Chadha, 2006: 66) that enables one to wear the clothes on different occasions, whether it be 'a student, office worker, housewife, office executive or anybody else regardless of age who cares about his or her personal image' (Chadha, 2006: 64). Focusing on one coordinated brand concept enabled the company to develop several brand extensions to further facilitate its international growth:

The identity of Mexx today is and always will be defined by its unique separateness and unity. We will be forever Dutch in Holland, German in Germany, British in the United Kingdom, American in the United States, Japanese in Japan and so on. In short, global but local. At the same time, our headquarters in Voorschoten, the Netherlands, is now home to at least twenty different nationalities. Yet there are no foreigners here. (Mexx, 1991)

Mexx was built around a global brand concept that not only incorporated its marketing strategy but stretched throughout the entire organisation from design and production to marketing and distribution.

In 2001, New York-based fashion group Liz Claiborne acquired a controlling interest in Mexx (Hooimeijer, 2001). The takeover was seen as an opportunity for Mexx to expand its business into the American market, while Liz Claiborne could expand in Europe. After Liz Claiborne's takeover, Mexx's founders stayed on as managing directors until 2006. However, several changes of management and corporate strategy turned the tide for the company: its growth stagnated, sales figures dropped and more and more unprofitable outlets had to be closed, until all US-based stores were shut by 2007 (Staps, 2007).

69. Emanuelle and Moustache catalogues in the 1980s. From *It Started with a Kiss: Twenty Years of Mexx*, by N. Chadha

70. Early Mexx campaign, 1980s.

Although it is hard to determine the exact causes for the company's struggles and recent bankruptcy, many sources, including press and (former) managers and employees, refer to Chadha's departure as a loss of Mexx's spirit. In 2004, MODINT – the Dutch trade association for fashion and textiles – had awarded Rattan Chadha with the Grand Seigneur award, praising his vision, guts, drive, style, and tremendous sense of organisation, marketing and PR (MODINT, 2004). When Chadha withdrew in 2006, followed by some 25 more managers, Mexx is said to have lost its 'heart and soul' (Probe and Wollenschläger, 2009). Chadha's successors – Australian Jeff Fardell (Nike), American Tom Fitzgerald (Liz Claiborne), German Thomas Grote (Esprit) and the Americans Doug Diemox (Gap) and Mark Stone (The Gores Group) – were unable to effectively cope with Mexx's growing competition and to continue its former success.

Nevertheless, Mexx can be considered as one of Dutch fashion industry's major success stories, especially in the 1980s and 90s. Part of its success is certainly due to Chadha's strategy to market the brand as a global lifestyle concept. But Mexx's global identity was more than a brand image; as we will see in the next section, it was facilitated by an organisational structure that was based on global sourcing, geographical spread of manufacturing, and a sophisticated system that coordinates design, marketing, production and sales at a distance.

ANJA KÖPPCHEN

Global Complexity: From Hong Kong to Amsterdam

The history of Mexx can be roughly divided into three different organisational phases: from private label in the 1970s, via two brands in the 1980s, to the Mexx lifestyle brand from 1986.

Amex Fashion – set up in 1980 – was a wholesale business involved in the design, production and sales of the two brands Moustache and Emanuelle. It started in a small apartment in The Hague, but quickly expanded to two nearby but separate offices in the early 1980s: a design office in Wassenaar and a sales office in an old printer factory in Leiden, both situated in the urban west of the Netherlands. Production was coordinated through two buying offices – one in New Delhi and one in Hong Kong. These offices spread manufacturing to several independent plants in India, Sri Lanka and the Far East. The number of plants grew from 20 in 1980 to 150 in 1985 (Bomers and Boudeguer, 1990). Manufacturing gradually shifted from India to Hong Kong and by 1984, Chadha decided to set up Amex's own production centre and sample factory in Hong Kong (Chadha, 2006). The Hong Kong production centre – Amex Hong Kong – became a wholly owned subsidiary in 1985 (Bomers and Boudeguer, 1990), and eventually expanded manufacturing for example to China, Taiwan and Korea (Chadha, 2006).

Amex was a branded producer (Faust, 2005) that controlled the entire value chain except manufacturing, which was subcontracted to independent plants in the Far East. However, Amex was not one single firm. The Amex Group consisted of a spatially fragmented collection of relatively independent sales and production operations. In the different countries where Emanuelle and Moustache were sold, locally embedded and autonomous sales organisations were responsible for marketing, distribution, sales and financial transactions with customers. The lead firm – Amex International – acted as a joint wholesaler of the two brands, and was set up to centralise design, production coordination, group image and financial concerns (Bomers and Boudeguer, 1990; Land, 1999).

Amex's fragmented structure was presumably a way to spread financial risks and increase flexibility in terms of manufacturing and sales, but it also posed a challenge in terms of smoothly connecting the design ideas at Amex's headquarters with the ways that the independent sales organisations priced, advertised, and merchandised these designs within their specific markets (Boudeguer and Van Leeuwen, 1994). One way to balance this fragmentation was explained in Amex's so-called *Concept Manual*, which would continue to play an important role at Mexx:

> [I]n all dimensions of the company: management, manpower, collections, advertising, point of sale material, offices, packaging material, promotion articles, etc. the style of Amex was to remain one and the same: casual, young and fashionable. Likewise, everywhere in the world Amex's facilities were to match this image [...] beginning by its corporate headquarters in Voorschoten. [...] To maintain Amex corporate identity, an eye is kept on all aspects: from the buttons on a shirt to the office buildings. (Bomers and Boudeguer, 1990: 8)

Amex (and later Mexx) can be considered one of the first Dutch fashion brands that explicitly aimed at building a strong corporate identity by creating a concept. While the Amex Group consisted of a collection of autonomous profit centres, considerable effort was put into building and maintaining one strong and recognisable brand identity that would not only define the brand's products, but also its organisational culture.

Mexx was built on the foundations of Amex and continued its main strategy of focusing on concept, brand identity, design, marketing and sales – while outsourcing manufacturing to the Far East. Mexx International – the headquarters of the Mexx Group – has been responsible for design and product development since 1986.

Between 1986 and 2004 Mexx's corporate headquarters were situated in a renovated former silver factory in Voorschoten; since 2004, Nissan Europe's former head office in Amsterdam has served this purpose. Also from the start, Mexx owned two buying offices: one in New Delhi and the production centre in Hong Kong. These offices distributed orders from the head office in the Netherlands to the factories abroad. Mexx did not work with independent agencies. In the 1980s and early 1990s, the majority of the collections were manufactured in the Far East, including China, Japan, Taiwan and Singapore:

> Production is controlled from Hong Kong where our staff of 250 work in a centralised office, co-ordinating production and quality. The business of actually producing the clothes is sub-contracted to some 95 factories all over the Far East which gives us an enviable degree of flexibility. Using our own basic raw materials we utilise factories that specialise in particular items which may vary from season to season, collection to collection. (Mexx International, 1987: 33)

At the beginning of the 1990s, changing fashions led Mexx to search for new suppliers that were able to produce high-quality formal wear. These suppliers were first and foremost to be found in Europe. Therefore, a third buying office was set up – Mexx Europroduction. It was located within the head office of Mexx International, but its function was similar to the buying offices in India and Hong Kong. Mexx Europroduction allocated orders to manufacturers, first in the Netherlands and Belgium and later to Portugal, Greece, Italy and Eastern Europe, accounting for approximately 30 per cent of Mexx's turnover (Boudeguer and Van Leeuwen, 1994).

While Mexx Europroduction was initially set up for constructed garments such as blazers and suits, Mexx started to source more types of products from its European suppliers. Mexx found that, for instance, 'Portugal excelled in producing quality knitwear, while

suppliers in Turkey were known for their innovative casual styles' (Chadha, 2006: 16). This led to a diversified supplier base of approximately 150 factories, on average, working for Mexx during the 1990s. Although Mexx in principle aimed at long-term partnerships, changing fashions and macroeconomic developments led to continuous shifts in supplier countries, moving to, for instance, Bangladesh, Vietnam and Korea and reducing European production in favour of Asian suppliers.

In 2008, Liz Claiborne decided to merge its own production operations with those of Mexx. Ultimately, this resulted in the closure of Mexx's own production centres, leaving production coordination to Hong Kong-based agency Li & Fung Ltd. A leading multinational corporation specialising in supply chain management for all kinds of consumer goods, Li & Fung has a network of manufacturing relationships with offices all over the world (Lane and Probert, 2009) and can control and coordinate 'all stages of the clothing supply chain, from design and production planning [...] to the final stages of quality control, testing, and the logistics of distribution' (Dicken, 2007: 262). By the end of 2008, Li & Fung and Mexx Europe announced that:

> they have entered into a Buying Agency Agreement whereby Li & Fung will act as the primary global apparel sourcing agent for the Mexx brand. Mexx's existing buying offices, which will be integrated into the Li & Fung organization, are located in Hong Kong, Bangalore, Shanghai and Shenzen. (anon., 'Liz to Outsource', 2008)

While Mexx could now draw on an immense global supplier base, this agreement resulted in Mexx depending on one exclusive agency. Thomas Grote, CEO from 2009 until 2012, regarded the exclusive relationship with Li & Fung as an unhealthy situation, and started to rebuild a more diversified supplier network (Textilia, 2010). The main focus was still Asia, though less in China and more in places such as Korea, Indonesia and Bangladesh. In recent years, a substantial part of production had gone 'back' to Europe, and Turkey in particular (Pels, 2010).

The development of Mexx's global production network thus indicates several geographical shifts in the location of supplying partners and subcontractors. Furthermore, my research revealed that Mexx's organisational complexity was not only manifested in its global production network, but also in its sales organisation. In the 1980s, Mexx started with a rather fragmented supply chain. Every country had its own independent sales office, and goods were delivered via several distribution centres throughout Europe. This resulted in a complex organisation of financial and commodity flows.

In the late 1980s and early 1990s, Mexx faced increased competition from big speciality chains such as P&C and M&S in the Netherlands and Belgium, and Kookoi in France (Boudeguer and Van Leeuwen, 1994). In addition to the prospect of a European single market policy, Mexx implemented a number of changes in its organisation of distribution from the 1990s onward. Mexx started to centralise its distribution and gradually closed several sales offices and related distribution centres. By centralising its distribution, Mexx became a more rational, efficient and cost-effective organisation.

Also in the 1990s, Mexx decided to set up its own retail organisation, as an answer to speciality chains' and department stores' increasing tendency to develop their own brands:

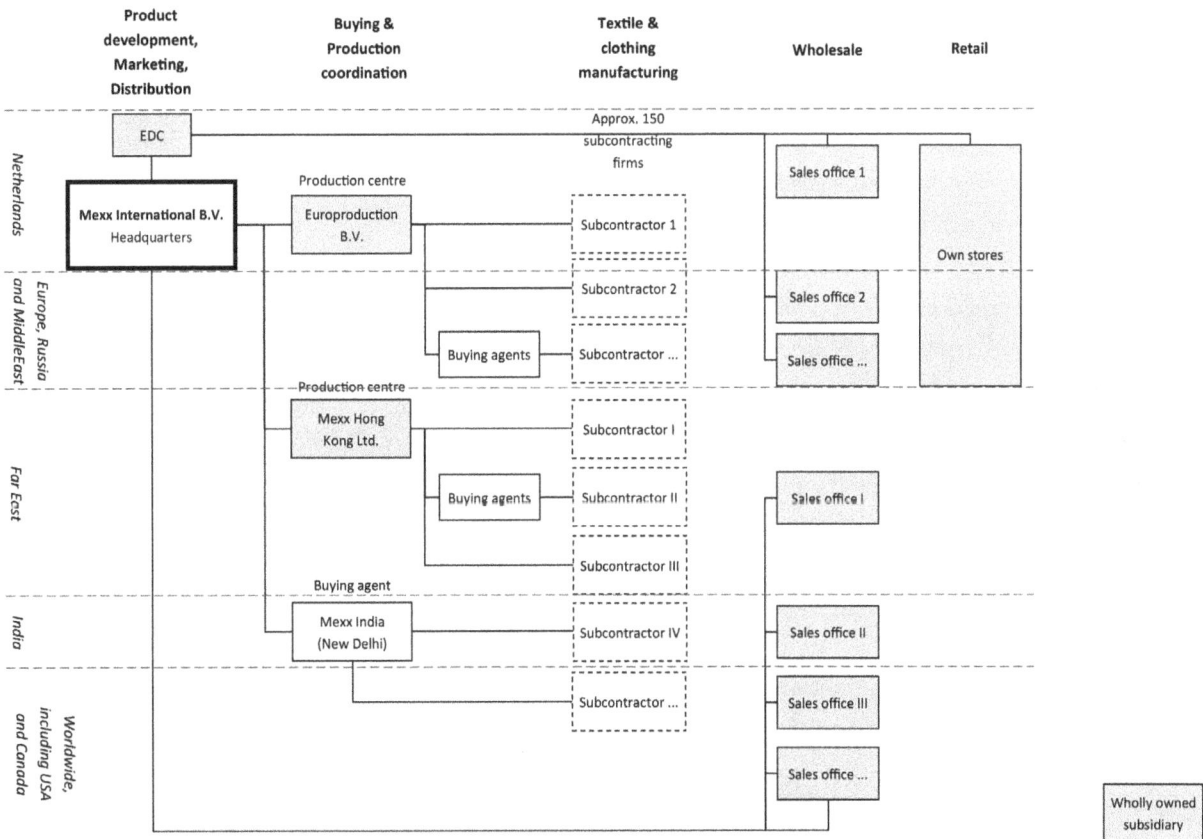

71. Organisational structure, Mexx, 2000: a Dutch firm with global organisational reach.

By 1992, it could no longer be denied that the fashion landscape was undergoing another major evolution. More and more department stores were developing their own house brands and increasingly high rents were forcing independent boutiques to move out of the high streets. In their place came a host of new specialty stores which concentrated on selling their own brands. (Chadha, 2006: 218)

After the opening of its first flagship store in Antwerp in 1997, Mexx expanded its retail operations significantly from the late 1990s onward:

We opened flagship stores in all of the major cities of Europe, including Amsterdam, Arnhem, Breda, Eindhoven, Groningen, Maastricht, The Hague, Rotterdam, Utrecht, Brugge, Brussels, Edinburgh, London, Manchester, Berlin, Bonn, Cologne, Düsseldorf, Frankfurt, Hamburg, Stuttgart, Vienna, Cannes, Bordeaux, Lyons, Marseille, Paris, Strasbourg, Toulouse and Oslo. (Chadha, 2006: 226)

Mexx thus became a 'branded marketer' (Lane and Probert, 2009), focusing on multiple channels of distribution. This strategy to combine retail and wholesale is related to the company's global reach. Retail landscapes differ from country to country, which means that own retail is more suitable for one market, while wholesale is suitable for another. Since Mexx operated in different markets through different channels of distribution, building and maintaining a strong recognisable brand image became even more important.

Figure 71 depicts the organisational structure of Mexx in its geographical context, based on the situation before the takeover by Liz Claiborne. It shows – albeit in a simplified way – how Mexx's offshore sourcing strategies connected the firm to a globally dispersed network of subcontractors. The organisational structure of Mexx reveals a complex and globally dispersed network of buying and production centres,

manufacturers and subcontractors, and sales organisations, coordinated by the company's headquarters in the Netherlands. Operating in the market of fast-changing fashions, this structure first and foremost poses logistical challenges to ensure that the right goods arrive at the right place at the right time. Mexx was remarkably strong at synchronising all operations from design to shop floor delivery. It introduced a new organisational structure to the Dutch fashion industry in which design, production and sales are strongly connected through a centralised system of information flows. The ways in which Mexx managed to make these connections will be discussed in the next section.

Making Connections: From Concept to Product

Before consumers can buy a Mexx garment, the product has travelled virtually around the world. The production process of the fashion industry can be broken up into several operations, which in principle can be performed independently. As Dicken explains:

The manufacture of clothing is an ideal candidate for international subcontracting. It is highly labour intensive; uses low-skill or easily trained labour; and the process can be fragmented and geographically separated, with design and often cutting being performed in one location (usually a developed country) and sewing and garments assembly in another location (usually a developing country). (Dicken, 2007: 276)

As we have seen above, Mexx has never owned any manufacturing plants and subcontracted manufacturing to the Far East right from the start. This means that design is geographically and organisationally separated from manufacturing. Design ideas have to be translated into physical garments at a distance. Managing distance is a crucial element of fashion firms' organisation of production, because a failure to manage distance can result in being too late, too expensive, or ending up with the wrong product – all of which mean severe risks for a fashion firm's performance.

My research has revealed that managing distance was one of Mexx's core competencies. Mexx was known for its sophisticated coordination system that aligns all corporate practices from creative concept to physical product and from the factories to the shop floor. When Chadha started with Amex in the early 1980s, he developed the so-called *Concept Cycle*:

a coordination system whereby the different disciplines of the company's operational structure are intertwined in a continuous and self-perpetuating cycle. The underlying philosophy is that all elements of Amex must operate like a clock; they must function synchronically. No element should run ahead nor stay behind. (Bomers and Boudeguer, 1990: 7)

Mexx developed an integrated planning tool from this concept cycle. This so-called 'Annual Schedule' contains non-negotiable deadlines for all operational activities 'from the moment that designers should start sketching to when the garments should be delivered to [the] customers' shop floors' (Chadha, 2006: 50).

The entire production and sales process, as outlined by the Annual Schedule, is based on the so-called 'sell-buy' principle. Mexx introduced this 'method of forward ordering' with the aim of eliminating inventory risks: '[A]ll units to be produced were already sold' (Bomers and Boudeguer, 1990: 7). Although this is now a common strategy in the clothing wholesale business, it was not so in the 1970s and 1980s; many fashion firms still produced first and tried to sell their stock afterward.

An integrated, company-wide planning tool, the Annual Schedule combines detailed schedules for each department (i.e. design, production, sales, etc.) with 'set

in stone' key dates that prescribe 'handover deadlines' between departments. As the organisation grew, the complexity of the Annual Schedule also increased. What had once started as a single sheet of paper had, by the twenty-first century, evolved into a book of more than 150 pages (Chadha, 2006).

The success of Mexx's schedule depends not only on the tool itself – every company deploys some kind of planning – but also on people who are willing and able to work according to this schedule. Discipline is such an important corporate value that almost everyone meets the agreed deadlines. In the words of Chadha:

The Annual Schedule codified the way we would do business for the next twenty years. It was consulted and followed down to the last detail by people all over the world (be they designers in the Netherlands, sales people in Germany or production people in Hong Kong). (Chadha, 2006: 50)

The Annual Schedule worked through the alignment of different yet connected practices throughout the entire value chain; Mexx had found a way to commit all actors from Hong Kong to Amsterdam to the same rhythm. This alignment was partly facilitated by the Hong Kong production centre, where Mexx employed its own, local experts with technical manufacturing knowledge, who were in charge of fabric sourcing and production coordination (Chadha, 2006). Moreover, due to the production centre's own small sample factory:

they had the expertise to manufacture an entire sample collection, as well as create their own fabric patterns. This convenience made research and development as well as communication between the designers in the Netherlands and the production people in Hong Kong a lot smoother. (Chadha, 2006: 39)

In fact, the Hong Kong production centre managed the entire sampling and manufacturing process. Designers visited the centre every season to discuss the prototypes and finalise the collection, facilitating direct communication between design and production during the product development phase. The production centre incorporated valuable technical skills and knowledge of pattern making and manufacturing; it had grown with Mexx, understood the brand's 'DNA', and had developed a certain aesthetic signature as well. This enhanced the 'seamless cooperation' between Mexx and the centre, which was considered one of Mexx's strengths as it played an important role for the brand's consistency in terms of product quality and fit. In the process of fashion production, every translation from sketch into prototype entails a risk of 'misinterpretation', which the ownership of a production centre can reduce to some extent. As designers at Mexx were in regular, direct contact with the production centre, the distance between design and manufacturing was narrowed both by frequent travelling and by the dedication of Mexx's own local workforce in Hong Kong.

By the end of 2002, something occurred beyond Mexx's control that would have an immense effect on its way of organising product development: Guangdong was struck by an outbreak of a virus causing a serious form of pneumonia called SARS (Severe Acute Respiratory Syndrome). As the disease spread quickly to Hong Kong and, due to increased world travel, towards other countries around the globe, Mexx's designers and product developers were no longer allowed to travel. They were therefore forced to find other ways of developing the collection. They had all the prototypes and samples sent to the Netherlands, finalised the collections there, marked changes on the product itself and sent it back together with the style sheets and remarks, and set up videoconferencing when necessary.

Remarkably, the new process worked just as well; after a few seasons – once the SARS-related travel restrictions were over – designers no longer wanted to travel that much. Along with the obviously immense cost reductions, this meant the end for Mexx's formerly highly valued practice of frequent travelling. The outbreak of SARS is thus a striking example of how an unexpected incident at the other end of the world can cause a sudden change of taken-for-granted practices in the Netherlands.

This change in travelling practices is also an illustration of a more fundamental change in the relationship between designers and the physical garments they create. New technologies such as computer-aided design (CAD) and the Internet contributed to Mexx's efficient organisation, but have also minimised designers' physical contact with the actual garments:

Whereas in the 1980s, designers had to physically handcraft, draw and paint their designs, today most sketches are made on the computer. Meanwhile, the Internet has vastly increased the amount of creative input into making a collection concept. While our designers still travel every season, the Internet allows them to be in five different places at once. Designers no longer have to physically attend every fair in Paris, London, Milan, New York and Tokyo. They can see videos, fashion shows and store openings, as well as read international colour and fabric trend forecasts, from their desks. (Chadha, 2006: 76)

Design at Mexx was always a team activity (Boudeguer and Van Leeuwen, 1994), with a clear division of labour, responsibilities and tight schedules. Today's generation of designers is much more used to designing on a computer screen, and to working with creative constraints – set not only by production but also planning, merchandising and marketing. To facilitate a smooth translation from design ideas into patterns, prototypes and samples, Mexx's own production centre in Hong Kong was indispensable. The 'destruction' – as

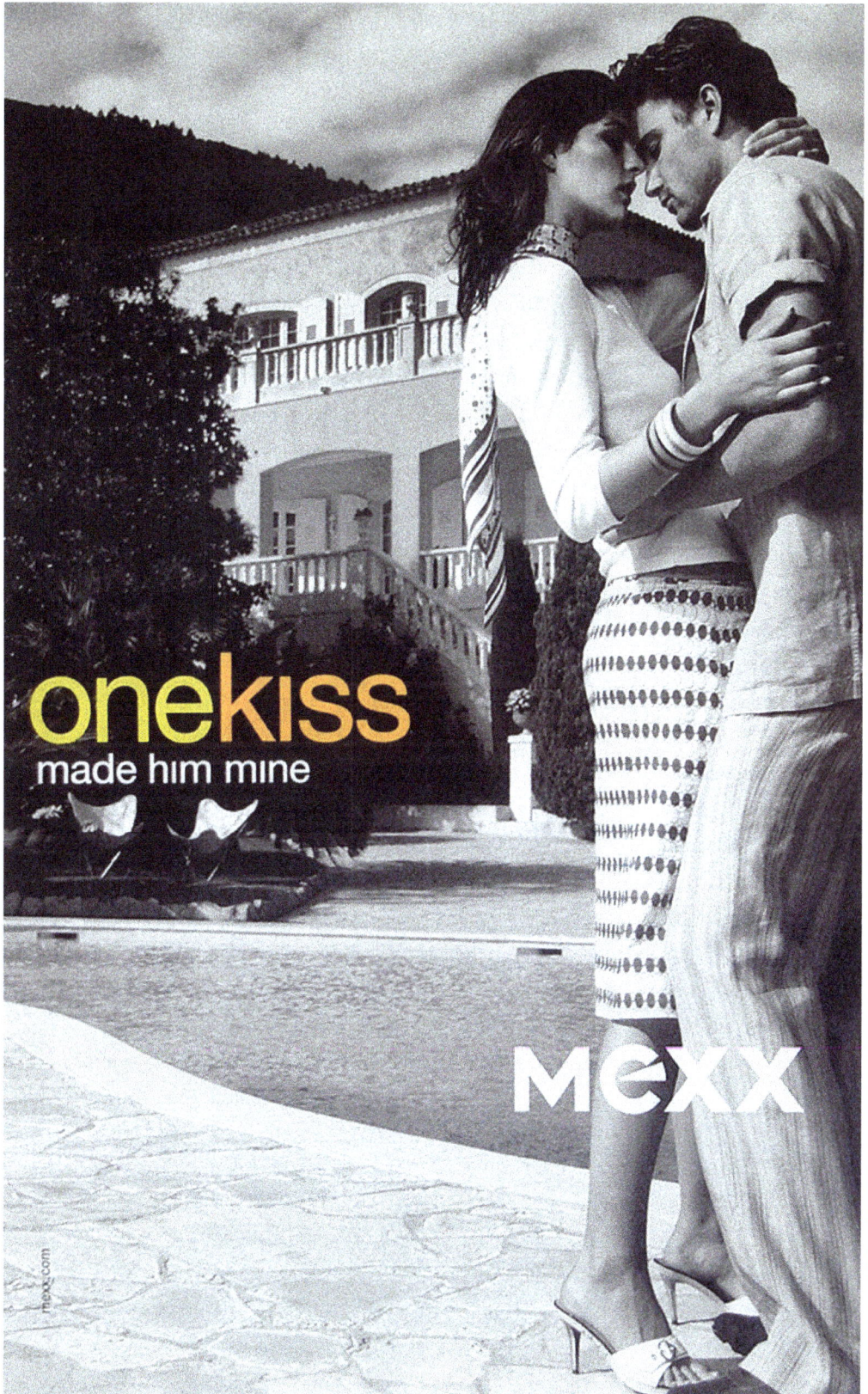

onekiss
made him mine

MEXX

72. Mexx
advertisement 2004.

one of Mexx's founders called it in an interview – of the production centre is considered by many (former) managers and employees as one of the main problems affecting the company ever since. The closure resulted in the loss of site-specific, technical knowledge and skills, and required different ways of organising the relationships between design and manufacturing. Since the divestment of the production centre, the connection between design and manufacturing has largely depended on the cooperation between individual designers and buyers, who now work with independent vendors instead of what Mexx used to call 'co-makers'.

While it is beyond the scope of this chapter to give a detailed analysis of how working with different types of suppliers and subcontractors has affected Mexx's global organisation of production, the significance of the Hong Kong production centre illustrates the interdependencies between design and production, between creative and industrial practices. Even though outsourcing manufacturing is common practice within the fashion industry, the organisation of production can play a considerable role in defining a brand's aesthetic signature. Or, in the words of Weller (2004: 173): 'Industrial development is not separate from aesthetic development.' Therefore, analysing Dutch fashion brands within a national context can only provide a partial understanding; the international context is needed for a fuller and richer comprehension of how Dutch brands have been able to develop their own distinctive style, freed from the technological limitations of domestic manufacturers.

A Dutch Brand with Global Reach

The fashion industry is a global industry. Globalisation does not only manifest itself in the worldwide spread of fashion trends and continuous shifts in manufacturing locations, but is also manifested in a proliferation of fashion or style centres beyond the traditional capitals of Paris, London, Milan, New York and Tokyo (Beard, 2011). These new centres of fashion are not necessarily cities, but increasingly include (small) Western European nations. As the contributions to a 2011 special issue of *Fashion Theory* clearly indicate, it is no longer inconceivable that 'fashion' can be preceded by 'Danish', or 'Scandinavian', 'Dutch', 'Belgian', or 'Australian' (Melchior, 2011; Skov, 2011; see also the Introduction). By way of a commercial strategy, fashion brands and designers may use their national heritage or background to communicate a unique, distinctive image in the global world of fashion (see also chapters 2 and 5). In this way, the nation becomes an instrument for product differentiation; as such, it functions as 'a value-adding factor in the merchandising of clothes' (Goodrum, 2005: 17).

Yet, as we have seen, Mexx strategically aimed to conceal its Dutch origin and to position itself as a truly global brand. Why, then, consider national fashion boundaries at all? How can a global brand like Mexx contribute to understanding the Dutch fashion industry? On the basis of my research, I argue that Mexx has both shaped and was shaped by the Dutch fashion landscape in at least three ways.

The first aspect concerns the brand's global sourcing strategies. The history of the Dutch fashion industry goes back to the 1960s, when clothing firms started to relocate and outsource manufacturing abroad. Although the decline of the clothing industry from the 1960s onward was a European phenomenon, the Netherlands underwent one of the most dramatic restructurings: '71% of jobs were lost between 1970 and 1980' (Scheffer, 1992: 93; see also chapter 3). Furthermore, the Dutch clothing industry is considered to have been an 'early mover into foreign outsourcing' (Levelt, 2010: 99), as Dutch firms were among the first in Europe to relocate and outsource manufacturing to low-wage countries. Considering Dutch fashion industry's 'early move', Mexx fitted in with a new generation of Dutch fashion brands starting in the 1980s without former manufacturing competencies. The majority of Dutch fashion is now designed in the Netherlands, but manufactured abroad.

Remarkably, in the 1990s Mexx expanded its manufacturing relationships from the Far East to Europe. Continuous shifts in production locations are common practice within the globalised fashion industries. However, while most Dutch fashion firms gradually moved from the Netherlands and Europe to the Far East, Mexx has moved in the opposite direction. The rationale for this locational shift is more informed by changing fashions – and thus changing manufacturing requirements – than by the search for lower costs. Particularly in its heyday, Mexx was a design-driven company, and production was geared to the demands of design. India was chosen for its hippie styles, Hong Kong for its casual-coordinates and Europe for its formal wear. Likewise, certain countries within Europe were selected on the basis of product specialisations. In the words of one of Mexx's founders: 'In Mexx we used to say "The first hierarchy of decision-making is produce where it is best available".' In the 1980s, manufacturing in the Far East was driven by Mexx's aim to create a total, coordinated, casual look: 'Our goal was not to make a better shirt, but to make something that matched: that was something you couldn't do here [i.e. in the Netherlands or Europe],' because every manufacturer was specialised in a certain product category.

Suppliers in the Netherlands and Belgium were mainly the relics of a once flourishing Dutch clothing industry, such as SAB Fashion and Interface Fashion, which were important manufacturers for large chain stores including C&A and Foxy Fashion in the 1960s. In

the 1990s, these producers were outsourcing manufacturing to Eastern European countries including Poland, Ukraine and Romania. They continued production for brands like Mexx, often keeping their own sample rooms in the Netherlands. Most of these firms went bankrupt between the late 1990s and the early 2000s as more and more manufacturers developed into more integrated suppliers that also offered pattern and sample making, and even design. This further enabled Dutch retailers and brands like Mexx to source directly from these manufacturers abroad, and cut out the middlemen in the Netherlands.

Second, in addition to its role within Dutch fashion industry's deindustrialisation, Mexx is an interesting case study as it has been a forerunner in a number of organisational strategies that are now considered the standard, such as the 'sell-buy' principle and its well-thought-out brand concept. The Annual Schedule in particular is widely known as a cornerstone of Mexx's organisational strategy. One of Mexx's founders explained the company's role in the history of the Dutch fashion industry as follows: 'We brought order to a chaotic industry.' While such a statement may sound somewhat conceited, overestimating the power of a single firm, it illustrates both an important aspect of Mexx's way of working and how this organisation related to the industry as a whole. Mexx is a 'deadline company' that put great emphasis on discipline (Kosterman, 2005), but the complex ways in which buyers and suppliers in the fashion industry are interconnected means that all aspects of the entire value chain needed to be aligned with each other.

For Mexx, working according to a tight schedule was only possible if suppliers followed the same schedule with the same discipline. Moreover, once a growing fashion firm like Mexx achieves on-time delivery rates of more than 98%, as several interviewees have claimed, customers' expectations are raised as well. While it may be difficult to substantiate the claim that Mexx was the first fashion company with such a well-organised chain – Esprit, for instance, had a similar approach – it is clear that Mexx played a substantial role in 'disciplining' the often emotion-driven fashion business. In the words of Rattan Chadha:

> I really wanted to leave behind the un-businesslike approach in fashion. I wanted to lead Mexx more like a computer company. In fashion too one just has to deliver goods at the start of each month. We have twelve collections a year and turnover rates are extremely high, which is very demanding for an organisation. Mexx is a deadline company. Everything is planned a year ahead. The factories know, everybody knows. (Chadha in Kosterman, 2005, my translation)

According to Chadha, people in the fashion business were not used to strict deadlines and reliable deliveries, and were therefore shocked when Mexx delivered ten thousand garments on time, in the right colours and the correct sizes (Kosterman, 2005).

Thirdly, Mexx played an important role in the history of the Dutch fashion industry by providing a training ground for many people working in the fashion business in the Netherlands. This case study is part of a larger comparative study of four Dutch fashion brands, drawing primarily on interviews with (former) managers and employees (Köppchen, 2014). Almost one-third of all interviewees had worked for Mexx at some point in their careers. Considering the growth of the company since the 1980s, in a country as small as the Netherlands and in a fashion industry that consists mainly of small and medium-sized enterprises, this is hardly surprising. People often started at Mexx in an early stage of their careers and were given the opportunity to learn the business through trial and error. Mexx was known

73. Career paths of interviewees.

for its horizontal organisation and a culture based on 'continuous development, taking up challenges, learning from each other, a positive attitude, mutual respect, joint achievements and individual responsibility/self-directed learning' (Land, 1999: 235).

While not representative for the entire population of Dutch fashion professionals, fig. 73 illustrates how Mexx was related to other Dutch fashion brands through labour mobility. It therefore indicates that by providing a training ground, Mexx affected ways of working in the Dutch fashion industry as a whole.

Although it is difficult, if not impossible, to determine the impact of a single firm on an entire industry and vice versa, Mexx is often considered a pioneering firm in the Netherlands that set an important example for many of today's fashion firms' way of organising themselves (Boudeguer and Van Leeuwen, 1994). Mexx developed a remarkably strong brand concept, knew how to reap the benefits of spreading production geographically, introduced the method of forward ordering and successfully met its logistical challenges through a meticulously executed Annual Schedule. By connecting every aspect of the value chain through this carefully designed Annual Schedule, Mexx codified fashion's rhythm of change.

Considering its global complexity on the one hand, and its significance for the Dutch fashion industry on the other, I want to conclude this chapter by arguing that an apparent local-global paradox is not paradoxical at all. Mexx understood relatively early that fashion is both global and local (Mexx, 1991). The Dutch fashion industry evolved with the globalisation of clothing production. Mexx is a highly significant case illustrating the ways in which design and manufacturing depend on and influence each other even at large geographical distance. The case study of Mexx thus shows that we have to take into account the industry's global dimension in order to understand how Dutch fashion is made.

Post scriptum

While we were working on the manuscript for this book in December 2014, Mexx Europe International went bankrupt. The empirical research for this chapter was conducted between 2010 and 2012 (Köppchen, 2014) and thus did not take into account the latest, rapidly moving developments. There were already some indications for the brand's downward trend: Mexx closed its Amsterdam flagship store in 2013, and discontinued its online store early in 2014. In the Dutch press it was argued that the middle-range sector of the fashion industry was having great difficulties maintaining its position. After Mexx's bankruptcy in December 2014 the interim CEO Herman Hovestad aimed at a swift restart, and by the end of January 2015 it was indeed announced that the Turkish Eroğlu Holding would take over Mexx. While these recent events may be considered a continuation of the struggles that Mexx had been facing since the withdrawal of the brand's co-founders, the rapid attempts to revive Mexx also indicate that the brand is still considered valuable and worthy of investments. The recent developments do not alter the important role that Mexx has played in the development of the Dutch fashion industry, as I argued in this chapter. If anything, they show that the fashion business is a dynamic and fast-changing industry.

Notes

1. For reasons of readability I do not refer to interview numbers in this chapter; more information on methodology can be found in my dissertation (Köppchen, 2014). Quotes without a reference have their source in the many interviews I conducted; all translations from Dutch are mine.

Claudia Sträter (1970–present)

Lianne Toussaint

When customers buy something with us they keep it for several years, because you just don't throw away a Claudia Sträter.

—M. Breij, quoted in M. Leistra, 2012

For many the name Claudia Sträter brings an image to mind of a dignified German woman in her forties. Yet, the brand's name does not refer to a person nor does the company originate in Germany. Claudia Sträter is a Dutch company with an almost exclusively Dutch team, which arose from a merger between the companies Claudia Fashion and fashion house Sträter in 1970 (Leeflang, 2010). The collections for this upper-middle-class womenswear brand are all designed, presented and exported from the Netherlands.

74. 'Open tomorrow: Claudia Sträter, a new fashion shop'. Advertisement for the opening of a new shop for Claudia Sträter in Alkmaar, 1975.

Claudia Sträter is known as a rather chic concern, catering to professional women with a good income. The brand is commended for its elegant style, eye for detail and good price-to-quality ratio. In the course of time, however, Claudia Sträter has increasingly been contending with the reputation of being predictable and outmoded. As business went well and the company grew along with its ageing clientele, it got out of touch with its original target group: fashionable professional women. Over the past few years, Claudia Sträter has therefore tried to renew itself and regain the reputation it once had. In 2007, Jan Taminiau (see profile in chapter 5) designed an exclusive collection for the concern. Another collaboration took place in 2009, when fashion duo Spijkers en Spijkers (see chapter 11) rejuvenated the classic Claudia Sträter look with a prêt-à-porter collection that included a tube skirt, blazer and dresses in bold colours and shapes. In addition to several popular guest designer collections, a fresh campaign strategy helped Sträter to gain publicity and brand recognition. Several Dutch celebrities, such as Olympic medallists, writers and actresses, were attracted as models for campaigns and fashion shows. More recently, a new webshop and website have been launched to support a more modern retail strategy.

Although it has known some rough times, Claudia Sträter seems to be back on track. While still true to its clean cut and a good price-to-quality ratio, Claudia Sträter now represents a modern-classic style that appeals to both young and old. Targeting the self-confident, modern and emancipated woman, the brand embodies the ultimate 'dress for success' mentality. Being classic and elegant, yet powerful and modern, Claudia Sträter designs for 'a woman that loves fashion without being a fashion victim' (J. Hübner quoted in W. van den Broek, 2005).

75. Claudia Sträter, Amsterdam Fashion Week (S/S 2007).

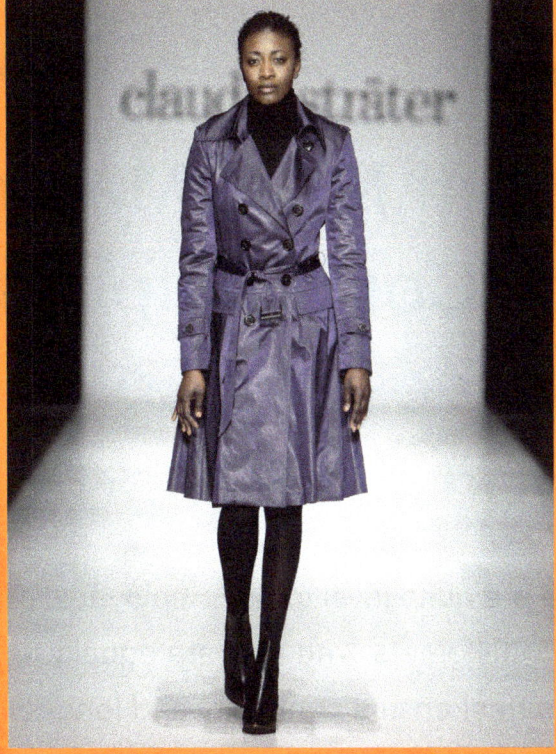

76 Claudia Sträter, Amsterdam Fashion Week (A/W 2010).

77. Claudia Sträter, Campaign 'Art of Fashion' (S/S 2016).

78 Detail, shawl 'paint à porter' by Evi Vingerling for Claudia Sträter (S/S 2016).

9.

From Mac&Maggie to ˉCoraKemperman: Successful Co-Creation in Production and Consumption

'We are quite loyal to our employees, manufacturers, partners and customers. And they are equally loyal to us. Mutual loyalty and trust ensure continuity and long-term cooperation.'

—Brigitte de Wilde & Saskia Kemperman, Business Brochure, ˉCoraKemperman, 2014

Anneke Smelik, Anja Köppchen and Constantin von Maltzahn

Dutch Designer Cora Kemperman

Wide, sweeping skirts, dashing colours or patterns in daring combinations, asymmetry, wraps and multiple layers – in chapter 5 we discussed the style of Cora Kemperman, the head designer of first Mac&Maggie and later ‾CoraKemperman. In this chapter we argue that Kemperman's unique style is the result of 'co-creation', that is, of the specific way in which production and consumption are organised by the brand. Cora Kemperman's wilful choice to remain a small business is based on her desire to entertain close relations with her suppliers as well as her consumers. The small scale of her enterprise allows for co-creation by combining buying and designing in the field of production, and for a particular relation in the field of consumption. This chapter therefore takes a close look at the organisation of the production and consumption of Mac&Maggie (1976–96) and ‾CoraKemperman (1995–2016). As this book went to press, news was announced of ‾CoraKemperman's unexpected bankruptcy; we were unable to process this latest news in our research. As negotiations about buyers are still going on, and we assume (or hope) that ‾CoraKemperman will survive, we write about the business in the present tense in this chapter.

Cora Kemperman is one of the foremost players and leaders in Dutch fashion. When the Dutch glossy *Avantgarde* celebrated its thirtieth anniversary in 2010, the editors considered her the most influential personality in the Dutch fashion world. Over a decade earlier, in 1987, Cora Kemperman earned the Grand Seigneur award for her significant contribution to the fashion industry in the Netherlands.[1] Until recently, ‾CoraKemperman was a successful small-scale womenswear retail business, operating within the higher middle-market segment and aiming at a target group of women between the age of twenty and sixty. To distinguish between Cora Kemperman as a person, and ‾CoraKemperman as a business, we have marked the brand with their distinctive ‾ followed by the name without a space. The

fashion designs of ‾CoraKemperman include basics like long-sleeve tops, leggings, or scarves as well as more complex garments like skirts, dresses, blazers and coats, the product style being characterised by a combination of basic black and white with an array of bold colours, versatile shapes and wide-cut silhouettes. Aiming to offer unique garments that are artful and wearable, affordable and adaptable, ‾CoraKemperman keeps its price range fairly moderate. As claimed in the brand's mission statement, ‾CoraKemperman strives for a 'distinguishing, original, personal, individual, innovative, anti-mainstream, and reasonably priced' product (‾CoraKemperman, 2002: 1). The business is also known for its focus on fair trade, sustainability and social responsibility.

In this chapter we will explain the success of Mac&Maggie and ‾CoraKemperman by analysing the production and the consumption of the fashion products in terms of co-creation.[2] After a short introduction to the businesses, the chapter consists of two main sections: an analysis of the production of Mac&Maggie and ‾CoraKemperman and a study of ‾CoraKemperman's consumers.

From Mac&Maggie to ‾CoraKemperman: A Short History

The unique style of ‾CoraKemperman has its roots in another retail concept: Mac&Maggie. The first Mac&Maggie store, a subsidiary of Peek & Cloppenburg, opened in 1976, at the initiative of marketing director Paul Mathesius. Mac&Maggie was a hip, young and trendy brand that sold 'super fashionable clothing for a very affordable price', as stylist Frans Ankoné related to us in an interview in 2012.[3] When Cora Kemperman was assigned as head of the buying department of womenswear, the popularity of Mac&Maggie rapidly grew. She contributed largely to the success of the brand, which has been described as 'accessible and exclusive

79. Cora Kemperman's wide, sweeping skirts, dashing colours or patterns in daring combinations, asymmetry, wraps and multiple layers (S/S 2011).

at the same time' (Verbeek in Bakker, 2010); 'daring, well-considered, and affordable' (Schenk, 1995); 'different, unique, alternative, and eye-catching [...] clothes to stand out, and affordable too' (Bos in Bakker, 2010). The idea was simple: 'translate designer fashion as shown in Paris and Milan as quickly as possible into affordable, wearable, but highly unique clothes' (Van den Brand, 1995). Frans Ankoné, stylist at Peek & Cloppenburg at the time and involved with Mac&Maggie from the very beginning (Plas, 1986: 48), even describes the brand as 'fast fashion *avant la lettre*', a precursor of contemporary chains like Zara and H&M.

Under the leadership of Cora Kemperman, Mac&Maggie developed its own unique look, supplemented with a collection by among others Nico Verhey and Frits Klarenbeek (Soap Studio). Mac&Maggie enjoyed its heyday in the eighties with dozens of shops and a high turnover. Then a slow downturn started, due to a range of interrelated factors: increased competition, changing consumer preferences, and a loss of its exclusivity and distinguishing style. In 1994 Mac&Maggie wanted to rejuvenate and decided to replace Cora Kemperman. However, after the head designer Kemperman had left, the company lost its unique style and went further downhill. In 1996, the company was running at a loss and was sold by Peek & Cloppenburg to the fashion chain The Sting Modes, who stopped the brand Mac&Maggie.

A year before, in 1995, Cora Kemperman – together with one of Mac&Maggie's suppliers, Gloria Kok – had founded her own retail business: ¯CoraKemperman. Gloria Kok became director of policy and finance, and Cora Kemperman director of design and buying. From the beginning, it has been a deliberate choice of both Kok and Kemperman to not open too many shops, so as to be able to manage their own production. They own and manage six shops in the Netherlands and three in Belgium. This reluctance to expand contributes to the exclusivity of the brand, which can be considered an important part of its identity. The limited size of the corporation also enables ¯CoraKemperman to maintain a profitable, yet close and enduring relationship of co-creation with its suppliers. Both Kemperman and Kok have left the business in recent years. Their successors Saskia Kemperman, Cora's niece, and Brigitte De Wilde continued the brand with fashion designs characterised by a distinctive and exclusive style until 2016.

Part I: Production

In order to understand how the unique and distinctive look of Cora Kemperman is intricately linked up with the organisation of production and consumption, we have made a thorough analysis of those two aspects of the companies involved, although, of course, we could not interview consumers of Mac&Maggie. As mentioned above, Mac&Maggie (1976–96) was a subsidiary company of the Dutch Peek & Cloppenburg Group. With a turnover of 405 million Dutch guilders (approximately 180 million euros) in 1993–4, the Peek & Cloppenburg Group then ranked fourth in the clothing business in the Netherlands (Simons et al., 1995: 166). Mac&Maggie operated relatively independently from its parent company as long as turnover targets were achieved, reaching the height of its success in the 1980s with 42 shops (Van Rossum, 2000; Teunissen, 2006) and a turnover of up to 60 million Dutch guilders (approximately 25 million euros) (Schenk, 1995).

At Mac&Maggie, Cora Kemperman led a small team of buyers who were responsible for everything from collection planning and styling to product development and sourcing. Even in the period of rapid expansion of Mac&Maggie, the buying department maintained these multiple functions. Our research has revealed that the buying department formed the heart and soul of Mac&Maggie, taking a significant part in shaping the image and nature of the brand. In this part of the chapter we therefore focus on the relation between buying and

ANNEKE SMELIK, ANJA KÖPPCHEN AND CONSTANTIN VON MALTZAHN

designing as a form of co-creation, which, in our view, is key to Cora Kemperman's success.[4]

Design

In her acceptance speech for the Grand Seigneur award in 1987, Cora Kemperman famously opened with the following words: 'before you stands a failed designer' (Verheyen, 2002: 43). Considering her sustained role in the successful collections for Mac&Maggie and later for ¯CoraKemperman, and in view of her training as a fashion designer at the renowned Gerrit Rietveld Art Academy in Amsterdam in 1967, how could Cora Kemperman describe herself as a failure? What does this statement tell us about her design practice?

A year later Kemperman explained her provocative statement in a lecture 'Commerce versus Creativity?'

80. Models in colourful clothes by Mac&Maggie in a typical Dutch scene: on a bike at the beach in the rain (year unknown).

(Kanteman et al., 1988: 6-10). She recalled how in the late 1960s design was an isolated process driven by vaguely defined tasks such as 'inventing new clothes'. Garment manufacturers were not used to thinking in terms of collections and only rarely hired trained fashion designers. In those days design was not yet considered a core value of the company. Buyers took the lead in determining the next collection, quite unrelated to production or consumers. Dutch clothing retailers simply did not yet have a vision about trends or a sense of fashion. Due to her earlier experience as a buyer at the Dutch department store Vroom & Dreesman (then comparable to Debenhams), Cora Kemperman realised how powerful buyers are in determining which garments get into the shops (Verheyen, 2002: 43; Kanteman et al., 1988: 6-7). In her view, their commercial responsibility often led to a rather conservative buying practice. Kemperman, however, was trained to use her own creativity for her designs rather than be driven by sales figures or other commercial considerations. She thus experienced a clash between the ambition for a highly personal and creative design and the commercial mentality of buyers.

Gradually, creative design acquired an increasing role within clothes manufacturing and retailing in the Netherlands, due to a growing awareness of international influences, the multiform and ephemeral nature of fashion, and the resulting importance of distinctive signature aesthetics (Krekel et al., 1972; Kanteman et al., 1988). However, it would still take years before design and styling were acknowledged as an expertise and added value of its own.

Buying

In the mid 1970s, Cora Kemperman and her small team of buyers at Mac&Maggie were dissatisfied with the traditional way of buying 'off the shelves', that is, making a selection of brands and garments that manufacturers and wholesalers have on offer. They developed a more integrated approach to buying, where the buyer is responsible for the entire process from first idea to final shop delivery. In fact, by getting more and more involved in the design process (Hahn, 2009: 138) – adding a pocket here or changing a sleeve there – Mac&Maggie's buyers gradually transformed buying into product development and even into creative design. At the time, product development by other chain stores that were developing private label collections was understood to consist of three separate activities executed by different people: styling, logistics and buying. Mac&Maggie uniquely combined these three functions within one person, Cora Kemperman (Schippers, 1988). We interpret this combination of functions as Kemperman's distinctive form of co-creation. Although co-creation originally defines a marketing approach that seeks to approximate, or make use, of the values of consumers (Payne et al., 2008; Prahalad and Ramaswamy, 2004; Rowley et al., 2007), here we extend the concept to include the special business-to-business relationship that Cora Kemperman has built with her suppliers. We understand co-creation in this particular case as the cooperative way in which retailer and manufacturer come together in the practice of buying. As buying is about connecting the creative side of fashion design with the world of manufacturing, garments are produced – co-created – in interaction between the buyer Cora Kemperman and her suppliers.

The Mac&Maggie buyer was then responsible for design, product development, buying, price negotiations, finance, maintaining supplier relations, quality control, control of commodity flows, markdowns and stock control. This entailed frequent travelling of three weeks or longer, especially to the Far East. A trip would, for instance, start with four or five days shopping in Tokyo. The clothes obtained served as a basis for new Mac&Maggie items: originals are copied, but with a different pocket or hood. In the words of a former buyer: 'you put it in a blender and something different came out of it'. With the 'new' designs the buyer went to

81. Mac&Maggie (A/W 1986).

Hong Kong, Bangkok, and India to have certain items manufactured. Back in the Netherlands, the buyers checked the prototypes, commented on style and fit, and eventually sent orders for production. These trips to the Far East occurred four times a year and were complemented with visits to Portugal (knitwear), Italy (sweaters), and fairs in London and Paris.

Creative design thus entered the buying system in the form of co-creation. The final Mac&Maggie designs were the result of a process lying somewhere between 'copying' and 'translating'. Says Kemperman about Mac&Maggie: 'We check whether we have any suitable samples left to use (a sample will always be "used" and hardly ever "copied"), or if we can transform old models into new samples.' Collections were based on the information from the ongoing and previous season, international fashion trends, competitors' behaviour and the buyers' own knowledge and taste. Four to six themes per season complemented traditional styling aspects of colour and shape. Inspiration for styling was mainly drawn from shopping at competitors in Tokyo, Paris, London, Italy and Amsterdam, but also from fashion magazines, fashion institutes, fairs and other cultural events. A major influence then and today was stylist Frans Ankoné, who worked for Mac&Maggie and ‾CoraKemperman, but also for the trendsetting Dutch glossy *Avenue* (1965–94) (for more information on this journal see chapter 4).

The Whole Package

By starting her own retail business together with Gloria Kok in 1995, Kemperman was able to continue developing her personal style as well as the integrated approach to buying. Drawing on her experience at Mac&Maggie's, Cora Kemperman can be described as a unique mixture of designer, stylist, buyer, retailer and manufacturer. In this mixture lies the key to the process of co-creation, as it renders the boundaries between the creative and the technical side of fashion production less definite. The designing and buying process at ‾CoraKemperman does not consist of well-defined, successive steps but is an ongoing process of parallel activities. Buying and design are controlled by one and the same person, Kemperman herself, who can boast more than thirty years of experience.

The design process itself resembles in many ways how it was done at Mac&Maggie. Orientation towards new trends happens throughout the year, supported by Kok and Kemperman travelling around the world, getting inspired by other fashion designers, buying samples, shopping in Paris and Tokyo, endlessly perusing fashion magazines and making numerous sketches. Drawing on these ideas, Cora Kemperman creates a colour chart that guides them in their search

for the right fabrics. Some garment suppliers source for fabrics in compliance with ‾CoraKemperman's wishes. Others offer a large range of fabric samples from which Kok and Kemperman can choose.

The actual design process involves Cora Kemperman making so-called 'size specs': size specifications. These are technical drawings with a scale of 1:10 indicating the measurements and other details of different items, which the suppliers use for pattern and sample making. For the translation of these drawings into actual samples, Kemperman visits her Indian and Italian suppliers twice a year. In India, Kemperman creates a 'library of styles' of drawings and prototypes. Every sample is then produced and shipped to the headquarters, because the final fitting will be done in-house on a live model. Subsequently, Kemperman decides whether or not the item will be ordered. A positive decision is followed by negotiating lead times, price, colour options and washing instructions.

Cora Kemperman draws from nine permanent suppliers in India and Europe with whom she has been working for twenty to thirty years. India can be regarded as ‾CoraKemperman's most important supplier country, not only in terms of volume but also in terms of the type and quality of the products, in addition to the fact that this country is an important source of inspiration for her designs. Portugal is the most important supplier in Europe. The selection of suppliers has been made from experience with former Mac&Maggie suppliers, based on requirements regarding price, type of product, small production runs and corporate social responsibility.

From the description of the design and development process, it is clear why Cora Kemperman worked with only a limited number of permanent suppliers; because it facilitated her co-creative practice of buying. Instead of sending her sketches to a wide range of suppliers, waiting for the prototypes and deciding where to have products manufactured, the translation from design to product would take place at the production

82. Colourful clothes
by Cora Kemperman
(S/S 2011).

site in close interaction with Kemperman herself. Even though ⁻CoraKemperman works with a buying agent in India – who founded his agency after Mac&Maggie had consulted him in a clothing factory – Kemperman herself would communicate with the suppliers directly, because, according to her agent, she 'believes in working like a family'. The close relationships based on mutual trust and interdependency enabled Kemperman to control the whole process without actually owning a factory. Furthermore, such long-term 'associative' relationships (Dawson and Shaw, 1990) between Cora Kemperman and her suppliers were a necessary precondition for co-creation in the processes of buying and product development.

Corporate Social Responsibility

For Cora Kemperman and Gloria Kok durable relationships with suppliers did not only enable a form of co-creation in product development; they are also part of their strategy to set corporate social responsibility (CSR) as the standard for the organisation of their firm (Kniese, 2001). The self-evident aim for taking care of people and environment is practised throughout the entire organisation, from shop personnel to seamstresses.

Cora Kemperman had been confronted with alarming working conditions in India during her work for Mac&Maggie, when she was in no position to improve the situation. For the new company ⁻CoraKemperman, Kok and Kemperman dedicated considerable time and effort to create 'responsible quality', meaning 'that we try to save the environment during our production processes as much as possible, in addition to taking care of good working conditions in the factories' (Kok in Müller, 2002). The company has taken the terms of the Fair Wear Foundation (FWF) as a point of departure and further developed these codes of conduct to train their suppliers in meeting the required conditions (Müller, 2002). Kok and

Kemperman have succeeded in helping their suppliers to receive the SA8000 certification, meaning that the suppliers have to comply with nine conditions: no forced labour, no discrimination, no child labour, the right to unionise, liveable wages, no excessive working hours, sanitary and safe working environment, freedom to negotiate terms of employment and employment contracts in compliance with local laws and international ILO terms (Kok, 2006). ⁻CoraKemperman has also set up a foundation called Amma, which supports local projects in India to provide, for instance, medical healthcare and education (Müller, 2002).

Cora Kemperman: The Designer?

Let us now return to the question why Cora Kemperman called herself a failed designer. The truth of this statement depends on one's understanding of design. If the definition of design is limited to working like an original artist, creating something entirely new, then the design practice of Cora Kemperman indeed does not qualify as such, although creative design was her professional training. Particularly in fashion, where novelty and recycling go hand in hand, it is difficult to claim that a certain design is really new. Her integrated and multifunctional approach to the job is both more and less than what we now understand by a 'high fashion designer' like Viktor&Rolf or Spijkers en Spijkers, discussed elsewhere in this book. She is *more* of a designer because she is artist, buyer, stylist and even retailer in one. She is *less* of a designer because she styles and designs together with her buyers, suppliers and manufacturers. This collective and dynamic process is what we have called co-creation. We suggest that her success in building this co-creation strategy is influenced, if not made possible, by her being a middlebrow (rather than high end) designer.

Cora Kemperman, is then a particular kind of fashion designer, who draws together the different roles of designing, buying, styling, as well as retailing and manufacturing. For the process of co-creation, Kemperman draws inspiration from her travels, fashion journals and favourite designers, using their ideas and adding something personal (Schoots, 1995). In terms of connecting practices and organising the translation process between the different phases of the production, Cora Kemperman combines creative and commercial skills with particular forms of knowledge. In a way, she is the personification of the translation process in fashion design. In this light, Cora Kemperman's styling is in fact very close to creative design. We want to conclude this section by claiming that Cora Kemperman is indeed a designer in her own right, understood in this particular combination of roles. Co-creation is at the heart of this combination as it both facilitates and presupposes close and long-term relationships with suppliers. Through these relationships, Kemperman is able to share and combine the different types of knowledge and skill that are involved in the design and production of her particular styles. Her designs are thus the product of cooperative buyer-supplier relationships in which a form of co-creation is accomplished in the practice of buying. As the brand ¯CoraKemperman was highly successful and had a large number of remarkably loyal consumers, it is time to look at whether co-creation is also a possibility between the brand and its consumers.

Part II: Consumption

In the second part of this chapter we explore how ¯CoraKemperman actively co-creates the identity concepts of its consumers. The way in which we use the term co-creation in this part is closer to innovation studies (Jacobs, 2013) and marketing theory (Payne et al., 2008; Prahalad and Ramaswamy, 2004; Rowley et al., 2007), where it describes a shift towards reciprocity in the relationship between consumers and companies. As Prahalad and Ramaswamy (2002: 1) argue:

For more than 100 years, a company-centric, efficiency-driven view of value creation has shaped our industrial infrastructure and the entire business system. [...] Now information and communications technology, the Internet in particular, is forcing companies to think differently about value creation and to be more responsive to consumer experiences.

According to this definition, the term co-creation describes the multiple ways in which companies try to account for interests or consumption behaviour of their main audience groups based on active engagement with consumers. In an attempt to appeal to the identity concepts of consumers, the goal is to develop and facilitate a joint experiential framework (Forsström, 2005). Instead of introducing ready-made and relatively inaccessible profiles, co-creation promotes the active integration of consumer input into the value proposition. Similarly, co-creation can be defined as a process where consumers have a direct impact on certain brands or products (Brown, 2007; Park et al., 2007). More often than not, however, it is hard to actually measure that influence. Cova et al. (2011), for example, question the role of consumers as 'active producers', arguing that in the majority of cases it might be much more appropriate to envisage the interface between supply and demand as a dialogue, thereby stressing its discursive function.

Small, Yet Strong

In an era of increasingly generic high-street fashion and fickle consumer behaviour, it is not always easy for brands to establish a strong position in the market. Yet, as a medium-sized firm with no more than nine shops, ¯CoraKemperman is remarkably successful in entertaining strong bonds with loyal consumers. Our research shows that the company capitalises on a comparatively large number of very loyal consumers who love the firm's unique style and strong identity.[5] Yet the firm hardly has a marketing strategy: it does not advertise

83. Colourful ensemble by Cora Kemperman (S/S 2010).

in media nor does it use other classic branding tools to create a high profile or attract public attention, such as advertisements, billboards, product placement or push marketing. The main channels to showcase the clothes are the – relatively few – shops and the brand's website, which has only recently been updated with a web shop.

Although ⁻CoraKemperman has chosen to keep a low profile on the high street, and a low-key presence in on- and offline media, the brand can boast a most loyal clientele. ⁻CoraKemperman's consumers can roughly be clustered into three main groups. The first and largest group is made up of women between 45 and 55 years, who enjoy the dashing colours and flowing lines of the clothes with an alternative edge. This group mostly comes from a middle-class background, with many involved in education, local politics or the creative industries. The second group is comprised of women between 30 and 55 years who generally sport a more subtle and sober look. The first two groups are usually the more loyal consumers who opt for a 'total look' with the majority of items obtained exclusively from ⁻CoraKemperman. The third, and smallest, group of consumers consists of women between 20 and 30 years. These women appear more oriented towards the latest fashion trends, assembling their outfits from a wide variety of different brands and sources and only picking specific pieces from the collection of ⁻CoraKemperman. From questionnaires and interviews with consumers and shop staff, we have distinguished three factors that moderate the successful relation of co-creation between ⁻CoraKemperman and its consumers: exclusivity, authenticity and individuality.

Exclusivity

The brand capitalises on clear-cut policies when it comes to limited production runs and retail margins, thus warranting a low profile in the market. By intentionally keeping the brand small and minimising the number of available items per shop, exclusivity is a property that is artificially created and sold to consumers. For one thing, the margin of available items is very small, so that many designs come in just one or two pieces per size. For another, the brand shows no ambition to expand the business beyond its current scale, with six retail outlets in the Netherlands and three in Belgium. With the goal of devising individual and outgoing products that appeal to a rather specific clientele, the firm nurtures a non-mainstream attitude and seeks distinction through limited sales points and product scarcity. In the words of Cora Kemperman herself:

> Almost every week we get requests about whether we wouldn't want to open a shop in New York or Israel. And I always say 'No, I don't want that'. [...] Once people have discovered us they will also have to make some effort to be able to buy our clothes. In return, they get the opportunity to wear a more exclusive type of garment and that's why people are loyal to us.

Kemperman's account should be read with a grain of salt. After all, it is questionable whether those 'weekly requests' are not to some extent rhetoric, helping to promote the brand in a certain way. Nevertheless, it is likely that the general argument actually holds. The fact that the firm receives much attention from other countries, in spite of its relatively small size and reach, is probably due to the fact that, for one thing, ⁻CoraKemperman offers a unique product with a strong visual identity and, for another, the firm consistently refuses to broaden its scope of retail channels. With no external merchandising and until recently no web shop, the product is the exclusive privilege of those living in, or travelling to, the Netherlands or Belgium. As American expat Jemitra Hairstom explains, 'My friends are just as mad about the stuff as I am. Sadly for them, I'm the only one who can buy it. I mean, they live in the States ...'

It is precisely this limited availability that speaks to ⁻CoraKemperman's consumers – partly because it makes the products all the more covetable. Without exception, all respondents during the interviews singled out aspects such as product exclusivity or the chance to purchase products that only a handful of other people have access to. Part of the brand's appeal, then, stems from the desire of consumers to perform their self-identity in unique ways. As appears from our research, ⁻CoraKemperman's audience uses the products as means to present a specific image of themselves. With a desire to communicate through clothes, the product is understood as an extension of personal identity and a means of self-expression. As Hairstom says,

> Of course, it's not really my identity, but this is the way that I like to look. [Points to her dress.] This dress is an extension of how I feel about myself. And it just so happened that ⁻CoraKemperman's stuff matches up with how I feel about me [sic].

Authenticity

Another aspect intimately related to the discussion of personal identity is that of authenticity. According to the results from the questionnaires, respondents place great emphasis on the degree to which the firm is considered to have an individual – and credible – value proposition. On the one hand, that image has to do with the fact that the firm is fairly transparent when it comes to production methods and sustainability issues, thereby offering consumers an honest no-nonsense product with a distinct aesthetic signature. On the other hand, that view is based on a streamlined and holistic display of ⁻CoraKemperman as a brand, encompassing products, shops, staff, as well as on- and offline presentation. Thriving on a high degree of internal cohesion, ⁻CoraKemperman presents itself as a seamless operation where the company's different facets harmoniously work together, the sum of which form a distinguished and convincing brand persona.

Considering the crucial role that both Cora Kemperman and Frans Ankoné played in the creation of Mac&Maggie's style, it is not surprising that their visual language further developed as their collaboration continued when Cora Kemperman started her company together with business partner Gloria Kok in 1995, developing into a more mature brand with a stronger emphasis on exclusivity, originality and authenticity. By fostering these values and successfully tapping into their consumers' desire for self-expression the company plays an active role in the co-creation of identities. Although resolute and outspoken in its design philosophy, ⁻CoraKemperman is responsive to consumer feedback and quick to adapt to changing demands. As our research demonstrates, the company is well versed in identifying the needs and wants of consumers, gearing the product slate and service in the shops towards these expectations. The dialectics between accessible and inaccessible, subdued and outspoken, colourful and muted all oscillate around a specific understanding of individuality: one that is honest and fair, open-minded and somewhat quirky, rational and down to earth. Or, as defined in the brand's mission statement: '[W]e want to dress women in a distinguishing, unique, creative way' (⁻CoraKemperman, 2002: 1).

It could even be argued that both brand and consumers inhabit a similar aesthetic position in that the brand's quest for individuality coincides with that of its consumers. Just like Cora Kemperman, the designer and entrepreneur, defies expansion and adaptation to the mass market, consumers seek to find clothes that are decidedly non-mainstream and off-the-beaten-path. Kemperman frequently expresses the extent to which she values creating a unique, individual identity: 'The only thing that the brand conveys is [...] that you are not part of the masses, that you have your own identity.' In this sense, Cora Kemperman actively engages in creating a paradoxical 'performance of authenticity' (Smelik, 2011: 76). As Smelik asserts, '[a]uthenticity is fashionable today. It is important to present oneself as an individual who stands out from the crowd.' (2011: 77). Authenticity is what consumers crave for (Gilmore and Pine, 2007). At the same time, '[a]uthenticity is nowadays constructed and performed, and it has therefore become an illusion that can no longer be true or genuine' (Smelik, 2011: 77). From this perspective, ˜CoraKemperman seems to provide an answer to the contemporary desire for authenticity by stressing the importance of having, or rather creating or performing, a unique identity.

Individuality

The previous aspects of ˜CoraKemperman's brand proposition, exclusivity and authenticity, also come into play in the focus on the individual consumer. The firm's retail policy to a large extent focuses on a decidedly consumer-centric approach where the individual needs and demands of consumers take centre stage. The brand advocates the endorsement of personal relations within the retail environment, which makes it possible to co-create the identity concepts of the main audience group by zooming in on the desires of each single consumer. The selection of staff is based on a set of strict criteria, by means of which ˜CoraKemperman seeks to establish a coherent and yet fairly diverse profile of different salespeople. The diversity among staff is motivated by the firm's eagerness to respond to its different consumer profiles, thus facilitating consumer relations in the best possible way. This approach produces an interesting dynamic in the retail environment: most patrons actually relate, and return, mainly to one assistant who caters to their every need, keeps track of their purchase portfolios, advises on certain items, and helps to build up a wardrobe with ˜CoraKemperman's clothes. Our research found that many of the firm's loyal consumers build a quite intimate relationship with the staff over time. ˜CoraKemperman demands from its personnel high levels of involvement, including that they stay abreast of more personal aspects, such as a consumer's family situation or problems at their workplace. As a long-time patron explains during an informal conversation on the shop floor:

It's quite like spending time with your friends. You come here and it just feels right. In the end, it just does not matter all that much whether or not I have bought a piece. Still, in the majority of cases I do, of course.

Such deliberate advocating of personal relations should not be understood as a mere by-product of the retail process. Indeed, it features as a strong tool in the brand's strategy of co-creation. During the period of observation and supported by internal documents (for example, guidelines clearly explaining the required code of conduct and consumer approach) it became clear that brand image, retail environment, as well as the experiences provided to consumers are subject to systematisation and a whole apparatus that sits behind their successful functioning. The brand's particular type of consumer pitch is subject to hardly any variation across the different shops. The company's coherent approach involves a number of policies concerning the corporate look of the shops and presentation of items, but primarily relates to in-store performances of staff – as reflected in their unreserved friendliness, openness, attention to detail, intimacy and an individually pitched sales approach.

Next to product-inherent aspects such as uniqueness, individuality and exclusivity, the staff's individual sales approach is strongly reflected in the interviews, indicating a tendency of the firm's regulars to accord significance to a wholesome shopping experience and high degrees of perceived personal involvement. This way, the brand establishes long-term buying relations that are, in however subtle ways, fostered through creating an atmosphere of personal relevance for each single consumer. ˜CoraKemperman co-creates the identities and needs of its clientele based on a model that puts the consumer first. Central in its positioning is an approach that actively integrates the voice of consumers in the sales process and that promotes a long-term perspective. Interestingly, that degree of reciprocity produces a climate of interdependence: the input of consumers helps ˉCoraKemperman to devise products and services that are right on message while consumers benefit from a 'priority treatment' that makes them an active ingredient in the overall process. The personalised sales pitch thus constitutes a mainstay in the firm's strategic set-up by extending the focus of clothing consumption away from material concerns and towards emotional and personal connections with brand and product.

Emotional Luxury as a Way of Co-Creation

Exclusivity, authenticity and individuality are, then, the three factors that we have distinguished as moderating the successful relation of co-creation between ˉCoraKemperman and its consumers. We believe those factors to be connected by the emotional quality of the loyal bond between ˉCoraKemperman and its consumers. In this respect, it may help to understand the specific relation of co-creation between brand and consumers through the concept of 'emotional luxury' that the French sociologist Gilles Lipovetsky introduced (2007: 31). He describes emotional luxury as a recent retail and marketing approach in the fashion and lifestyle industries. Emotional luxury is defined by a sense of uniqueness that becomes an integral part of the value creation chain. Fastening on the guiding principles of the luxury industry – such as appealing to sensual experiences and emotional values – firms create bonds with their main audience groups by transcending the merely functional or aesthetic properties of a product. In a period of rampant individualism there is a desire to stand out from the crowd, to be different, to feel special. An elitist motivation remains, but is founded less on honour and social ostentation than on a distancing from the other, the pleasure of differentiation achieved through the consumption of rare luxury and the resultant contrast with the mundane (Lipovetsky, 2007: 32).

Following Lipovetsky, luxury above all has become an issue of emotional relevance, speaking to consumers in a tone that translates individual motifs and aspirations into material culture (Von Maltzahn, 2012). Co-creation can be seen as part of that paradigm as well. In fact, it is the active integration of consumer needs that first and foremost appeals to the emotional level as it communicates a feeling of appreciation and equality. Applied to the fashion industry, that means to account for emotional needs and translate those into organisational concepts. Indeed, patron-status and store atmosphere are

84. Ensemble in white by Mac&Maggie (S/S 1981).

ANNEKE SMELIK, ANJA KÖPPCHEN AND CONSTANTIN VON MALTZAHN

important aspects of this new understanding of luxury (cf. Husic and Cicic, 2009: 236; Okonkwo, 2007: 78-81; Tynan et al., 2008: 5). Letting consumers experience fashion brands on multiple sensorial levels consequently extends the point of exchange away from material to emotional concerns. By means of facilitating brand experiences that in the first place appeal to their sense of self or reflect certain values connections, firms enhance their sales pitch by directing the focus from concrete products to company philosophies or entire lifestyle concepts. Instead of restricting fashion branding to products and services the approach calls for a broadening in scope towards a multitude of symbolic and emotional anchors that consumers can identify with (Lipovetsky, 2007: 32-33).

Labelling ˉCoraKemperman as a luxury brand would not be entirely correct, because it is a (small) high street brand. The leading edge of Lipovetsky's argument, however, is useful for understanding the inherent dynamics at play in the consumption experience that is provided to consumers. While the brand does not fulfil certain criteria of a true luxury label, its value proposition strongly hinges on aspects like limited availability, individuality and authenticity as main selling arguments. The results from the questionnaires and interviews reflect the tendency of ˉCoraKemperman's consumers to consider exclusivity, authenticity and individuality important consumption motifs. Limited production runs and a deliberately small number of sales points guarantee that the clothes do not turn into generic high-street products. In fact, it can be argued that the scarcity principle advocated by the brand produces a feeling of aesthetic and emotional kinship: consumers see themselves as being part of an intimate circle of people 'in the know'. Authenticity largely conforms with this dynamics as well. Used as means for expressing personal identity, ˉCoraKemperman's clothes moderate the contemporary desire for performing a distinctive, 'unique' identity. The firm's streamlined and transparent

brand persona helps feeding that need in that it represents a relevant site of individual identification. The personal sales approach in the stores, finally, establishes a direct connection between the products' material properties and emotional value that is created during the act of consumption. Actively engaging with consumers, the staff is trained to elevate the purchase act from a merely interactional process to an emotionally charged experience.

The manner in which the firm co-creates the life-worlds of its clientele thus produces a shared aesthetic and emotional territory that is reflected in the value proposition just as much as in the sales approach and the actual identities of consumers. We have also seen how the brand relies on long-term relationships with consumers that are fostered by the reinforcement of personal ties with sales staff in order to establish a more complex grid of possible points of connection. Much in line with Lipovetsky's argument to extend the focus from merely buying or selling products to charging them with emotional relevance for individual identity constructions, ˉCoraKemperman relies on a number of strategies emphasising these characteristics. The deliberate advocating of personal relations consequently features as a strong device in the brand's co-creation of values as well as of consumer's identities.

Conclusion: Successful Co-Creation

In the Dutch fashion market ˉCoraKemperman is a medium-sized enterprise with a limited number of outlets and until recently no retail channel other than the actual shops on the high street. ˉCoraKemperman does not own a production centre or factory, but fully relies on the production skills and knowledge of its suppliers. Keeping full control over the production cycle, the company capitalises on long-term relations with manufacturers and employees and is distinguished by handling the entire value-creation chain in-house. In this way, a co-creation of styles is facilitated through sharing and combining knowledge and skills of the buyer ⁻CoraKemperman and the company's suppliers. ⁻CoraKemperman has become well known for its sustainable approach towards clothing consumption, which allows customers to combine items across several seasons and complement an existing wardrobe. The company is equally appreciated for its sustained effort to achieve corporate social responsibility, setting a high standard in taking care of people and the environment, both at home and in the supplying countries. Kemperman and Kok's desire to maintain a team spirit and remain in close contact with everyone working for them is one of the main reasons for firmly resisting to expand their business and keep it small-scale (Müller, 2002).

It will be recalled from chapter 5 that ⁻CoraKemperman has developed a unique aesthetic vocabulary defined by the use of vibrant colours, flowing shapes, and the juxtaposition of graphic elements and plains. In this chapter we have traced the basic concept and product philosophy of ⁻CoraKemperman back to the designer's earlier career as a successful buyer and designer for Mac&Maggie. First as a buyer and gradually incorporating aspects of styling and designing into the process, Cora Kemperman learned to combine creative and commercial knowledge and skill, while she literally moved between sites of creation and manufacturing, thus enabling a process of fruitful co-creation between buyer and supplier.

Our research reveals that Kemperman's particular integrated buying practice was the source of the success of first Mac&Maggie and later ⁻CoraKemperman. The outcome of Kemperman's buying practice was in both cases a successful brand, but with the success and the growth of Mac&Maggie the organisation changed and Cora Kemperman became redundant to the system. When we compare Mac&Maggie to ⁻CoraKemperman,

we see that Cora Kemperman did not change the integrated buying practice, but pursued a multifunctional approach where buying spills over into styling and designing. In fact, the structure of the new company was organised in such a way as to maintain her unique buying practice. We described Cora Kemperman as a particular kind of fashion designer, drawing together the different roles of designer, buyer, stylist and retailer. Her unique way of making fashion has been facilitated by the small scale of the company and the close relationship with a limited number of permanent suppliers, enabling a form of co-creation in the process of buying.

By keeping down the number of outlets as well as the supply inside the shops, the clothes are given an exclusive edge which makes them more covetable and attractive for the clientele. Promoting exclusivity as an asset, ⁻CoraKemperman successfully creates a 'buzz' around its products, thus augmenting their desirability. We saw that the audience puts a premium on the brand's distinguished avant-garde style. Consumers buy into the value proposition based on the fact that they are given the opportunity to be part of a rather small and somewhat exclusive group of people: it is a non-mainstream type of clothing that is actively sold to consumers as 'not for everyone'. The relation with the company not only depends on product-intrinsic aspects, but is also related to personalised and individual inter-action between consumers and staff members. Instead of traditional promotion strategies, the company works by a well-orchestrated, consumer-centric sales pitch, producing an atmosphere of belonging and individuality for its consumers. ⁻CoraKemperman co-creates the identities of its consumers by appealing to emotional values and a sense of well-being and being in good hands. While the effort is meant to appear casual and natural, its successful functioning depends on a set of well-designed strategies to retain consumer loyalty and build a relationship with the firm based on personal ties between consumers and salespeople.

In this chapter we have shown how ⁻CoraKemperman has developed two forms of co-creation that are based on reciprocity: on the one hand the firm has established an intense cooperation between buyer, manufacturer and retailer, resulting in garments that are co-created in interaction between the buyer Cora Kemperman and her suppliers. On the other hand the firm has capitalised on patronage and long-term relations with consumers, creating a high level of emotional involvement with the brand. That unique two-pronged approach to co-creation comprises the success of the Dutch brand ⁻CoraKemperman.

Notes

1. Since 2001 the Grand Seigneur award has been granted by MODINT, the trade association for the Dutch apparel industry. Between 1984 and 1998 the prize was awarded by MODAM, the Association of the Dutch Fashion Fair.

2. The research was done by Anja Köppchen and Constantin von Maltzahn with a multi-method approach: questionnaires for clients; interviews with consumers and shop staff; participatory research in stores; interviews with buyers, stylists, designers, directors; archival research into newspaper articles and corporate documents, business archives and data of the Chamber of Commerce; literature review and theoretical background. The rich data and methodological details can be found in the dissertations of the co-authors (Von Maltzahn, 2013; Köppchen, 2014). This chapter brings the results of the research together in a synthetic interpretation.

3. For reasons of readability we do not refer to coded interview numbers. If a quote remains without a reference, the source is derived from an interview with one of us. All quotes are translated from the Dutch by us.

4. For more detailed information on other elements of the organisational structure, such as sourcing and suppliers, we refer the reader to Anja Köppchen's dissertation, 2014.

5. For more detailed information on the methodology of the research and for a more detailed discussion of the findings, we refer the reader to Constantin von Maltzahn's dissertation, 2013.

The People of the Labyrinths (1984–present)

Lianne Toussaint

Fashion has become a snack. It's all about status or
cheap products, but no longer about creativity.
— Geert de Rooij, quoted in Esser, 2014

To stand out in the world of fashion calls for a free-minded and alternative approach. Designers Geert de Rooij (b. Vogelwaarde 1959) and Hans Démoed (b. Ede 1959) are the 'outsiders within' Dutch fashion design. With a quirky oeuvre for their label The People of the Labyrinths (often abbreviated as POTL), de Rooij and Démoed created a world of its own. The high fashion label has a signifying style of multicoloured, richly decorated and fantastical designs. Quite independent from reigning fashion trends and the Dutch bent for soberness, their looks rather fit with the colourful aesthetics of brands like Oilily, Mac&Maggie and ˉCoraKemperman (see chapter 5).

Right from its start in 1984, The People of the Labyrinths have specialised in handmade, hand-printed and hand-dyed garments. To produce the exact right colour or print, Démoed and de Rooij do everything themselves. Démoed does the dyeing, de Rooij the printing. Their designs attract a loyal following of clients worldwide, varying from skaters and rich old ladies to celebrities including Elizabeth Taylor, Cher, Sarah, The Duchess of York and Elton John. Fans of The People of the Labyrinths can be recognised by their profuse and fairy-like garments with intense prints and earthly colours. 'People wearing our clothes greet each other. And they become friends,' de Rooij explains (quoted in Wouters, 2013).

The style of The People of the Labyrinths is often labelled as sixties and hippie-like, a characterisation that Démoed and de Rooij have never really identified with, apart from the free spirit it connotes. Their graphic prints and lines are inspired by heraldry, art, history, photography, nature and science. 'Caravaggio flavours and Van Dyck elegance' for example inspired the 'Golden Age' (A/W 2005–6) collection; the writings of eighteenth-century philosopher Montesquieu led to 'Democrazy' (S/S 2008); and the alchemic formulas and astrological drawings from the Middle Ages inspired 'Alchemy' (A/W 2013–14). No matter what the source or time of inspiration is, the labyrinth is a recurring and eponymous motif in their work (Van den Berg, 2006: 170). It is present in the many silkscreen prints and patterns of brains, ancient symbols, genes, road networks and fingerprints. 'We're not exactly minimal', Démoed drily notes (quoted in Koning, 2013).

Their entrepreneurial spirit turned The People of the Labyrinths into a world-famous lifestyle label with its own accessories, interior fabrics and perfume. Yet, because of their growing dislike of the stressful and unsustainable fashion system, the designers now no longer produce biannual collections. As De Rooij says: 'Even French fries cost more than a pair of shoes from Primark. I just think that is disrespectful: towards the planet, the natural resources and the people that make it' (quoted in Esser, 2014). Today, The People of the Labyrinths solely focuses on the design of interiors, photography, art and exhibitions. And maybe, if their labyrinth incidentally happens to lead them back to their point of origin, a wayward and handmade fashion collection.

86. The People of the Labyrinths. 'Magic' (S/S 2012).

87. A colourful design from the 1980s by The People of the Labyrinths, (1984).

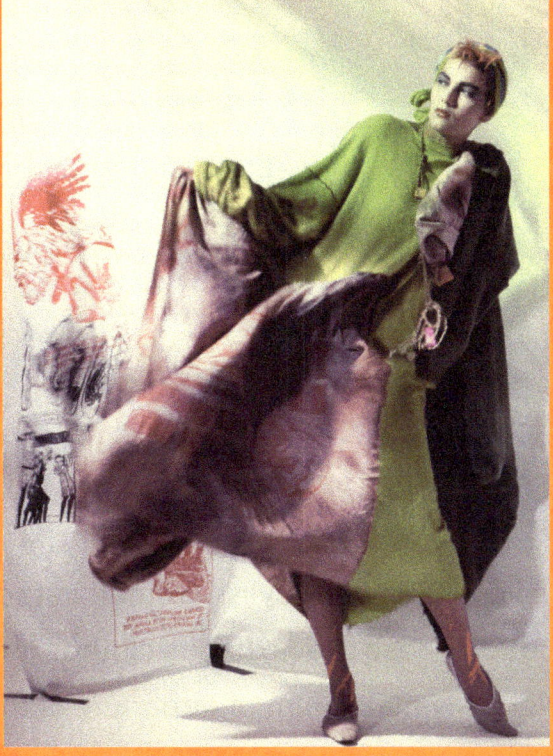

85. A design from the 1980s by The People of the Labyrinths, (1984).

88. A design from the 1980s by The People of the Labyrinths, (1984).

10.

Vanilia: High-Street the Dutch Way

'I make clothing for stylish women in their thirties. I'm proud of the product. These are luxurious clothes, not some mainstream top sellers. My main point of departure is that clothing should make women more beautiful. At the end of the day, fashion is a form of adornment.'

—Michel Hulzebosch, owner of Vanilia, quoted in Lampe, 2011: 4 (translation CvM)

Constantin von Maltzahn

Introduction

The Dutch fashion market is peculiar in a number of ways. At some level, and contrary to popular belief, the Dutch actually do like fashion and fashionable clothing, even though their style may not be the most sophisticated. At the same time it is also true that a set of underlying cultural principles such as a stylised sense of moderation or a distinct eschewing of unnecessary extravaganza do dictate how the local market operates, to some extent. Partially, this is to do with the fact that the purchasing behaviour of Dutch consumers is defined by a balance of fashion cachet and practical considerations, not least connected to the preferred mode of transportation, the bicycle. A short dress made out of delicate raw silk does quite literally not sit too well with the local crowd, because it requires a fair amount of maintenance and is hard to go on a bike with. By the same token, it is probably no coincidence that the Dutch have been able to develop with relative ease the image – or myth actually – of the Netherlands as a 'denim country', with Amsterdam as its epicentre, where everyone from politicians to top models wears jeans, as Maaike Feitsma and Anneke Smelik demonstrate in chapter 6. Clothing products should be durable, hardwearing, and reasonably priced just as they should look smart but not outrageous. In chapter 3, Michiel Scheffer points out that the amalgam of these factors has produced a special type of company, if not business model, in the more popular segments of the Dutch fashion market, combining an adaptable and well-designed product range with relatively affordable prices and clever marketing and branding.

Based on ethnographic research carried out between 2010 and 2011, this chapter identifies the Dutch fashion firm Vanilia as one of the more successful and recognisable players in this market. Medium-sized and with a product portfolio that translates international fashion styles for a local audience, the company is renowned for its clothing products as much as for its distinctive retail environments that, all bar one, are set in monumental listed buildings across the country. Originally a purveyor of mostly business wear, in recent years Vanilia has eagerly taken on the challenge of developing a brand identity alongside a more particularised range of products, streamlining much of its offerings for a style-conscious, low-key clientele.

The first part of this chapter unpacks Vanilia's coming of age as a brand and focuses on the firm's business tactics as well as the different levers of its business model contributing to its continued success. The second part will take a closer look at the relationship between the firm and its audience group to understand the drivers of consumption and the value connections governing the relay between supply and demand. Employing a mixed-method approach of quantitative data in the form of questionnaires[1] and qualitative data in the form of semi-structured in-depth interviews,[2] conversation protocols and participant observation, the results show that the firm's strength lies in its knowledge and understanding of local consumer needs and market preferences. Vanilia has stayed true to its origins with balanced and adaptable collections while continuing to develop its brand profile across different demographics and sites of identification.

Dutch a Gogo

As of 2015, the Dutch womenswear brand Vanilia has 18 single-brand stores and about 100 points of sale across the Netherlands. With about 55 people working at the headquarters and another 200 in the shops, it is a medium-sized enterprise with a strong foothold in the local fashion market. Arguably, this has not always been the case. Originally a supplier of business clothing, the focus of Vanilia used to be not quite what is commonly considered 'fashion'.[3] In fact, much of the original range of products was comprised of twinsets, trouser suits, blouses, and other basics, most of them subject to only marginal seasonal variation. After a change of ownership

89. Vanilia (A/W 2007).

in 1991 the company started to slowly venture into more trend-driven clothing styles and a broader target market. It was not until the mid 2000s, however, that things took a more radical turn, with the introduction of collections that had a decidedly more fashion-forward tone and punctuated the company's more traditional lines. Peculiarly enough, while it seems clear that Vanilia actively opted to redefine its product proposition and venture into a different market, throughout all the interviews I conducted with management and sales staff, consumers and designers, no one could really pinpoint what the shift was motivated by or where it even came from. As Rotterdam store manager Wendy B. explains:

> It was a strange thing, really. All of a sudden, some two or three years ago, we received all those new items in the store. The style was different — more edgy and slightly younger. [...] I never quite knew why this was actually done. [...] From all I hear this is the direction the brand is now going in.

Whatever the true motives may have been, it is clear that ever since, Vanilia has been eager to establish the image of a trend-oriented quality fashion brand.[4] By extending its focus from business wear to up-to-the-minute fashion clothing the firm has made a sustained effort to pack more cachet, with collaborations, events, and a rebranding strategy for the firm's logo, packaging, signature colours, and web presence. Powered by the trending (and slightly overused) theme of 'affordable luxury' (Za and Suzzi, 2014), the primary goal of that process was to prompt a shift from 'a mere clothing firm towards a lifestyle brand,' as Vanilia's former PR and marketing manager, Tatiana Striekwold, discloses. She further explains:

> Just now, the women who come to the shops are on average older and a bit more 'frumpy' than we would actually like. [...] So my task is to change that by means of PR and the like. [...] We are now trying to make a conscious effort to connect Vanilia's name and brand image to a different audience group — so, basically all things the company stands for or is being associated with.

With Vanilia's venturing out into new terrain, the brand has also become a frontrunner for a typically Dutch brand proposition and business model. Much in line with the concept of 'cosmopolitan nationalism' (Beck, 1997; Melchior, Skov & Csaba, 2011) put forward in the introduction to this book, 'typically Dutch' in this context does not actually stand for a clichéd idea of stylised nationalism that seeks to present certain facets of cultural production as unparalleled and downright original. Rather, it signifies a hybrid approach that cleverly manoeuvres between local ingenuity and international appeal. Vanilia uses a business vernacular that is influenced and inflected by a plurality of factors to carve out its very own niche in the market and, because of this hybrid character, has been able to develop a somewhat unique and inspired brand proposition.

If we put Dutch fashion in a broader perspective it appears that the local industry is shot through with womenswear brands such as Turnover or Sandwich that operate, and capitalise on, business formulas where the design process is structured around quick response mechanisms and a swift and flexible assimilation of international fashion trends. Factoring in clever marketing techniques and attractive merchandise to their advantage, the aim of this 'creative middle class' of brands is to offer accessible and democratic products at affordable prices. Perhaps more than in other fashion economies, a substantial number of Dutch fashion houses seek to marry a mid-market business approach to an original and distinguished design identity.

Vanilia's market approach, as of 2015, is designed for a target audience situated somewhere between high-octane fast-fashion players like H&M or Zara who address an audience aged from 12 to 30 years (excluding childrenswear), and pared-back, less fashion-driven firms like Karen Millen in the UK or Claudia Sträter in the Netherlands. The range of products, the marketing initiatives, the service, and the brand identity are all geared towards a specific consumption profile centring around (business)women who combine work and leisure time, family and social life, culture and socialising and who put a premium on the brand's trademark assets of good fit, tailored yet comfortable proportions, quality fabrics, and original style. This ambition is translated into four different product lines: 'Celebrate', which encompasses fashionable and slightly more formal pieces; 'Sport Couture', which comprises a variety of sporty and streetwear-oriented styles; 'Modern Business', which offers a broad selection of fashion-inspired business pieces; and 'Vanilia Accessories', where consumers can find everything from sunglasses and brooches to scarves and gloves.

With this all-round approach Vanilia is fairly versatile, which probably resonates well with a particular cultural spirit: for the Dutch, clothes ideally work across a wide variety of contexts, so versatility and adaptability are key to the product proposition. The separation between business clothing and more fashion-inspired items is a crucial part of that ambition in that it allows Vanilia to function as something of a one-stop destination where consumers can source entire outfits, complete with accessories and even cosmetics, without spending too much time dashing from store to store. In business terms, this approach represents a blueprint for an economically powerful part of the national fashion industry as a whole. Vanilia's product range and marketing strategy both accommodate a decidedly varied cachet; the following sections will unpack the relation between the firm's product proposition and its marketing and branding formula.

Supply-Chain Management and Vertical Integration: Towards Fast Fashion

The first, and probably most powerful, ingredient in Vanilia's success stems from its product proposition. As stated in the previous section, the company is well known for a wide selection of different items and styles. What is less well-known is the fact that the elements around which that variety is built are dynamic replenishment and quick product adaptation, i.e. a selection of items that is continuously being adapted and complemented. The way this is achieved is through workflow dynamics and a vertically integrated supply-chain that eliminates long lead times and long-term advance planning. With a company-owned factory in Turkey the firm is able to respond to fast-emerging trends and new ideas almost instantaneously, thereby operating a near fast-fashion dynamic for a local clientele.

With the aim to translate the latest fashion trends into the company's very own design vocabulary, Vanilia employs an in-house design team that regularly sets out for research trips to fashion capitals such as New York, London, Paris or Hong Kong. Quite obviously, these travels are aimed at finding inspiration and modelling the firm's collections on the latest clothing styles from across the globe. With the adoption of a supply-chain management that is vertically integrated from start to finish, Vanilia thrives on a flexible business model and fast transactions in the stores. Beyond merely product-related factors, however, this way of working also enables the firm to exercise control over a variety of internal processes, for example working conditions and quality control. The combination of these two factors puts Vanilia in an interesting position in the local fashion market: on the one hand, the products are 'on-trend', well made, and relatively affordable, while, on the other, the approach stresses corporate social responsibility and in-house design, sourcing, and quality assurance. According to Michel Hulzebosch, owner and director of Vanilia:

CONSTANTIN VON MALTZAHN

90. Vanilia (A/W 2007).

We are now able to respond to trends much quicker. Of course, I don't mean to just copy trends – the fashion world is full of that anyway. At the same time, I don't want to be stubborn and sell one and the same folklore print for over 20 years. I just have a keen eye on current developments. (Lampe, 2011: 4, my translation)

Despite Vanilia's modest size this way of working enables the firm to introduce 14 collections per year with a supply of new styles in the stores virtually every week. In doing so, Vanilia has managed to realise something quite remarkable for an outfit of local reach: a fast-fashion business model *en miniature* that allows for the same quick-response mechanisms and transactions as some of the bigger players in the market. In the words of Anna-Maartje van der Veen, one of the head designers, 'The whole system we introduced is a big change [...] and comes with a host of new challenges. But overall I believe that we are [...] able to do something really interesting that not many other companies of our size and standing can offer or have access to.'

Where most fast-fashion players outsource production to faraway places such as Vietnam or Bangladesh to keep manufacturing costs down to a minimum, Vanilia chose the opposite route. An actual proprietor of a factory in Turkey, Michel Hulzebosch makes clear that his ambitions reach beyond mere control of the supply chain, as he is concerned with minimum wages and problematic working conditions. The result, according to him, pays off:

I very much believe that treating your workers respectfully produces a return on investment – both literally and figuratively. If you offer them the right basis for carrying out their tasks – and by that I mean both the physical conditions inside the factory as well as food and regular working hours – it can only be beneficial because [your employees] will automatically work better and more efficiently.

Admirable though his efforts may be, Hulzebosch is first and foremost a businessman who puts his assets to good use. Compliance with corporate social responsibility standards may be just as important as control over the supply chain at some level, but whereas the former is mainly connected to brand image and proliferation across various media channels, the latter is an actual conduit to success. As we will see in the second part of the chapter, it is precisely the combination of contemporary collections and a certain degree of humility and understatement that constitutes a main driver of consumer involvement. The structural set-up behind the actual product proposition allows Vanilia to stay ahead of the curve and deliver fresh clothing styles with little dead time from conception to execution.

Store Atmospherics and Consumption Experience

The second key factor in Vanilia's brand proposition is its retail environments. Unlike the majority of high-street fashion firms, whose store layouts tend to be somewhat generic and nondescript, Vanilia puts a premium on shop design and service inside the shops. Across the board, including store interiors, online activities and events, the company makes a concerted effort to present itself as an accessible and smart alternative to competitors in the same segment by blending Dutch ingenuity and flair with quality clothing and in-store atmospherics.

Over the past two decades, the company has built up a reputation for preserving and restoring monumental buildings as retail destinations across all major Dutch cities. Since 2008 Vanilia's headquarters have been located in a magnificent national monument, the former soap factory De Adelaar in Wormerveer, 20 km north-west of Amsterdam. With one exception, all of the firm's retail destinations are located in exquisite spaces, rich with period details and vintage furnishings, and decked out with vast arrangements of plants and flowers.

Defining the firm's brand and product identity through contemporary, sophisticated retail spaces that evoke the impression of high-end boutiques more than high-street shops, the stores do have the look and feel of concept stores where products are presented shoulder to shoulder with mid-century vintage furniture, art works, earthenware and *objets d'art*.

In an effort to produce a coherent brand image across all the stores and create a trademark style and familiar atmosphere, Vanilia opts for a highly systemised approach to the presentation of the items, the decoration of the shop windows, and the styling of staff. Each of the stores is renewed on a regular basis with a fresh and updated visual identity. Periodically, the respective store managers receive detailed briefs from Vanilia's visual merchandise team on how to arrange the shop and window displays. These instructions include photographs of a model scenario, directions as to which flowers to buy or how to dress the windows – even to the point of specifying the clothes that should be hung in the display windows and those that should be put on the shelves. As Birgit Groot, head of Vanilia's visual merchandise team, explains, service and retail atmospherics are used strategically as ploys to distinguish the brand from competitors:

> For some time now we have worked with this whole theme around cosiness and a homey atmosphere – a place where people simply like to spend time. So, we have all kinds of paraphernalia like old trunks, huge planters, ladders, sailing hawsers and what not. Also, the coffee corners we are now trying to install in all the shops are part of that [approach]. Consumers can sit down, have a cup of decent coffee, and take a rest. There's no rush, no crowds, no pushy service. I believe our consumers appreciate that a lot, because it makes them feel welcome.

In doing so, Vanilia aims to create a quality that reaches beyond the product as a stand-alone item. Rather than exclusively focusing on the goods on display, the firm's spaces are designed not only for functional purposes, but to create a sensory experience where the product is part and parcel of a grander scheme. Through the creation of nooks and little corners consumers are invited to rest or read a magazine, thereby stimulating the idea of retail as pastime; i.e. an opportunity to spend time alone or in a group in an environment that blends the worlds of consumption and relaxation. The process of making a purchasing decision is embedded in a framework where consumption is part of a set of possibilities and where the different variables cross-fertilise each other. As 27-year-old customer Nanda R. told me in an interview, 'Certainly, the music, the service, [...] the stores

91. Vanilia (F/W 2015–16).

and the location: [...] all of that plays a role. [...] For me, it's a complete package that works very well and that makes shopping here a pleasant experience.'

The general high-street experience is likely to be governed by functional goals and designed to maximise display and not retail space (Newman and Patel, 2004). Vanilia, on the contrary, inverts that relationship and stimulates a retail climate where buying becomes part of an experience and where the store functions as a 'hangout'. By setting the firm apart as a fashionable and edgy alternative to competitors through sensory spaces and the provision of personal, tailored service, Vanilia's in-store approach is geared towards a distinct brand and business identity across all its retail destinations.

Welcome to the Club! Are You in ... or Out?

In an attempt to complement, and expand on, the idea of activities and initiatives beyond the actual selling process, several years ago Vanilia established a tradition of organising special events for its consumers in a bid to develop a relationship away from the functionality and aesthetics of the product – or even the sales act. With the aim to create an atmosphere of belonging and personal relevance, the brand makes use of sales promotions 'by invitation only' and orchestrates events that elevate the relationship between the brand and its consumers from a functional to an emotionally charged one. The most interesting bit of this is the special night-time events the firm has been organising periodically for a number of years now. During these sessions, dubbed 'Vanilia Night Out' or 'Vanilia Champagne Night', a number of happenings are organised around the collection in order to involve consumers more directly and thoroughly with the brand and its products. For example, for the 'Champagne Night' a team of stylists and make-up artists was hired, so consumers could choose a full makeover, complete with make-up,

image consulting or professional styling in Vanilia clothes while being treated to champagne and nibbles. The results were caught on Polaroids and given to customers to take home for free. In another instance, the company teamed up with a producer of vodka to design a special-edition bottle with the Vanilia logo and custom labels that was then handed to customers as a give-away.

Each of these efforts is meant to connect the firm's portfolio to a lifestyle context and give consumers the opportunity to experience the collection in an exclusive and stimulating setting. Shifting the point of value exchange from product-centric to lifestyle-related properties, Vanilia's initiatives can be considered an integrated approach for tapping into the life-worlds of consumers and facilitating a different experience of the brand. To augment that feeling of 'we-ness', most of the events are connected to the firm's own members' club, a term that Vanilia uses rather liberally and that does not require much more than filling in a form with personal and contact details. In the past this club was primarily a one-way relay with emails sent regularly to all members of the club. With changing consumption habits, however, communication and brand experience have increasingly shifted to online contexts where different environments allow consumers to get a taste of the company around and beyond the actual product. As a result, the members' club has been upgraded to a more contemporary format. Not too long ago, Vanilia introduced the 'Membercard' app, which, essentially, is a rebate system that connects purchases online or in-store with discounts proportional to the retail prices of the individual items bought. Connecting on- and offline sales environments, the app is a tool to stimulate purchase behaviour as well as a response to changing consumption dynamics.

CONSTANTIN VON MALTZAHN

Business Model Generation

Probably a good way to summarise all the aspects described in the previous sections is that the main conduit to Vanilia's success, and hence what makes the firm such an interesting study case, is a combination of factors that are somewhat unexpected or even unusual for the very segment it operates in. Over the years Vanilia has developed and refined a vocabulary that is designed for the Dutch market and adapted to the needs of a local clientele. Pooling all aspects together it appears that the firm has made a vested effort to create a particular brand identity by complementing its product proposition with various other assets, some of which might be surprising while others are more intuitive.

The retail environments evoke an atmosphere of sophistication, distinctiveness, and belonging that probably does not quite compare to that of the average nondescript high-street brand. The spaces are chic, individualistic, and inviting, but they are also understated and down to earth, utilitarian and functional. The combination of these factors tells us something about the Dutch market and, perhaps, even about the firm's uniquely Dutch business model. Vanilia's formula is very much about finding the right balance between seemingly opposite poles: upstream vs downstream, luxurious vs utilitarian, fashionable vs timeless, outspoken vs demure. The same logic applies to the actual product proposition, which is modelled on emerging trends from across the globe, but translated for the local market. By developing the collections in-house from start to finish Vanilia actually emulates the driving rationale behind some the most successful fast-fashion chains worldwide (Petro, 2012). Finally, the firm's orchestrating of after-hours events and targeted promotions is an attempt to decrease the gap between supply and demand, allowing consumers to experience and participate in the brand and provide playful (consumption) experiences away from the actual purchasing process. It is important to note that these initiatives are rather casual affairs that are tailored to the needs of the local market. They are understated, easy-going endeavours that do not require strong commitment or even longstanding purchase history.

With openness to change and an ability to look for unexpected solutions the company has successfully built a distinct business identity. In doing so, Vanilia's strategy is about finding a balance and developing a rationale for sustained success. Perhaps a good way to describe the firm's business model is a combination of business acumen and Dutch ingenuity. Vanilia has been looking for gaps in the market, possibilities to make a difference and provide goods and services that – at least in that unique combination – other outfits do not have access to or cannot compete with.

Consumption Dynamics: Who, What and Why?

In the preceding sections I have sought to define the main pillars of Vanilia's business identity and structural set-up. Rather than looking at them exclusively as levers of success it is my contention that they illustrate a cultural tendency to do things differently and in a somewhat individual manner. Vanilia may not be a nonconformist brand by any means, but it surely is a company that is not afraid of trying out different ideas and, as a result, is able to bring to market a unique combination of features.

Having developed an understanding of the firm's business model and market position, in the following sections I will provide an overview of the actual value connections that govern the relationship between the brand and its main audience groups. In so doing, my aim is to facilitate a perspective on the overall consumption dynamics as well as the different levels of involvement. Based on a set of in-depth interviews (n=8) and question- naires (n=294) that were carried out with consumers between 2010 and 2011, the following sections will discuss in more detail the main drivers of purchasing

92. Vanilia (S/S 2016).

behaviour and the level of brand and product involvement, respectively.

Soon after I had started my in-store research it became clear that Vanilia's audience, perhaps unsurprisingly, is fairly heterogeneous in terms of age distribution and consumption interests. From young women in their early twenties to ladies in the 50-and-above age bracket, Vanilia attracts a wide spectrum of consumers, although most of them are involved with the firm's products for similar reasons. The younger consumers do probably have more of an interest in state-of-the-art pieces while the older ones may rather look for clothes that are chic, understated, and contemporary. What unites them, however, is their interest in smart and adaptable products that travel easily across a wide range of occasions.

My results indicate rather convincingly that the level of fashion involvement may be moderate at best. The firm's audience in general is not interested in dressing according to the latest trends or following catwalk buzz through fashion magazines or blogs. They are neither active online in forums, nor do they follow the most recent developments on blogs or other fashion-related websites. In a manner of speaking, the general impression was that Vanilia's consumers are rather unconcerned with the whole notion of fashion altogether. That, however, does not mean they would not have a pronounced interest in clothing and style (which are not necessarily the same as fashion). In the absence of an explicit interest in 'trending' products or fashion media, Vanilia's audience group does actually nourish an interest in clothing and aesthetics. The firm's consumers search for garments with a certain edge, a 'twist'. With subtler notes than straightforward adaptations of current fashion trends governing their stylistic preferences, more obvious fads tend to be ignored in favour of fashion-inspired yet timeless looks that are not bound by default to a specific seasonal style.

The quantitative work I carried out in the form of questionnaires inside the stores helped further refine these insights in terms of the attitudes and beliefs consumers have towards the brand. One of the questionnaire items was designed to identify the primary drivers in product perception ('Please name three characteristics you associate with Vanilia's clothing') in order to understand the very nature of their involvement with the firm's products. After clustering and analysing the results, a pattern emerged identifying three variables as key components in the relationship: (1) quality/price, (2) style, and (3) comfort/wearability. The first attribute is rather obvious and is to do with an apparently favourable ratio between product quality and purchase price ('value for money'). The second one picks up on the style of

Vanilia's products, which can be summarised as chic and versatile, smart and subdued. The third is to do with the products' comfortable fit and adaptable aesthetics and can be interpreted as an indicator of the more functional 'blend-in' qualities of the garments.

Having established a basic understanding of the attributes that consumers in the main connect with Vanilia's products, I wanted to find out how this variable relates to their perception of the brand. A second questionnaire item was designed presenting respondents with a multiple-choice question comprising 15 pre-conceived response options ('Which three of the following fifteen attributes are most suited to describe Vanilia as a brand?'). The question was created to compare the independent variables tested through the previous item and a number of standardised brand values to identify similarities and divergences between the two. With the help of frequency-analysis methods a fairly uniform pattern emerged across all response options. As the results indicate, the vast majority of consumers see Vanilia as (1) fashionable, (2) stylish, and (3) reliable. We might say, therefore, that the firm's general image among consumers is very much in line with the company's product portfolio and overall business strategy. Fashionable and stylish appearance have mostly to do with the actual product appeal and the identity of the brand, whereas reliability probably reflects a quality that is more to do with purchase satisfaction, positive post-purchase evaluation, or even a long-term buying history. It is crucial to note that fashionable appearance in this context is not necessarily synonymous with copycat styles gleaned from the international catwalk shows, but relates more to a certain zeitgeist or contemporary feel of the clothes, as the insights from the in-depth interviews with patrons below clarify. Many of Vanilia's consumers use the clothes as all-round garments in private but also specifically in professional contexts where overly fashionable attire is usually not quite *comme il faut*.

While the questionnaires were aimed at developing a more general, quantifiable understanding of the relays running back and forth between Vanilia and its audience, the in-depth interviews were geared towards exploring the life-worlds of consumers and identifying the deeper meaning and motifs behind their consumption choices. Across these different conversations consumers highlighted the connection between style, versatility, and price as a key variable in their individual relationships with the firm. As Nanda R., a communication strategist, explains:

I wear it a lot to work [because] I think it's always a good choice. I think that the type of clothes you wear to work makes a lot of difference [...] so I do take that into account. For me, Vanilia is more business-like. But I also think that certain items [can be worn in different ways]. Just take a pair of jeans and slippers and it looks great, too. You can combine the clothes in a number of ways.

The research showed that most of Vanilia's consumers are working women whose clothes need to serve a variety of purposes. For many, the outfits need to 'look the part' in many different environments throughout the day and be suited to professional and private contexts alike. The combination of stylish and versatile attire has particular relevance for women who search for understated products that impart feminine and sophisticated traits without overpowering, or conflicting with, their professional appearance. A working mother who first brings her children to kindergarten, then cycles to work, shops for groceries on her way back, and meets with friends for a drink before returning home probably does not have the time to change several times a day. Vanilia's average consumer searches for a type of product that supports, or even enhances, the performance of social roles, regardless of the occasion. As 31-year-old Jessica J. explains:

It's a nice brand because it fits both leisure and business contexts. That suits me well because I'd rather have clothes that work well in both parts of life. I'm a lawyer and it's just very handy. It's a style that does not look dowdy but stylish and fashionable. I like this combination a lot because it allows me to express myself within a certain framework.

It is this matrix of practical considerations, stylish appeal, and flattering proportions that defines much of the relationship between Vanilia and its clientele. The firm's consumers generally appreciate the products and do actually return for repeat purchases, which probably attests to the fact that they have developed some kind of rapport with the firm and its products. At the same time, their level of emotional involvement is fairly moderate. Most of Vanilia's consumers maintain a rather diverse consumption attitude and source their clothing from a variety of brands with a similar aesthetic register. In that sense it is probably fair to say that the relationship with the company is mostly functional, certainly so when it comes to the main drivers of the purchase decision-making process. The purchase act primarily satisfies functional and aesthetic needs, but does not involve a lot of product-extrinsic arousal factors, as can be the case with real 'brand fans' whose purchases tend to be motivated by an ownership experience first before practical or rational considerations (cf. Brown, 2007; for an example of fandom among fashion consumers, see chapter 9 in this book on ⁻CoraKemperman).

This is not very surprising, because the firm's rather generalist set-up and selection does not focus on a specific clientele. Indeed, Vanilia's orientation is intentionally broad and seeks to cater to a wide range of consumption interests in order to keep the brand profile accessible for a wide range of people. As designer Anna-Maartje van der Veen explains:

We do have a certain target group. These are women between 30 and 40 [years], independent, with a working background and their own income. That said, we do try to reach a rather diverse group of people. That's why we have the different labels. That's the reason behind that strategy.

For the consumers the diversity of styles on offer holds the promise of finding products they like and that are likely to look good on them without having to scour many different shops. Vanilia's clientele has a keen interest in clothes with an articulate look. And yet, while they favour fashion-inspired, up-to-the-minute products and while consumers are well aware of the expressive potential of their clothes, their preferred type of garment has a rather temperate flavour. Rather than generic high-street fashion as in, for instance, fast-fashion copycat products that adopt styles from international catwalks with only minor adjustments, it is fashion as an expression of subtle personal style they are looking for. As a customer from Rotterdam explains:

The thing is this: I do like fashion and I do like to dress in a feminine, trendy way. And yet I'm 58 years old and there are limits to what I can wear. Certain pieces — however beautiful they may be — simply won't work. They will look ridiculous on me, because they are made for people who are much younger. Vanilia is a great option, because the clothes are trendy and understated. They look decent on me. You know, fashionable but not hip.

As this and comparable statements suggest, Vanilia's audience gravitates towards an aesthetic repertoire that is understated, flexible and discreetly distinctive, i.e. a signature style that is smart, functional, and versatile without unnecessary pomp or loud, conspicuous details. It is this combination of factors that is central to the involvement of consumers with

CONSTANTIN VON MALTZAHN

the firm. 'The clothing is fashionable but surely not too extravagant because that is never going to work [in the Netherlands],' as van der Veen explains. The clothing is modelled on, and inspired by, the latest trends, but it is designed in a way that is appealing for a clientele looking for a middle ground between fashion and moderation, between edgy and understated clothing pieces. In the words of 33-year-old film-maker Iris O.:

> I'm not too much into super-fashionable, loud clothes. But I do like clothes that are chic and wearable. [...] What I like about Vanilia is the fact that it's accessible, but not in the way H&M or Zara is. The quality is better and the clothes are not as generic. At this stage of my life I feel that I've outgrown that look. Already as a student I liked Vanilia, but back then I wasn't able to afford it. Now I can, and I think it's in line with the face I want to show to the world.

Consumer involvement, we can conclude, is largely dependent on the differentiating qualities of Vanilia's products. Although the clothes blend in easily, Vanilia's style is nevertheless defined by a vernacular that merges international influences with local taste, resulting in a product proposition that is smart and adaptable as well as refined and recognisable. The firm's structural set-up, encompassing four individual fashion lines and 14 collections per year, establishes the company as a consummate supplier of diversified and distinguished fashion products. Vanilia capitalises on a nuanced range of products, offering ample choice and encouraging a wide variety of combinations. As with many of the firm's initiatives, also in design terms Vanilia has potentially carved out a particular niche by giving the products a low-key trademark twist.

Conclusion

Throughout this chapter I have argued that Vanilia represents a blueprint for a type of high-street fashion firm and business model that in a number of respects can be considered 'typically Dutch'. As explained earlier, this notion does not so much reflect the cliché of stylised nationalism that portrays certain qualities or cultural tendencies as unique and original to a specific cultural background. Rather, it is the hybrid character inherent in Dutch cultural heritage and many so-called 'typically Dutch' artefacts that we encounter also in this context. It is a fusion – or perhaps recoding – of factors that is unique in that very combination. If we look at the product proposition the style is fairly international, but then adapted to the tastes and preferences of the Dutch local audience, which – most broadly speaking – tends to be practical and slightly more sober. The firm's business identity, meanwhile, epitomises an economically powerful part of the national fashion landscape. The local industry knows more than a few womenswear brands that operate under a similar flag as Vanilia (see also Michiel Scheffer's arguments in chapter 3). With a design process structured around a swift and flexible assimilation of international styles, Dutch companies like Turnover or Sandwich capitalise on quick response mechanisms and a specific trademark style. Seeking distinction through clever marketing puffery and attractive merchandise, the aim is to offer accessible and democratic products at affordable prices. It is in this way that quite a few Dutch fashion firms marry their mid-market business approach to original and distinctive design identities, and perhaps in a more articulate manner than is the case in other fashion economies.

With products and services that are inspired, smart, and accessible, Vanilia's value proposition resonates with an all-round cultural spirit. Vanilia aims for sophistication on the shop floor with stylish and accomplished retail environments, and puts an emphasis on in-store atmospherics and service. Similarly, in its marketing strategy the company has developed an image as a distinguished and smart alternative for young career women who divide their time between work, family, and social life. By allowing consumers to experience the brand in one-off marketing events inside the stores away from the actual purchasing process, the firm creates a sense of belonging and community (even though, as we have seen, this does not translate into strong emotional involvement with the firm for most consumers). Across these different sites of identification, Vanilia has developed a specific business identity that ties in numerous facets that have relevance for the Dutch market. Clearly, it is not so much the individual components that are worthy of attention, but the compound they jointly come to represent. Vanilia has designed its brand identity across a number of pillars, the sum of which boosts its cachet in terms of product and retail aesthetics as well business acumen.

The latter part of the chapter elaborated on these findings from a consumer perspective. Focusing on the relays between Vanilia and its clientele, my analysis demonstrates that the relationship is first and foremost defined by product-intrinsic values. The firm's clothes are adaptations of emerging international fashion styles that are framed and translated in near-real time for the Dutch market. Despite this speed to market the nucleus of the product proposition is not so much fashion as it is style. Vanilia above all translates a certain mood of the moment rather than the exact same shapes and colours that have been shown on the runways shortly before. The firm's consumers look for an accommodating type of garment that is contemporary and sophisticated and can be worn effortlessly across a variety of occasions as well as social and/or professional contexts. The analysis identified product attributes including stylishness, versatility, product quality and comfort as the main drivers of brand and product involvement, respectively. The firm's consumers want their clothes to be simultaneously distinguished and functional while not requiring too much care to maintain. With four complementary lines and a constant influx of new items in the stores, the profusion of styles guarantees a wide enough range to satisfy multiple consumption interests. The downside of this broad-based set-up is that consumers tend to not develop a strong sense of emotional involvement. While many consumers do return for purchases on a regular basis, they maintain a rather broad-based consumption attitude and purchase their clothing pieces from a selection of different brands.

The odds are that strong emotional involvement in this context does not matter all that much. The high street, regardless of the type of business strategy that is being adopted, is a rather unlikely place to develop strong feelings towards a brand. Chapter 9 on ¯CoraKemperman analyses the coming of age and success factors of a decidedly smaller outfit where the commitment and loyalty of consumers are unusually strong. Unlike Vanilia, however, that firm presents only one (very unique) offering that, together with a personalised service variable, is responsible for the cult following. In the more fiercely contested trenches of the high-street market such dynamics are few and far between. Vanilia has carved out a different niche that is designed to speak to several different types of consumers. Through quick assimilation and translation of international fashion styles for the local market, Vanilia's products may not be ahead of the curve, but rather, perfectly aligned with it, as Dutch fashion journalist Bregje Lampe (2011: 4, my translation) summarises: 'Vanilia certainly is not overly progressive. The clothes are modest, elegant, feminine and in some cases sporty or a bit coarse. In other words, it is a type of product that is eminently suited for the Dutch market.'

Notes

1. The results were analysed with a frequency-analysis model. For a detailed methodology, I refer to my doctoral dissertation (von Maltzahn, 2013).

2. All the interviews were recorded digitally with permission of the interviewees, transcribed, and analysed based on a clustering method after Mayring (2000). For a detailed methodology, see my doctoral dissertation (von Maltzahn, 2013).

3. There is also a German fashion label of the same name. However, no relation exists between the two.

4. Although speculative, one possible explanation might be the onset of the financial crisis in 2007–8. Coinciding with a climate of trembling economic uncertainty at the time, it stands to reason that Vanilia's change of direction was at least partially motivated by a desire to address the challenge head-on and give the brand a new direction rather than waiting for the firm to nosedive because of imminent socio-economic changes.

5. The response options were: authentic, reliable, personal, innovative, extravagant, stylish, individual, fashionable, responsible, cool/hip, recognisable, sporty, interesting, special, other.

Marlies Dekkers (b. Oosterhout 1965)

Lianne Toussaint

Innerwear becomes outerwear.

—Marlies Dekkers, 2015

For Marlies Dekkers, lingerie is not just about underwear. It is a way to boost and express the power, beauty and self-confidence of women. With her provocative and famous designs, like the 'bare-bottom-dress' and 'spider-web-bra', Dekkers radically breaks with the stereotypical image of demure and obedient women who adorn themselves in cute lingerie to please men. In Dekkers' world, a woman takes the lead in a never-ending play of revealing and concealing. She is the one who takes the initiative to seduce, because *her* desires and fantasies are central to the game of sexuality. The most important motive behind Dekkers' lingerie designs is to make women proud of their bodies and get them in touch with suppressed desires and fantasies. Marlies Dekkers aims at empowering women, making them feel better about themselves, and expressing themselves more confidently.

Dekkers' visual language is innovative in the conventional field of lingerie. She daringly combines some of the more traditional ingredients of erotic lingerie like ruffles, bows and lace with strong shapes, ingenious straps and refined cutaways in unexpected parts of the designs. It is a 'signature' look that has become world-famous, especially because of the bras with extra straps above the cups (Arts, 2006: 52).

After studying at the The Academy of Art and Design St. Joost and the Charles Montaigne Fashion Academy, Dekker started her own label in 1993: 'Undressed' by Marlies Dekkers. Back then erotic lingerie was mostly associated with prostitution and pornography. The seamstresses of the Belgian atelier that produced her first collection initially rebelled against what they considered indecent and unnecessarily intricate designs (Ibid.). In the years that followed the interest in Dekkers' design slowly but steadily grew. She produced a collection for the Dutch lingerie chain Hunkemöller and had her first solo exhibition. When a company from Hong Kong was willing to invest in the still quite small brand, her work suddenly gained momentum. Through better production techniques and professional distribution, her high-end lingerie label (by then called marlies|dekkers) became a major player on the global market. By 2008, the brand owned stores in many Dutch cities, Antwerp, Bangkok, Paris, New York and Berlin and also created its own swimwear ('Sundressed') and special collections for men and young women. However, as debts rose and the economic crisis hit, the company was declared bankrupt in 2013. Dekkers decided to make a restart, downsizing the company and shifting its focus to the webshop and online stores (Persad, 2013).

Business is going well again and Dekkers is not taken aback. Her recent projects include haute couture lingerie collections inspired by iconic 'power-women' such as Jeanne d'Arc, Indian poet-princess Mirabai, and Greek goddess Pallas Athena. Dekkers' work is as daring and extravagant as before, yet still clearly communicates her strong vision: lingerie is there to be seen and admired just like the beautiful, strong and self-confident women it adorns (Bruggeman, 2013).

93 Marlies Dekkers, 'The Victory' (A/W 2014).

94. Marlies Dekkers (A/W 2009).

95. Marlies Dekkers (S/S 2008).

96. Marlies Dekkers, 'The Firebird' (A/W 2015).

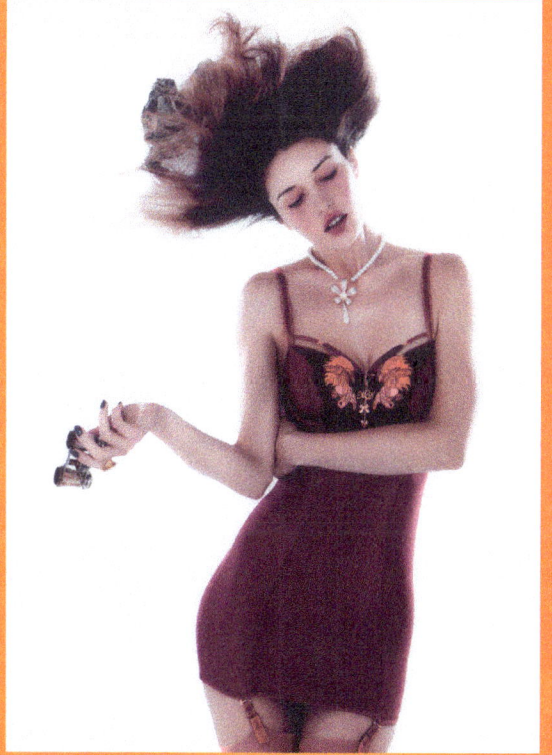

11.

Spijkers en Spijkers:
A Cut Above

'Spijkers en Spijkers are building up their business and learning as they go along. They are always gaining new experience, consolidating the lessons they learn in practice and they consider the following step. They are very ambitious. Unlike many people with businesses in the creative sector, they really want to grow. Yet, they are aware of the weaknesses and seek to overcome them.'

—D. Jacobs (2011b: 119)

Constantin von Maltzahn

Introduction

Since 2001, Dutch luxury label Spijkers en Spijkers has been a stellar fixture on the international fashion scene in Milan and London. With a cutting-edge design identity and a headstrong business approach, twin sisters Truus and Riet Spijkers have shaped their brand in their very own way. Interestingly, without any well-oiled marketing apparatus to spice up their product slate, in its development Spijkers en Spijkers has mainly relied on what was possible with a team of only a handful of people, carefully extending the brand by looking for opportunities to drive the business forward.

Known for its playful blending of modernist shapes and patterns with vibrant colours and edgy materials, the company appears typically Dutch in its conceptualist take on design, resonating with the country's artistic past in early twentieth-century architecture and painting, as José Teunissen explains in chapter 2. These cultural borrowings notwithstanding, it took quite some time for Dutch consumers to come to appreciate the products – and probably even longer to start actually purchasing them. As opposed to most other fashion companies, the firm has undergone a reverse development in that the driving force of its business was first of all through sales abroad, and only at a later stage did it establish a foothold in the home market.

This chapter traces the development of Spijkers en Spijkers in terms of market adaptation and maps out how the firm – in quite an implicit way – has managed to adopt an increasingly consumer-oriented approach by moulding its product slate through collaborations and brand extensions. The research was based on in-depth interviews with Truus and Riet Spijkers and an interview with Chananja Baars, the manager of concept store Arnhem Coming Soon; knowledge obtained during a four-day research trip with the designers to Iaşi (Romania), which served the purpose of exploring new possibilities in manufacturing; and an extensive study of the literature.[1] This chapter presents a comprehensive sketch of Spijkers en Spijkers' coming of age as a brand – as well as of the designers as self-taught entrepreneurs – and identifies the tools that were necessary to develop a business identity and secure a steadier and more permanent market position. In so doing, the brand's trajectory has also proved representative of the struggles of smaller independent fashion labels that have to carve out a niche and position for themselves next to the established names in the market.

Twenty-first Century Fox: Moving Target

Before actually delving into the firm's business it seems worthwhile to quickly introduce the two designers and the kind of aesthetic their label has come to be known for. Early recipients of the Hyères Awards, a prestigious annual design competition in the South of France, twin sisters Truus and Riet Spijkers started their own label in 2001, following a stint with a capsule collection at Carole de Bona's Paris showroom. From the very beginning their work has been marked by a juxtaposition of stark, austere cuts and glamorous, delicate fabrics. The marriage of these two worlds gives the garments a poetic, almost fragile quality that produces a perplexing image of old-world glamour in a twenty-first-century disguise. Deceptively simple in appearance, the collections are rich in construction and attention to detail and combine the clean-cut lines of modernism and Art Deco with startling prints and eye-catching finishes (Teunissen and Van Der Voet, 2011: 12).

In their work, the designers' ambition is simple yet challenging: 'Youth, that's what we want. Everyone's got that secret, but you need to bring it to the outside. Our clothes can help with that.' Although perhaps a tad idealistic, it seems that they try to appeal to some kind of spirit or mindset rather than a specific target audience. As Truus Spijkers says: 'It doesn't matter whether it's a woman of 18 or 80 – our understanding

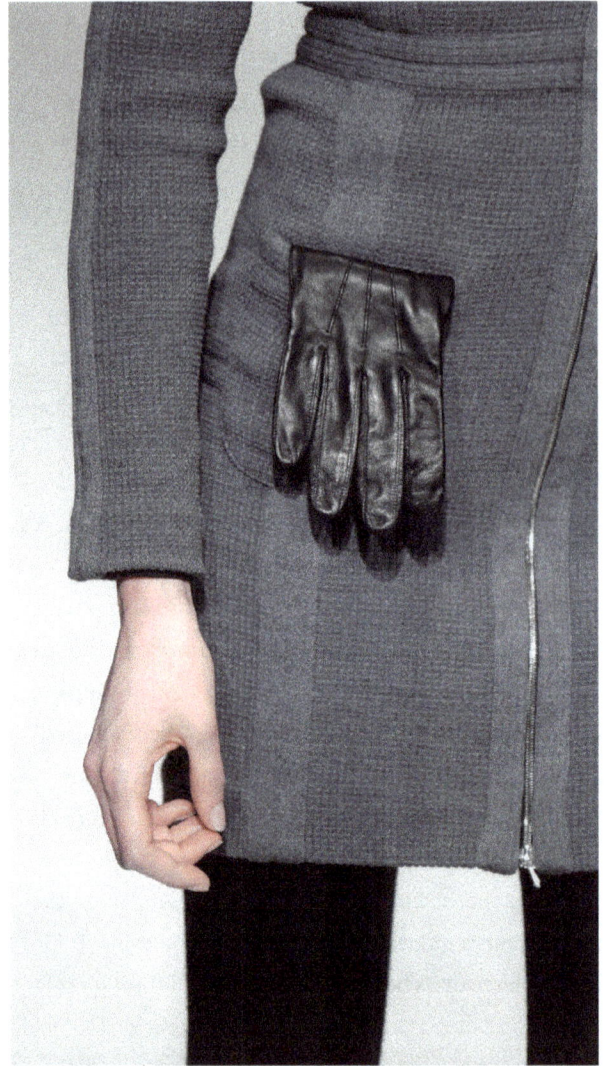

97, 98. SIS by Spijkers en Spijkers (A/W 2011-12).

of beauty has more to do with a certain attitude than with age.'

It could be said that such an undiscerning approach sounds nice. Still, the question is whether it is reasonable and in line with the firm's actual ambitions. With towering prices of 800–1200 euros for their signature dresses and jumpsuits, the clothes are clearly positioned in the higher echelons of the womenswear market, which makes them unattainable for the vast majority of consumers to start with. It may be true, then, that the collections are not driven by an articulate marketing strategy that seeks to address specific consumer profiles, but it appears rather doubtful that the designers do not envision their actual end consumer falling within certain demographic or sociographic parameters.

A similar brand of romantic idealism is echoed by the claims of certain authors who have argued that the image of femininity evoked through the clothes challenges gender stereotypes such as eternal youth, sexual objectification or the industry's almost exclusive reliance on reed-thin looks (Mumby-Croft, 2010: 5; Teunissen and Van Der Voet, 2011). While there may be a grain of truth to it, it appears that some putting into perspective is needed. Granted, the clothes are probably more graceful and feminine than laden with sexual innuendo. Still, the idea of aesthetic criticism seems to be a somewhat over-optimistic view considering that the designers operate within the rather narrow confines of the high-end market.

After this short insight into the firm's product and the designers' approach to their collections, the following sections will map out the business development of the Spijkers en Spijkers brand, defining in what way and by what means it has developed over the past couple of years.

Creative Evolution: The Designers as Entrepreneurs

Traditionally, smaller fashion labels operate on a small-order basis. This is also true in the case of Spijkers en Spijkers, where average production runs are of no more than one hundred pieces per style and in fact, in some cases the limit is down to 10 or 20 pieces. This has important consequences for the set-up of the company. First, unusually small order sizes mean that most of the production can only be done in specialised factories and/or workshops. Second, small production units lead to relatively high manufacturing costs per piece, which in turn leads to a rather tight gross margin. Ordinarily, the easiest way to make up for the asymmetry between liquidity and profitability is by taking one or more investors on board. Interestingly, Truus and Riet Spijkers deliberately chose against collaboration with a backer since, in their view, it would have curtailed their creative freedom too severely. As Truus recounts:

We've had quite a number of talks with potential investors, [but] the people we spoke to asked impossible things. I'm realistic and I understand that collaborating with a partner means they will ask something in return. What we don't want is someone who thinks: I want to get out of this as much money as possible as quickly as possible, or who wants a majority stake in our company. That's just not interesting for us [since] we have built this [brand] for the past ten years. (Truus Spijkers in *Husslage*, 2011: 3, my translation)

By not working with an investor, the designers chose to develop the brand independently and free from liabilities. With zero overheads, only two permanent employees, three people on a zero-hour contract basis and a handful of interns, the operation is run by an exceptionally small team – specifically if we take into account that the products are sold in no less than twelve countries across the world (Jacobs, 2011b). In spite of – or perhaps because of – the firm's rather small size the two sisters have had to take a more entrepreneurial role themselves. In the words of Truus: 'We really had to get into the whole business side of things ourselves. At times that was pretty tough, as we did not have any training in that regard. At the art academy, the focus is purely on creativity, not entrepreneurship' (Truus Spijkers in *Husslage*, 2011: 2).

Since establishing the firm in 2001, Truus and Riet Spijkers have gone from strength to strength operating their brand with business acumen and a good intuition for interpreting and translating signals from the market. Nonetheless, building the business has not been without its problems. In particular, their move – probably not quite deliberate at the time – to first explore markets abroad turned out to be both curse and blessing at the same time. On the one hand, reaching out to a global audience has opened markets for the firm which smaller labels tend to enter only at a much later stage in their development, if at all. This manoeuvre has greatly boosted the firm's reputation as an internationally operating high-end fashion house. On the other hand, while the designers were able to attract an international buying public, they did not succeed in retaining much long-term loyalty in any of these markets. As Jacobs (2011b: 121) argues:

> From the start, their operations have been very international. Their first buyers have been Japanese, followed by the British, Russians, Chinese, plus buyers from the Gulf States [...]. All went extremely well for some time. But sales were never stable. On average, they sell to some twelve countries, but those often vary and their shares in overall sales fluctuate constantly.

With a miniscule team operating out of Arnhem, thousands of miles away from their sales territory, it turned out to be a hazardous task to understand and cater to the needs of these different consumer groups all at once, which meant a lack of control over the actual market they meant to target. Conversely, in the Netherlands, where the designers intuitively understood the culture and consumption behaviour much better, there was little interest in the products initially – partly so because the country does not have any real tradition in the luxury goods sector and consumers tend to have quite different spending habits.

Over the years, however, a peculiar development set in: while in their home country sales were at best moderate, the designers' successful appearances during fashion weeks in Milan and London gradually started adding cachet to their status as iconic designers in the Netherlands. With their edgy signature style and somewhat peculiar status as identical twins, Truus and Riet Spijkers have in time come into their own. Arguably, Spijkers en Spijkers is no fast-track success story. And yet, it is precisely this aspect that makes the brand an exemplary case for many small independent fashion houses, most of which are forced to fathom gaps and opportunities in the market in order to advance business and sales.

The Quest for Awareness

Stubbornly, in a way, Spijkers en Spijkers neither advertises in magazines nor employs any other explicit kind of consumer marketing. As Truus Spijkers told me: 'We've got only a limited budget to spend on a number of different things. Advertising is rather costly, and personally I'm not sure whether our brand would actually profit from it.' From this perspective it seems that the firm's rather marketing-averse stance is dictated by economic means and financial scope. When compared to the large multi-label corporations that rule a good deal of the high-fashion industry (such as Kering, Louis Vuitton Moët Hennessy, Compagnie Financière Richemont) there appears to be a striking difference in budget, leverage and economic reach, but also in the

CONSTANTIN VON MALTZAHN

99. SIS by Spijkers en Spijkers (A/W 2013-14).

100. SIS by Spijkers en Spijkers (S/S 2011).

determining variables of a collection's success or failure. A company like Prada, for example, launches its products with the help of an enormous marketing apparatus, including large-scale advertising in all important magazines, million-dollar budgets for fashion shows, costume designs for blockbusters, or – as happened in July 2011 – renting five floors of Park Hyatt Shanghai to stage a three-day fashion-show-cum-exhibition for Miu Miu's F/W 2011/2 collection (Martin, 2011: 97-100).

The Spijkers en Spijkers brand by contrast, is actually forced to rely on a comparatively low-key approach by foregrounding the product and looking for opportunities beyond the luxury mainstream. Rather laconically, Truus Spijkers sums up the situation saying: 'Brands like Prada are our direct competitors. And you just can't compete with them. It's impossible. Those are mega teams and mega budgets, you see …' From an early point in their career it was clear that the choice against investors made it imperative to find an alternative strategy to advance the business. For the two designers that meant finding ways to create awareness and devise a brand narrative around the main constituents of the brand as a whole: high design (as the designers would call it), modernist aesthetics and individuality (personal interview; see also Teunissen and Van Der Voet, 2011: 58). The first and foremost way to do that was, and still is, to make the product the linchpin of all business thinking. As Riet Spijkers contends: 'After all, it's quite an expressive product. [...] And I think in our case it has to be, because we don't have the marketing apparatus [of the bigger brands]. We have to make the cut with our products, not by placing nice campaigns in fashion magazines.'

It goes without saying that awareness by itself is what all brands, regardless of size and turnover, strive for and profit from. Basically any type of marketing, be it high-profile advertising, artist sponsorships, or ritzy locations for fashion shows, is nothing but a means to raise awareness. What is interesting about Spijkers en Spijkers' rather low-key approach to 'marketing' (if one wants to call it that) is the fact that even without actively practising the art of marketing the designers have successfully raised their stakes by exploiting their rather peculiar status as identical twins and by connecting their name and signature style to different, and sometimes unexpected, contexts. The following sections will provide a more detailed account of their activities and how they have built their business.

Sister Act

In some way, their status as identical twin sisters who are also their own best models has served Truus and Riet Spijkers well in establishing a growth platform for their brand. Since they don their own products day in and day out, all creations are made to their own liking with the garments' proportions modelled on their own physique. Despite the fact that they do not advertise explicitly with spreads in magazines, they do actually capitalise on the presence they have as designers. As explained above, it took a fair amount of time for Dutch consumers to appreciate the brand's products. In fact, somewhat ironically it was not until the credit crunch of 2008 that the designers seriously started considering opportunities closer to their own base of operations. Two years in the making, the designers introduced a diffusion line, SIS, in 2010, which at present has eleven points of sale in the Netherlands.

SIS originally made its debut at the Amsterdam International Fashion Week as an extra pre-collection with the aim to test the firm's potential in the home market (Teunissen and Van Der Voet, 2011). Apart from creating a more accessible product, the brand expansion was aimed at exploring new possibilities and steering the brand into a different direction. The financial crisis between 2008 and 2010 had left deep marks on the sales volume abroad, with rather alarming economic drop-offs in the brand's markets in Russia and Ukraine. Lower purchasing quantities and a changing consumption

101. Spijkers en Spijkers, group photo of V-dress for beer brand Bavaria on the occasion of the UEFA European Championship (2012).

mentality meant a change of direction for the company to prevent floundering and to keep the business sustainable (personal interview; see also Teunissen and Van Der Voet, 2011: 57-58).

Rather unexpectedly, the collection became an instant commercial success with critics and buyers from the Netherlands and abroad, which made it quickly turn into a mainstay of the firm's business operations. As the designers state, SIS was the result of two developments that were happening almost simultaneously at the time. In their markets abroad consumption was becoming increasingly unpredictable, which made a transformation necessary to respond with a different type of product. In the Netherlands, meanwhile, the main collection – but also the twins as a brand in their own right – started receiving more media attention and interest in the products:

> At the time, we were getting more and more requests for affordable clothing from Dutch retailers. With our main collection it was impossible to satisfy that demand, so we introduced a 'little sister'. Originally, SIS was developed specifically for the Dutch market because we wanted to be able to also sell our products in stores closer to where we live. (Truus and Riet Spijkers in *Elle.nl*, 2010: 1, my translation)

From the initial idea to establish SIS as an exclusive line for the Dutch market, it was only a small step to extend it to other countries as well, with large parts of the production now going to Japan, Russia and the UK (Teunissen and Van Der Voet, 2011: 65).

The difference between the main collection and the commercially more viable distribution line is basically that SIS features more accessible looks and is produced in higher quantities, which in turn allows for a larger target market and lower retail prices. By turning their products into more everyday items, the designers directly responded to a shifting consumption mentality at the time. As it appears, the decision to introduce a more

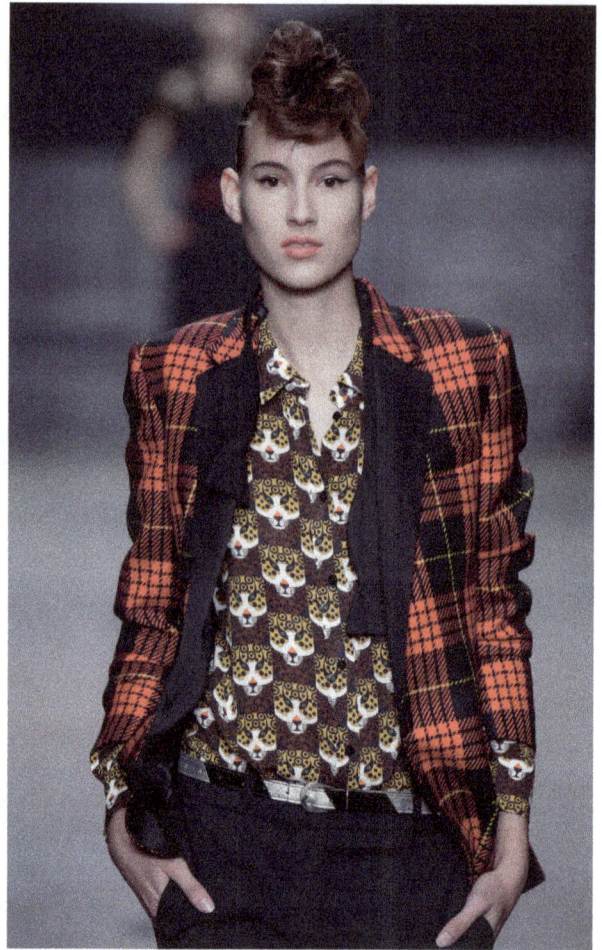

102. Spijkers en Spijkers (A/W 2016).

wearable, mainstream kind of look reflects a more general shift in pre- and post-crisis luxury consumption. According to Delpal (2014), the financial crisis basically led to a bifurcation of the market. At one end, long-time industry heavyweights like Louis Vuitton or Gucci started withdrawing several of their cheaper lines in favour of developing their portfolio towards even more expensive markets. In most cases, those endeavours went hand in hand with the introduction of a different kind of iconography in the campaigns foregrounding craftsmanship and artisanal technique. At the other end, 'accessible' luxury brands like Michael Kors and Tory Burch that fill the gap between the high-street and high-end market started gaining more and more

CONSTANTIN VON MALTZAHN

momentum by offering a luxury experience at much lower entry prices.

Driving up retail prices even further was not an option for Spijkers en Spijkers since their sales volume proved to be rather unstable already and the demand in the Netherlands was also not calling for high-ticket price ranges, but for an affordable, everyday kind of product. The introduction of SIS therefore was as much a reaction to a trend that was going on in the market at the time as it was an attempt to explore their potential in the Netherlands, serving the double purpose of creating demand in their home country and stabilising sales volume abroad.

Joining Forces

Another interesting example of how Spijkers en Spijkers has successfully advanced its business comes from a number of collaborations connecting the label's name and signature aesthetics to popular high-street firms in the Netherlands. In this case, too, the efforts allowed the designers to address a more mainstream kind of market and make their signature style available to a mass-market public. In 2009, Truus and Riet Spijkers designed a capsule collection for Dutch high-street chain Claudia Sträter, featuring fifteen styles in total, each available in a number of different colours. In 2010, this was followed by a successful series of spectacle frames (24 regular models and 10 sunglasses) called 'A Touch of the Roaring Twenties' for the Dutch branch of UK optician chain Specsavers.

Soon after, Dutch beer brand Bavaria teamed up with the duo on the occasion of the European Football Championship in 2012 to design a low-budget item for women called 'Victory Dress' (see also the Introduction).

In each of these cases, the growing popularity of the designers in the Netherlands made them interesting candidates for the joint venture, and for both parties the effort turned out to be a win-win situation. The commissioning houses took advantage of the fact that

their name became connected to a high-end fashion label, which helped add fashion cachet to the brand and product proposition. Truus and Riet Spijkers, for their part, capitalised on the media impact of these large-scale projects, which meant free advertising and further financial resources to back and develop their label. As Truus recalls: 'For us these projects have been great opportunities in the sense that they taught us to venture out and try our hands at different things. [...] For the future, we'd love to see what we could do in different creative fields. It's a great opportunity for us.'

Across these collaborations the designers have developed and adapted their brand profile to the needs and wants of a mainstream public by making the brand more accessible through offering multiple points of connection. Beyond the rather uniform appeal of high-end fashion, which tends to be attractive for many while excluding most as actual consumers, these collaborations have ensured that their move towards a more democratic type of product did not affect their kudos as high-end designers, simply by 'outsourcing' the locus of their efforts to brands other than their own.

Private Affairs

Another way in which the designers have sharpened and extended their business profile – this time by venturing further up- rather than downmarket – is by offering a bespoke service to private clients. By channelling their own aesthetics through a dialogue with clients, Truus and Riet Spijkers seek to translate the individual wishes and ideas of their consumers into custom-made pieces of clothing. As Riet says: 'We work a lot with private clients and there you get a first-hand experience of what clothes can do to a person. You see that, of course, only when you're actually one-on-one with a client.'

In a sense, this Paul Poiret-like way of working is reminiscent of the heyday of the couturier who dresses socialites in his studio rather than designing entire collections for a wider audience. Unlike their forefathers, however, for Truus and Riet Spijkers a sole reliance on private clients would not be a route worthwhile pursuing – even if it were financially viable. According to them, it is precisely the polarity between collection-based work for a larger audience and individual commissions that excites them, as it allows them to work in both broad and narrow experiential frames (personal interview).

While the collections are usually a translation of the designers' own ideas for the coming season, their bespoke work is dialogue-based and requires adaptation skills. On the one hand, the direct interaction in the workroom allows them to profit from hands-on experience and gain insight into their consumers' desires. On the other hand, the intimate setting and close contact call for sensitivity and tact to establish rapport. Perhaps fittingly for a label that has gained notoriety for its 1920s and 1930s leanings, an ideal situation for the designers would be to strike a golden mean. As Riet Spijkers confesses:

> Actually, the nicest thing is a small-scale presentation in a showroom like it used to be back in the day. Take Chanel, for example: there is Marlene Dietrich sitting on the staircase and you have a number of models, dressed in the latest collection, walking around with number boards in their hands. You know, here's your customer and it's nice and direct. I'd love to work like that.

In their capacity to bestow on the wearer a sense of self-assuredness, clothes can help define a personality in a certain way, or so the designers claim. And while their vision is not entirely free from idealism, there might be a grain of truth to it. As 34 year-old customer Lisa T. told me during an informal conversation: '[W]ell, that whole talk about empowerment I'm not so sure about, but the clothes are certainly powerful. I own a few of their dresses and when I put them on they really do something

to me.' Obviously, such statements do not have the advantage of lending themselves to deep generalisations since whatever sensation clothing may evoke will always be a highly individual and intimate affair. Nevertheless, it appears that part of Truus and Riet Spijkers' success is owed to their ability of striking a chord with their customers in devising a product that is sensual and powerful, poetic and hard-edged. In their business, it is the same sort of polarity that has allowed them to develop their brand name and create a rather diverse portfolio for a rather small operation. Switching gears between their high-end line, Spijkers en Spijkers, and SIS as a more accessible counterpart as well as entering into different kinds of collaborations at lower and mid-range mass-market level in connection with a bespoke service, the company's set-up is designed to establish multiple points of connection via alternative economic bases.

Dutch Luxury?

Earlier we saw that the Spijkers en Spijkers imprint has enjoyed great, albeit unstable, success abroad while in the Netherlands it took quite some time for the label to catch on. The firm's cheaper diffusion line, SIS, on the other hand, went to become a crowd favourite in both markets almost instantaneously. At face value this may not seem all that surprising considering that more affordable goods are usually accepted more easily by the buying public, due to a lower threshold. And yet, the apparent asymmetry between those two developments allows us to understand an important part of the Dutch fashion landscape and the predominant consumption mentality of local consumers. What is it, then, that makes selling high-end products in the Netherlands so difficult? Or, put another way, why is there hardly any market for luxury products in the Netherlands?

One explanation for the absence of a luxury-goods market in the Netherlands has indeed to do with the country's cultural leanings and historical progression. As

103, 104. A wink to Dutch heritage: a dress with prints of seventeenth-century ships, after the style of Delft Blue earthenware. SIS by Spijkers en Spijkers (S/S 2011).

Jacobs (2011c) argues, Holland has no actual foothold in the high-end sector partly because of its Calvinistic heritage. During the Golden Age, moderation was stylised as a cultural virtue with the result that the Dutch, despite their wealth, decried pomp and splendour in favour of a more unassuming take on material possessions – at least those visible to the outside world. In his book *The Embarrassment of Riches* (1988) British cultural historian Simon Schama takes a similar stance. With Dutch trade, art, science and military propelling the country to the highest global rungs at the time, the Dutch found themselves in a perplexing situation: with a population of only a million and hardly any paupers among them, wealth had become an almost uncomfortable cultural condition. Dutch citizens were attacked and threatened by the country's moral institutions until a compromise was found: being rich as though you were not. Schama traces this moral predicament with an analysis of Golden-Age still lifes. Vermeer's paintings show hats made from Canadian beaver fur and expensive Oriental rugs and tapestries – obvious markers of wealth and affluence. These, however, the artist often paired with vanitas motifs of death and decay as if to suggest moral turpitude hidden behind those pleasures. The basic rationale, although surely extenuated, prevails to this day: showiness – be it in clothes or architecture or interiors or art – is not very much *en vogue* in the Netherlands.

Another more prosaic explanation has to do with the rather egalitarian socio-cultural climate in the Netherlands, which, along with a wider array of cultural ramifications, also pertains to income distribution. The Netherlands is a largely middle-class-driven society with relative socio-economic wellbeing distributed among a large number of people. According to the International Monetary Fund (2014), the Netherlands ranks sixth in the European nations, with the highest purchasing power parity per capita (PPP), after Luxembourg, Norway, Switzerland, San Marino and Austria. In other words, the country's (relatively) high gross domestic product goes together with a fairly democratic income distribution. One effect produced by the rather high average amount of discretionary money in the Netherlands is that the country has a well-established and economically strong middle market. Unsurprisingly perhaps, the demand for luxury products is somewhat lower because the super-high income groups are fewer as well (Jacobs, 2011b: 122). Conversely, in markets abroad, notably the moneyed nations of the Far and Middle East, we can observe an inverse development. On a global scale, Qatar or Brunei rank in the top five of countries with the highest gross domestic product per capita. In this case, however, the figures are partly produced by the high density of the super-rich rather than a democratic overall income distribution.

In light of these figures it is probably not altogether surprising that the Spijkers en Spijkers brand has fared much better in markets with a higher density of extremely affluent consumers, because the scope of spend-active consumption is of a different calibre. Fittingly, Truus and Riet Spijkers make a distinction between their markets in countries from the Middle East and those in Europe, stating that motivations and consumption behaviour are subject to quite different premises. As they say, in a place like Dubai people will purchase a product 'just because they like it', whereas in Europe luxury shopping is often connected to occasion-specific purchases. International differences aside, even within Europe the spending activity on luxury goods is distributed rather unevenly: in Italy the annual expenditure on luxury goods was 16.6 billion euros in 2011, while in France it was 12.6 billion and in Germany 8 billion (Altagamma, 2011: 5). Compared to that, the Dutch luxury sector has perhaps grown during the past couple of years, but it remains a gradual (and rather slow) shift that is connected to a changing consumption mentality over time.

Coming back to the difference in leverage in the Netherlands between the Spijkers en Spijkers mainline and SIS, both of the above factors explain part of the rather hesitant uptake on high-ticket products in the Netherlands. While Queen Máxima has been spotted in their designs on more than one official occasion, the Dutch in general are rather casual in choosing their wardrobe: garments need to be comfortable and travel across a variety of contexts. You need to be able to go to work by bike, do groceries afterwards at a local street market, and go directly from there to have dinner with friends (Von Maltzahn, 2013). The reason the label never picked up steam as much as it did abroad is mainly due to the fact that most Dutch consumers are not willing to spend large amounts of money on a garment that can only be worn for special occasions and requires intensive care. A dress or jumpsuit, entirely made out of delicate silk, as are regularly featured in a Spijkers en Spijkers collection, is simply at odds with the day-to-day requirements of the local audience. As Chananja Baars, manager of the Arnhem-based concept store Arnhem Coming Soon, says:[2] '[T]he clothes are difficult to sell, actually. Here in the Netherlands it's not so easy to find consumers for this type of clothing. It's not practical – and expensive. That combination ... doesn't sit too well with the local audience.'

Spijkers en Spijkers: Dutch Fashion Between the Chairs

In the previous section we established that much of the structural set-up of the local fashion industry, and hence consumer demand, is directly or indirectly connected to national history and a number of socio-economic currents. If we take that knowledge one step further, where and how can we place Spijkers en Spijkers in the Dutch fashion market?

If we look at the Dutch fashion narrative more generally, it appears that much of the country's design and fashion identity used to be viewed mainly in conceptualist terms, or as a continuation of the country's modernist heritage, as explained in chapter 2 (see also Teunissen and Van Zijl, 2000; Feitsma, 2011). More recent research, however, suggests that there are at least two 'fashion identities' (Feitsma, 2011; Jacobs, 2010; Jacobs, 2011a). The first kind is indeed very much steeped in tradition and takes recourse to the country's past in modernist design, painting and architecture (Teunissen and Van Zijl, 2000). At the other end of the spectrum, however, we find a style of fashion that is defined by colour, pattern and playfulness – characteristics that date back to the times of Dutch folklore and traditional local dress (Feitsma, 2011). According to Jacobs (2010: 20), the former can be found mostly in the upper-middle and high segment, while the latter is mainly connected to the more popular ranges of the fashion market.

The work of Truus and Riet Spijkers takes its cues from both realms, merges them, and gives a new twist to it all. Many of their products are inspired by modernist aesthetics on the one hand, especially when it comes to graphic composition, make use of patterns and fields of colour. On the other hand, the vibrancy and edgy appearance of the collections is mainly driven by the way the Dutch fashion narrative is inflected by various cultural influences. Merging elements of both traditions into a new whole, the garments resume conceptualist roots in terms of proportion and graphic composition, while a predilection for animal prints and metallic tones, for instance, evidences a more playful and experimental stance. Put another way, much of the clothing is about achieving a balance between two poles: symmetry and asymmetry, colourful and colourless, exposed and hidden, patterns and planes.

In a country like Italy, for instance, we find a clear opposition between companies catering to either end of the spectrum. At one end there are brands such as Armani or Prada, whose trademark style is sleek, pared down and somewhat technical. At the other end, houses such as Versace, Cavalli or Dolce e Gabbana are known for a classy yet aggressive and erotically charged type of fashion. In general, the former reflect the kind of understatement and austerity we also find with many Dutch upmarket fashion labels like orson+bodil, Saskia van Drimmelen or Marcha Hüskes. Reflecting the lascivious panache of the latter, however, we find designers like Bas Kosters whose work is a smorgasbord of colour, pattern and frivolous exuberance. In a manner of speaking, the work of Truus and Riet Spijkers occupies a space that combines these two extremes. The brand is typically Dutch in the sense that it blurs the boundaries between reprised conceptualism and playfulness, graphic composition and edgy looks: it juggles with different disciplines and aesthetic repertoires and merges them into a new whole.

Conclusion

For Spijkers en Spijkers the journey has been anything but predetermined in business terms. In fact, with a miniscule team operating out of Arnhem in the east of the Netherlands, with no ritzy advertising campaigns and no major financial backing to allow for a great deal of entrepreneurial freedom, much of the firm's journey has been tacit manoeuvring by responding to signals from the market. Rather than riding the branding wave, Truus

and Riet Spijkers have made their own face and signature style the figurehead of the company. As this chapter has demonstrated, the firm's 'marketing approach' is implicit and primarily product-based.

Brand awareness is created through a number of strategies that, on the face of it, might seem only remotely related to putting the consumer front and centre. On closer inspection, however, it has been shown that the different ventures the firm has been tied in with are in fact tacit ways of integrating consumer and market needs into the brand proposition. When there was demand for a different, more affordable type of product, SIS was created as a more accessible alternative in the designers' trademark style. The moment Truus and Riet Spijkers understood that their own media profile was a marketing tool in its own right, they put themselves more into the limelight and started connecting their name to well-known high-street brands. The same is true for their fashion designs. On the one hand, these are resolutely built around what the two sisters call 'high design'. On the other hand, they take wearability into consideration and develop their collections to be smart and versatile. The designs are creative with an eye on the market; exclusive, but not out of reach; conceptual in approach, yet playful in appearance. In short, Spijkers en Spijkers is many things at the same time – and perhaps it is precisely that eclectic quality that makes it typically Dutch.

Notes

1. All interviews were recorded digitally with permission of the interviewees, transcribed and analysed based on a clustering method after Mayring (2000). For a detailed methodology, please refer to my doctoral dissertation (Von Maltzahn, 2013). Unless noted otherwise, all direct quotes of Truus and Riet Spijkers are taken from an interview conducted in the summer of 2011 as well as a number of more informal conversations.

2. Arnhem Coming Soon used to own three stores in the Netherlands retailing the Spijkers en Spijkers mainline. With the introduction of SIS, however, the store's management decided to focus on the commercially more viable diffusion line and eliminate Spijkers en Spijkers from its selection of products.

Alexander van Slobbe (b. Schiedam 1959)

Lianne Toussaint

Fashion is the here and now, while I design
from a specific mentality.

—orson + bodil (2013)

Alexander van Slobbe regards himself as a designer
who never belonged to the world of fashion. Putting
quality and skilful craftsmanship centre stage, his work
stands for a modest and 'everyday' luxury that defies
the whims of a volatile and industrialised fashion
industry. Labelled as one of the pioneers of 'Dutch
Modernism' in fashion (see chapter 2), van Slobbe
founded the exclusive womenswear line Orson & Bodil
together with Nannet van der Kleijn in 1988. The small-
scale label set the stage for the timeless, restrained
and minimalist design style that still characterises van
Slobbe's work today. Back then, Orson & Bodil was not
even considered to be 'real fashion': once embraced
by the fashion world, it became fashion. The mostly
handmade, relatively simple and high quality designs
soon attracted a select group of loyal customers and
the label increasingly gained recognition. While Orson
& Bodil still ran on subsidies and failed to arouse the
interest of investors, van Slobbe's men's label SO soon
started to demand his full attention (Van den Berg,
2006: 196).

Changing from local to global, handmade to
industrial, and small-scale to large-scale, SO was
in many ways the opposite to Orson & Bodil. With
its groundbreaking combination of sporty and
classic, represented in famous designs like the
pinstriped jogging bottoms, SO almost instantly
became a huge international success and one of
the best-selling designer labels worldwide. After
ten years of travelling back and forth between the
Netherlands and Asia, however, van Slobbe decided
it was time to go back to basics. He took the radical

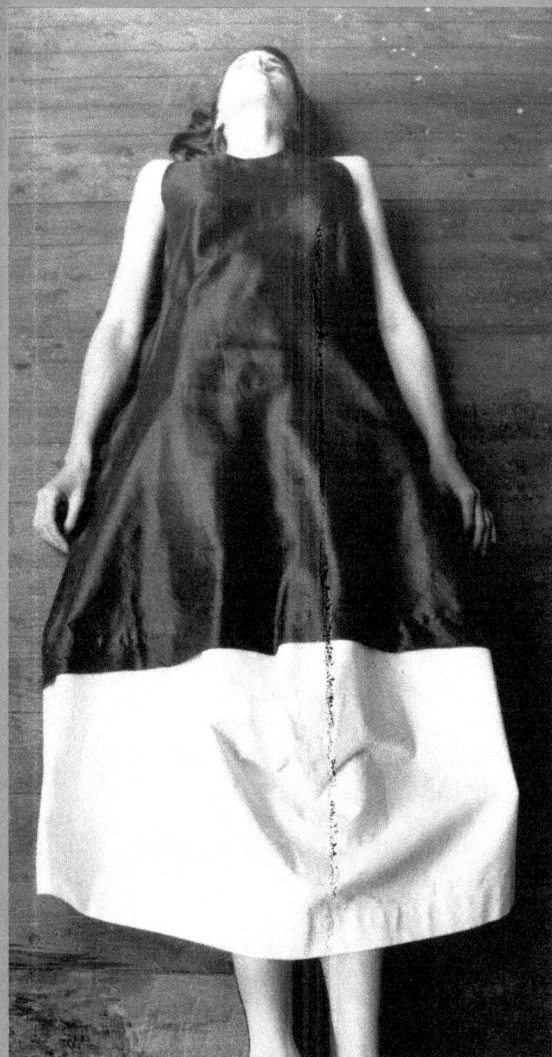

105. Orson & Bodil (1993).

106. SO by Alexander van Slobbe (1999).

107. orson + bodil, 'Dress' (S/S 2010).

decision to sell SO to Japanese investors. Happy to refocus on the actual design process, he revitalised orson + bodil – now written with a plus sign – and opened an exclusive concept store in Amsterdam. Meanwhile, he continued to broaden his horizon with numerous special collaborations. His strong belief in the mixing of sport and couture resulted in a shoe collection for sports giant Puma (Ibid.). Several special collaborations led to the design of big porcelain 'pearls' for renowned Dutch ceramics company Royal Tichelaar Makkum (see fig. 16) and, more recently, the new staff uniforms for the restored Rijksmuseum in Amsterdam.

Another milestone in van Slobbe's career was the Fashion stipend of the Prins Bernhard Cultuurfonds in 2003. Being the first fashion designer to receive the highly esteemed prize, van Slobbe proudly considered it a breakthrough for Dutch fashion (Lampe, 2005: 2). Yet when the prize money ran out and the economic crisis hit, he had to exchange his expensive workspace in Amsterdam for a modest 1960s house in a small and drowsy village in the north of Holland. Though his company is now smaller than ever, van Slobbe is content with the way things are: 'It has always been about designing for me. I could continue like this until I'm eighty' (quoted in Van Rossum, 2013: 13). This loving devotion to the design process is also what drove van Slobbe to recently join forces with Francisco van Benthum (see profile in chapter 6) in establishing VAN SLOBBE VAN BENTHUM; a small-scale label using the remnants of the fast-fashion industry to counter the hegemony of the big fashion chains.

Novel
Perspectives

III

12.

Dutch Fashion Photography:
Liquid Bodies and
Fluid Faces

'Identities are more like the spots of crust hardening time and
again on the top of volcanic lava which melt and dissolve again
before they have time to cool and set.'

—Zygmunt Bauman (2000: 83)

Daniëlle Bruggeman

Introduction

Black leather jackets, white or striped T-shirts, skinny jeans and hair styled to create the perfect messy out-of-bed look. These are characteristics of the 'French touch boys' (fig. 108), one of the many social groups photographed by Dutch photographer Ari Versluis and stylist Ellie Uyttenbroek for their project *Exactitudes*.[1] Versluis and Uyttenbroek are known for the special way in which they have systematically documented numerous social identities since 1994, always photographing twelve persons against a white background and arranging them on one page by four rows of three models. Random people they encountered on the streets of various cities are categorised into many different social groups with shared dress codes and characteristics of their appearances, which is emphasised by their similar poses. In addition to the French touch boys, Versluis and Uyttenbroek categorised, for example, madams, homeboys, skaters, hipsters and hundreds more social groups. *Exactitudes* visualises the power of the fashion system to label and construct subcultural groups, simultaneously codifying identities. The sartorial surfaces that 'fashion' our human bodies can thus shape codified, seemingly static and fixed social group identities.

Yet, as I will argue, the material objects of fashion simultaneously allow for a creative play with individuality, experimenting with identity as a fluid and flexible dimension. Fashion photography can serve as a mirror of these socio-cultural dynamics in contemporary consumer culture. In contrast to *Exactitudes*, which demonstrates how clothing can fix identity, there are numerous fashion photographers who focus first and foremost on the inherently *dynamic* nature of identity. These photographers often move between experimental and commercial work and regularly create alienating imageries of 'fashioned' bodies. For example, in her artistic photograph 'Sasja 90-60-90' (1992) renowned Dutch photographer Inez Van Lamsweerde presents a model dressed in a bikini with a so-called perfect body and with the ideal bust, waist and hip measurements of 90-60-90 centimetres (fig. 109). However, by using digital technologies her head has been turned 180 degrees, with the front facing backwards.

In this sense Van Lamsweerde illustrates as well as criticises most fashion photography, that 'in following the suggestion of the fashion industry about the latest figure, measurements and proportions, declares a new beauty each season; a beauty that is fugitive, ephemeral and insubstantial, yet exerts a powerful hold on corporeal ideals' (Lehmann, 2002: 14). While undermining the idealised body and pointing out the ephemerality of these concepts of beauty by subverting them, Van Lamsweerde also challenges normative conceptions regarding the body. She explores and transgresses the boundaries of the body by liberating certain body parts from their predetermined position, embracing the freedom of the virtual realm of photography to re-imagine what a body is. Van Lamsweerde's artistic imagery represents a trend among contemporary fashion photographers who are set free by digital technologies from the limitations imposed by the corporeal body or biological realities (De Perthuis, 2008: 172).

Fashion photography has gained significance in the fashion system as well as in contemporary culture (Lehmann, 2002; Shinkle, 2008). Rather than merely representing clothes with the main objective of selling them, fashion photography 'is increasingly treated on a par with contemporary works of art; where it is consumed like autonomous art objects' (Lehmann, 2002: 12). The current proximity of fashion photography to contemporary art allows photographers to experiment with bodies and identities in an artistic sense, regularly resulting in imagery that is all the more thought-provoking. Moreover, as Karen De Perthuis argues in her exploration of digital fashion photography, the idea of endless possibilities – inherent in digital manipulation – 'is applied to the human body, which is treated as if it is made from the same material as clothing and can henceforth be cut, shaped, pasted and stitched in

108. *Exactitudes*, Ari Versluis & Ellie Uyttenbroek: 'French Touch Boys' (2006).

any imaginable way' (De Perthuis, 2008: 176). Digital post-production thus turns fashion photography into a fictional realm, offering infinite possibilities to play with the body as a fashion object.

In this chapter I focus on a selection of Dutch fashion photographers whose editorial and artistic work regularly questions, subverts and mobilises dominant representations of men and women, transgressing boundaries and transforming bodies and identities.[2] The Netherlands has a strong tradition in photography and also in fashion photography, with many renowned names operating internationally, such as Inez Van Lamsweerde and Vinoodh Matadin, Anton Corbijn, Erwin Olaf, Freudenthal/Verhagen, Viviane Sassen, and Anuschka Blommers and Niels Schumm. These photographers have often presented their work in Dutch magazines such as *Avenue, Dutch, Fantastic Man, Blvd.* and *Blend*, and are closely linked to Dutch fashion culture and to the rise of Dutch fashion (Teunissen, 2015: 6-14; see also Bruggeman, 2015). Fashion photography offers an interesting perspective on fashion in relation to identity, because it is in the imaginary, virtual, representational realm of fashion that photographers often have the artistic freedom to visualise certain dynamics that otherwise remain invisible in daily life on the actual, material level of dressed bodies. Moreover, due to the use of digital technologies in representations it is possible to visually experiment with bodies and identities far beyond what is possible in daily life.

My analyses of Dutch fashion photography point to a paradoxical double dynamics of identity. On the one hand, fashion images regularly categorise, label and commodify individuals, suggesting that we can purchase this kind of appearance and identity, and selling the idea 'that we are what we wear' (Bauman, 2000: 74). On the other hand, contemporary fashion photographers often play with the flexibility of (clothed) bodies and identities. As Anneke Smelik argues in the Introduction, identity is increasingly understood as a flexible, fluid or 'liquid'

dimension that can be shaped through fashion's material objects (see Bauman, 2000; Lipovetsky, 2005). The idea that identity is 'under construction' and that clothes contribute to that lifelong process confirms that identity is, at least to a certain extent, not predetermined, static and fixed, but rather mouldable, variable and fluid. These identity dynamics clearly find expression in fashion (Bauman, 2011: 22-25). In this chapter Dutch fashion photography serves as a magnifying glass to illuminate identity dynamics in the field of fashion, shedding light on the ways in which fashion as an imaginary realm produces a fluidity of identity.

In the first part of the chapter I elaborate on the project *Exactitudes* by the Dutch duo Ari Versluis and Ellie Uyttenbroek. In the second part I discuss the work of fashion photographers Inez Van Lamsweerde, Edland Man, Erwin Olaf, Marcel Van Der Vlugt and Bart Hess, who all experiment, albeit in different ways, with the fluidity of identity in relation to the (clothed) body.

109. Inez Van Lamsweerde, 'Sasja 90-60-90' (1992).

Momentary Fixations

For their project *Exactitudes* Versluis and Uyttenbroek categorised hundreds of social group identities, such as goths, skates, punks or hipsters. These photographic series visually epitomise Georg Simmel's argument that fashion entails two contradictory social tendencies: the need for union through imitation on the one hand, and the desire for isolation through individual differentiation on the other (1957: 543-44); or in other words, the desire to belong while striving for individuality. 'This artwork of typology', as Anneke Smelik argues, 'makes us realise that there is very little originality in dressing: rather than being a distinctive individual we are part of a social group or fashion tribe' (2011: 77), which points to the paradoxical relationship between individual and group identities. In *The Times of the Tribes* (1996) Michel Maffesoli discusses these paradoxical dynamics in his post-modernist analysis of the 'interplay between the growing massification and the development of micro-groups', which he calls 'neo-tribes' (1996: 6). He asserts that these tribes characterise sociality at the end of the twentieth century, as they are 'preferably [...] expressed through lifestyles that favour appearance and form' (Maffesoli, 1996: 98). It is thus through one's outer appearance that tribes, social groups, are formed and express themselves. Fashion plays an important role in relation to these identity dynamics.

Exactitudes illustrates the way in which specific identities may be '"caught", frozen, temporally fixed by fashion' (Entwistle, 2000: 32). Fashion, as a system, is a realm of standards, ideal forms, codes and meanings. These dominant codes, circulating in the fashion system, contribute to the coming-into-being of certain codified identities. This is clearly exemplified by certain subcultural groups, such as goths, skaters and punks, who perform already codified identities by wearing certain clothes and adopting a specific outer appearance. As Joanne Finkelstein argues,

Fashion provides a shortcut by which we can adopt an identity and join a subculture that in turn can variously insulate us from others or promote our social stakes. [...] Fashion segments the social world, it localizes social groups by tastes and possessions, it transforms identity into a material commodity. (2007: 211)

From this perspective one can argue that *Exactitudes* shows how the fashion system functions as a 'supermarket of identities', from which one can select an identity (Bauman, 2000: 83). Yet, the idea of adopting an identity as a material commodity might falsely suggest that fashion can affect every aspect of identity or each facet of the self, or that one can completely change identity by simply changing clothes. Therefore, I prefer to use a more nuanced notion of identity, as something that consists of numerous socially formed concepts of who we (or others) are, for example: 'I am a woman', 'I am Dutch', or 'I am stylish'.[3] As *Exactitudes* shows, numerous different concepts can potentially be created, and clothing has a great impact on the performative communication as well as the formation of these concepts. In addition, *Exactitudes* illustrates that these concepts are always defined in relation to other people and other concepts.

Material objects of fashion may thus help to create, frame, fix and express specific identity concepts. For instance, the concept 'I am a goth' may be materialised and simultaneously produced by means of clothes, which reinforces one's concept of oneself as well as the concepts others have of this particular person. It is important to emphasise that dressing obviously pertains to only *one* concept of self. Someone's identity is much more complex, consisting of numerous different concepts, some of which are more stable, and some more variable and fluid. The identity of a goth is undeniably formed by a wide variety of different factors, of which clothing is only one – yet overtly visible – element. Yet, in the case of *Exactitudes*, clothes shape and visually signify

DANIËLLE BRUGGEMAN

110. *Exactitudes*, Ari Versluis & Ellie Uyttenbroek, 'Ghoullies'(2002).

one particular concept, which reduces identity to merely one visible codified concept. This reduction of identity is accentuated by the similar poses and age groups, and by neutral, white backgrounds providing no environmental context. *Exactitudes* thus demonstrates how the socio-cultural system of fashion operates: codifying social groups based on shared dress codes, deliberately reducing the complexity of identity to mere fixed concepts.

While showing the way in which fashion objects may frame and create specific identity concepts, I want to argue that *Exactitudes* simultaneously confirms the fluid dimension of these concepts: it is precisely *because* of an underlying fluidity of specific identity concepts that clothing has the power to shape these concepts. Specific concepts – especially the ones that are easily affected by the material objects of fashion – follow the identity dynamics described poetically by Bauman, which I used as a motto for this chapter: 'identities are more like the spots of crust hardening time and again on the top of volcanic lava which melt and dissolve again before they have time to cool and set' (2000: 83). Whereas some identity concepts have set more than others and one can obviously choose to hold on to certain concepts and thus let these concepts harden, I want to point out the momentary status of concepts that can be shaped through clothes. The role that age may play in the formation of specific identity concepts demonstrates the ephemerality of particular concepts. For example, it is rare for people in their forties and fifties to continue dressing up as goths – which confirms the temporary status of concepts such as 'I am a goth', while other concepts may remain stable. As *Exactitudes* shows, clothing – when it is used to shape and express identity concepts – can be viewed as the temporary materialised form of numerous possible fluid concepts.

In addition to this momentary status of certain formed concepts, it is important to think in terms of *semi*-fixed concepts. In my view these identity concepts are even more fluid than they seem at first sight. When

taking a closer look at the categorisations of specific concepts visualised in *Exactitudes,* we see numerous minor differences between different people within these social groups. For instance, within the category 'Ghoullies' – who look somewhat comparable to goths – we can distinguish a wide variety of corsets, gloves, accessories, jewellery, or hairstyles (fig. 110).

Even when choosing to express a particular recognisable 'fixed' identity concept, individuals tend to make minor changes or play with certain codes in order to differentiate themselves, which is, again, an illustration of the contradictory social tendencies that Simmel describes (1957: 543-44). Moreover, this emphasises the fluidity *within* seemingly 'fixed' concepts. Bauman's analyses of the cultural dynamics of identity help to explain this illusionary coherence and fixity of different concepts of the self and of others:

'Seen from a distance, [people's] existence seems to possess a coherence and a unity which they cannot have, in reality, but which seems evident to the spectator.' [Camus, 1971: 226-27] This, of course, is an optical illusion. The distance (that is, the paucity of our knowledge) blurs the details and effaces everything that fits ill into the *Gestalt*. [...] We struggle to deny or at least to cover up the awesome fluidity just below the thin wrapping of the form [...]. Identities seem fixed and solid only when seen, in a flash, from outside. (Bauman, 2000: 82-83)

The fixity of identity, or in this case rather the fixity of a particular concept expressed and created by means of clothes, is thus an optical illusion as well as a sign of the desire for stability, solidity and a coherent self. While *Exactitudes*' categorised identities seem rather fixed from a distance, there are numerous minor differences at the micro-level of details, indicating the intrinsic fluidity of these concepts. Even the boundaries of these concepts are rather porous in some cases: when are you a ghoully, when a goth? In addition, as such categorisations may develop over time, or may differ from country to country, these framed social groups are relatively variable. Yet, while implicitly revealing the flexibility of certain concepts, *Exactitudes* nevertheless primarily visualises the ways in which the fashion system produces semi-fixed and codified identity concepts, which may be materialised and performed through material objects of fashion.

Fluid Bodies and Identity Concepts

Transforming Bodies

Whereas *Exactitudes* shows how clothing can fix and solidify identity concepts, I will now elaborate on the work of fashion photographers who explore the inherently *dynamic* nature of identity – even though they employ different strategies to do so. I will first continue to discuss the photography of Inez Van Lamsweerde, who, with her partner Vinoodh Matadin, works for international brands such as Dior, Gucci and the Dutch designer duo Viktor&Rolf. As we have seen in the introduction to this chapter, Van Lamsweerde's early artistic work in the 1990s revealed her desire to play with the boundaries of the body as well as the boundaries of identity – questioning and subverting dominant commercial representations of idealised subjects. She was one of the first Dutch fashion photographers who used digital technologies to criticise, for instance, the myth of female beauty in western culture (Smelik, 2004: 299). Whereas she contributes to the construction of the image of ideal bodies and subjects in her commercial work, she critically assesses these idealised imageries in her artistic photography. As argued above, 'Sasja 90-60-90' shows that the virtual and imaginary realm of fashion offers the opportunity to play with the idea that 'the body is a cultural construct rather than a natural entity that is fixed and immutable' (Negrin, 2008: 83). This image exemplifies the ways in which the body

in fashion photography is often 'underwritten by the idea of metamorphoses. In other words, it contains the possibility, inherent to fashion, of reinventing itself in a constantly changing form.' (De Perthuis, 2008: 174). The body plays a crucial role in fashion photography, and is especially relevant in relation to the constantly changing dynamics of fashion and the creation of identities.

In an even more radical way, Van Lamsweerde experiments with the body in her series 'Thank you Thighmaster' (1993). In this series Van Lamsweerde displays women whose genitalia have been removed by using digital technologies and while they still have breasts, they no longer have nipples (fig. 111).

Their bodies have an unnatural metallic gloss, which make them look quite artificial and plastic. By so doing, Van Lamsweerde highlights and criticises the artificiality of contemporary unattainable standards of beauty that people try to meet by, for instance, using exercise products such as the Thighmaster. Furthermore, digital technologies have made these bodies sexless, almost beyond humanity, creating an image in which human and machine are merged (Smelik, 2004: 299). As we can sometimes see the veins in hands and feet, there is a clash between the humanity and the artificiality of these bodies. Here, as Anneke Smelik (2012) argues, Van Lamsweerde presents the image of a cyborg (cybernetic organism) – 'a hybrid of machine and organism' (Haraway, 1991: 149) – which moves in between human and machine, biology and technology, real and artificial, and thus blurs and transgresses the porous boundaries of these categorical distinctions (Smelik, 2012: 183). As cultural images of cyborgs move in between these binary oppositions, they mobilise certain fixed categorisations of the self, opening up opportunities to play with what the body is, or what human beings are. Dutch photographers Anuschka Blommers and Niels Schumm view the artificial images of sexless 'posthuman beings' in fashion photography as an expression of the 'prevailing fear of the gradual loss of identity in a society that seemed to have come adrift and in which nothing was what it seemed' (2007: 96). In a more positive sense, these imageries explore a dynamic state of the self, which could be understood as 'new model for a liberated conception of the self' (Negrin, 2008: 83). From this perspective, 'Thank you Thighmaster' can be read as a visual exploration of the fluidity of the concept of the self as a natural organism, or of the concept of a woman in a visual culture that emphasises female beauty ideals.

It is important to emphasise that here, in her artistic work, Van Lamsweerde is playing with the naked, undressed body in contrast to the crucial role that clothes play in her commercial fashion photography. Ulrich Lehmann argues that the body in fashion photography often disappears behind a complex system of signification of fashion, which makes it a non-body, devoid of sex, bearing no relation to the sensual body (2002: 13-14). Along these lines, Van Lamsweerde's representation of highly artificial sexless bodies may be understood as an implicit reflection on the vital part that clothes – with numerous symbolic codes and meanings attached – play in the subjectification, or even sexualisation of the human body. As Lehmann continues, 'the body in its "natural" (i.e., naked) state is asexual in fashion photography; only through the addition of commodified fashion does the body obtain sexuality within the image' (2002: 14). It is this asexuality of the body – before being dressed and commodified – in fashion photography that Van Lamsweerde highlights, while pointing out the artificiality of that asexuality at the same time. By doing so, it is implicitly suggested that the body is subjectified, given meaning, a sexuality or an identity through clothes – while (concepts of) the naked, undressed bodies in 'Thank you Thighmaster' find themselves in a more fluid state of becoming cyborgs.

Such photography confirms the inherently dynamic nature of certain identity concepts – even those regarding the body – while suggesting that clothing may

solidify these fluid concepts. Especially in her artistic work Van Lamsweerde has experimented with different ways of transforming bodies, to transgress seemingly static imageries and ideal subjects, visually playing with the fluidity of concepts of the body.

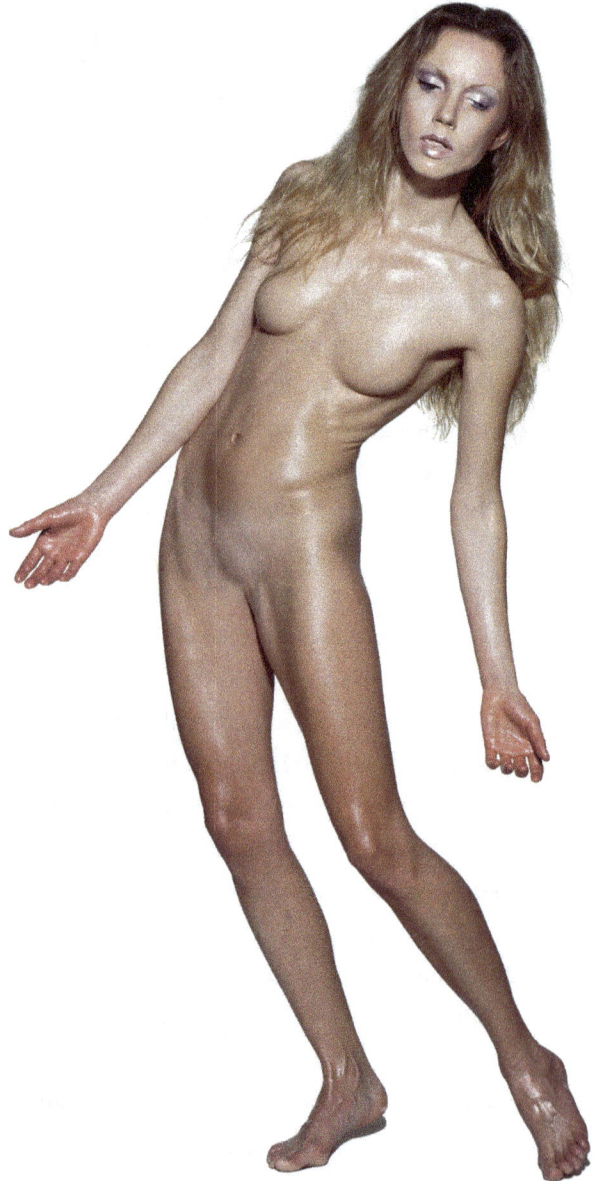

111. Inez Van Lamsweerde, 'Thank you Thighmaster' (1993).

112. Edland Man, 'Metals 5' (2002).

Liquid Bodies and Fluid Faces

Some fashion photographers play with liquidity and fluidity in quite a literal sense. In his artistic work, Dutch fashion photographer Edland Man, who has worked for renowned magazines such as *Vanity* and Italian *Vogue*, uses the possibilities of digital technologies to literally visualise a certain liquidity of our bodies.

In his artistic photographic series 'Metals' (2002) and 'Liquids' (2011) he offers a peek into the fluid substances inside bodies. Although these are different photographic series, the bodies are visualised in similar ways. It is remarkable that we see the bodies of both a black woman in 'Metals' and (at least the suggestion of) a white woman in 'Liquids', consisting of similar fluid substances. As we see the ethnic identity of the black woman dissolve into liquidity (fig. 112), it is suggested that

humans are all made up of a comparable 'fundamental' fluidity irrespective of, for instance, ethnic background or skin colour. An important part of the woman's body finds itself in a state of formlessness. Only her face, which is often taken as emblematic of our self-identity in Western culture (Negrin, 2008: 87; Deleuze and Guattari, 1987 [1980]: 167-91), still reveals her ethnic identity. This photograph shows fluidity differently: rather than presenting the body as something that can easily change shape, the image visualises an intrinsic liquid substance *within* the body, as if it is a human-shaped glass form filled with water. In one of the images in 'Liquids' we see a similar human form with a naked upper body and white trousers that presumably have just been taken off, thus dressing a part of the body below the buttocks. The undressing of the body reveals the complex mechanism and the intrinsic fluid dimension of the body, which is usually covered by clothes. By literally playing with and visualising the fluidity inside bodies, Edland Man liberates these bodies from fashion, and thus from certain fixed codes, labels and identity concepts.

In a similar vein, Dutch photographer Erwin Olaf explores the liquidity of the body in his editorial series 'New York Times Couture' (2006), published in the *New York Times Magazine*. Whereas in Edland Man's photography we can still see the contours of the bodies, Erwin Olaf lets different body parts of the models melt and dissolve into, for instance, a stone floor or staircase. He thus renders certain 'solid' materials fluid – the substance of the body, the material of the floor – playing with the flexibility of certain fundamentals of our being. The contours of some body parts become blurred, fluid, and can barely be discerned from the walls or floors they dissolve into.

The models wear dresses by famous designer brands such as Chanel, Lacroix, Versace or Valentino. Remarkably, in several images in this series, it is primarily the models' heads and faces that fuse with the walls or floors. For instance, in the photo with the dress by Versace, the stone floor is making a wave-like motion with the model's face as its epicentre (fig. 113). In the photo presenting garments by Chanel, the model's head is about to be absorbed into the swirling movement of the wall.

This play with the fluidity of the face is crucial. Drawing upon the work of Gilles Deleuze and Félix Guattari, Llewellyn Negrin argues that 'in our culture, the face is deemed the most precious characteristic of human identity and therefore enjoys a privileged status to the rest of the body. It becomes the site of signification and subjectification' (2008: 87). By liquefying faces and letting them dissolve into certain walls and floors, Olaf breaks with the face as the centre of signification, and hence with certain meanings and codes inscribed into the face. The bodies in these photographs are moving towards 'the realms of the asignifying, asubjective, and faceless' (Deleuze and Guattari, 1987: 187; Bruggeman, 2009: 6). We see part of the models' bodies literally disappear 'behind the fashions that adorn and conceal it' (Lehmann, 2002: 14), which could be an expression of the depersonification of the models that 'allows the clothing to become the body' (Khan, 2000: 125). While bodies become liquid and faces become fluid, the couture dresses stand out by themselves and function as sartorial signifying 'sur-faces'.[4]

Since the face plays an important part in the codification of identity, I want to briefly draw attention to a few photographic series by Marcel van der Vlugt in which he dresses faces with different kinds of materials. Especially, his artistic photographic series 'I like ...' (2002) and 'Hoshii' (2004) are noteworthy in relation to the face. In this series, the faces of the models with different ethnicities are dressed with a wide variety of materials, such as miso, cheese, or coffee.

Such a visualisation raises questions about the ways in which adorned and dressed faces – using dress in its broadest sense – refer to certain ethnic identities. For instance, in one image of the series 'Hoshii' (fig. 114), the face of an Asian woman is covered with dark brown seasoning, miso, which changes the shape of her face and causes it to resemble that of an African woman. Yet, as she is still recognisable as an Asian woman because of her eyes, we observe an almost alienating combination of different visualised identity concepts as specific ethnicities are mixed up.

In such artwork we encounter fluid faces in the sense that they can easily change shape (Bauman, 2000: 1-2) through the addition of different kinds of materials. Whereas clothes can solidify specific identity concepts, certain materials dressing the body also enable concepts relating to, for instance, ethnicity to be played around with. In another image from 'I like ...', a white woman's face is covered with a slice of cheese

113. Erwin Olaf, '*New York Times* Couture: Versace' (2006).

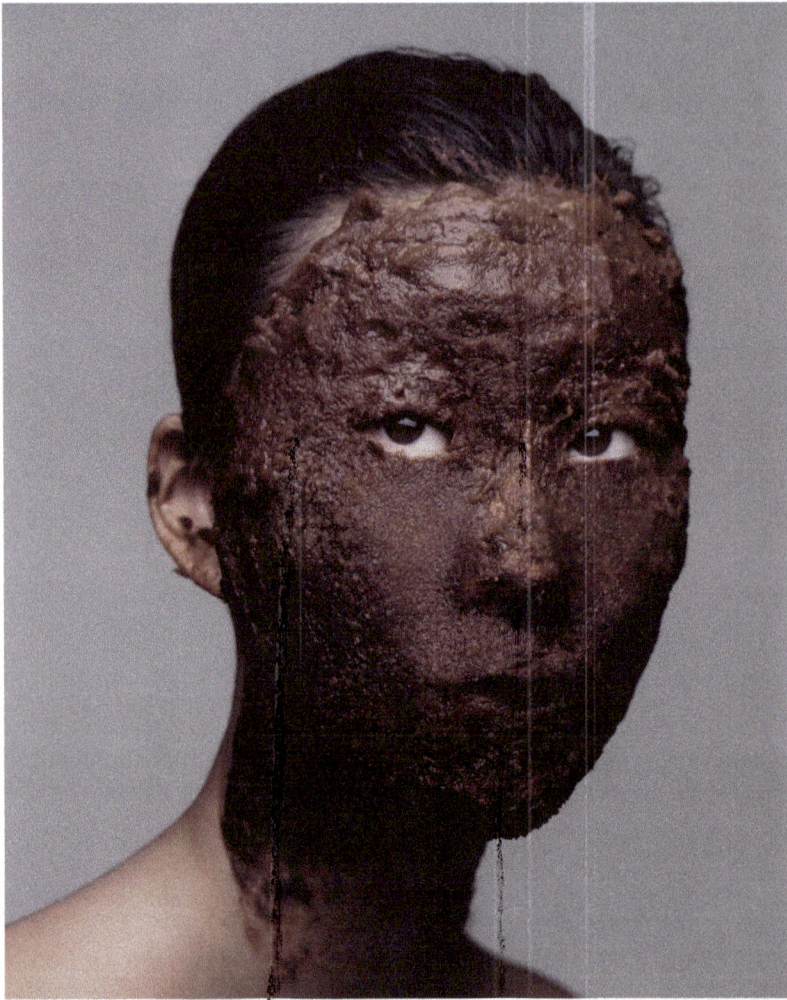

114. Marcel van der Vlugt, 'Miso' (2004) from the series 'Hoshii'.

– often conceived of as a typical element of Dutch national culture – in such a way that it resembles part of an Islamic niqab, a cloth covering the face below the eyes. Van der Vlugt thus uses different ways to cover faces in order to both expose and blur the boundaries between different ethnicities and cultures. He explores how different material objects 'fashion' – i.e. give meaning to – the clothed physical body, such as the labelling of an Arabic identity, which confirms that the covered face plays an important part in processes of subjectification and signification. At the same time, he reflects in a more general sense on the ways in which dressing certain body parts affects the identity concepts that we form of ourselves and of others. Clothing in its broadest sense is thus a sur-face 'fashioning' the physical form.

Alienating Imageries

In an even more alienating way, designer, video artist and photographer Bart Hess experiments with dressing the body with different kinds of materials – which he regularly does in collaboration with the artist Lucy McRae (see also chapter 14). As mentioned on Hess' website: 'Lucyandbart imagine physically transformed bodies and faces with sometimes shocking artistic realism. They work instinctively, using at first various materials on the body, exploring volumes and remodelling the human silhouette very quickly to expulse all creative energy.'[5] In his work Hess explores several fields, such as material studies, animation and photography. It is particularly interesting with regard to the porous boundaries between fashion, identity and the clothed body that he plays with, for instance, certain unexpected materials as a second skin, and with the fusion between fashion and the human form. In their series for the fashion magazine *AnOther Man* (A/W 2010), Hess and McRae take their investigation of the fluidity of concepts of the self/others to an extreme by exploring the boundaries between humans and animals.[6]

A few photographs in this series depict male bodies dressed with different kinds of sculptural shapes and with animalistic hair-like materials also covering the face, which function as surrealistic extensions of the human body. By doing so, they visually explore, stretch and transgress the boundaries of who we are as humans. The otherness of the men in this series is emphasised as they visually move towards the animalistic, almost beyond humanity. The artists play with the notion that certain material objects of fashion function as a second skin (Entwistle, 2007: 93-104), which raises questions about the porous boundaries between clothes and the physical body. In two other, even more alienating, images of this series we can hardly tell the difference between human bodies and the other materials, pointing to an exploration of the fluid boundaries between the body and material objects (fig. 115). Such an artistic approach is an expression of the relative freedom – although possibly constrained by commercial interests – of contemporary fashion photographers to create 'imaginary forms where body and garment dissolve into one another' (Shinkle, 2008: 10). The bodies merge with a variety of different materials that can barely be identified, but are presumably foam, paint, and long hair. Only a few body parts – two legs, and a face – can still be recognised in this fusion between the physical form of the male body

and an estranging combination of materials functioning as a second skin.

The images in this series move beyond certain pre-categorised identity concepts, such as, for example, are visualised in *Exactitudes*. Instead, such photographs move the human body and thus identity towards the indefinable, the inconceivable, and the realms of fluidity. In a Deleuzean perspective Smelik (2016: 175-6) reads such images as radically undercutting 'any notion of an idealised, stratified, body,' and revealing the human body as a 'constant flux of becoming' (2016: 176; see also chapter 14). Although part of a fashion editorial, and thus in fact commercial work, the photographic series present radically different forms of the human body – dressed by strange and alien material objects – than usually prevail in the representational realm of fashion. This could be understood as a countermovement to representations and discourses surrounding idealised bodies and identities in contemporary fashion imagery. As Bart Hess is an artist rather than a fashion photographer, he works in the virtual realm of fashion in quite an artistic sense. This confirms the current proximity of fashion photography to contemporary art. In my view, Hess explores the possibilities of the imaginary realm of fashion to transgress boundaries and experiment with the liquidity of certain concepts that pertain to the physical body and material objects in an often surrealist way.

Conclusion

In showing liquid bodies and fluid faces, the work of the Dutch photographers Inez Van Lamsweerde, Edland Man, Erwin Olaf, Marcel van der Vlugt and Bart Hess demonstrate the different ways in which fashion photographers visualise the liquidity of the human body while simultaneously playing with the fluidity of specific identity concepts. In a broader cultural sense, such images can be read as an expression of identity in times of hypermodernity – 'characterized by movement,

115. Bart Hess
and Lucy McRae,
'AnOther Man'
(2010).

DANIËLLE BRUGGEMAN

fluidity and flexibility,' as Gilles Lipovetsky writes (2005: 11). In the liquid world of today notions of the self are pushed in the direction of fluidity and flexibility (Bauman, 2000). In contemporary culture the dynamics of fashion are all-encompassing in the process of liquefying identity (Lipovetsky, 1994 [1987]: 131; Bauman, 2011). Within such a context, it is perhaps no surprise that the virtual realm of fashion photography expresses these forces of movement, fluidity and flexibility to which identities are subjected. The artworks visualise the ways in which both the dynamics and the material objects of fashion have become an inextricable part of contemporary individual subjects. While the selected fashion photographers may also reflect on the ways in which clothing as a signifying surface helps to define, enhance and shape specific identity concepts, in my view they primarily reveal the inherently dynamic nature of identity – often taking its fluidity to an extreme beyond any kind of realism. This is, again, an expression of one of the paradoxes inherent in Dutch fashion.

Dutch fashion photography shows a continuous oscillation between the fixing of specific visible identity concepts through clothes (*Exactitudes*) and the potential undoing of these concepts by visualising liquid bodies and fluid faces (Van Lamsweerde, Man, Olaf, van der Vlugt and Hess). Fashion images thus show, on the one hand, that sartorial surfaces have the power to subjectify individuals and shape codified identities. On the other hand, we have seen that fashion photography can also allow for a continuous experimentation with the clothed body and the boundaries of the self, revealing the underlying fluid dynamics of human identity. Taken together they show the two paradoxical sides of the relation between fashion and human identity in a 'liquid modernity' (Bauman, 2000): the sense of belonging to a group and the desire to shape an individual, fluid and flexible identity. The imaginary realm of fashion photography thus takes us from the fixed measures of 90-60-90 centimetres and the rigid framework of *Exactitudes* to the liquid bodies and fluid faces of models with their heads turned around, covered in foam or hair, dressed in miso or cheese, or melted into walls and floors. Let's continue to mobilise the seemingly immobile, conceive the inconceivable, and create the unimaginable. Experiment, play, and liquefy what is solid and frozen!

Notes

1. See www.exactitudes.com.

2. This chapter is based on the research for chapter 2, 'Fluid Concepts of the Self: Dutch Fashion Photography', of my dissertation (Bruggeman, 2014).

3. See my dissertation (Bruggeman, 2014) for an elaborate discussion of the way in which I propose to use the notion of 'identity' in terms of 'concepts of the self' and a 'conceptual self' as defined by psychologist Ulric Neisser (1988).

4. In my dissertation (Bruggeman, 2014) I expand on the role of the face – both conceptually and as a body part – in relation to the fashion system by drawing upon Gilles Deleuze and Félix Guattari's work on the 'face', 'faciality' and 'becoming faceless' (1987).

5. See http://www.barthess.nl/lucyandbart.html.

6. The series 'AnOther Man' (A/W 2010) involved a collaboration between artists Hess and McRae, with stylist Alister Mackie and photographer Nick Knight, presenting fashion designs by Rick Owens, Comme des Garçons and Vivienne Westwood.

Studio JUX (2008–present)

Lianne Toussaint

MY NEPALI TAILOR IS A ROCKSTAR

—http://studiojux.com/products/rockstar-t-shirt

A garment with a 'made in Nepal' label typically brings images of child labour and sweatshops to mind. Not when Studio JUX is involved. Being 'cool as Nepal ice', Studio JUX designs, produces and sells minimalistic fashion in a sustainable and eco-friendly way. Minimalistic, because of the sober, comfortable and often loose-fitting designs with surprising accents like bright coloured stitching or sharp contrasts. Eco-friendly, because of the use of sustainable materials like organic cotton, hemp and recycled cola bottles (Aalderink, 2013: 12).

Jitske Lundgren (b. Hilversum 1980) started Studio JUX in 2008 out of a growing disappointment over the polluting and exploitative fashion industry. Carlien Helmink (b. Hilversum 1983) soon joined as the company manager. Jux means 'fun' or 'joke' in German, which represents the company motto: fashion should be fun. Not just for the consumer or the designer, but also for the tailors and everyone else involved in the production chain: 'We like to do good and look good at the same time' (Helmink quoted in video by Noordhoek and Zwartepoorte, n.d.).

Studio JUX produces the majority of garments in its very own garment factory in Kathmandu, Nepal. Each garment made in that factory contains a numbered label, which corresponds to one of the Nepali tailors that buyers can 'shake hands with' on the company website. The skirt made of a sustainable substitute for silk from Japan was for example 'stitched by' tailor no. 5: Manesh, who 'comes from the jungle area of Saptari, where he goes to see his family once a year for the Hindu Dasain festival'. The jacket of recycled hemp and organic cotton was made by tailor no. 4, Kamal, who 'loves to ride his motor bike, going to the cinema or outside of Kathmandu with friends and likes to listen to sentimental Nepali or Hindi music' (www.studiojux.com/handshake). For those customers eager to grant just that little bit of extra fame and status to the tailors, the Studio JUX web shop also offers a 'My Nepali tailor is a rockstar' T-shirt.

Studio JUX makes clothing for the so-called network generation: higher educated, idealistic youngsters of about 25 to 35 years old. This strategy has proved to be highly successful. The clothes are now sold in about 80 shops in 16 different countries around the world, including Germany, the United Kingdom and Australia. What once started with the production of a few hundred garments a year now represents an annual turnover of over 10,000 items. Nevertheless, it is not just commercial growth that indicates that Studio JUX is on the right track. The company also won several prices over the past few years, including the Ethical Fashion Award in 2010, the Green Fashion Competition in 2012 and most recently the Village Capital Competition, an investment programme for sustainable businesses. For Lundgren and Helmink there is no doubt about it, thinking green is the way forward: 'Sustainable fashion is the future and that is why Studio JUX is there' (Helmink quoted in video by Noordhoek and Zwartepoorte, n.d.).

116. T-shirt 'My Nepali Tailor is a Rockstar' (2013).

117. Studio JUX Catwalk Fashion Show A/W 2013.

118. Studio JUX Amsterdam Catwalk Fashion Show S/S 2013.

119. Dress from collection A/W 2015–16.

13.

Fashion as a New Materialist Aesthetics:
The Case of Viktor&Rolf

'A materialist aesthetic [...] situates the aesthetic as a relationship
"between" — between the human and non-human, the material
and immaterial, the social and physical.'

—Barbara Bolt (2013: 6)

Daniëlle Bruggeman

Introduction

In Viktor&Rolf's fashion show 'Long Live the Immaterial' (A/W 2002–3), garments seem to transform into the Manhattan skyline, fireworks, traffic, cloudy skies, or dissolve into the warm and intense colours of a sunset: the blue screen technology – often used in the film and television industry – enabled Viktor&Rolf to project different imageries onto bright blue garments (fig. 120). As the title of this fashion show explicitly expresses, Viktor&Rolf like to emphasise the immaterial aspect of their work. Indeed, they are often praised for their conceptual approach to fashion, which is in line with a Dutch modernist tradition, as José Teunissen argues in chapter 2. In this chapter I want to address the question to what extent their work actually is immaterial and conceptual.[1] While the projected visuals in 'Long Live the Immaterial' express a sense of immateriality of the clothes as they seem to dissolve into moving images, at the same time the *materiality* of the garments come to the fore as the intense, bright blue colour bursts out. In addition, rather heavy materials, such as velvet, wool, and crochet, are used in the designs, highlighting the tactile quality of the garments. The fashion show exemplifies the ways in which Viktor&Rolf, since the start of their career, have explored the possibilities of the medium of fashion, simultaneously playing with its materiality and immateriality.

120. Viktor&Rolf, 'Long Live the Immaterial' (A/W 2002–3).

By focusing on the case of Viktor&Rolf, in this chapter I offer an alternative perspective on the dominant focus of Dutch fashion as conceptual and modernist (Teunissen, 2008; Feitsma, 2014). In doing so, I argue for the importance of highlighting fashion's matter and materiality, by which I mean not only the material objects of fashion but also the matter of the human body. Ever since Roland Barthes published *The Fashion System* (1990 [1967]), fashion has generally been regarded as a system of signification in which clothing objects can signify social, cultural and political structures. Fashion is thus often conceived as an *immaterial* realm of codes, signs and meanings. As a result, clothing 'becomes reduced to its ability to signify something that seems more real – society or social relations – as though these things exist above or prior to their own *materiality*' (Miller, 2005: 2). Although fashion is to some extent a system of immaterial meanings and concepts, this understanding fails to take into account the physicality of the body and the materiality of clothing (Entwistle, 2000). Discourses around fashion have consistently asked 'what does it mean?', often disavowing the actual materiality of fashion. Since fashion presents itself through the dominant discourse of media and visual communication, the actual material objects of fashion seem to have disappeared. Moreover, 'while fashion has been embraced as an embodied art form [...], its evolution in Western culture has to a large extent been predicated on a disavowal of the body' (Negrin, 2013: 141). There is an urgency to bring back the body – the embodied subject – and materiality into fashion discourse, and vice versa. It is therefore important to develop an alternative, and more material, reading of fashion. In my view, Viktor&Rolf's work inspires to do so, which simultaneously offers a fresh perspective on the much-lauded conceptualism of Dutch fashion.

Viktor&Rolf started their collaboration after graduating from the Arnhem Academy of Art and Design in the Netherlands in 1992. As José Teunissen pointed out in chapter 2, it was due to the Dutch subsidy system that fashion designers such as Viktor&Rolf in the Netherlands became eligible for art grants, which allowed them to enter the world of international fashion. As part of Le Cri Néerlandais, Viktor&Rolf started showcasing their work in Paris in 1994. Their style was soon dubbed 'Dutch Modernism', which highlighted their minimalist and conceptual design approach (Teunissen, 1994; Huygen, 2007: 429). Viktor&Rolf always experimented with different ways of subverting the established fashion system. They created, for instance, posters stating 'Viktor&Rolf on strike' instead of releasing a collection for the next season, sell expensive fake and scentless perfume in bottles that cannot be opened (Smelik, 2007: 67-68), or let models on the catwalk throw porcelain accessories to the ground, breaking them into pieces (De Baan, 2005: 16). Yet, Viktor&Rolf's presentation of 'statement collections' is not an exceptional phenomenon within the fashion world; designers such as Hussein Chalayan, Alexander McQueen and John Galliano, for instance, are also known for it. While Viktor&Rolf keep criticising the fashion system, they are at the same time willingly partaking in it (De Baan, 2008: 10-11). In 2000 they presented their first prêt-à-porter show 'Stars and Stripes' (which gave them their breakthrough), showcased their work in an exhibition at the Louvre in Paris, and signed a contract with L'Oréal to develop their perfume Flowerbomb. They keep creating spectacular fashion shows and notable designs, such as a white blouse with five collars, dresses stuffed with balloons resembling the mushroom cloud shape of nuclear bombs, or clothes worn upside down. Although they now evidently work within the context of commercial fashion, the media as well as scholars usually still conceive of them as (conceptual) artists or performance artists (see e.g. Boelsma, 2000; Kuijpers, 2003; Evans, 2003; Smelik, 2007; Sheffield and Bush, 2008). As stated by the organisers of the Viktor&Rolf exhibition at the Barbican in London in 2008, 'Viktor&Rolf understand that great art is not simply about creating great and original works, but is in itself a philosophical exploration of the limits and possibilities of the medium' (Sheffield and Bush, 2008: 6).

It is precisely this exploration of the medium of fashion itself that I focus on in this chapter. Whereas Viktor&Rolf are typically regarded as conceptual designers in line with a Dutch modernist and conceptual tradition, I want to foreground their experimentation with the materiality of fashion (see also Bruggeman and Van de Peer, 2016). Their concepts and artistic ideas are inextricably linked to the matter that brings it to expression. In order to develop an alternative and more material perspective on Viktor&Rolf's fashion practices, I draw upon the philosophy of Gilles Deleuze and Félix Guattari and on the theoretical discourse of 'new materialism' (e.g. Coole and Frost, 2010; Bennett and Joyce, 2010; Dolphijn and Van Der Tuin, 2012; Barrett and Bolt, 2013; Rocamora and Smelik, 2016). As a cultural theory, new materialism proposes a renewed focus on materiality that incorporates bodily matter. A new materialist approach to fashion thus allows us to take into account living, fashioned bodies, embodied subjects, and the actual materiality of fashion objects. Moreover, drawing upon Anneke Smelik's work on Deleuze and Guattari in relation to fashion (2007, 2014, 2016), I will show that the analytical tools offered by Deleuze and Guattari enable rethinking of the aesthetic power and the dynamics of fashion in a more material sense.

Deleuze and Guattari's (1994) work on aesthetics and art is particularly valuable in this regard, as they argue for a return to the specific material expression of art. In their view, the artistic medium is expressive in itself – 'the smile of oil, the gesture of fired clay, the thrust of metal' – regardless of its content (1994: 166-67). This helps to rethink the expressivity of the medium of fashion as well. From a Deleuzean perspective, the ideas of the artwork are indivisible from the medium that brings it to expression: 'Great artists are also great thinkers, but they think in terms of lines and colors, just as musicians think in sounds, filmmakers think in images, writers think in words, and so on' (Smith, 2012: 125-126). Following this line of thought, I argue that Viktor&Rolf's fashion practices should first and foremost be understood as material practices, as they are thinking in terms of textiles, fabrics, patterns, shapes, colours, etc. Although this may seem evident to fashion designers or pattern cutters, this materialism is often disregarded in the journalistic and academic discourse of fashion (Van de Peer, 2014).

In this chapter I will reflect on different elements of Viktor&Rolf's work, while shedding light on fashion in new materialist terms. Instead of searching for meanings or concepts, I will discuss a selection of fashion shows that exemplify Viktor&Rolf's exploration of the physicality of the body as well as the materiality of fashion. First, I will continue to discuss the fashion show 'Long Live the Immaterial' (A/W 2002–3), and expand on how the designers play with embodiment and disembodiment and with the materiality and immateriality of fashion objects and clothed bodies, while exploring fashion as a theatre of metamorphoses. Secondly, I will discuss the fashion show 'Upside Down' (S/S 2006), which demonstrates how Viktor&Rolf often search for ways to escape the fixed orders of fashion. I will argue that their subversive practices open up ways of rethinking fashion in terms of material connections and transformative encounters between the body and cloth. In the last part of this chapter I will expand on these material encounters and on the transformational element of Viktor&Rolf's work by offering an in-depth analysis of their fashion show 'Glamour Factory' (A/W 2010–11). The theoretical notions that I use will help to understand their fashion practices in more depth and in new materialist terms.

121. Viktor&Rolf, 'Long Live the Immaterial: Karolina' (A/W 2002–3).

Fashion as a Theatre of Metamorphoses

As mentioned above, in their fashion show 'Long Live the Immaterial' Viktor&Rolf use the blue screen technology to project different imagery onto the blue garments. The title of this fashion show refers to the French artist Yves Klein's exclamation 'Long Live the Immaterial!' in his *Chelsea Hotel Manifesto* (1961). In addition, the blue colour Viktor&Rolf use in their garments has the same brightness and intensity as the 'International Klein Blue' – a colour comparable to ultramarine, mixed and patented by Klein himself (Bourriaud, 2000: 35). Klein worked with this colour of blue in different artworks, such as his *Monochrome* paintings in the 1950s and early 1960s. His use of the blue is frequently interpreted as an exploration of pure artistic sensibility (Perlein, 2000: 13). One of the curators of the Musée d'Art Moderne et d'Art Contemporain in Nice (France), a museum that devotes an entire section to Klein's work, describes one of his *Monochromes* as follows:

> A single painting, offered to our gaze. A lone blue rectangle stands out against the white wall. A single color, fragment of matter, asserting at once a presence and an absence. Thus begins the ambiguity; the trusted reference points have vanished. The painting has evacuated the image by refusing 'the tyranny of representation'. [...] In 1913, when Malevich proposed a black square, he was seeking the trace of a sensorial space by foregoing any representation of the outside world. It is as if the artist's objective were to lay bare the material itself, to strip the means of production down to the extreme. Once this degree of purity is attained, the work is complete: there is nothing further to say. (Perlein, 2000: 13)

In this description, curator Gilbert Perlein draws attention to the way in which this single coloured painting creates a sense of pure materiality and full intensity as that which refuses representation. Reference points vanish so all that is left is the pure materiality of the artwork and the full intensity of the colour blue. In his preface to *Yves Klein: Long Live the Immaterial* (2000), the director of the museums of Nice, Jean-Francois Mozziconacci, argues that Klein approached 'what Delacroix called "the indefinable"' (in Perlein and Corà, 2000: 9). Klein's artwork thus escapes representation, figuration and signification, while he explores the sensibility of colours, the indefinable dimension of art. By explicitly referring to Klein's work, Viktor&Rolf put themselves in an honourable tradition of experimentation in the art world. In their own designs and shows they try to escape from the fixed orders of fashion, specifically breaking with fashion as a realm of representation and a system of signification.

In 'Long Live the Immaterial' the usage of the blue screen technology that projects imageries onto the garments, creates the somewhat surrealist effect of the models wearing and almost becoming these moving images. On screen, parts of the models' bodies seem to become, for instance, Egyptian pyramids, cityscapes, blue skies or ocean waves. Birds are flying through the body, or so it seems. As Caroline Evans and Susannah Frankel note, it looked as if certain sections of the garments 'came to life on giant screens on either side of the stage, the blue replaced by breathtaking footage from the natural and urban worlds' (2008: 126). Each garment is designed to express this imagery in a different way. Sometimes trousers become landscapes, scarves become cloudy skies, or dresses become fireworks.

Seen on screen, these projections cause a continuous transformation of the clothes, presenting fashion as a '*theatre* of metamorphoses and permutations', which Deleuze ascribed to the role of modern art in *Difference and Repetition* (1994 [1968]: 56), challenging systems of representation and signification. In this show Viktor&Rolf fully explore the possibilities of both the immateriality and the materiality of the medium of fashion. As mentioned in the introduction to this chapter, the garments seem to dissolve into the moving imagery on screen, yet at the same time the bright blue colour and the materiality of the garments stand out on the catwalk. For example, the garment of the 'Long Live the Immaterial' collection entitled 'Karolina' is made of cotton, silk, wool and leather, which points out the focus on the heavy and contrasting materials used in the garments (fig. 121).

In 'Long Live the Immaterial' Viktor&Rolf play with the themes of embodiment and disembodiment, by emphasising the materiality of the garments and visually exploring the physicality of the body onstage. In some cases, the collars of the garments are bright blue, which seemingly detaches the face from the rest of the body on-screen. This creates an almost extraterrestrial effect of disembodied faces as they are surrounded by different movements of colours. In other cases, complete garments are made of the same intense blue coloured fabric, with only the models' faces and hands remaining visible in their natural physical state. During the fashion show's finale, Viktor&Rolf enter the catwalk, dressed in matching blue pyjamas. On-screen their heads and hands are floating in the darkness of a starry sky. By using the blue screen technology and the moving imagery, they visually explore the possibilities of dressed bodies to potentially become something else. On-screen the clothed body undergoes a continuous change as the images, as body and clothes are incessantly folding into each other, thereby liberating 'the materiality of the body into something continuously changing, mobile and fluid' (Smelik, 2014: 51). Certain body parts become invisible, fluid or flowing and find themselves in a continuous state of movement. These clothed body parts are visually subject to continuous processes of metamorphoses and permutations, escaping signification and representation. In contrast to the transforming clothed bodies seen on-screen, the physicality of the bodily self and thus the bodily matter of the embodied subjects walking on the catwalk come to the fore.

At a certain point during the fashion show one of the models opens her long coat to reveal its bright blue lining. As her dress is made of a similar radiant blue colour, the images projected onto the inside of the coat and onto the dress surround her entire body with approximately a metre of intense, warm, shifting colours. The contours of her dressed body become blurred, fluid and can barely be discerned from the clothing items as they have both dissolved into the moving images. It is impossible to tell where the body ends and where the clothes begin. There is only movement and hardly any fixity. Interestingly, only her face – a very coded part of the body, as I pointed out in the previous chapter – is still visible. The other dressed body parts are absorbed into the movement and intensity of the imagery, subject to constant transformation. As the images and the dressed body keep changing, they cannot be grasped. Viktor&Rolf visually experiment with the possibilities of dissolving the clothing items and the dressed bodies into a continuous state of movement – perhaps a step towards the indefinable, which is a step beyond the 'tyranny of representation', to borrow Perlein's terms. In their investigations of both the materiality and immateriality of fashion in 'Long Live the Immaterial', they let the dressed body dissolve into the intensity of the fields of colours and the expressivity of the projections. By doing so, Viktor&Rolf liberate the dressed body in fashion from its representational function by 'undoing its codes, unsettling its regularities, inducing metamorphoses' (Bogue, 2007: 147). The designers are thus engaged in the practice of experimenting with materiality and immateriality of fashion objects and physical bodies, playing with the transformational potential of the medium of fashion itself, pointing to fashion as 'a process of transformation and metamorphosis' (Smelik, 2016: 168).

Fashion's Material Encounters

While Viktor&Rolf are evidently working within the capitalist system of fashion, they frequently search for ways to escape its fixed orders and its focus on representations and significations. Another example of Viktor&Rolf's exploration of ways to subvert the established system of fashion is the fashion show 'Upside Down' (S/S 2006). An analysis of this show will also open up ways to rethink fashion in terms of material encounters between, for example, the body and cloth.

When this show starts and the audience anticipates the first model to showcase the first piece of the new collection, surprisingly, the designers Viktor&Rolf enter the catwalk. Their logo and names are displayed and positioned upside down behind them. The designers walk halfway down the catwalk, applaud and go off the stage again. Subsequently, all the models appear in a 'final' parade on the catwalk, walking in a straight line and clapping. The lights are turned off. Uncertain about what will happen next, the audience sees a model wearing the final signature look. The second model to appear wears the exact same dress but she wears it upside down. This principle continues during the entire fashion show (fig. 122 and fig. 123).

Dresses are worn upside down, for example with the straps hanging down loosely, almost touching the floor. As Evans and Frankel observed, '[t]he "Upside Down" collection showcased couture pieces that could be worn bottom up or bottom down; on the catwalk they were presented first one way and then the other' (2008: 172). At the end of the show, instead of the finale with the appearance of the designers, we see the last model leaving the catwalk, striking a pose at the beginning of the catwalk, while the lights are slowly turned off. During the show Diana Ross's song 'Upside Down' is played in reverse, emphasising the 'absurd logic' (Evans and Frankel, 2008: 172) of the presentation of this collection. The fashion show 'Upside Down' (S/S 2006) refers to the boutique that Viktor&Rolf opened in Milan

in 2005 (and closed in 2008), in which the interior also hung upside down.

'Upside Down' is illustrative of Viktor&Rolf's subversion of the conventions of the fashion show and, in a more general sense, of fashion as a system. As the designers stated in an interview, a 'constant questioning of fashion itself as a system – and our own place in it – is always the root of our work' (cited in Frankel, 2008: 33). Furthermore, as Evans argues, 'a sense of inversion and reversal also finds expression in much of their design work. [...] In a more diffuse way, all their work has an upside-down or distorted quality' (Evans, 2008: 15). In this 'Upside Down' show Viktor&Rolf reverse the normal procedure of the catwalk, thereby unsettling expectations of the audience. While Viktor&Rolf subvert the meaning of the fashion show, they also break with the conventional function of material objects of fashion. Since the models wear the couture pieces bottom up and bottom down, the audience is stimulated to reconsider the possibilities of the clothes being worn differently, upside down, or maybe even inside out. Skirts, for example, are in some cases detached from the lower part of the body, and re-encounter the upper part of the body. The skirts then become mere pieces of cloth again, ready to make new connections to other parts of the body, and thus temporarily lose their representational function of signifying femininity. Viktor&Rolf experiment with the flexibility and possibilities of cloth being continuously remade into different clothes and shapes, irrespective of their seemingly indexical relationship to certain body parts. By so doing, the material independence of cloth is foregrounded as the clothes are freed from their attachment to particular body parts or to certain meanings and codes. It is demonstrated that cloth can enter into a composition with the body in many different ways, emphasising fashion as a site of infinite variations.

In order to gain a deeper insight into these fashion practices, I want to draw attention to the distinction that Simon O'Sullivan (2006), inspired by Deleuze and

122. Viktor&Rolf, 'Upside Down' (S/S 2006).

DANIÉLLE BRUGGEMAN

123. Viktor&Rolf,
'Upside Down'
(S/S 2006).

Guattari, makes between 'objects of encounter' and 'objects of recognition' in relation to art and aesthetics. He argues that the latter is a mere confirmation of our knowledge, beliefs and values, and thus a '*re*presentation of something always already in place' (2006: 1, original emphasis). On the contrary, 'objects of encounter' disrupt our systems of knowledge, forcing us to think, while simultaneously affirming ways of seeing and thinking this world differently (O'Sullivan, 2006: 1). Viktor&Rolf's subversion of the conventions of fashion does have an effect similar to O'Sullivan's definition of 'objects of encounter' to the extent that it breaks with the concept and principle of 'the fashion show' and with 'the clothing object' as we know it, and at least temporarily unsettles our habitual mode of thinking and seeing fashion. I thus propose to think of Viktor&Rolf's subversive fashion shows and collections as potential 'objects of encounter', momentarily unsettling our expectations and systems of knowledge, beliefs and values, maybe even offering a way of thinking fashion and material clothing objects differently.

Moreover, the term 'encounter' leads to another possible viewpoint, which is an understanding of fashion in terms of material encounters. We may think of fashion as a process of endless transformative encounters between, for instance, fabrics, textiles, shapes, patterns, the hands and tools of the designers and pattern cutters, or the bodies of the wearers. In this regard, Brian Massumi's material perspective on the notion of 'meaning', following Deleuze and Guattari, is noteworthy. He views meaning as a material process of encounters: 'meaning is precisely that: a network of enveloped material processes' (Massumi, 1992: 10). Meaning, here, is not based on semiotics and immaterial systems of signification, but is rather understood as a material 'meeting' between different forces. As O'Sullivan explains, Massumi's notion of meaning is a relation, a process, a dynamic encounter between 'two (or more) forces acting on one another in a reciprocal

and transformative relationship' (O'Sullivan, 2006: 21). Massumi reflects on a woodworker encountering a piece of wood and bringing the qualities of wood to a certain expression. He discusses the relationships between, for example, tools and wood – 'tool meets wood' (Massumi, 1992: 11) – but also relationships with the woodworking body. Following Massumi's line of thought, O'Sullivan proposes to think of 'the artist's "meeting" with his or her materials', which he views as an encounter of the same fundamental nature (O'Sullivan, 2006: 21). I would argue that this material process also holds true for fashion designers and pattern cutters who continuously 'meet' with different fabrics, transforming the (qualities of the) materials, and experimenting with different possible ways to let cloth encounter the body. As Viktor&Rolf play with these different encounters between cloth and the models' bodies on the catwalk in their show 'Upside Down', they create meaning as a dynamic process of material encounters.

In their fashion practices, Viktor&Rolf are thus – both conceptually and materially – experimenting with fashion's potential 'objects of encounters'. Their subtle subversions and disruptive practices open up ways to rethink fashion in terms of material connections and transformative encounters.

Transformational Assemblages

In this section I expand on the ways in which Viktor&Rolf produce creative connections and material encounters, while again highlighting the transformational element of their work. I will do so by focusing on Viktor&Rolf's show 'Glamour Factory' (A/W 2010–11) and by drawing upon Deleuze and Guattari's notion of 'assemblages', which is, as I will argue, a productive next step in thinking of fashion in terms of encounters and connections.[2]

This fashion show echoes one of Viktor&Rolf's early haute couture shows, 'Russian Doll' (A/W 1999–2000). For 'Russian Doll' the model Maggie Rizer was dressed by Viktor&Rolf real time onstage with nine layers of couture dresses, placed on top of each other. As Viktor&Rolf dressed Rizer with increasingly larger-sized dresses, the materiality and the tactility of the clothes as well as the model's physicality were increasingly foregrounded (Smelik, 2007: 69). A similar transformational process takes place in 'Glamour Factory'. Whereas in 'Russian Doll' Rizer entered the catwalk wearing just one outfit before being dressed with nine layers, 'Glamour Factory' opens with the model Kristen McMenamy wearing ten layers (fig. 124). Because of this physically demanding task, she is wobbling on her high heels while stepping onto a rotating platform in the middle of the catwalk. As viewers we become aware of the heavy weight as well as the warmth of all the layers of clothes that she must experience. Our attention is thus drawn to the physical aspect of this show. Viktor&Rolf take centre stage, stand beside her, and take off her tweed cape while a second model in a body stocking appears, and also steps onto the rotating platform. Subsequently, the designers dress the second model with the clothing item they had just taken off McMenamy, creating an interesting dynamic between the processes of undressing and dressing at the same time. During this process the cape becomes a coat for the second model. While McMenamy stays on the revolving platform, the

124. Viktor&Rolf, 'Glamour Factory' (A/W 2010–11).

DANIËLLE BRUGGEMAN

125. Viktor&Rolf, 'Glamour Factory' (A/W 2010–11).

second model walks down the catwalk before going offstage again, and a third model appears. This turns into a repetitive practice with different models and clothing items. Systematically, McMenamy is undressed layer after layer, while Viktor&Rolf are simultaneously dressing the other models with the items they have just taken off. At a certain point, when McMenamy is wearing no more than a pink bodysuit (fig. 125), the same process continues in reverse: McMenamy is dressed again with layers of clothing items taken off the other models. Cloth continuously meets and makes transversal connections with other bodies and with other fabrics, while undergoing transformations itself as the function of the garments changes in the process: capes become coats, coats become dresses. Here, we can again understand Viktor&Rolf's fashion practices as a '*theatre of metamorphoses and permutations*', in the words of Deleuze (1994: 56).

With mechanical precision and meticulous timing, Viktor&Rolf dress and undress the models, as if they are operating in a factory of transformation, constantly producing new connections between different bodies and material fabrics. In their *Glamour Factory*, they are engaged in an almost machine-like process of assembling, disassembling and reassembling. In order to grasp this way of producing new creative connections, I propose to bring into play Deleuze and Guattari's notion of 'assemblages'. The French original, *agencement*, can be translated as an arrangement of things, and moreover as the active *act* of arranging; the *process* of arranging, assembling, or fitting together (Macgregor Wise, 2005: 77; Bogue, 2007: 145). An assemblage results from the connections between different heterogeneous elements, such as 'materials, colors, odors, sounds, postures, etc.' (Deleuze and Guattari, 1987: 323). Different elements meet and form a temporary 'holding together' (ibid.: 242). An important principle of the ways in which assemblages function is that they are 'in constant variation'; they are

'themselves constantly subject to transformations' (ibid.: 82). Thus, an assemblage may always be disassembled again and is itself always undergoing transformations. In Viktor&Rolf's show 'Glamour Factory', we see the *act* of arranging, the *process* of assembling. Onstage, Viktor&Rolf let different clothes encounter each other as well as the models' bodies, producing new momentary assemblages; temporary 'holdings together' of different models' bodies and clothing items. Evidently, in the process of actually making this collection prior to this fashion show numerous creative, transformative connections had already been made between different heterogeneous elements, such as different materials, textiles, patterns or colours. The material garments are evidently manufactured in actual textile factories, yet, in contrast, in the fashion show we see *performances* of assemblages.

As Viktor&Rolf strip McMenamy of her layers of clothes, they engage in a process of disassembling. At the same time, when the removed clothing item is connected in a different way to another model's body, new assemblages are formed. By doing so, Viktor&Rolf invent their own laws of assemblages, which are created from the transversal connections between the physical bodies of the designers, of the models and the materiality of the clothes. In this process the nature of the assemblages also transforms. The pieces of cloth undergo metamorphoses as their function changes through the encounters with different bodies (capes become coats, coats become dresses). In addition, the dressed models transform as they are constantly assembled, disassembled and reassembled. By performing this 'machine-like' process onstage, Viktor&Rolf affirm the transformational potential of cloth to continuously enter into different assemblages with different bodies.

This inspires and opens up a different way of conceiving, in a broader sense, what happens whenever a physical body (an assemblage) encounters a material piece of cloth (another assemblage). This functions as follows: firstly, a human body is already an assemblage in itself. As Claire Colebrook, following Deleuze and Guattari, notes, '[a]ll life is a process of connection and interaction. Any body or thing is the outcome of a process of connections. A human body is an assemblage of genetic material, ideas, powers of acting and a relation to other bodies' (2002: xx). Secondly, a clothing item is also already an assemblage in itself, as it is made up of, for instance, different materials, textiles, colours, threads and fibres. When a human body then encounters an object of cloth, two assemblages meet, make a connection and form a new assemblage, a new temporary 'holding together': a dressed body.

As Tony Bennett and Patrick Joyce point out in their introduction to *Material Powers* (2010), the notion of 'assemblages' contributes to a material understanding of how social life operates. They particularly emphasise Deleuze and Guattari's 'contention that social life is to be understood in terms of the operation of assemblages made up of "semiotic flows, material flows, and social flows simultaneously"' (Bennett and Joyce, 2010: 5). The notion of 'assemblages' thus offers an interesting perspective on the semiotic, material and social dynamics of fashion. In the realm of fashion, material objects and physical bodies are continuously related to socio-cultural meanings, signs and codes. While pointing out the entanglement of matter and meaning, the notion of 'assemblages' highlights the *material* dimension of this entanglement. This is essential for a materialist reading of fashion, which entails the relationships between 'the human and non-human, the material and immaterial, the social and physical' (Bolt, 2013: 6). When different heterogeneous elements meet and set up relations, new material assemblages are formed in which social and semiotic flows are also intertwined. It is within these assemblages that cloth and bodily matter are inextricably interrelated to meanings, codes or signs. A dressed body can thus be viewed as an assemblage made up of semiotic, material and social flows.

We could say that the fibres of cloth, in their pure material state, are in themselves pre-individual, a-subjective, a-signifying and a-conceptual. In the process of the production of actual clothes, the conceptual identity of the cloth – e.g. a dress, trousers, cowboy boots – comes into being due to the formation of assemblages in which material, semiotic and social flows meet. Simultaneously, a process of signification may start, connecting immaterial meanings to these clothing items, for instance, attributing femininity to a dress and masculinity to cowboy boots – which confirms the new materialist view on the inextricable 'entanglement of materiality and meaning' (Dolphijn and Van Der Tuin, 2012: 91). When pieces of cloth – that have become fashionable commodities – then encounter human bodies in a social context, these clothes can become individualised.

A new materialist perspective opens up ways to think fashion differently, which is, in Deleuze and Guattari's terms as well as in Viktor&Rolf's work, 'very much a materialist practice' (O'Sullivan, 2006: 16). To move away from the dominant mode of viewing fashion, we could – instead of asking what it means – explore in more depth the ways in which fashion can be understood as a network of transformational assemblages in which material, semiotic and social flows are woven together.

Conclusion

Viktor&Rolf's experimentation with the medium of fashion inspires to think (Dutch) fashion differently. Instead of privileging the artistic idea or the concept of a collection, in this chapter I emphasised the importance of foregrounding the matter of fashion. I have done so by using a Deleuzean and new materialist vocabulary. Rather than merely asking 'what does it mean?' or 'what is the idea behind it?', I have suggested that we look at fashion in terms of encounters, connections and 'meetings' between different materialities. A new materialist approach to fashion helps to do more justice to the complexities of cloth in itself and of (dressed) bodies, moving beyond the dominant way of reading fashion in terms of what it signifies and represents (cf. Rocamora and Smelik, 2016: 11–15). I focused on the designers Viktor&Rolf, because their fashion practices provide insight into what lies at the heart of the dynamics of fashion. Rethinking fashion as a new materialist aesthetics helps to liberate fashion's materiality, its colours, threads, fabrics from its mere representational function. In addition, rethinking Dutch fashion from a new materialist perspective offers an alternative to the dominant reading of Dutch fashion as conceptual fashion.

Viktor&Rolf's play with fashion as a theatre of metamorphoses still takes place within the realm of fashion as a system of representation and signification. Although it is important to give special attention to fashion's materiality and to the medium of fashion, in the field of fashion we will need to look at the ways in which 'material and semiotic relations are entangled with one another' (Bennett and Joyce, 2010: 9). As new materialism accentuates the entwinement of matter and meaning, matter and discourse, matter and concept, and the material and immaterial, this perspective can greatly contribute to the journalistic and academic discourse of fashion.

Meanwhile, the conceptual aspect of Viktor&Rolf's work continues to be highlighted, by the designers themselves and by fashion journalists. 'High concept it was' (Phelps, 2013) are the words of a review of Viktor&Rolf's A/W 2013–14 collection, which they presented in Paris to celebrate their 20-year collaboration. Yet, immaterial ideas and concepts are always inextricably intertwined to their material expression. In this chapter I have stressed the importance of rethinking fashion through material lens: Dutch fashion needs a new materialist vocabulary: *Long Live the Material!*

Notes

1. This chapter is based on the research of chapter 5, 'Towards a New Materialist Aesthetics: The Case of Viktor&Rolf', of my dissertation (Bruggeman 2014).

2. An analysis of the fashion show 'Glamour Factory' can also be found in Bruggeman and Van de Peer (2016). In this article we reflect on the entanglement of concept and materiality.

Bas Kosters (b. Zutphen 1977)

Lianne Toussaint

IS THAT A COCK OR YOUR LEGS?

—www.baskosters.com/webshop/product/is-that-a-cock-or-your-legs

Bas Kosters is best described as the humorous, provocative and outspoken *enfant terrible* of Dutch fashion design (anon., *Het Parool*, 2012: 11). His style is highly distinct: chaotic, colourful and carnivalesque, with bold prints of stickers, portraits, penises and – Kosters' self-invented trademark – fictional dolls called 'munchies'. Media phenomenon Kosters is more than just your average fashion designer. He paints, makes art pieces, illustrations and graphic designs, does music and dance shows with his performative punk band, DJs and publishes his quarterly 'Extra Kak' magazine (in Dutch 'kak' can mean both 'snobbish' and 'shit'). Though his label is seldom found on the street, that doesn't bother Kosters at all: 'I wish to be famous for what I do, that does not necessarily have to be fashion' (Ferwerda, 2006: 118). Fashion, for him, is just another way to tell stories about the Bas Kosters universe.

After graduating from the Academy for Art & Design in Enschede and the ArtEZ Institute of the Arts, Kosters established Studio Bas Kosters in 2005 as an umbrella for his various activities as independent fashion designer and artist. Annually hosting an 'Anti-Fashion Event' during the Amsterdam Fashion Week, Kosters does not exactly live by the rules of the fashion world. His Studio is a 'brand' that hardly creates any sellable clothes; it primarily stands for Kosters' ever-excessive style. As a great lover of second-hand clothing, the seventies and do-it-yourself clothing, Kosters considers the innovative character of fashion 'rather unnecessary' (Ibid.). When it is time to produce another series of his one-of-a-kind garments he just calls some of his friends, family and acquaintances to come by and help sew or knit for a day.

Everything produced under the name of Kosters' 'house of fashion-related activities' has two distinct sides. It either exhibits a dark humour that warns against alarming social issues, or a friendly and positive feeling of happiness. The happy and playful style has led to various collaborations with commercial partners. Kosters created a limited edition buggy covered with his characteristic 'munchies' for the globally successful Dutch stroller brand Bugaboo, designed a cartoonish series of pyjamas for low-budget store Zeeman, a Barbie-outfit for Mattel and a 'post-pop-art' collection packed with vintage beer-can prints for Heineken (Bas Kosters Studio, n.d.).

The more socially engaged and punkish side of Kosters' work is mostly reflected by his independent collections and designs. They bear names like 'Clowns Are People Too', 'Love, Fuck, Yeah' and 'Ugly Collection'; or 'Eat Fries Xerox dress', 'Protest Dolls legging' and 'Is That An Eye Or Your Vagina? trousers'. What unites everything that sprouts from the dazzling fantasy of this rebellious entertainer is his unique and nonconformist signature: festive, extreme, psychedelic and playful, yet critical, sensitive and sincere to the core.

126. Bas Kosters, 'Red Monster Dress'.

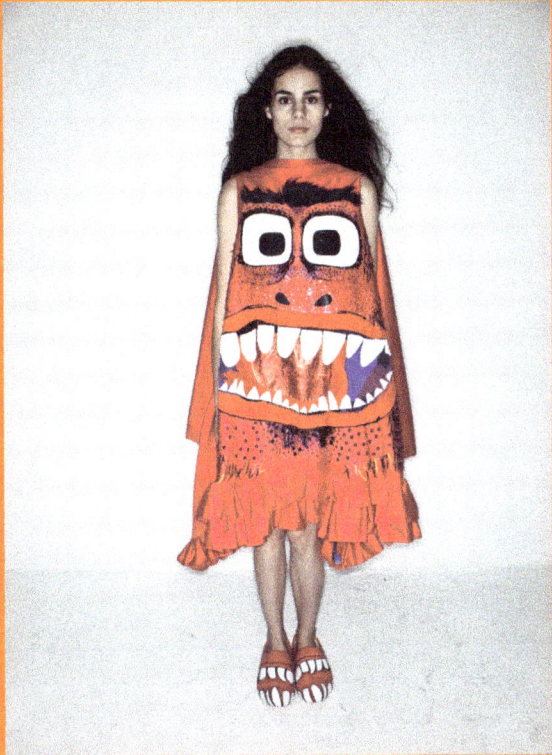

127. Bas Kosters, 'Fashion Mutant Polkadot Monster'.

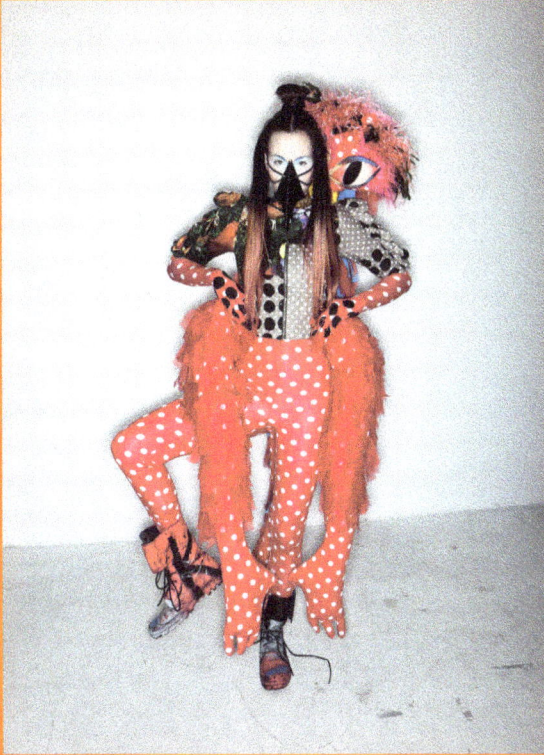

128. Bas Kosters, 'Icons Heart Dress'.

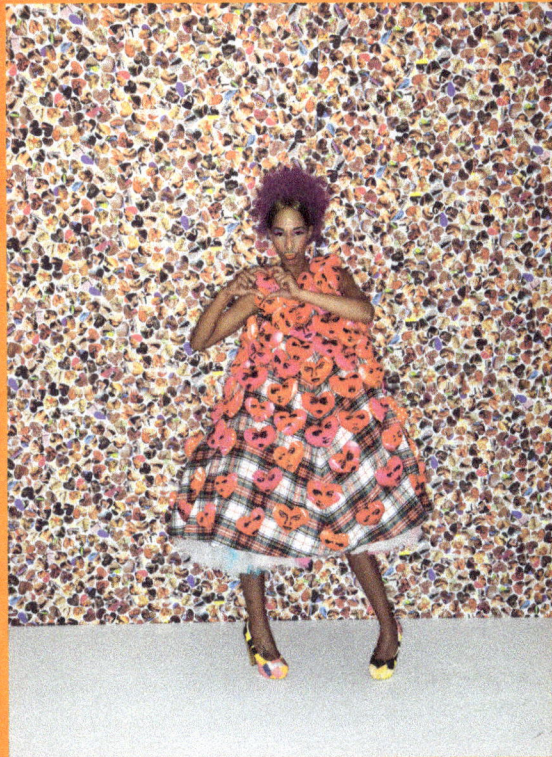

129. Bas Kosters, 'Blue Velvet Self-Portrait Pantsuit'.

14.

Cybercouture:
The Fashionable Technology
of Pauline van Dongen,
Iris van Herpen and Bart Hess

'[Technology] is an open-ended beginning, an infinite game
calling us to play.'

—Kevin Kelly (2010: 345)

Anneke Smelik

Introduction

One of the exciting new fields in the creative industry is the integration of fashion and technology. Wiring complex systems of microprocessors, motors, sensors, solar panels, (O)LEDs or interactive interfaces into fabric, textile or clothing turns them into smart garments that have a certain agency of their own. Designers experiment with these 'smart materials' to create thrilling examples, like a dress that connects you to Twitter, a catsuit that visualises your emotions and trousers that change colour or measure your vital functions. These examples show how '[t]echnology is now evolving faster than fashion trends,' as designer Katrina Barillova claims (in Quinn, 2002: 73). This new field is called 'wearable technology' or simply 'wearables'. Although I use both of these labels interchangeably in this chapter, I prefer the term 'fashionable technology', following Sabine Seymour (2009, 2010), to bring the field of advanced technology more decidedly to the field of fashion. Given the futuristic look of many designs, perhaps the term 'cybercouture' is even more apt (Smelik, 2012).

If the 'future of fashion is now,' as a Dutch exhibition (Autumn 2014) in the Museum Boijmans van Beuningen in Rotterdam was called, it is fitting to finish this book with a chapter on cybercouture. Interestingly, Dutch artists and designers such as Pauline van Dongen, Iris van Herpen, Bart Hess, Daan Roosegaarde, Marina Toeters, Karin Vlug and Anouk Wipprecht form the vanguard in the international field of fashionable technology. Some recent examples are the 3D-printed designs of the collection 'Escapism' by Iris van Herpen (2011), wearable robotics in the 'Robotic Spider Dress' by Anouk Wipprecht (2012) or wearable solar panels in the 'Wearable Solar Dress' by Pauline van Dongen (2013). In this chapter I first situate research on fashionable technology in the Netherlands by giving a short sketch of the field. I then evaluate how fashion and technology become more and more integrated and how this development changes the cultural value of fashion, especially in the transformative relation to the human body and identity. In the second part of the chapter I therefore pay particular attention to the intriguing nexus of the relation between fashionable technology and the human body and identity. I do so by discussing the work of three Dutch designers, Pauline van Dongen, Iris van Herpen and Bart Hess, who each move between art, fashion and technology.

Dutch Experiments

In the last few decades, interdisciplinary research has been carried out at the crossroads of art, fashion, sports, gaming, medicine and many industrial branches of technology. In the Netherlands research takes place at a variety of places, often working in close cooperation: art and fashion academies; cultural institutions; laboratories of small companies, large companies, big corporations, and technical universities; and finally in so-called 'fab labs' that allow students to use expertise in the labs in exchange for their designs. The experiments are presented at quite different locations, sometimes on the catwalk, sometimes as a performance at a cultural festival, or in games, at sports events or academic conferences.

There is one Dutch city in particular that presents itself as the design city: Eindhoven, with its Faculty of Industrial Design, the Design Week, the many artist, designer and architect ateliers in the old Philips factories in 'Strijp' and the High Tech Campus of the Dutch electronics and light multinational, Royal Philips. Philips Design runs a laboratory where artists, designers and scientists work together on the interaction between body, clothing and environment. These are experiments for what they call 'the far future', not with the aim of developing technological clothing that is wearable but rather to study emergent trends and behaviour. In 2006, artist Lucy McRae, for instance, created the 'Skin Probe Dress' in conjunction with Philips. Through biometric sensors the dress explores the space between the body

130. Bubelle Blush Dress, developed by Lucy McRae for Philips Design, 2006.

and the near environment. Electrons in the fabric can register and visually represent the emotions of the wearer: the dress will turn green when you are jealous or red when you are in love. McRae also produced the 'Bubelle Blush Dress' for Philips in the same year, exploring what they call 'sensitive' technology through biometric sensors. This dress is surrounded by a delicate 'bubble', which responds to skin contact by illuminating various patterns. In probing the skin, such designs behave differently depending on who is wearing them and therefore exhibit non-programmed behaviour.

Working in the far future design research programme of Philips, McRae met Dutch artist Bart Hess in 2007, and they launched several projects together as the duo LucyandBart. For Philips they worked on an 'Electronic Tattoo' project, a digital tattoo augmented by touch. In 2008, a collaboration between Philips and designer Anouk Wipprecht (see profile in this chapter) resulted in the 'Lumalive' dress with flexible displays. Most recently, Pauline van Dongen created 'Mesopic' (2014), a project that aims to increase human visibility and safety in low-light outdoor scenarios. For this garment, Philips' textile LED ribbons have been integrated in the fabric, resulting in a light-emitting jacket that merges with the city-lights glowing in the nocturnal surrounding.

These are just a few examples to illustrate the vibrant climate for experiments in fashionable technology, in this particular case stimulated by a big cooperation, Philips. The Dutch fashion academies are also at the forefront of new developments. The Amsterdam Fashion Institute, for example, has integrated 3D virtual prototyping in its curriculum (Boekman, 2012: 53-54). The students learn how to digitally create a better fit, which costs less time, leads to less need for samples, less transport and less use of material. While virtual prototyping thus enhances sustainability, it also allows more freedom in the design process by digitally creating variations in form, material, prints and details. Pushing the boundaries of software capability, students research how complex designs can be developed.

As such, students and designers continue an honourable tradition in Dutch product design and industrial design dating back to the beginning of the twentieth century (De Rijk, 2003; Simon Thomas, 2008). Dutch product design has always been more successful and internationally better known than Dutch fashion, although as Maaike Feitsma (2014) argues, Dutch fashion has ridden the successful wave of Dutch design since the 1990s. The point here is that the Netherlands can boast some very successful Faculties of Industrial Design and several renowned art, design and fashion academies in major cities across the country. This has created a generation of young designers who are eager to cross the disciplines of art, design, fashion and technology.

The Smart Materials of Fashionable Technology

Fashionable technology is versatile and can therefore be quite bewildering: it can range from e-fashion, smart materials, wearable electronics, solar energy and 3D printing to bio-couture and nanotechnology.[1] Recent studies in the field provide an overview of techniques and applications (Mattila, 2006; Cho, 2010), or summarise its developments and actors (Quinn, 2002, 2010, 2012; Seymour, 2009, 2010), but, to date, few studies critically reflect on the socio-cultural dimensions of fashionable technology (Toussaint and Smelik, 2016).

Like most technology – the internet, for instance – wearable technology has its origin in military research and space travel (Quinn, 2002: 98). While most innovations have not been incorporated into our daily clothes (yet), others have been successful in, for instance, sports gear. One of the most successful markets for wearables in the Netherlands is the field of safety, such as the military, police and fire brigades.[2] Fabrics and textiles have been developed to protect soldiers, police officers or firemen from all kinds of impact, be it fire, water, bullets, knives or debris. An example is the European Prospie project that produced a garment measuring core body temperature as an efficient method for monitoring heat stress amongst workers in hot conditions; it was tested at Tata Steel (Niedermann et al., 2014).

A second major market for wearables is healthcare. Hein Daanen, professor of Fashion and Technology at the Amsterdam Fashion Institute, has developed a measuring Knee Brace with sensors for wireless feedback on movement and automatic self-calibration, a Runalyser with sensors for wireless feedback on gait analysis and walking and running techniques, and a Smart Shirt that allows for 3D monitoring of the human trunk to improve posture (Daanen and Ter Haar, 2013; McLellan et al., 2013). New developments in microbiology and nanotechnology have opened up new applications for smart materials in healthcare and beauty care. Think for instance of the antibacterial qualities of cleaning cloths or a mattress – but researchers also experiment with smart materials that can have vitamins, sun creams or deodorant embedded into the fabric itself (Quinn, 2010).

A third possible market for wearable technology is communications, involving the integration of mobile technology into the clothes. This may be the fastest-moving area in the field of wearables, and perhaps also the 'coolest' one. Take for example the 'Twitdress' that singer Imogen Heap donned for the Grammy Awards in 2010. This dress had a big flashing collar and a transparent bag that functioned as a television screen. The digital collar showed real-time tweets from her fans that were transmitted through a wireless router in her dress. In her handbag was an iPhone with pictures that she was being sent online. The wearable technology allowed the singer to be in constant contact with her fans and communicate with them. In order to perpetually collect, process and exchange data, wearables like the Twitdress should be able to generate and preserve its own energy. Researchers aim to integrate wireless systems into the

fibre, yarn or fabric, thus allowing the piece of clothing to become interactive. While there are promising developments, as the discussion of Pauline van Dongen's 'Wearable Solar Dress' will show, there remain practical problems like washing or day-to-day wear and tear.

Remarkably, *fashion* is seldom mentioned as a possible market for wearables. This goes to show that the field of wearables is still dominated by a strong push from technology and little or no pull from fashion. However, wearables will never make it commercially if the prototypes are not translated into an aesthetics of fashion. It is for that reason that fashion designer Pauline van Dongen worked on a prototype for a knitted cardigan called 'Vigour', designed by Martijn ten Bhömer as a tool that enables geriatric patients, physiotherapists, doctors and family to gain more insight into the exercises and progress of a rehabilitation process. Van Dongen made the cardigan with integrated stretch sensor monitors more comfortable to wear and more aesthetically pleasing. The point of fashionable technology, after all, is to merge fashion with technology in such a way that it becomes wearable and fashionable at the same time. If we take the term 'wearable technology' on its own merits, it is rather obvious that it should be precisely that: wearable. In other words, it should be comfortable to wear on the body like any piece of clothing. Moreover, the term 'fashionable technology' suggests that fashion and technology should blend together, turning geeky or nerdy garments fashionable.

While the future of fashionable technology has been announced time and again (Quinn, 2002; Seymour, 2009), the praxis, however, lags behind. Wearables rarely leave the lab or catwalk and have not yet conquered the street in spite of many prophecies (Smelik, 2012). This is partly because the innovation of wearable technology needs to be connected more to the aesthetic value of fashion than is the case now. Wearable technology is mostly still in an experimental phase, allowing fashion designers to use and apply new

131. Aynouk
Tan wearing an
'emotional catsuit'.

materials and technologies, but this has been the case for decades without its ever making it to the shops or streets. The main exception is some success of integrating smart materials and new technologies in sports clothing and sports shoes. Generally, there are practical reasons for the lack of success of wearable technology: for example, how to wash fabrics with embedded LEDs, solar fibres or batteries? Then there is the issue of comfort: some of the materials, fabrics or outfits are not particularly 'wearable'. When Dutch model and fashion journalist Aynouk Tan tried out a trial version of Philips' 'skin probe dress' mentioned above, she loved it, but complained about the electrodes sticking into her skin (Tan, 2009).

There are also more profound cultural reasons why wearable technology has not been that successful.[3] In the first place, wearable technology often only focuses on functionality, ignoring the social or cultural value of the new technology (Pakhchyan, 2008). Yet, for successful innovation it is more important to look for added value in the form of social interaction and cultural practices. As Ann Balsamo argues, any technological innovation is a 'work of cultural reproduction' (2011: 6) and the 'outcome of social interactions' (ibid.: 11). A design should add value to its functionality; otherwise it remains forever in the realm of mere gadgetry. A garment that charges my mobile phone remains functional, but if it allows me to communicate with others it brings me into a social network, and if it gives me information about the energy levels of my body it can enter a cultural practice of health and fitness. In other words, for fashionable technology to become socially successful and commercially viable, it should involve a process of meaning-making.

Secondly, many wearables are not fashionable enough because the aesthetics of the design is not integrated in the technology. Too often they remain a gadget without taking into account the wearer's body or identity or adding to the quality of life. Comfort, beauty and fashionability should also be part of the design. Thirdly, as the body of the wearer will itself become

a form of interface, it is highly probable that wearable technology will blur the boundaries between computer and body. The notion of fashionable technology suggests that bodies are enhanced by the garment, thus increasingly becoming a platform for sensitive and interactive technology. As Fortunati et al. argue, 'the main battleground between the forces of culture and technology is becoming the human body' (2008: 216). On the one hand, cultural fears of technology getting intimately connected to the human body may hamper the further implementation of wearables. On the other hand, an uncritical embracement of technology may obscure ethical issues of privacy or sustainability. In my view, fashionable technology produces cyborg-like figures that will inevitably shift the notion of our own body and identity (Smelik, 2012). The development of cybercouture therefore calls for a renewed and critical understanding of the relation between technology, the body and identity.

Body and Identity

Smart materials and smart garments can be understood as protecting the body or extending its physical functions. Although cultural anthropology claims that clothes function first and foremost as decoration and adornment, clothes are also an extension of the skin, protecting it against nature and society (see for instance Flügel, 1950). Within a context of technology this idea derives from media guru Marshall McLuhan (2002 [1964]: 129-30). In the beginning of the 1960s he suggested that all technology is in fact an extension of the human body. We have now entered an age in which technology is not only a bodily extension, but also a physical improvement, enhancement and expression. We use technology with the idea that we can control, improve and enhance both our lives and our own bodies. By wearing it directly on our bodies, we relate intimately to technical objects and materials. As Lucy Dunne writes, 'Through technology, garments are now becoming dynamic, responsive, and aware; thus, they are better able to express our individuality and meet our needs and wants' (2011: 616). Integrating technology into our clothes will therefore have an impact on how we experience our bodies and our selves.

Dressing happens literally on the body, and fashion is thus an important way of performing identity in its many facets. As Joanne Entwistle and Elizabeth Wilson (2003) argue, the body is not so much a submissive object to be draped in accordance with the dictates of the social or cultural field, but dressing is rather an active embodied practice. The body, then, is not a given, but something we can put in shape or dress up for what I call a 'performance of identity' (Smelik, 2011). The bodily practice of dressing is an important factor in constructing one's identity. The idea that one 'performs' rather than 'is' one's identity, refers to a constructivist notion of identity: rather than an unchanging essence, identity is a social and cultural construction that slowly transforms over time. As Kelly reminds us, 'Homo sapiens is a tendency, not an entity' (2010: 128). Identity should thus be understood as a process of continuous becoming: not rigid and fixed from cradle to grave, but fluid and flexible throughout life (Smelik, 2016: 167). Becoming is taken here as a practice of change in the way that philosopher Gilles Deleuze and psychoanalyst Félix Guattari approached it. The continuous process of creative transformations is what Deleuze and Guattari (1987) understand by 'becoming'. One does not just become, but one always becomes something else; life is thus a process of 'becoming-other'.

In the context of this chapter, identity can be likened to the performance of a constant dress rehearsal. Or, to put it differently: our identity is 'wearable'. Technology is indeed one of the major factors in affecting our identity and changing the relation to our own body, and wearable technology even more so because of its closeness to the body. This is not entirely new, because human beings have always been intimately connected to technology. The scientist who launched the term 'cyborg' in 1960, Manfred

Clynes, says: 'Homo sapiens, when he puts on a pair of glasses, has already changed' (in Gray, 1995: 49, original emphasis). If this is the case for normal glasses, just imagine how the human body and identity change with Google glasses; the new 'geek chic' (Quinn, 2002: 97) that Diane von Furstenberg brought to fashion in 2012. A few decades after Clynes coined the term 'cyborg', the philosopher of science Donna Haraway launched the idea of the cyborg as a figure that typically embodies fluid identity, because it has 'made thoroughly ambiguous the difference between natural and artificial, mind and body, self-developing and externally designed, and many other distinctions that used to apply to organisms and machines' (1991 [1985]: 152). This is particularly relevant for wearables, because they shift and push the boundaries between body and technology. As Fortunati et al. argue, 'the body continually abolishes the border between nature and technology by converting one into the other' (2008: 216). Understanding identity as a bodily practice that is performed time and again, fashionable technology offers alternative and new ways of transforming identities. Exploring the wearer's corporeal and sensorial boundaries, fashionable technologies enable the body to perform identity in and through smart clothes. In my view, therefore, cybercouture extends the possibilities and functions of fashion as an embodied performance of identity.

Today, some avant-garde designers experiment with the ways in which we can shape our bodies or perform our identities beyond our wildest dreams. They seem to have taken Haraway's plea at heart; an appeal 'for pleasure in the confusion of boundaries' (1991 [1985]: 150; original emphasis). In the next part of this chapter I further explore the work of Pauline van Dongen, Iris van Herpen and Bart Hess, whose futuristic designs blur the boundaries between art, fashion and technology. They not only share a sculptural, technological and artisanal approach to clothes, but also a fascination for stretching the form and shape of the human body and playing with human identity.

Pauline van Dongen: Morphogenesis and Solar Dress

For her graduation at the ArtEZ Fashion Academy in Arnhem in 2010, Pauline van Dongen created a futuristic shoe, 'Morphogenesis', that was designed and manufactured with a 3D printer.[4] It was then still a new technology in the fashion world, which received a lot of media interest. The particular design of the 'Morphogenesis' shoe was sponsored by the Amsterdam design studio 'Freedom of Creation' that is completely dedicated to the technology of 3D printing, also known as rapid prototyping. The result was so successful that van Dongen received various awards for her shoe. It was the intention to take it into production, but she ran up against the limits of the technology: the choice of materials was then quite limited and the polyamide material was too hard and inflexible for a wearable shoe and it was still a too expensive technique to take into commercial production.

The interesting point of 3D printing is that the entire design process takes place in the computer, without using a mould, prototype or moulage on a tailor's dummy. The virtual design is directly transferred from the computer and printed as a three-dimensional object, which can be made of plastic, metal, ceramic and even glass. The technique of 3D printing opens up new possibilities of designing shapes that are impossible to create by hand. Van Dongen was thus able to discover new

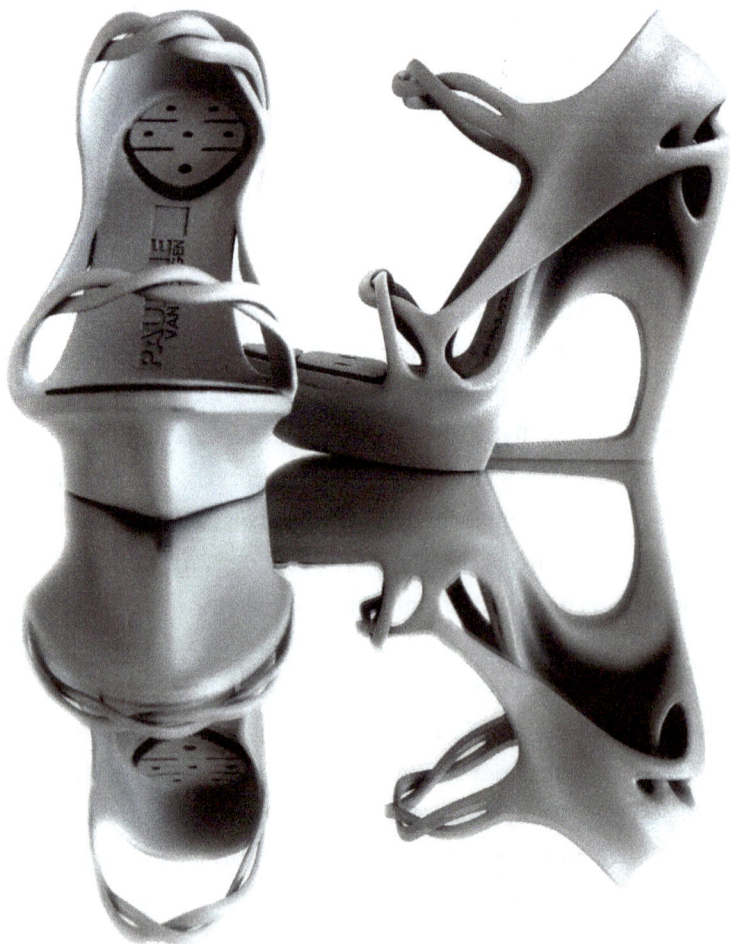

132. Pauline van Dongen, Shoe 'Morphogenesis' (2010).

133. Pauline van Dongen, 'Wearable Solar Dress' (2013).

spatial forms and repetition of structures for the design of the shoe 'Morphogenesis', as the inimitably intertwined loops in the heel show. The technology enables an architectural approach to design, which she now applies to clothes.

Van Dongen believes that wearable technology should move beyond mere gadgetry, by integrating the technology into the clothes to give it a social or communicative function. Pauline van Dongen conducts a meticulous research on the behaviour of experimental and hi-tech materials, combining new technologies with traditional techniques to constantly renovate the practice of craftsmanship. Above all, she is interested in how to make her sculptural and artistic design wearable by

combining technology with industrious workmanship. Paradoxically, then, the example of van Dongen shows that technological innovation in the field of cybercouture is sustained by craftsmanship and workmanship.

Working closely with companies from the field of science and innovation, especially small firms such as Solar Fiber, Elitac, Inntex and Xsens, van Dongen also seeks to integrate solar energy or hardware into the fabrics and clothes. The integration of different expertise has been fundamental for the realisation of projects such as 'Wearable Solar Dress' (2013), an example of wearable technology that integrates solar cells into garments. The project again stimulated a lot of media interest; van Dongen was asked to explain on many a

Dutch television show how the body can become a source of energy by exposing the garment to sunlight for two hours so as to, for example, charge your smartphone. The Wearable Solar Dresses thus feature not only fashionable, but also sustainable technology.

The 'Wearable Solar' dresses contain solar cell modules that are made of flexible thin-film solar cells. As the cells cannot be stitched, Van Dongen worked with leather to create slits in a pre-defined grid, creating pockets for the thin films that are connected on the inside with thin electrical wires. This technology inspired the aesthetics of the dresses: by noticing the layered construction of the solar cells, she then created a layered garment, where the solar cells are placed in modular compartments that can be unfolded to reveal them to light or worn invisibly when they are not needed (Smelik, Toussaint, van Dongen, 2016).

As becomes clear from these examples, Pauline van Dongen's collections create an aesthetics of technology. Her cybercouture refers to what I have called elsewhere a 'becoming-machine' (Smelik, 2016). Deleuze and Guattari introduced this term to indicate a new process of becoming (1987 [1980]). The abstract fluid volume and hyperbolic surfaces of van Dongen's collections 'Kinetic Landscapes' (S/S 2012) and 'Oloid' (S/S 2014), for example, show the possibilities of transforming the human body. Her designs of fashionable technology invite a reflection on new forms of embodiment. The becoming-machine of such fashion designs suggests a dynamic engagement with the technology that surrounds us and vice versa.

Iris van Herpen: Form Follows Emotion

Also a graduate from ArtEZ Fashion Academy in Arnhem, Iris van Herpen has made it to the international platform of high fashion since she was invited to show her collections in Paris as of 2011, as a guest member of the Parisian Chambre Syndicale de la Haute Couture. In 2014, she received the prestigious ANDAM Award that included a year's training under François-Henri Pinault and in 2016 she received a big Dutch award, the Fashion Stipendium from the Prins Bernhard Fund for Culture.

Iris van Herpen's fashion designs are hailed as 'futuristic, sculptural and experimental', in the words of fashion curator Ninke Bloemberg for an exhibition of her work in the Central Museum in Utrecht in 2011 and in the Groninger Museum in 2012 (Bloemberg, 2011: 7). Perhaps no wonder that none other than Lady Gaga and Björk have been spotted in van Herpen's designs. Van Herpen herself refers to her designs as 'organic futurism' because they are characterised by new technologies as well as by detailed handwork (Bloemberg, 2011: 13). Bloemberg describes the designs as 'avatar-like' (2011: 7), and indeed most designs seem to find their inspiration in a science-fiction or fantasy world that is closely related to science and technology.

To understand the special and often alien designs of van Herpen, the term 'becoming' in its sense of becoming-other can help (Smelik, 2016).[5] Throughout her collections, the 3D printed designs seem to be made of wafts of smoke, falls of water, rings of twisted leaves, or folds of bones. In a unique play of endless loops, folds, waves, bends, curls, wrinkles and circles, baroque shapes open and close. Forms undulate and fluctuate. Materials ripple, waver and swing. Van Herpen's sensitive visual language is not captured in traditional flowing fabrics like silk, satin, tulle or organza, but in hard materials such as leather, metal, plastic, synthetic polyesters and hi-tech fabrics. She

134. Iris van Herpen, 'Capriole' (A/W 2011).

135. Iris van Herpen, 'Capriole' (A/W 2011).

succeeds in catching a wave of water in an intangible form, a becoming-water in 'Crystallization' (2011), or a becoming-smoke in a design from the collection 'Refinery Smoke' (2008). Dressed in van Herpen's designs, the models cross the boundaries of what a body can look like and become in-between characters: between humans and animals in 'Fragile Futurity' (2008), between mummy and doll in 'Mummification' (2009), between skeleton and body in 'Capriole' (2011), between man and cyborg in 'Chemical Crow' (2008), between the virtual and material in 'Escapism' (2011) and between organic and artificial in 'Hybrid Holism' (2012) or 'Wilderness Embodied' (2013). In 'Biopiracy' (2014) the models are caught in things that look like spiders' webs. In her latest collections van Herpen pursues her signature in combining 3D-printing patterns with hand-woven textiles mixed with unlikely materials such as steel. 'Magnetic Motion' (S/S 2015) was inspired by the power of magnetic fields that she discovered during her stay as artist-in-residence at the European Organization for Nuclear Research CERN. As she did for 'Hacking Infinity' (A/W 2015–16), she worked together with artists and architects to create a fractal look that fuses nature and technology.

Van Herpen's designs come across as futuristic, morphing new silhouettes, inviting the wearer to inhabit the freedom of co-creating the body into new shapes. In her experiment with form and matter she calls for a different relation to the, mostly female, body. As van Herpen says:

I just do not subscribe to the slogan 'Form follows function'. Instead, I look for shapes that complement and change the body and thus the emotion. Movement, so essential to and in the body, is just as important in my work. (Van Herpen quoted in Bloemberg, 2011: 11)

Looking at any one of her innovative designs one can see how the human body is invited to become dynamic, opening up to a multiplicity of lines, notches, gaps, holes and fissures.

Van Herpen's style does not only derive from her talent and imagination, but is also made possible by new technologies. She is always on the lookout for new forms, materials and techniques, with which she then experiments in her studio (Bloemberg, 2011: 13). Her work is thus an example of the blurring of boundaries between fashion and technology, or as Ava Chin writes: 'Indeed, technology *is* the fashion' (2010: 35, original emphasis). As we read above, 3D design and printing has brought about a revolution in design practice, opening up possibilities of creating new forms which would have been impossible when designing by hand on a flat sheet. Yet, importantly, as for Pauline van Dongen – and Bart Hess, as we shall see below – craftsmanship remains important to van Herpen's work. Each garment, however much technologically designed and manufactured, is finished with the finest detail by hand. In other words, the fusion between technology and craftsmanship is paramount. As Iris van Herpen comments:

The combination of craftsmanship and new technology is crucial for me, because it gives a tension between the possibilities of technology and the redundancy of traditional techniques. I do not want to resolve this tension by only designing clothes in a high-tech way, but I sustain the tension by giving ample space to manual workmanship. (Van Herpen quoted in Bloemberg, 2011: 11)

More recently, she claims that she is 'still searching for a way to fill the gap between the computer process and the traditional craftsmanship that is done by hand' (Lampe 2015: 36). For her, science, technology and craftsmanship should come together into a fusion where they can enhance one another.

Bart Hess: Organic High-Tech

As a graduate from the Design Academy in Eindhoven, Bart Hess is perhaps more of an artist than a fashion designer, although he has made textiles, photographs and animations for American *Vogue*, and for fashion designers Walter van Beirendonck (with whom he did an internship in 2006), Iris van Herpen (2011) and Thierry Mugler (S/S 2013). With his fascination for manipulating the human body, Hess pushes the boundaries of textile design by extending the materials through other media such as film, photography and animation. His futuristic materials blur the boundary between textile and skin. He has dressed the naked, often male, body not so much in clothes, but in a range of textures including toothpicks, shaving foam, grass, pins and needles, earth, shards of plastic and even slime. To create the latter he mixes hundreds of small pots of slime, which he purchases in children's toy shops, with latex, paint and other materials. Hess then pours the coloured slime over a model in the studio or during live performances. While the model stands dripping for ten or fifteen minutes, Hess takes pictures or makes

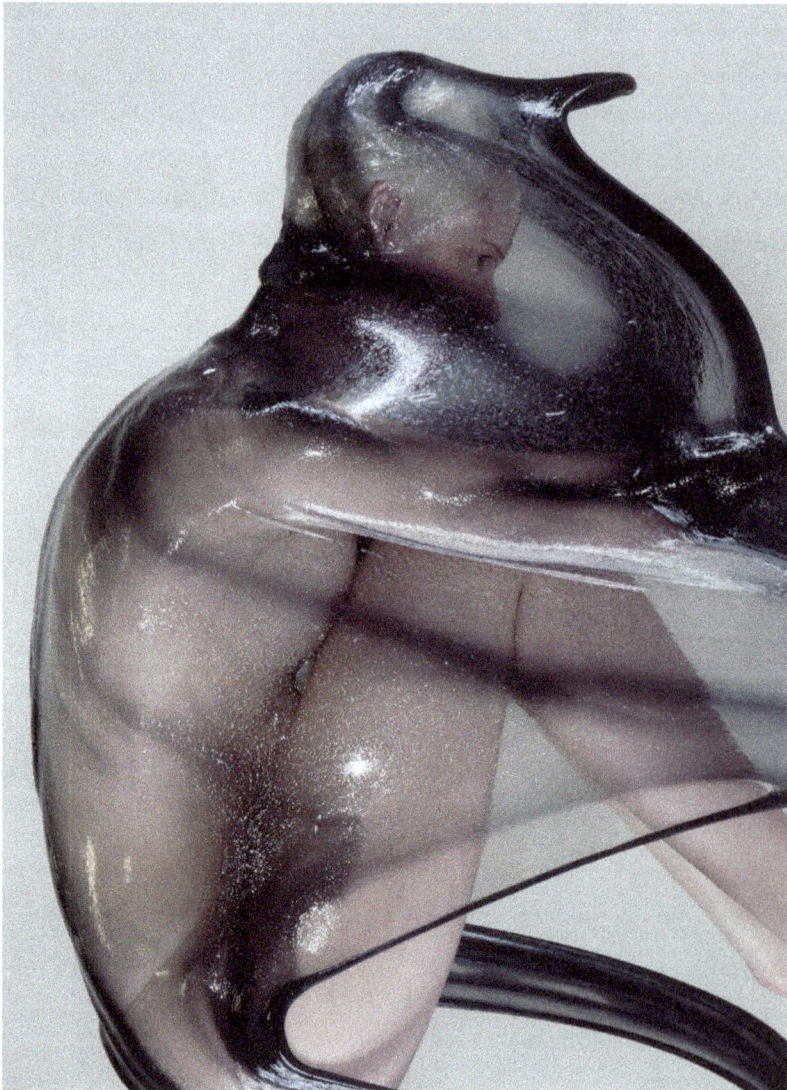

136. Bart Hess, 'Slime' (2010).

ANNEKE SMELIK

137. LucyandBart,
'Exploded View 2' (2010).

videos of the slow slimy process. One of the more famous designs is his 'Slime Outfit' for Lady Gaga's album *Born This Way* (2010).

Here we find an image that expresses perfectly, if not literally, the becoming of an identity in flux. This is a human body dressed almost beyond recognition; a body without a pre-ordained meaning or function. As the slime drips down, the body reveals its constant state of flux, of transformation, of becoming.

Slime is not particularly technological, but I have used the example here to show how art can push the boundaries of what a body can become, unleashing normative ideas of what a body should look like. Bart

Hess has also produced many high-tech images of cyborg-like figures, for example in his projects 'Pins and Needles' (2014), where he adorns the body in pins, studs and needles, 'Echo', where he dresses the body in liquid glass (2011) or 'Mutants' where he clothes the body in latex (2011). Like the work of Iris van Herpen, his work is often referred to as 'futuristic'.

In the exhibition *A Hunt for High Tech* (2013) the Rijksmuseum Twente in Enschede showed a collection of such futuristic designs by Bart Hess. The collection of photography, animations and live performances shows conceptual textiles that blur the boundaries between nature and technology in an effort to create new human/animal/cyborg-like figures. Hess manipulates inorganic materials, such as plastic, foil, silicone, latex and clothing pins, to create synthetic skins and furs, magnifying and exaggerating their characteristics. The result is an ambiguous mix of biological organisms and technological devices in a futuristic-looking collection. This is a very different kind of wearable technology to what I have discussed so far in this chapter. The 'wearables' in this case are not really wearable, because they are often made of materials that are temporarily glued to or poured over the human body, but they do explore the corporeal and sensorial boundaries of the human body. What strikes the viewer is the suggestion of tactile qualities; it takes a moment to realise you are not looking at hair, fur or scales, but at a range of strange materials such as foam, balloons, needles or toothpicks. As in the case of the textiles that Bart Hess created for Iris van Herpen, they show the vast amount of handicraft that is implicated in his work.

Despite the futuristic appearance of many of his works, there is, in fact, very little technology involved. He has created many images through traditional craftsmanship and basic photographic and video-editing techniques. The outlandish forms that he creates are based on painstaking manual labour, while the textures often suggest the possibility of organic growth in a hi-tech lab. The paradoxical effect is that he thus points to the *im*possibility of such lab-grown materials. Like in his earlier work with Lucy McRae, as the duo LucyandBart that I mentioned above, Bart Hess alters the appearance of the human body or the human face into fascinating forms beyond recognition. Again, the notion of 'becoming-other' of Deleuze and Guattari (1987 [1980]) comes to mind: becoming-animal, becoming-cyborg, becoming-alien, becoming-fluid.

The Future of Cybercouture Is Now

In the first part of this chapter I discussed the context and practice of fashionable technology in the Netherlands, while in the second part I focused on the work of three young Dutch designers. In this concluding section I want to draw out several points: the emphasis on craftsmanship, the importance of materiality and the play of identity.

To begin with, Pauline van Dongen, Iris van Herpen and Bart Hess share an intense love for crafts-manship; each of them likes to engage hands-on with the materiality of textiles and textures. In my view, the renewed focus on craftsmanship is intimately connected to the technological world we live in. As Richard Sennett writes, 'technical understanding develops through the powers of imagination' (2008: 10). The qualities that are imbibed in craftsmanship bring the technologies within the grip of our hands, making the hi-tech world more human and accessible. Where for Sennett it seems to be impossible or utopian for craftsmen to work with the machines productively (2008: 118), the Dutch designers are keen to combine craftsmanship with technology; it is not a question of one excluding the other – they go hand in hand. Here we can hark back to the original Greek meaning of the word *techne*: art, skill, craft. The focus on craftsmanship betrays a new interest in the materi-ality of matter in a hi-tech world of virtual technologies (Barrett and Bolt, 2012). While van Dongen, van Herpen and Hess focus first and foremost on the materiality of textiles, as fashion designers they are also interested in the materiality of the human skin and body. Moreover, they extend their fascination for matter and materiality to the technologies that they use; they have developed what Sennett calls a 'material consciousness' (2008: 119).

I draw attention to the issue of materiality, because matter is precarious in an age of digital and virtual technologies (Coole and Frost, 2010; Bennett and Joyce, 2010).[6] The notion of materiality allows us to focus on the actual matter of technology and how our – material

– bodies relate, often intimately, to the technical objects that enhance our clothes and our selves. There is no doubt that technological innovations will have a deep impact on the meaning and communication of clothes and fashion. If technologically enhanced clothes can measure temperatures, chemical processes or vital functions, sense movement and position, or have expressive qualities, they will change the relation of the wearers to themselves as well as transform the communication to and with others. The fact that the garments are worn on the body increases the urgency to take into account the body's materiality. Perhaps fashionable technology can develop ways of integrating the body's tactility and sensitivity into the design. This is where I think the futuristic designs of van Dongen, van Herpen and Hess can help us to shape and change our identities differently.

Moving in between art, fashion and technology, Pauline van Dongen, Iris van Herpen and Bart Hess experiment with the ways in which we can shape our bodies or perform our identities. Clearly, they move us out of our comfort zone or our wardrobes into a fantasy world, where they take pleasure in confusing boundaries between human and cyborg, or human and animal, but also shift ambiguous borders between skin and textile, organic and technological, material and digital. Their cybercouture shares a futuristic outlook, opening up a horizon beyond conventional fashion. In their shared fascination for stretching the boundaries of the human body, they tempt the viewer or wearer to put his/her identity at play. As I argued in this chapter, this play with identity can be understood – following Deleuze and Guattari – as a process of 'becoming'. As Kelly writes, 'we are nothing more and nothing less than an evolutionary ordained becoming' (2010: 128). In his view technology is part and parcel of that open-ended process. The three Dutch designers that I discussed in this chapter ask us to engage affectively with the fusion of art, fashion and wearable technology, embarking on the transformative process of becoming. The strange shapes, forms, textiles and materials invite a reflection on new forms of both embodiment and human identity. By reshaping the human body beyond its finite contours, cybercouture offers an encounter between fashion and technology, opening up to a future world where garments are merged with human skin, body and identity.

Notes

1. I thank Lianne Toussaint for her valuable input in this paragraph.

2. Personal communication with professor Hein Daanen, June 2014.

3. In this context it may be interesting to mention that I am currently (2013–2018) running a research project on fashionable technology at the Radboud University Nijmegen, together with the Technical University Eindhoven (Oscar Tómicó Placencia) and the ArtEZ Fashion Academy Arnhem (José Teunissen), financially supported by the Netherlands Organisation for Scientific Research. The interdisciplinary research project is called *Crafting Wearables* and aims at designing wearables that are robust, fashionable as well as commercially viable within the production chain. It brings together the different fields of fashion, technology, industry and academic scholarship, by working with the following private and public partners: Philips Research, Textile Museum Tilburg, MODINT, Freedom of Creation, Solar Fiber, Inntex, and Xsens. The two PhDs are Pauline van Dongen as designer and Lianne Toussaint for the social-cultural perspective. See for more information: www.craftingwearables.com.

4. The information for this section is based on several conversations with Pauline van Dongen between 2011 and 2015.

5. In the article 'Gilles Deleuze: Bodies-without-Organs in the Folds of Fashion' I have analysed the work of Iris van Herpen and Bart Hess more systematically with several of Deleuze's concepts (Smelik, 2016).

6. In the 'Introduction' to *Thinking Through Fashion*, Agnès Rocamora and I have elaborated on the use of theories of materialism for fashion studies (Rocamora and Smelik, 2016).

Anouk Wipprecht (b. Purmerend 1985)

Lianne Toussaint

What does fashion lack? Microcontrollers.

—www.anoukwipprecht.nl

'Fashion-tech designer' Anouk Wipprecht epitomises a futuristic and exciting new field of 'fashionable technology': fashion that integrates technology of all sorts (see chapter 14). Her work offers a glimpse of what the future of Dutch fashion might hold.

Wipprecht's work represents a rare combination of fashion design, engineering and science and interaction design. She brings fashion and technology together by designing garments that are fashionable and artistic, but also contain high-tech systems or functions. Having a background in fashion design and interaction design, Wipprecht aims to establish thought-provoking encounters between these two formerly separate domains. Fashion particularly interests her because of the emotional, intellectual and sensual experiences it can convey, as well as the close physical and psychological relation it may have to its wearer. Based on this fascination, Wipprecht designs garments that trigger certain experiences, behaviour and interactions.

After graduating in 2010, Wipprecht worked with Studio Roosegaarde to create 'Intimacy': a dress made of opaque smart foils that become more or less transparent in response to the wearer's heart rate. It was the first of many interdisciplinary collaborations with programmers, engineers and artists. Like 'Intimacy', most of Wipprecht's designs establish a playful interaction through reacting to the emotions or behaviour of the wearer and her environment. 'Daredroid 2.0' (2011) is a robotic dress that is able to make cocktails for party guests. The dress, however, does not serve the alcohol until the drinker personally interacts with the wearer by playing a touch screen game of 'truth or dare'. The 'Smoke Dress' (2012) and 'Robotic Spider Dress' (2012) use ideas of personal space, embarrassment and defence. When someone comes too close these dresses will suddenly react by respectively veiling the wearer in thick smoke or protectively 'attacking' the intruder with a set of robotic arms (Pakhchyan, 2012).

Wipprecht's innovative designs radically redefine what fashion is and can be in the future. Will fashion be able to reflect, trigger or even correct our behaviour? Will it extend our inner and interpersonal experiences, helping and challenging us to deal differently with certain social, emotional or physical issues? Whatever the case, Wipprecht's 'fashiontech' designs reveal that fashion is on the verge becoming much more than just fashion.

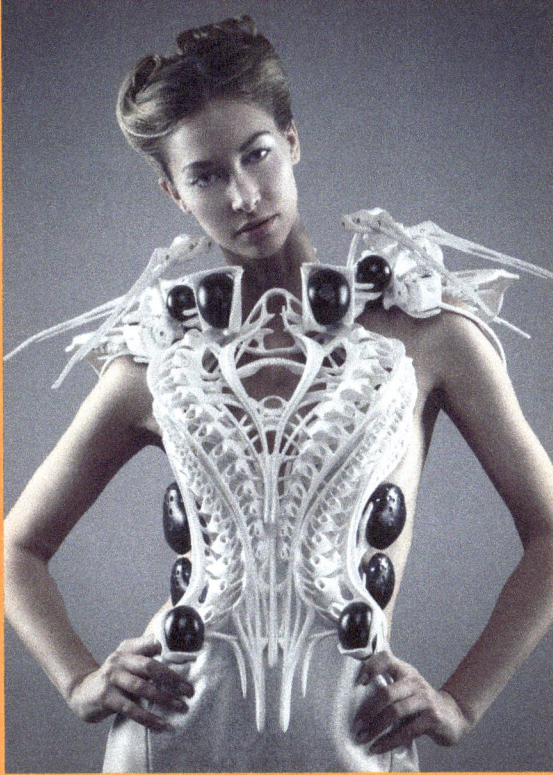

138. Anouk Wipprecht, 'Spider Dress 2.0' (2015).

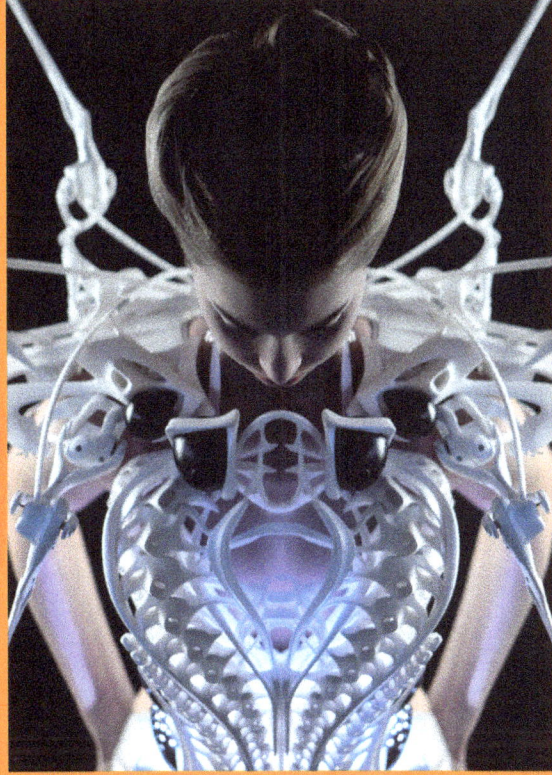

139. Anouk Wipprecht, 'Spider Dress 2.0' (2015).

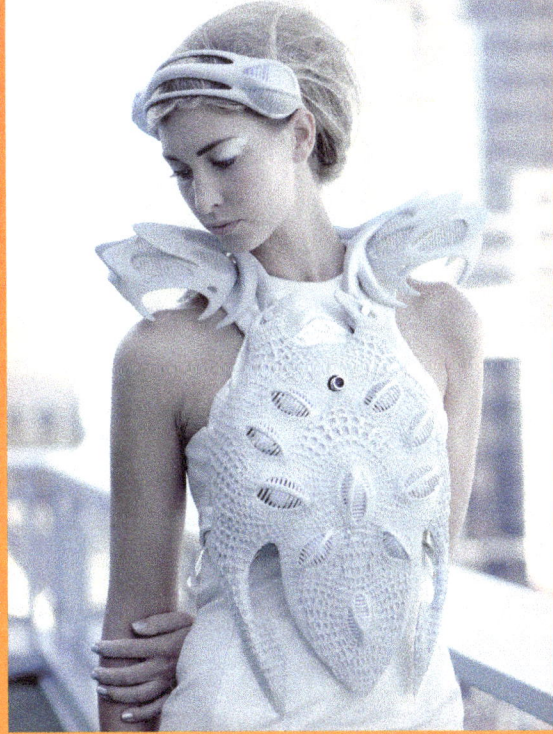

140. Anouk Wipprecht, 'Synapse' (2014).

141. Anouk Wipprecht, 'Detail of Synapse' (2014).

Bibliography

Aalderink, R. (2013) 'Jurken van Houtpulp en Colaflessen' in *Het Parool*, Specials, 6 June: 12.

Allen, J. (2000) 'Power/Economic Knowledge: Symbolic and Spatial Formations' in J.R. Bryson, P.W. Daniels, N. Henry and J. Pollard (eds), *Knowledge, Space, Economy*, London: Routledge.

Altagamma (2011) 'Worldwide Luxury Markets Monitor: Spring 2011 Update', Milan, May 3 (retrieved through http://www.altagamma.it/download/Altagamma_Worldwide_Markets_Monitor_Spring_2011_Update.pdf on 1 October 2014).

Amin, A. and P. Cohendet (2004) *Architectures of Knowledge: Firms, Capabilities, and Communities*, Oxford: University Press.

Amsterdams Blauw (n.d.) 'About Us' (retrieved through http://amsterdamsblauwabdc.blogspot.com/p/about-us.html on November 15 2011).

Anderson, B. (2006 [1983]) *Imagined Communities: Reflections on the Origin and Spread of Nationalism*, London and New York: Verso.

anon. (1986) 'De Visie van "Grand Seigneur" Jacques Van Gils op het Ontwerpen van Mode' in Confectie & Tricotage: 395-97.

anon. (2008) 'Liz to Outsource Mexx Global Sourcing Operations to Li & Fung' in *Fibre2fashion*, 12 November (retrieved through www.fibre2fashion.com/news/fashion

anon. (2010) 'Interview: Spijkers en Spijkers' in *Elle.nl* (retrieved through http://www.elle.nl/Maybelline

anon. (2010) 'Redding Mexx Nabij?' in *Textilia*, 12 May.

anon. (2010) 'We Willen het Merk weer Terugbrengen naar zijn Kracht' in *Fashion United*.

anon. (2012) 'Ik ben mijn eigen icoon' (Bas Kosters quoted in) *Het Parool*, 14 January: 11.

anon. (2012) 'Jeans: Van Mijnen naar Haute Couture' in *De Gelderlander*, 24 November.

anon. (2012) 'Verslaafd aan Bluejeans' in *Haarlems Dagblad*, 4 December.

anon. (2012) 'In het Land van Mest, Mist en Denim' in *Trouw*, 23 November.

Arts, J. (2006) 'G-Star' in J. Teunissen (ed.), *Mode in Nederland*, Arnhem: Terra.

Arts, J. (2006) 'Marlies Dekkers' in J. Teunissen (ed.), *Mode in Nederland*, Arnhem: Terra.

Arts, J. (2010) *Oilily*, Arnhem/Zwolle: d'jonge Hond/ArtEZ Press.

Assmann, J. (1992) *Das Kulturelle Gedächtnis: Schrift, Erinnerung und Politische Identität in frühen Hochkulturen*, München: Beck.

Bakker, A. (2010) 'Mooie Tijden: Mac & Maggie' in *Flow*, 6 (retrieved through http://www.corakemperman.nl/content.asp?path=k7k3vw5s on 23 September 2014).

Baks, E. (2012) 'Eerbetoon aan Spijkerstof' in *Dagblad van het Noorden*, 5 December.

Balsamo, A. (2011) *Designing Culture: The Technological Imagination at Work*, Durham: Duke University Press.

Barker, C. (2008) *Cultural Studies: Theory and Practice*, London: SAGE.

Barrett, E. and B. Bolt (eds) (2013) *Carnal Knowledge: Towards a 'New Materialism' through the Arts*, London/New York: I.B.Tauris.

Barthes, R. (1990 [1967]) *The Fashion System*, M. Ward and R. Howard (trans.), Berkeley and Los Angeles: University of California Press.

Barthes, R. (1991 [1957]) *Mythologies*, J. Cape (trans.), London: Paladin.

Bas Kosters Studio (n.d.) 'Biography Bas Kosters' (retrieved through www.baskosters.com/bas-kosters/biography on 12 February 2016).

Baudrillard, J. (1993 [1976]) *Symbolic Exchange and Death*, I. Grant (trans.), London: SAGE.

Bauman, Z. (2000) *Liquid Modernity*, Cambridge: Polity Press.

Bauman, Z. (2005) *Liquid Life*, Cambridge: Polity Press.

Bauman, Z. (2011) *Culture in a Liquid Modern World*, Cambridge: Polity Press.

Bauman, Z. (2013) *Does the Richness of the Few Benefit Us All?*, Cambridge: Polity Press.

Beard, N. (2011) 'Defining the Fashion City: Fashion Capital or Style Centre' in A. de Witt-Paul and M. Crouch (eds), *Fashion Forward*, Oxford: Inter-disciplinary Press.

Beck, U. (2007) 'The Cosmopolitan Condition: Why Methodological Nationalism Fails' in *Theory, Culture & Society*, 24 (7-8): 286-290.

Bennett, T. and P. Joyce (eds) (2010) *Material Powers: Cultural Studies, History, and the Material Turn*, London/New York: Routledge.

Berger Hochstrasser, J. (2007) *Still Life and Trade in the Dutch Golden Age*, New Haven: Yale University Press.

Bernheim, N. et al. (2015), *The Belgians. An Unexpected Fashion Story*. Hamburg: Hatje Cantz.

Betlem, R. (2012) 'Amsterdam Is in Opkomst als Vestigingsplaats voor Jeansindustrie' in *Financieel Dagblad*, 21 November.

Billig, M. (1995) *Banal Nationalism*, London: SAGE.

Bloemberg, N. (2012) 'Dutch Jeans' in N. Bloemberg and H. Schopping (eds), *Blue Jeans*, Utrecht: Centraal Museum, exhibition catalogue.

Bloemberg, N. (ed) (2011) *Het Nieuwe Ambacht: Iris van Herpen en Haar Inspiratie*, Utrecht: Centraal Museum.

Blommers, A. and N. Schumm (2007) 'State of Uncertainty' in E. Bippus and D. Mink (eds), *Fashion Body Cult*, Stuttgart: Arnoldsche Art Publishers.

Blue Blood (2009) 'Blue Blood Packs Amsterdam in Denim' (retrieved through http://bluebloodblog.wordpress.com/2009/07/17/blue-blood-packs-amsterdam-in-denim/ on 12 February 2016).

Boekman (2012) thematic issue on the Creative Industry in The Netherlands, 24 (93).

Boelsma, M. (2000) 'Viktor & Rolf Staren en Zwijgen' in *Algemeen Dagblad*, 6 November: 23.

Bogue, R. (2007) *Deleuze's Way: Essays in Transverse Ethics and Aesthetics*, Aldershot: Ashgate.

Bolt, B. (2013) 'Introduction: Toward a "New Materialism" through the Arts' in E. Barrett and B. Bolt (eds), *Carnal Knowledge: Towards a 'New Materialism' through the Arts*, London/New York: I.B.Tauris.

Bomers, G.B.J. and R.M. Boudeguer (1990) *The Mexx Group (A)*, Breukelen: Nijenrode University Press.

Bosman, L. (2012) 'Ik Geloof in Evolutie, Niet in Revolutie' in *Textilia*, 91 (18/19): 6-7.

Boucher, F. (1987 [1965]) *20,000 Years of Fashion: The History of Costume and Personal Adornment*, New York: Thames and Hudson.

Boudeguer, R.M. and M.M. van Leeuwen (1994) 'Mexx' in G.F. Jonkergouw and F.J. De Vries (eds), *Strategic Issues for Management in an Integrated European Context*, Heerlen: Open University.

Bourriaud, N. (2000) 'Blue Company: Or, Yves Klein Considered as a World-Economy' in G. Perlein and B. Corà (eds), *Yves Klein: Long Live the Immaterial!*, New York: Delano Greenidge Editions.

Bovone, L. (2012) 'Fashion, Identity and Social Actors' in A.M. González and L. Bovone (eds), *Identities Through Fashion. A Multidisciplinary Approach*. London: Berg: 67-93.

Brand, J. and J. Teunissen (eds) (2006) *The Power of Fashion: About Design and Meaning*, Arnhem: Terra.

Brands, M. (2006) *Avenue van A tot Zero*, Rotterdam: Veenman.

Breukink-Peeze, M. (2000) 'Sitshandel en Aspecten van Sits in Mode en Streekdracht' in G. Arnolli et al. (eds), *Kostuum. Relaties: Mode en Streekdracht*, Amsterdam: Nederlandse Kostuumvereniging.

Breward, C., B. Conekin, and C. Cox (eds) (2002) *The Englishness of English Dress*, Oxford/New York: Berg.

Brown, S. (2007) 'Harry Potter and the Fandom Menace' in B. Cova, R.V. Kozinets, and A. Shankar (eds.), *Consumer Tribes*, Oxford: 177-193.

Brubaker, R. and F. Cooper (2000) 'Beyond "Identity"' in *Theory and Society*, 29: 1-47.

Bruggeman, D. (2009) 'Ontsnappen aan het Gezicht van de Blanke Man' in *Raffia*, 21 (3): 3-6.

Bruggeman, D. (2013) 'The Invisible Presence of the Internalised Corset: Post-Feminist Values Materialised in Marlies Dekkers' Lingerie'. In: Marco Pedroni (ed.) *From Production to Consumption: The Cultural Industry of Fashion*. Oxford: Inter-Disciplinary Press: 37-56.

Bruggeman, D. (2014) 'More than Meets the Eye: Dutch Fashion, Identity and New Materialism', doctoral dissertation, Nijmegen: Radboud University (accessible through http://repository.ubn.ru.nl/bitstream/handle/2066/132976/132976.pdf?sequence=1).

Bruggeman, D. (2015) 'Questioning Identity Through Digital "Imaginings"' in J. Lamoree, J. Teunissen, and H. Van Der Voet (eds), *Everything but Clothes: Fashion, Photography, Magazines*, Arnhem/Houten: ArtEZ Press and Terra Lannoo.

Bruggeman, D. and A. Van de Peer (2016) 'Long Live the (im)Material: Concept and Materiality in Viktor & Rolf's Fashion' in *International Journal of Fashion Studies*, 3 (1): 7-26.

Bryson, P.W. Daniels, N. Henry, and J. Pollard (eds) *Knowledge, Space, Economy*, London: Routledge.

Butler, J. (1990) *Gender Trouble*, London: Routledge.

Carvalho, H. (1996) 'Frans Molenaar en de Nederlandse Modetraditie: Een Beetje Knippen en Plakken' in *NRC Handelsblad*, 15 May: 3.

Chadha, N. (2006) *It Started with a Kiss: Twenty Years of Mexx*, Amsterdam: BIS.

Chin, A. (2010) 'Technology Shapes Fashion' in R. Scapp and B. Seitz (eds), *Fashion Statements: On Style, Appearance and Reality*, London/New York: Palgrave Macmillan.

Cho, G. (ed) (2012) *Smart Clothing: Technology and Applications*, Boca Raton: CRC Press.

Clark, H. (2009) 'Fashioning "China Style" in the Twenty-first Century' in E. Paulicelli and H. Clark (eds), *The Fabric of Cultures: Fashion, Identity and Globalization*, New York: Routledge.

Clark, J. (2004) *Spectres: When Fashion Turns Back*, London: V&A Publications.

Clynes, M. (1995) 'Interview' in C.H. Gray (ed), *The Cyborg Handbook*, London: Routledge: 43-54.

273

Colebrook, C. (2002) *Understanding Deleuze*, Crows Nest: Allen & Unwin.

Conrads, M. (1992) 'De Mythe van de Denim' in H. Diederiks (ed) *Textielhistorische Bijdragen* 32 (1992), Enschede: Stichting Textielgeschiedenis.

Coole, D. and S. Frost (eds) (2010) *New Materialisms: Ontology, Agency and Politics*, Durham: Duke University Press.

Costin, S. and P. Grotenhuis (1989) *Vijftig in Veertig: Modebeurs Amsterdam*, Amsterdam: Vereniging Nederlandse Modebeurs.

Cotton Incorporated (2005) 'Return of the Dragon: Post Quota Cotton Textile Trade' in *Textile Consumer*, 36 (Summer): 1-4.

Cova, B., D. Dalli, and D. Zwick (2011) 'Critical Perspectives on Consumers' Role as "Producers": Broadening the Debate on Value Co-creation in Marketing Processes' in *Marketing Theory*, 11 (3): 231-41.

Craik, J. (2009) 'Is Australian Fashion and Dress Distinctively Australian?' in *Fashion Theory: The Journal of Dress, Body & Culture*, 13 (4): 409-442.

Crane, D. (2000) *Fashion and its Social Agendas: Class, Gender, and Identity in Clothing*, Chicago University Press.

Crill, R. (2008) *Chintz: Indian Textiles for the West*, London: V&A Publishing.

Daanen, H. and F.B. Ter Haar (2013) '3D Whole Body Scanners Revisited' in *Displays*, 34 (4): 270-75.

Dartmann, L. (2011) 'Tulips, Cheese and Pickled Herrings in Amsterdam?' in *Sportswear International*, (238): 50-54.

Davis, F. (1992) *Fashion, Culture, and Identity*, Chicago: Chicago University Press.

Dawson, J.A. and S.A. Shaw (1990) 'The Changing Character of Retailer-Supplier Relationships' in J. Fernie (ed), *Retail Distribution Management: A Strategic Guide to Developments and Trends*, London: Kogan Page.

De Baan, E. (2005) 'Ooit hadden ze kritiek op de modewereld. Maar ook Viktor & Rolf hebben de commerciële mode omarmd' in *Trouw*, 4 January: 16.

De Baan, E. (2006) 'Max Heymans' in J. Teunissen (ed), *Mode in Nederland*, Arnhem: Terra.

De Baan, E. (2008) 'Meesterlijke Mode-popjes; Kunst' in *Trouw*, 16 June: 10-11.

De Baan, E. (2012) 'Nederlands Blauw' in *Trouw*, 15 December.

De Beus, J. (1996) 'The Value of National Identity' in A. Klamer (ed), *The Value of Culture*, Amsterdam: Amsterdam University Press: 166-186.

De Feijter, I. (2014) '"Het zijn de mensen die de kleren maken": C&A Herpositioneert zich met Hippe Winkels' in *Trends*, 6 February: 82.

De Jong, A. (1998) 'Dracht en Eendracht: De Politieke Dimensie van Klederdrachten, 1850-1920' in D. Verhoeven (ed), *Klederdracht en Kleedgedrag: Het Kostuum Harer Majesteits Onderdanen, 1898–1998*, Nijmegen: SUN.

De Jong, A. (2001) *De Dirigenten van de Herinnering: Musealisering en Nationalisering van de Volkscultuur in Nederland 1815–1940*, Nijmegen: SUN.

De Jonge, J. (2010) 'Dressed in Radiant Black' in K. Debo (ed), *Black: Masters of Black in Fashion and Costume*, Tielt: Lannoo.

De la Fressange, I. (2011) *La Parisienne*, Paris: Flammarion.

De la Haye, A. (ed.) (1996) *The Cutting Edge: 50 Years of British Fashion, 1947–1997*, London: V&A Publications.

De Leeuw, K. (1991) 'Local Costume in the Netherlands, 1800–Today: An Out-of-date Position or a Collective Stance?' in *Economic and Social History in the Netherlands*, 3: 61-81.

De Leeuw, K. (1998) 'Voorschrift, Verandering en Variatie in de Streekdracht' in D. Verhoeven, *Klederdracht en Kleedgedrag: Het Kostuum Harer Majesteits Onderdanen 1898–1998*, Nijmegen: SUN.

De Leeuw, K. (2000a) *Jong! Jongerencultuur en Stijl in Nederland 1950–2000*, Zwolle: Waanders.

De Leeuw, K. (2000b) 'Van Spijkerbroek tot Cocktailjurk: De Invloed van Amerika op het Kleedgedrag in Nederland, 1944–1969' in *Jaarboek Nederlands Openlucht Museum*, (6): 104-21.

De Perthuis, K. (2008) 'Beyond Perfection: The Fashion Model in the Age of Digital Manipulation' in E. Shinkle (ed), *Fashion as Photograph: Viewing and Reviewing Images of Fashion*, London/New York: I.B.Tauris.

De Rijk, T. (2003) *Designers in Nederland: Een Eeuw Productvormgeving*, Amsterdam: Ludion.

De Vries, F.J. (eds), *Strategic Issues for Management in an Integrated European*

De Winkel, M. (2006) *Fashion and Fancy: Dress and Meaning in Rembrandt's Paintings*, Amsterdam: University Press.

De Witt-Paul, A. and M. Crouch (eds) (2011) *Fashion Forward*, Oxford: Inter-Disciplinary Press.

Dekkers, M. (2015) 'I believe in Innerwear becomes Outerwear' in 'Maison Marlies: Get Dressed' (retrieved through https://eu.marliesdekkers.com/nl-nl/maison-marlies/i-believe-in-innerwear-becomes-outerwear.html on 10 February 2016).

Deleuze, G. (1994 [1968]) *Difference and Repetition*, London: Athlone Press.

Deleuze, G. (2006) 'What is the Creative Act?' in D. Lapoujade (ed), *Two Regimes of Madness: Texts and Interviews 1975–1995*, New York: Semiotext(e).

Deleuze, G. and F. Guattari (1987 [1980]) *A Thousand Plateaus: Capitalism and Schizophrenia*, B. Massumi (trans.), Minneapolis: University of Minnesota Press.

Deleuze, G. and F. Guattari (1994 [1991]) *What is Philosophy?*, London/New York: Verso.

Delpal, F. (2014) 'New Luxury? How Luxury Customer Behavior Redefines Companies' Strategies' in *New Conversations in Fashion—23-24 January*, Amsterdam, conference proceedings, Fashion Colloquia.

Dicken, P. (2007) *Global Shift: Mapping the Changing Contours of the World Economy* (5th ed.), London: SAGE.

Dolphijn, R. and I. van der Tuin (2012) *New Materialism: Interviews and Cartographies*, Open Humanities Press.

Dunne, L.E. (2011) 'Wearable Technology' in L. Welters and A. Lillethun (eds), *The Fashion Reader* (2nd ed.), Oxford/New York: Berg.

Duyvendak, J.W. and M. Hurenkamp (eds) (2004) *Kiezen voor de Kudde: Lichte Gemeenschappen en de Nieuwe Meerderheid*, Amsterdam: Van Gennep.

Emmer, P.C. (2006) *The Dutch Slave Trade: 1500–1850*, New York: Berghahn Books.

Entwistle, J. (2000) *The Fashioned Body: Fashion, Dress and Modern Theory*, Cambridge: Polity Press.

Entwistle, J. (2007) 'The Dressed Body' in L. Welters and A. Lillethun (eds), *The Fashion Reader*, Oxford/New York: Berg.

Entwistle, J. and E. Wilson (eds) (2003) *Body Dressing*, Oxford/New York: Berg.

Es, G., A. Govaerts, and S. van Riel. (1989) *België: Mode in de Lage Landen*, Antwerpen: Cantecleer.

Esser, Y. (2014) 'The People of the Labyrinths: De Toekomst Ligt Weer Open' in *Fashion United*, 29 April.

Evans, C. (2003) *Fashion at the Edge: Spectacle, Modernity, and Deathliness*, New Haven/London: Yale University Press.

Evans, C. (2008) 'Introduction' in C. Evans and S. Frankel (eds), *The House of Viktor & Rolf*, London/New York: Merrell.

Evans, C. and C. Breward (eds) (2005) *Fashion and Modernity*, Oxford/New York: Berg.

Evans, C. and S. Frankel (eds) (2008) *The House of Viktor & Rolf*, London/New York: Merrell.

Faust, M. (2005) *Reorganization and Relocation in the German Fashion Industry*, Cambridge: University of Cambridge, conference paper

Feitsma, M. (2011) 'Don't Dress to Impress: The Dutch Fashion Mentality' in J.L. Foltyn (ed), *Fashions: Exploring Fashions Through Culture*, Oxford: The Inter-Disciplinary Press.

Feitsma, M. (2012) 'Colour me Drab? Colours in Dutch Regional Wear and Fashion' in J. Berry (ed), *Fashion Capital: Style Economies, Cities and Cultures*, Oxford: Inter-Disciplinary Press.

Feitsma, M. (2014) 'Nederlandse Mode: Een Verkenning van Mythevorming en Betekenissen (Dutch Fashion: An Exploration of Myths and Meanings)', Nijmegen: Radboud University, doctoral dissertation (accessible through http://repository.ubn.ru.nl/bitstream/handle/2066/127127/127127.pdf?sequence=1).

Fermont, H.M.A. (2009) *Het Faillissement van Vilenzo: Teloorgang van een Hollandse Modereus*, Rotterdam: Erasmus University, MA thesis.

Ferwerda, J. (2006) 'Bas Kosters' in J. Teunissen (ed) *Mode in Nederland*, Arnhem: Terra.

Ferwerda, J. (2006) 'C&A' in J. Teunissen (ed), *Mode in Nederland*, Arnhem: Terra.

Ferwerda, J. (2006) 'Jan Taminiau' in J. Teunissen (ed), *Mode in Nederland*: Arnhem: Terra.

Finkelstein, J. (2007) *The Art of Self Invention: Image and Identity in Popular Visual Culture*, London/New York: I.B.Tauris.

Finlayson, I. (1990) *Denim: An American Legend*, New York: Simon & Schuster.

Fiske, J. (1989) 'The Jeaning of America' in *Understanding Popular Culture*, London: Routledge.

Flügel, J.C. (1950) *The Psychology of Clothes*, London: Hogarth Press.

Forsström, B. (2005) *Value Co-Creation in Industrial Buyer-Seller Partnerships*, Turku: Åbo Akademis Förlag.

Fortunati, L., J.E. Katz, and R. Riccini (eds) (2008) *Mediating the Human Body: Technology, Communication, and Fashion*, New Jersey: Lawrence Erlbaum.

Frankel, S. (2008) 'Interview' in C. Evans and S. Frankel (eds), *The House of Viktor & Rolf*, London/New York: Merrell.

Frijhoff, W. and M. Spies (2004) *Dutch Culture in a European Perspective: 1650, Hard-won Unity*, Basingstoke: Palgrave Macmillan.

Frowein, C. (2008 [1941]) *Vier Eeuwen Kleeding in Nederland*, Utrecht: Spectrum.

Geuze, S. (2012) 'Spijkerdoek Is Niet Alleen Goed' in *Nederlands Dagblad*, 30 November.

Gilmore, J. and J. Pine (2007) *Authenticity: What Consumers Really Want*, Boston: Harvard Business School Press.

Gimeno Martinez, J.C. (2006) 'The Role of the Creative Industries in the Construction of Regional/European Identities (1975–2002): Design and Fashion in Belgium and Spain', Leuven: KU Leuven, doctoral dissertation.

Gimeno Martinez, J.C. (2008) 'Fashion, Country and City: The Fashion Industry and the Construction of Collective Identities (1981–2001)' in *Symposium 1: Modus Operandi*, Antwerp: MoMu.

Giroux, H. (1994) 'Consuming Social Change: The "United Colors of Benetton"' in *Cultural Critique*, (26): 5-32.

Goedkoop, H. and K. Zandvoort (2012) *De Gouden Eeuw: Proeftuin van onze Wereld*, Zutphen: Walburg Pers.

Goldgar, A. (2007) *Tulipmania: Money, Honour and Knowledge in the Dutch Golden Age*, Chicago: Chicago University Press.

Goodrum, A. (2005) *The National Fabric: Fashion, Britishness, Globalisation*, Oxford/New York: Berg.

Grabher, G. (2003) 'Switching Ties, Recombining Teams: Avoiding Lock-In Through Project Organization?' in G. Fuchs and P. Shapira (eds), *Rethinking Regional Innovation and Change: Path Dependency or Regional Breakthrough?*, Dordrecht: Kluwer.

Grijpma, D. (2001) *Ich bin ein Mantelmann: Duits-Joodse confectionairs in de Amsterdamse Kledingindustrie 1933–1968*, Zutphen: Walburg Pers.

Groeneweg, I. (1995) 'Regenten in het Zwart: Vroom en Deftig?' in *Nederlandsch Kunsthistorisch Jaarboek*, 46: 198-251.

Gundtoft, D. (2013) *Fashion Scandinavia: Contemporary Cool*. London: Thames and Hudson.

Hahn, B. (2009) 'Cora Kemperman: "Dat Ik Zwart Draag Is Gemakzucht"' in *Elsevier*, September: 138.

Hall, S. (1997) 'The Spectacle of the "Other"' in S. Hall (ed), *Cultural Representations and Signifying Practices*, London: SAGE.

Hall, S. (2002) 'Whose Heritage? Un-Settling "The Heritage", Re-imagining the Post-Nation' in R. Araeen, S. Cubitt, and Z. Sardar (eds), *The Third Text Reader on Art, Culture and Theory*, London/New York: Continuum.

Haraway, D. (1991 [1985]) 'A Cyborg Manifesto: Science, Technology and Socialist-Feminism in the Late Twentieth Century', reprinted in D. Haraway, *Simians, Cyborgs, and Women: The Reinvention of Nature*, London: Free Association Books.

Hartkamp-Jonxis, E. (1987) *Sits: Oost-West Relaties in Textiel*, Zwolle: Waanders.

Hartley, J., J. Potts, T. Flew, S. Cunningham, M. Keane, and J. Banks (2012) *Key Concepts in Creative Industries*, London: SAGE.

Hemels, J. and R. Vegt (1997) *Het Geïllustreerde Tijdschrift in Nederland: Bron van Kennis en Vermaak, Lust voor het Oog: Bibliografie, 2 (1945-1995), part A (Lemmata A-L)*, Amsterdam: Cramwinckel.

Hesmondhalgh, D. (2013) *The Cultural Industries* (3rd ed.), London: SAGE.

Hesselink, H.J. (2010) *Strategische Besluitvorming in een Neergaande Bedrijfstak*, Delft: Eburon Academic Publishers.

Heymans, M. (1997) 'Max Heymans: Verfijning, Elegantie en Humor' in *Algemeen Nederlands Persbureau ANP*, 20 September.

Hill, A. (2005) 'People Dress so Badly Nowadays: Fashion and Late Modernity' in C. Breward and C. Evans (eds), *Fashion and Modernity*, Oxford/New York: Berg.

Hobsbawm, E. and T. Ranger (eds) (1983) *The Invention of Tradition*, Cambridge/New York: Cambridge University Press.

Hol, E. (2013) 'Designer Denim Rukt Op' in *Spits*, 3 January.

Hooimeijer, M. (2001) 'Perfectionist met Passie: Rattan Chadha wil het Mooiste en het Beste' in *Forum*, 7 (17): 18-21.

Hülsken, M. (2006) '*Margriet*' in M. van Delft and N. van Dijk (eds), *Magazine! 150 Jaar Nederlandse Publiekstijdschriften*, Zwolle: Waanders.

Husic, M. and M. Cicic (2009) 'Luxury Consumption Factors' in *Journal of Fashion Marketing and Management*, 13 (2): 231-45.

Husslage, K. (2011) 'Interview: Spijkers en Spijkers' in *Sprout* (retrieved through http://www.sprout.nl/artikel/internationaal/interview-spijkers-spijkers on 3 October 2014).

Huygen, F. (2007) *Visies op Vormgeving*, Amsterdam: Architectura & Natura Pers.

International Monetary Fund (2014) 'World Economic Outlook Database' (retrieved through http://www.imf.org/external/pubs/ft/weo/2014/01/weodata/index.aspx on 3 October 2014).

International Monetary Fund / Saxion (2006) *Competitiveness of the EU textile, clothing, leather, shoe and furniture industries*, Brussels, study for the EU Commission.

Jacobs, D. (2010) 'Looking Good or Being Fashionable?' in *Fashion: Sustainability and Creativity*, Taipei: Fu Jen Catholic University, conference proceedings IFFTI.

Jacobs, D. (2011a) 'Niet Één Nederlandse Mode-identiteit, maar Twee!' at *Amsterdam International Fashion Week*. Expert Meeting: Labelling Dutch, 28 January, presentation.

Jacobs, D. (2011b) 'The Quest For Further Growth and a Firmer Basis: Spijkers en Spijkers' Ambitions' in J. Teunissen and H. van der Voet (eds), *Spijkers en Spijkers*, Arnhem: d'jonge Hond/ArtEZ press.

Jacobs, D. (2011c) 'Fashion and National Identity: The Case of the Netherlands', unpublished draft paper, used by permission of the author.

Jacobs, D. (2013) *Adding Values: The Cultural Side of Innovation*, London/New York: Routledge.

Janssen, S. (2006) 'Fashion Reporting in Cross-National Perspective 1955–2005' in *Poetics*, 34 (6): 383–406.

Jensen, L. (2004) 'Geheel aan de Vrouwelijke Kunne Toegewijd: Nederlandse Vrouwentijdschriften in de Achttiende en Negentiende eeuw' in A. Sens (ed), *Van Zeep tot Soap*, Amsterdam: Persmuseum.

Jensen, L. (2012) 'Bluejeans, van armoebroek naar wereldfaam' in *BN/De Stem*, 1 December.

Joosten, C. (2004) '"Wij Waren de Eersten met Witte Streepjes"' in *Elsevier*, 18 December: 202-207.

Kanteman, C.A., C. Kemperman, E. Lamaker, and P. Mertz (1988) *Stylist (m/v) Ont(k)leed*, Amsterdam: Stichting Kennistransfer Mr. Koetsier.

Kattenburg, A. and M. Verdenius (1959) *Met de Regen als Vriend ...: Herinneringen uit een Halve Eeuw Regenkledingindustrie*, commemorative book published on the occasion of the 50th anniversary of Hollandia Kattenburg N.V., 15 January 1909–1959.

Kawamura, Y. (2005) *Fashion-ology. An Introduction to Fashion Studies*, Oxford/New York: Berg.

Kelly, K. (2010) *What Technology Wants*, London: Penguin Books.

Kemperman, C. (2002) *Mission Statement*, Sleeuwijk: ˉCoraKemperman.

Khan, N. (2000) 'Catwalk Politics' in S. Bruzzi and P. Church Gibson (eds), *Fashion Cultures: Theories, Explorations and Analysis*, London/New York: Routledge.

Klein, Y. (1961) 'The Chelsea Hotel Manifesto' in G. Perlein and B. Corà (eds), *Yves Klein: Long Live the Immaterial!*, Nice: Musée d'Art Moderne et d'Art Contemporain.

Kniese, M. (2001) *Maatschappelijk Verantwoord Ondernemen in de Productieketen van T-shirts*, Consumentenbond: Afdeling Onderzoek.

Kok, G. (2006) *Lezing van Gloria Kok tijdens Landelijke India Werkgroep*, Utrecht, speech, 13 May.

Koning, G. (2010) 'Nederlands eerste Couturier' in *Elsevier*, 17 February, 66 (7): 108.

Koning, G. (2013) 'Gewaden van een andere Planeet' in *Het Parool*, sectie Amsterdam, 24 January.

Koolhaas-Grosfeld, E. (2010) *De Ontdekking van de Nederlander: In Boeken en Prenten rond 1800*, Zutphen: Walburg Pers.

Köppchen, A. (2014) 'Mind the Gap: Balancing Design and Global Manufacturing in Dutch Fashion', Nijmegen: Radboud University, doctoral dissertation (accessible through http://repository.ubn.ru.nl/ bitstream/handle/2066/129879/129879. pdf?sequence=1).

Kops, H. (2010) 'Love for Denim' in *Proud Magazine*: 10-13.

Kosterman, R. (2005) 'Ik Wilde Mexx Leiden als een Computerbedrijf' in *Elsevier*, 9 March.

Kosters, B. (n.d.) 'Is that a cock or your legs?' (retrieved through www.baskosters.com/ webshop/product/cock-or-your-legs on 12 February 2016).

Kromer, F. (2012) 'Het Bewogen Leven van Max Heymans' in *Nieuw Israëlietisch Weekblad*, 7 April.

KSA, Kurt Salmon Associates (1982) *Richtlijnen voor een beleidsplan voor de kleding- en tricotage industrie*, policy report.

KWW, Krekel van der Woerd Wouterse BV (1972) *De Nederlandse Kledingindustrie in Perspectief: Eindrapport van de Eerste Fase van het Perspectief Onderzoek Confectie-industrie*, policy report.

Kuijpers, K. (2003) 'Een Artistiek Stelletje' in *Algemeen Dagblad*, 11 October: 2.

Kuijpers, K. (2009) 'G-Star: Groei zonder Glitter' in *Het Financiële Dagblad*, 11 April.

Kuitenbrouwer, J. (1985) 'De Van Gils-man Zou de Kruisraket Zeker een Mooi Kleurtje Geven' in *De Volkskrant*, 21 September.

Kwant, E. (ed) (2006) *Het Tijdschriftenboek*, Zwolle/Den Haag: Waanders and Koninklijke Bibliotheek.

Lampe, B. (2005) 'Mode houdt je...' in *Het Parool*, interview, PS van de Week, 6 August: 2.

Lampe, B. (2011) 'De Man Achter Modemerk Vanilia' (retrieved through http://www. bregjelampe.nl/de-man-achter-modemerk-vanilia on 16 October 2012).

Lampe, B. (2012) 'Nederland Denimland' in *De Volkskrant*, December 8.

Lampe, B. (2014) 'Rauwe Kracht' in *De Volkskrant Magazine*, 28 June.

Lampe, B. (2015) "Prêt à Paris", interview with Iris van Herpen in *Holland Herald*, June 2015: 30-41.

Land, R.F. (1999) 'Van Hiërarchie naar Zelfsturing en Partnership', Enschede: University of Twente, doctoral dissertation.

Lane, C. and J. Probert (2006) 'Domestic Capabilities and Global Production Networks in the Clothing Industry: A Comparison of German and UK Firms' Strategies' in *Socio-Economic Review*, 4 (1): 35-67.

Lane, C. and J. Probert (2009) *National Capitalisms, Global Production Network: Fashioning the Value Chain in the UK, USA, and Germany*, New York: Oxford University Press.

Laver, J. (1996 [1969]) *Costume and Fashion: A Concise History*, London: Thames & Hudson.

Lawler, S. (2008) *Identity: Sociological Perspectives*, Cambridge: Polity Press.

Lechner, F. (2008) *The Netherlands: Globalization and National Identity*, New York: Routledge.

Leeflang, G. (2010) 'Claudia Sträter Vult Witte Vlek in Apeldoorn' in *De Stentor*, 23 December.

Lehmann, U. (2002) 'Fashion Photography' in U. Lehmann (ed), *Chic Clicks*, Boston: The Institute of Contemporary Art and Hatje Cantz Publishers.

Leistra, M. (2012) 'Oudjes Scoren bij Claudia Sträter' in *Brabants Dagblad*, 1 May.

Levelt, M. (2010) 'Global Trade and the Dutch Hub: Understanding Variegated Forms of Embeddedness of International Trade in the Netherlands: Clothing, Flowers, and High-Tech Products', University of Amsterdam, doctoral dissertation.

Lipovetsky, G. (1994 [1987]) *The Empire of Fashion: Dressing Modern Democracy*, New Jersey: Princeton University Press.

Lipovetsky, G. (2005) *Hypermodern Times*, Cambridge: Polity Press.

Lipovetsky, G. (2007) 'Modern and Postmodern Luxury' in J. Teunissen and J. Brand (eds), *Fashion & Accessories*, Arnhem: Terra Lannoo.

Little, D. (1996) *Vintage Denim*, Salt Lake City: Gibbs Smith.

Little, D. (2007) *Denim: An American Story*, Atglen: Schiffer.

Macgregor Wise, J. (2005) 'Assemblage' in C. Stivale (ed), *Gilles Deleuze: Key Concepts*, Bucks: Acumen.

Maffesoli, M. (1996) *The Times of the Tribes: The Decline of Individualism in Mass Society*, London: SAGE.

Martin, J.J. (2011) 'Shanghai Surprise' in *Wallpaper*, November: 97-100.

Massumi, B. (1992) *A User's Guide to Capitalism and Schizophrenia: Deviations from Deleuze and Guattari*, Cambridge/London: MIT Press.

Mattila, H.R. (2006) *Intelligent Textiles and Clothing*, Boca Raton: CRC Press.

Mayring, P. (2000) 'Qualitative Inhaltsanalyse' in *Forum Qualitative Sozialforschung/Forum: Qualitative Social Research*, 1 (2).

McDowell, C. (2000) *Fashion Today*, London: Phaidon.

McIlveen, V. (2003) 'Interview with Adriano Goldschmied' in *Denim Specialist*, March 20.

McLellan, T., H. Daanen, and S. Cheung (2013) 'Encapsulated Environment' in *Comprehensive Physiology*, 3: 1363-91.

McLuhan, M. (2002 [1964]) *Understanding Media: The Extensions of Man*, London: Routledge.

Meij, I. (2000) 'Relaties: Mode en Streekdracht' in G. Arnolli et al. (eds), *Kostuum. Relaties: Mode en Streekdracht*, Amsterdam: Nederlandse Kostuumvereniging.

Melchior, M.R. (2010) '"Doing" Danish Fashion: On National Identity and Design Practices of a Small Danish Fashion Company' in *Fashion Practice: The Journal of Design, Creative Process & the Fashion Industry*, 2 (1): 13-40.

Melchior, M.R. (2011) 'Catwalking the Nation: Challenges and Possibilities in the Case of the Danish Fashion Industry' in *Culture Unbound: Journal of Current Cultural Research*, 3 (6): 55-70.

Melchior, M.R. (2011) 'From Design Nations to Fashion Nations? Unpacking Contemporary Scandinavian Fashion Dreams' in *Fashion Theory: The Journal of Dress, Body & Culture* 15 (2): 177-200.

Melchior, M.R., L. Skov, and F.F. Csaba (2011) 'Translating Fashion into Danish' in *Culture Unbound: Journal of Current Cultural Research* 3: 209–228.

Mexx (1991) *Global Locals*, Houten.

Mexx International (1987) *Mexx, a Lifestyle*, Wassenaar.

Micheels, P. (2009) 'Regenjassen en Oorlogsleed' in *Ons Amsterdam* (3).

Miller, D. (1990) 'Persons and Blue Jeans: Beyond Fetishism' in *Etnofoor*, 3 (1): 97-113.

Miller, D. (2005) 'Introduction' in S. Küchler and D. Miller (eds), *Clothing as Material Culture*, Oxford/New York: Berg.

Miller, D. (2011) *Global Denim*, Oxford/New York: Berg.

Miller, D. and S. Woodward (2007) 'Manifesto for a Study of Denim' in *Social Anthropology*, 15 (3): 335-51.

Mirande, R. (2008) 'Van Gils Durft Weer Brutaal te Zijn' in *Adformatie*, 23 October: 38.

MODINT (2004) *Grand Seigneur 2004 voor Rattan Chadha (Mexx)*, Zeist, jury's report.

Montagne, C. (2011) *How to Dress Like a French Woman: The Beginner's Guide to Dressing Classic, Chic, Sexy and Elegant Just Like the French*, e-book: Amazon Direct Publishing.

Moons, A. (2008) 'To Be (in) or not to Be (in): The Constituting Processes and Impact Indicators of the Flemish Designer Fashion Industry Undressed' in *Symposium 1: Modus Operandi State of Affairs in Current Research on Belgian Fashion*, Antwerp: MoMu.

Muggleton, D. (2000) *Inside Subculture: The Postmodern Meaning of Style*, Oxford/New York: Berg.

Müller, J. (2002) *Het Verhaal van Cora Kemperman*, Wormerveer: Mercurius.

Mumby-Croft, S. (2010) 'London Fashion Week S/S 2011 Catwalk Review: Spijkers & Spijkers' (retrieved through http://www.ameliasmagazine.com/fashion/london-fashion-week-ss-2011-catwalk-review-spijkers-spijkers/2010/09/19/ on 1 October 2014).

Narinx, C. (2014) 'En Toen Was er Denim' in *ELLE Denimbijbel*, Summer.

Negrin, L. (2008) *Appearance and Identity: Fashioning the Body in Postmodernity*, London/New York: Palgrave MacMillan.

Negrin, L. 'Fashion as an Embodied Art Form' in E. Barrett and B. Bolt (eds.) *Carnal Knowledge: Towards a "New Materialism" through the Arts*. London: I.B.Tauris: 141-154.

Neisser, U. (1988) 'Five Kinds of Self-knowledge' in *Philosophical Psychology*, 1 (1): 35-56.

Newman, A.J. and D. Patel (2004) 'The Marketing Directions of Two Fashion Retailers' in European Journal of Marketing, 38 (7): 770-89.

Niedermann, R., E. Wyss, S. Annaheim, A. Psikuta, S. Davey, and R.M. Rossi (2014) 'Prediction of Human Core Body Temperature Using Non-invasive Measurement Methods' in *International Journal of Biometeorology*, 58 (1): 7-15.

Niessen, S. (1998) 'Joanne Eicher, *Dress and Ethnicity [...]*', *Anthropologica* Vol. XL (1) 129-131.

Niessen, S. (2005) 'The Prism of Fashion: Temptation, Resistance and Trade' in J. Teunissen and J. Brand (eds), *Global Fashion, Local Tradition: On the Globalisation of Fashion*, Arnhem: Terra Lannoo.

Noordhoek, C. and B. Zwartepoorte (n.d.) 'Studio Jux', video, The Green Fashion Competition Season 2 (retrieved through https://vimeo.com/36131820 on 16 February 2016).

O'Sullivan, S. (2006) *Art Encounters Deleuze and Guattari: Thought Beyond Representation*, London/New York: Palgrave Macmillan.

Okonkwo, U. (2007) *Luxury Fashion Branding*, London: Palgrave Macmillan.

Olde Monninkhof, E. (2012) Personal Email, August 15.

Olsthoorn-Roosen, M. and D. Michielsen (1992) *Over Kinderkleren*, De Bilt: Cantecleer.

orson + bodil (2013) 'Frequently Asked Questions to Alexander', 25 September (retrieved through http://www.orson-bodil.com/news/frequently-asked-questions-to-alexander on 12 February 2016).

Pakhchyan, S. (2008) *Fashioning Technology: A DIY Intro to Smart Crafting*, Sebastopol: Make Books.

Pakhchyan, S. (2012) 'TECHNOSENSUAL Review + Interview with Anouk Wipprecht', blog post in fashioningtech, 12 November (retrieved through http://fashioningtech.com/profiles/blogs/technosensual-review-interview-with-anouk-wipprecht on 12 February 2016).

Park, D.J., S. Deshpande, B. Cova, and S. Pace (2007) 'Seeking Community Through Battle: Understanding the Meaning of Consumption Processes for Warhammer Gamers' Communities Across Borders' in B. Cova, R.V. Kozinets and A. Shankar (eds), *Consumer Tribes*, Oxford: Butterworth-Heinemann.

Paulicelli, E. and H. Clark (eds) (2009) *The Fabric of Cultures: Fashion, Identity and Globalization*, New York: Routledge.

Payne, A.F., K. Storbacka, and P. Frow (2008) 'Managing the Co-creation of Value' in *Journal of the Academy Marketing Science*, 36: 83-96.

Pels, D. (2010) 'Het Was Helemaal Mis bij Mexx' in *Trouw*, 28 August.

Perlein, G. (2000) 'Given a Monochrome...' in G. Perlein and B. Corà (eds), *Yves Klein: Long Live the Immaterial!*, Nice: Musée d'Art Moderne et d'Art Contemporain.

Perlein, G. and B. Corà (eds) (2000) *Yves Klein: Long Live the Immaterial!*, Nice: Musée d'Art Moderne et d'Art Contemporain.

Persad, R. (2013) 'Marlies Dekkers: Declared Bankrupt by Rotterdam Court' in *Troubled Company Reporter – Europe* (14), 30 September.

Petro, G. (2012) 'The Future of Fashion Retailing: The Zara Approach (Part 2 of 3)'. (retrieved through http://www.forbes.com/ sites/gregpetro/2012/10/25/the-future-of-fashion-retailing-the-zara-approach-part-2-of-3 on 22 September 2014).

Phelps, N. (2013) 'Viktor&Rolf Fall 2013 Couture: Review' in *Style.com*, 3 July (retrieved through http://www.style.com/fashion-shows/ fall-2013-couture/viktor-rolf on 26 September 2014).

Plas, R. (1986) *20 Seizoenen Mac&Maggie: Van 1976 tot 1986*, Rijswijk.

Plate, L. and A. Smelik (eds) (2009) *Technologies of Memory in Art and Popular Culture*, Basingstoke: Palgrave Macmillan.

Plate, L. and A. Smelik (eds) (2013) *Performing Memory in Art and Popular Culture*, New York: Routledge.

Pleij, H. (1991) *Het Nederlandse Onbehagen*, Amsterdam: Prometheus.

Pleij, H. (2010) '*Moet Kunnen': Een Kleine Mentaliteitsgeschiedenis van de Nederlander*, Diemen: Veen Magazines.

Polhemus, T. (1994) *Streetstyle: From Sidewalk to Catwalk*, London: Thames & Hudson.

Polhemus, T. (2005) 'What to Wear in the Global Village?' in J. Teunissen and J. Brand (eds), *Global Fashion: Local Tradition: On the Globalisation of Fashion*, Arnhem: Terra Lannoo.

Prahalad, C.K. and V. Ramaswamy (2002) 'The Co-Creation Connection' in *Strategy and Business*, 27: 50-61.

Prahalad, C.K. and V. Ramaswamy (2004) 'Co-Creation Experiences: The Next Practice in Value Creation' in *Journal of Interactive Marketing*, 18 (3): 5-14.

Prak, M. and J.L. van Zanden (2013) *Nederland en het Poldermodel: De Economische en Sociale Geschiedenis van Nederland. 1000-2000*, Amsterdam: Bert Bakker.

Probe, A. and U. Wollenschläger (2009) 'Der Purpurne Faden' in *Textilwirtschaft*, 49 (20).

Quinn, B. (2002) *Techno Fashion*, Oxford/New York: Berg.

Quinn, B. (2010) *Textile Futures: Fashion, Design and Technology*, Oxford/New York: Berg.

Quinn, B. (2012) *Fashion Futures*. London: Merrell.

Raes, S. (2000) *Migrating Enterprise and Migrant Entrepreneurship: How Fashion and Migration have Changed the Spatial Organisation of Clothing Supply to Dutch Consumers*, Amsterdam: Het Spinhuis.

Righart, H. (1995) *De Eindeloze Jaren Zestig: Geschiedenis van een Generatieconflict*, Amsterdam: De Arbeiderspers.

Robertson, R. (1992) *Globalization: Social Theory and Global Culture*, London: SAGE.

Robertson, R. (1995) 'Glocalization: Time-Space and Homogeneity-Heterogeneity' in: M. Featherstone, S. Lash, and R. Robertson (eds.), *Global Modernities*, London: SAGE: 25-44.

Rocamora, A. and A. Smelik (eds) (2016) *Thinking Through Fashion: A Guide to Key Theorists*, London: I.B.Tauris.

Rooijakkers, G. (1998) 'Dragers van Traditie? Klederdracht als Culturele Constructie' in D. Verhoeven (ed), *Klederdracht en Kleedgedrag: Het Kostuum Harer Majesteits Onderdanen, 1898-1998*, Nijmegen: SUN.

Rowley, J., B. Kupiec-Teahan, and E. Leeming (2007) 'Consumer Community and Co-Creation: A Case Study' in *Marketing Intelligence & Planning*, 25 (2): 136-46.

Rubinstein, R. (2001) *Dress Codes*, Boulder: Westview.

Ruigrok Netpanel (2008) *Second Site/Denim*, market research report.

Said, E. (1979 [1978]) *Orientalism*, New York: Vintage Books.

Saxion (2012) *Study on the European textiles and clothing industry*, led by M. Scheffer. Brussels, study for the EU Commission (retrieved through http://ec.europa.eu/ enterprise/sectors/textiles/documents/ index_en.htm#h2-4 on 28 January 2015).

Schama, S. (1987) *The Embarrassment of Riches: An Interpretation of Dutch Culture in the Golden Age*, New York: Knopf.

Scheffer, M. (1990) *Kijken naar de Toekomst: De Positie van de Nederlandse Kledingindustrie in de Jaren '90*, policy report.

Scheffer, M. (1992) 'Trading Places, Fashion, Retailers and the Changing Geography of Clothing Production', Utrecht University, doctoral dissertation.

Scheffer, M. (1994a) *Patronen voor Morgen: Een Perspectief voor Nederlandse Confectie- en Tricotage-ondernemingen*, Amsterdam, policy report.

Scheffer, M. (1994b) *The Changing Map of European Textiles: Production Policies of EC Textiles and Clothing Firms*, Brussels, policy report.

Scheffer, M. (2009) 'Fashion Design and Technologies in a Global Context' in E. Paulicelli and H. Clark (eds), *Fabric of Cultures: Fashion, Identity and Globalization*, Routledge, New York: 128-144.

Scheffer, M. (2009) 'Fatal Clusters Tilburg: The Evolutionary Pathway of the Tilburg Wool Industry' in H. Mommaes et al. (eds), *Comeback Cities*, Rotterdam: NAI Publishers.

Scheffer, M. (2012) 'Growth Regimes and Innovation in the Current Decade' in R. Shishoo (ed), *The Global Textile and Clothing Industry*, Cambridge: Woodhead Publishing.

Scheffer, M. and M. Duineveld (2004) 'Final Demise or Regeneration? The Dutch Case' in *Journal of Fashion Marketing and Management*, 8 (3): 340-349.

Schenk, W. (1995) 'Mac en Maggie en de Strijd om het Bestaan: Trendsetter van Weleer is op Drift Geraakt' in *De Volkskrant*, 23 September: 6.

Schippers, R. (1988) *Inkopen voor Mac & Maggie*, internal report.

Schoots, E. (1995) 'Er Is Meer tussen Mantelpak en Spijkerbroek: De Grote Ontwerpers Vertaald' in *NRC Handelsblad*, 3 August.

Schriemer, R. (2013) 'Mode' in *Leeuwarder Courant*, 18 May: 4.

Schuyt, K. and E. Taverne (2004) *1950: Prosperity and Welfare: Dutch Culture in a European Perspective, Vol. 4*, Basingstoke: Palgrave Macmillan.

Scotch & Soda (n.d.) *Let's Talk About Denim* (retrieved through http://www.scotch-soda.com

Scott, J. (2012) *Lessons from Madame Chic: 20 Stylish Secrets I Learned While Living in Paris*, New York: Simon & Schuster.

Segre Reinach, S. (2011) 'National Identities and International Recognition' in *Fashion Theory: The Journal of Dress, Body & Culture*, 15 (2): 267-72.

Sennett, R. (2008) *The Craftsman*, London: Penguin Books.

Seymour, S. (2009) *Fashionable Technology: The Intersection of Design, Fashion, Science and Technology*, Vienna: Springer.

Seymour, S. (2010) *Functional Aesthetics: Visions in Fashionable Technology*, Vienna: Springer.

Sheffield, G. and K. Bush (2008) 'Preface' in C. Evans and S. Frankel (eds), *The House of Viktor & Rolf*, London/New York: Merrell.

Shinkle, E. (ed) (2008) *Fashion as Photograph: Viewing and Reviewing Images of Fashion*, London/New York: I.B.Tauris.

Sim, S. (ed) (1998) *The Icon Critical Dictionary of Postmodern Thought*, Cambridge: Icon Books.

Simmel, G. (1904) 'Fashion', reprinted in *The American Journal of Sociology* (1957), 62 (6): 541-58.

Simmel, G. (1919) 'Die Mode' in *Philosophische Kultur*, Leipzig: Alfred Kröner Verlag.

Simon Thomas, M. (2008) *Dutch Design: A History*, London: Reaktion Books.

Simons, M., F. Koning, and C. van Dooren (1995) *Aangekleed, Uitgekleed: Consumentenwijzer over Kleding*, Amsterdam: Alternatieve Konsumenten Bond.

Skov, L. (2011) 'Dreams of Small Nations in a Polycentric Fashion World' in *Fashion Theory: The Journal of Dress, Body & Culture*, 15 (2), 137-56.

Skov, L. and M.R. Melchior (2011) 'Letter from the Editors' in *Fashion Theory: The Journal of Dress, Body & Culture* 15 (2): 133–36.

Smelik, A. (2004) 'Zwemmen in het asfalt: het behagen in de visuele cultuur' in *Tijdschrift voor Communicatiewetenschap*, 32 (3): 292-304.

Smelik, A. (2006) 'Fashion and Visual Culture' in J. Brand and J. Teunissen (eds), *The Power of Fashion: About Design and Meaning*, Arnhem: Terra, Artez Press: 152-171.

Smelik, A. (2007) 'Het Intermediale Sprookje van de Modeshow' in H. Oosterling, H. Slager, and R. Van De Vall (eds), *Intermediale Reflecties: Kruisbestuivingen en Dwarsverbanden in de Hedendaagse Kunst*, Rotterdam: DAF Cahiers: 64-72.

Smelik, A. (2011) 'The Performance of Authenticity' in *Address: Journal for Fashion Writing and Criticism*, 1 (1): 76-82.

Smelik, A. (2012) *Ik Cyborg: De Mens-machine in Populaire Cultuur* (I Cyborg: The Human-Machine in Popular Culture), Delft: Eburon.

Smelik, A. (2014) 'Fashioning the Fold: Multiple Becomings' in R. Braidotti and R. Dolphijn (eds), *The Deleuzian Century: Art, Activism, Society*, Amsterdam: Brill Rodopi: 35-49.

Smelik, A. (2016) 'Gilles Deleuze: Bodies-without-Organs in the Folds of Fashion' in A. Rocamora and A. Smelik (eds), *Thinking Through Fashion: A Guide to Key Theorists*, London: I.B.Tauris: 164-183.

Smelik, A. and M. Feitsma (2015) 'Jeans: From an American Icon to Dutch Denim' in

C. Decker and A. Böger (eds), *Transnational Mediations. Negotiating Popular Culture between Europe and the United States*. Heidelberg: Universitätsverlag Winter: 73-89.

Smelik, A., L. Toussaint and P. van Dongen (2016), 'Solar Fashion: An Embodied Approach to Wearable Technology' in *International Journal of Fashion Studies* 3 (2): 287-303.

Smith, D. (2012) *Essays on Deleuze*, Edinburgh: University Press.

Solomon, M. and N. Rabolt (2004) *Consumer Behavior in Fashion*, Upper Saddle River: Prentice Hall.

Sommers, S. (1988) *French Chic: How to Dress Like a Frenchwoman*, New York: Villard Books.

Sponselee, M. (2005) '2005 is het Jubileumjaar van Frans Molenaar' in *Amersfoortse Courant*, 28 April.

Stahl, G. (2003) 'Tastefully Renovating Subcultural Theory: Making Space for a New Model' in D. Muggleton and R. Weinzierl (eds), *The Post-Subcultures Reader*, Oxford/New York: Berg.

Stamkot, S. (2012) 'Nederland Denimland' in *Spits*, 26 November.

Staps, F. (2007) 'Bomvolle Straten, Maar Bij Mexx Bleef het Stil' in *NRC Handelsblad*, 1 September: 21.

Steele, V. (1988) *Paris Fashion*, New York: Oxford University Press.

Studio JUX (n.d.) 'Find your tailor' (retrieved through www.studiojux.com/handshake on 16 February 2016).

Studio JUX (n.d.) 'My Nepali tailor is a Rockstar' (retrieved through: http://shop. studiojux.com/rockstar on 16 February 2014).

Sturken M. and L. Cartwright (2001) *Practices of Looking: An Introduction to Visual Culture*, Oxford: Oxford University Press.

Sullivan, J. (2006) *Jeans: A Cultural History of an American Icon*, New York: Gotham Books.

Svendsen, L. (2006) *Fashion: A Philosophy*, London: Reaktion.

Taminiau, J. in s.n. (2013) '"Als kind was ik al anders dan de anderen"', interview in *Het Financiële Dagblad*, 14 December: 18.

Tan, A. (2009) Column 'Emotional catsuit' in *NRC*, May, 16.

Tap, R. (1986) 'Afstudeeronderzoek naar Turkse ateliers in de loonconfectie in Amsterdam', University of Groningen, MA thesis.

Teunissen, J. (1990) '*Margriet* en *Avenue* als Modemakers' in P. Terreehorst (ed), *Modus: Over Mensen, Mode en het Leven*, Amsterdam: De Balie.

Teunissen, J. (1994) 'Mode in Parijs: "Made in Holland"' in *NRC*, March 3.

Teunissen, J. (2005) 'Introduction' in J. Teunissen and J. Brand (eds), *Global Fashion: Local Tradition: On the Globalisation of Fashion*, Arnhem: Terra Lannoo.

Teunissen, J. (2006) 'Frans Molenaar' in J. Teunissen (ed), *Mode in Nederland*, Arnhem: Terra.

Teunissen, J. (2006) *Mode in Nederland*, Arnhem: Terra Lannoo.

Teunissen, J. (2008) 'The Netherlands' in L. Skov (ed), *Berg Encyclopedia of World Dress and Fashion. Vol 8: West Europe*, Oxford/New York: Berg.

Teunissen, J. (2009) 'The Dutchman Exists' in *Gone with the Wind*, Enkhuizen: Zuiderzee Museum.

Teunissen, J. (2015) 'Everything but Clothes: The Connection Between Fashion Photography and Magazines' in J. Lamoree, J. Teunissen, and H. Van Der Voet (eds.), *Everything but Clothes: Fashion, Photography, Magazines*, Arnhem/Houten: Terra Lannoo / ArtEZ Press.

Teunissen, J. and H. van der Voet (2011) *Spijkers en Spijkers*, Arnhem: d'jonge Hond / ArtEZ Press.

Teunissen, J. and I. van Zijl (2000) *Droog and Dutch Design*, Utrecht: Centraal Museum.

The Makers (2012) 'Philosophy' (retrieved through http://www.the-makers.nl/

TM.asp?taal=EN&breedte=1366 on 1 October 2012).

Thomas, I. and F. Veysset (2013) *Paris Street Style: A Guide to Effortless Chic*, New York: Abrams Image.

Toussaint L. and A. Smelik, 'From Hardware to "Softwear": The Future Memories of Techno-Fashion' in: D. Jaffé and S. Wilson (eds.), *Memories of the Future*, Bern: Peter Lang, 2016.

Tynan, C., S. McKechnie, and C. Chhuon (2010) 'Co-Creating Value for Luxury Brands' in *Journal of Business Research*, 63 (11): 1156–63.

Van de Peer, A. (2014) 'Re-artification in a World of De-artification: Materiality and Intellectualization in Fashion Media Discourse (1949–2010)' in *Cultural Sociology* (retrieved from http://cus.sagepub.com/content/early/2014/07/14/1749975514539799 on 22 May 2016).

Van de Peer, A. (2015) 'Geknipt voor het moderne. Beoordelingscriteria, tijdspolitiek en materialiteit in geschreven modejournalistiek', University of Gent, doctoral dissertation.

Van den Berg, N. (2006) 'Alexander van Slobbe' in J. Teunissen (ed), *Mode in Nederland*, Arnhem: Terra.

Van den Berg, N. (2006) 'Keupr/VanBentm' in J. Teunissen (ed), *Mode in Nederland*, Arnhem: Terra.

Van den Berg, N. (2006) 'The People of the Labyrinths' in J. Teunissen (ed), *Mode in Nederland*, Arnhem: Terra.

Van den Berg, N. (2008) *Alexander van Slobbe*, Arnhem: d'jonge Hond/ArtEZ press.

Van den Boom, I. (2012) 'De Spijkerbroek is het Nederlandse Mao-kostuum' in *Algemeen Dagblad*, November 23.

Van den Brand, A. (1995) 'Trendsetter Zonder Uitverkoop Is Zelf in de Verkoop' in *Trouw*, 2 November.

Van den Broek, W. (2005) 'Claudia Sträter: Een Nederlandse Succesformule' in *FashionUnited*, 1 April.

Van Grinsven, J. (1988) '"Van Gils is Merk-waardig"' in *Het Nieuwsblad*, 8 April.

Van Loon, E. (2014) 'Pauze voor Francisco van Benthum: Wel Nieuwe Brillen' in *FashionUnited*, 18 July.

Van Rossum, M. (2000) 'De Royale Rokken van Cora Kemperman' in *De Volkskrant*, 5 August.

Van Rossum, M. (2008) 'Ik Wil Gewoon Dat Mijn Werk Meetelt' in *De Volkskrant Magazine*, 3 May: 40.

Van Rossum, M. (2012) 'Hollands Blauw' in *NRC Handelsblad*, 24 November.

Van Rossum, M. (2013) 'Ik Maak Saaie Kleren' in *NRC Handelsblad, Lux*, 7 December: 13.

Van Rossum, M. (2015) 'Eerste Echte Nederlandse Couturier: Necrologie Frans Molenaar (1940-2015)' in *NRC Handelsblad*, 12 January: 2.

Van Slooten, R. (2009) 'Van Gils: It's all about DNA' in *New Style: modevakmagazine*, 6 (2): 120-121.

Van Zuthem, H. (1987) 'Boeren en Burgers in Katoen' in E. Hartkamp-Jonxis (ed), *Sits: Oost-West Relaties in Textiel*, Zwolle: Waanders.

Veenhoff, J. (2011) 'De Toekomst Lonkt en is Bright Blue' in *PS Magazine*, 1 (1): 34-35.

Vegt, R. (2004) 'Vriendinnen van Papier: Vrouwentijdschriften tussen 1934 en 2003' in A. Sens (ed), *Van Zeep tot Soap*, Amsterdam: Persmuseum.

Vegt, R. (2006) '*Elegance*' in M. van Delft and N. van Dijk (eds), *Magazine! 150 Jaar Nederlandse Publiekstijdschriften*, Zwolle: Waanders.

Veld, M. (2009) 'Amsterdam Denim Brands', 21 December (retrieved through http://www.wgsn.com

Verheyen, Y. (2002) 'Van Grand Seigneur tot Grande Dame: Betaalbare Designkleding van Cora Kemperman' in *Textilia*, January: 43.

Viktor&Rolf (2008) 'For the Moment | Viktor & Rolf' in *T Magazine*, 12 June (retrieved through http://tmagazine.blogs.nytimes.com/2008/06/12/for-the-moment-viktor-rolf on 12 June 2008).

Von Maltzahn, C.F. (2012) 'Shopping for Emotions: "Dutch Luxury" in High-Street Fashion Retail' in J. Berry (ed), *Fashion Capital: Style Economies, Sites and Cultures*, Oxford: Inter-Disciplinary Press.

Von Maltzahn, C.F. (2013) 'Dutch Identity in Fashion: Co-Evolution Between Brands and Consumers', Amsterdam: University of Amsterdam, doctoral dissertation (accessible through http://dare.uva.nl/document/2/123753).

Weller, S. (2004) 'Fashion's Influence on Garment Mass Production: Knowledge, Commodities and the Capture of Value', Melbourne: Victoria University, doctoral dissertation.

Windels, V. (ed.) (2001) *Young Belgian Fashion Design*, Antwerp: Ludion.

Wipprecht, A. (s.n.) 'What Does Fashion Lack? "Microcontrollers"' (retrieved through www.anoukwipprecht.nl on 12 February 2016).

Wishaupt, M. (2006) *'Avenue'* in M. van Delft and N. van Dijk (eds), *Magazine! 150 Jaar Nederlandse Publiekstijdschriften*, Zwolle: Waanders.

Wouters, N. (2012) 'De Draagbare van Benthum' in *NRC Handelsblad Lux*, 28 April.

Wouters, N. (2012) 'Ultra Kort, Skinny en Gekleurd' in *NRC Handelsblad Lux*, 17 March.

Wouters, N. (2013) 'Wees tégen iets!' in *NRC Handelsblad, Lux*, 19 January.

WRR, Wetenschappelijke Raad voor het Regeringsbeleid (2007) *Identificatie met Nederland*, Amsterdam: Amsterdam University Press.

Za, V. and S. Suzzi (2014) 'Italy's Furla Plans Sales Push to Cash in on Affordable Luxury Boom' (retrieved through http://www.reuters.com/article/2014/09/17/us-italy-furla-idUSKBN0HC11C20140917 on 28 September 2014).

List of Illustrations

Fig. 32. Frans Molenaar, image made for fashion show Summer 2013 (95th show); two dresses and cape, inspired by Molenaar's collection 1976. Courtesy Frans Molenaar. Photograph by Sabrina Bongiovanni, art direction by Maarten Spruyt. © Gemeentemuseum The Hague.

Fig. 33. Colourful clothes designed by Cora Kemperman (A/W 2005). © ¯CoraKemperman.

Fig. 34. Bold colours for Mac&Maggie (Summer 1986).

Fig. 35. Oilily: colourful children's clothes (1986). © Oilily.

Fig. 36. Colourful regional dress of the fishermen's village Marken (no year). M. Olsthoorn-Roosen, *Over kinderkleren* (1992).

Fig. 37. Women's collection by Oilily (A/W 2008). Photograph by Peter Stigter.

Fig. 38. Coloured engraving, plate 10 from Evert Maaskamp's book *Images of Clothes, Customs and Traditions in the Batavian Republic* (1804). © Atlas van Stolk, Rotterdam.

Fig. 39. Cora Kemperman, collection 'Jump Around the World' (A/W 2010). © ¯CoraKemperman.

Fig. 40. Regional wear from fishermen's village Marken. Gouache made by Jan Duyvetter, 1948. © Nederlands Openluchtmuseum.

Fig. 41. Cover of *Oilily magazine* (A/W 1993–4). © Oilily.

Fig. 42. Cover of *Oilily magazine* (A/W 1994–5). © Oilily.

Fig. 43. Cover of magazine *Mac&Maggie* (Summer 1986).

Fig. 44. Image from the book *20 Seasons Mac&Maggie* (1986).

Fig. 45. JANTAMINIAU, Mailbag jackets (2009). Photograph by Peter Stigter.

Fig. 46. JANTAMINIAU, Couture Collection (S/S 2013). Photograph by Peter Stigter.

Fig. 47. JANTAMINIAU, Couture Collection (S/S 2014). Photograph by Duy Vo.

Fig. 48. The cover of a vinyl record with an ad to celebrate ten years of Levi's in the Netherlands.

Fig. 49. Jacket by G-sus (A/W 2013–14). Photograph by Peter Stigter.

Fig. 50. Women's jeanswear by Blue Blood (S/S 2009). Photograph by Peter Stigter.

Fig. 51. House of Denim logo (2014). Photograph by Peter Stigter.

Fig. 52. Interior Exhibition *Blue Jeans*, 24 November 2012–10 March 2013. Photograph by Ernst Moritz. © Centraal Museum Utrecht.

Fig. 53. Streetwear during the Amsterdam Denim Days (2015). Photograph by Peter Stigter.

Fig. 54. G-Star shop in Amsterdam (2014). Photograph by Peter Stigter.

Fig. 55. Wolf/van Benthum (S/S 2008). Photograph by Peter Stigter.

Fig. 56. Francisco van Benthum, 'Marlin' (S/S 2014). Photograph by Peter Stigter.

Fig. 57. Francisco van Benthum, 'Marlin' (S/S 2014). Photograph by Peter Stigter.

Fig. 58. Francisco van Benthum (A/W 2014). Photograph by Peter Stigter.

Fig. 59. Advertisement Van Gils Strictly for Men (1990), collection Reclame Arsenaal. © Van Gils Fashion.

Fig. 60. Development of production network Van Gils, 1950s–80s, © Anja Köppchen, 2014.

Fig. 61. Van Gils 'No Stitch No Story' (Van Gils A/W 2014 campaign). © Van Gils Fashion.

Fig. 62. Developments of production networks, Van Gils and The Makers, 1990s–2000s. © Anja Köppchen, 2014.

Fig. 63. Van Gils 'No Stitch No Story' (Van Gils A/W 2014 campaign). © Van Gils Fashion.

Fig. 64. The original C&A shop in 1841 in Sneek, a town in Friesland. © C&A.

Fig. 65. Advertisement for C&A in a newspaper from 1970. © C&A.

Fig. 66. Opening of C&A's flagship store in Amsterdam in October 2015. © C&A.

Fig. 67. Interior C&A shop in Amsterdam (2016). © C&A.

Fig. 68. Interior C&A shop in Amsterdam (2016). © C&A.

Fig. 69. Emanuelle and Moustache catalogues in the 1980s, from N. Chadha (2006) *It Started with a Kiss Twenty Years of Mexx* (Amsterdam BIS Publishers).

Fig. 70. Early Mexx campaign (1980). © Chico Bialas, www.chicobialas.com.

Fig. 71. Organisational structure, Mexx, 2000. © Anja Köppchen, 2014.

Fig. 72. 'One Kiss', Mexx advertisement (2004). © JC Decaux, collection ReclameArsenaal.

Fig. 73. Career paths of interviewees. © Anja Köppchen, 2014.

Fig. 74. Advertisement for the opening of a new shop for Claudia Sträter in Alkmaar (1975). © Regional Archive Alkmaar, Province of Noord-Holland.

Fig. 75. Claudia Sträter, Amsterdam Fashion Week (S/S 2007). Photograph by Peter Stigter.

Fig. 76. Claudia Sträter, Amsterdam Fashion Week (A/W 2010). Photograph by Peter Stigter.

Fig, 77. Claudia Sträter, Campaign 'Art of Fashion' (S/S 2016). Artist Evi Vingerling painted on silk shawls: 'paint à porter'. Photograph by Louise te Poele (2015).

Fig. 78. Detail, shawl 'paint à porter' by Evi Vingerling for Claudia Sträter (S/S 2016).

Fig. 79. A design in striking patterns by Cora Kemperman (S/S 2011). © ¯CoraKemperman.

Fig. 80. Colourful clothes by Mac&Maggie in a typical Dutch scene (year unknown).

Fig. 81. Mac&Maggie (A/W 1986).

Fig. 129. Bas Kosters, 'Blue Velvet Self-Portrait Pantsuit' ('Permanent State of Confusion' collection, A/W 2015). Photograph by Marc Deurloo, © Bas Kosters Studio.

Fig. 130. Bubelle Blush Dress, developed by Lucy McRae for Philips Design, 2006.

Fig. 131. Aynouk Tan wearing 'emotional catsuit'. Photograph by Dennis Duijnhouwer.

Fig. 132. Pauline van Dongen, Shoe 'Morphogenesis' (2010). Photograph by Mike Nicolaassen.

Fig. 133. Pauline van Dongen, 'Wearable Solar Dress' (2013). Photograph by Mike Nicolaassen.

Fig. 134. Iris van Herpen, 'Capriole' (A/W 2011). Photograph by Peter Stigter.

Fig. 135. Iris van Herpen, 'Capriole' (A/W 2011). Photograph by Peter Stigter.

Fig. 136. Bart Hess, 'Slime' (2010). © Bart Hess.

Fig. 137. LucyandBart, 'Exploded View 2' (2010). © Bart Hess.

Fig. 138. Anouk Wipprecht, 'Spider Dress 2.0' (2015). Photograph by Jason Perry, © Anouk Wipprecht.

Fig. 139. Anouk Wipprecht, 'Spider Dress 2.0' (2015). Photograph by Jason Perry, © Anouk Wipprecht.

Fig. 140. Anouk Wipprecht, 'Synapse' (2014). Photograph by Jason Perry, © Anouk Wipprecht.

Fig. 141. Anouk Wipprecht, 'Detail of Synapse' (2014). Photograph by Jason Perry, © Anouk Wipprecht.

Contributors

Daniëlle Bruggeman is a cultural theorist, specialised in research on fashion and identity. She is a lecturer in Art and Fashion Philosophy at the Department of Textile & Fashion of the Royal Academy of Art (KABK) in The Hague. Her most recent research project focused on the Dutch company Vlisco, which designs, produces and distributes wax fabrics for the West- and Central-African market. In 2014 she successfully defended her PhD dissertation 'More Than Meets the Eye: Dutch Fashion, Identity and New Materialism'. She has been a visiting scholar at Parsons, the New School for Design (NYC), and at the London College of Fashion. She has published on topics including the performative power of fashion, Dutch fashion photography, and lingerie as an expression of post-feminist values (see www.daniellebruggeman.nl).

Maaike Feitsma is a lecturer and researcher at the Amsterdam Fashion Institute and the Fashion Masters of ArtEZ Institute of the Arts in Arnhem, where she teaches Fashion History and Fashion Theory. In 2014 she successfully defended her PhD dissertation 'Nederlandse mode: een verkenning van mythevorming en bete-kenissen' ('Dutch Fashion? An exploration of myths and meaning'). Feitsma won the International Foundation of Fashion Technology Institutes (IFFTI) Postgraduate Award in 2011 and the Hermesdorf Young Talent Prize for media attention for her dissertation in 2014.

Anja Köppchen is an interdisciplinary researcher in the fields of human and economic geography, fashion, design and technology. She is a researcher and coach at Cube design museum in Kerkrade (NL), and a graduation coach at the Amsterdam Fashion Institute. In 2014 she successfully defended her PhD dissertation 'Mind the Gap: Balancing Design and Global Manufac-turing in Dutch Fashion'. Her current research focuses on theories of design practice, in particular on design thinking and co-creation.

Constantin-Felix von Maltzahn is a research fellow and assistant professor of consumer behaviour at the Amsterdam Fashion Institute. In 2013 he successfully defended his PhD dissertation 'Dutch Identity in Fashion: The Co-Evolution between Brands and Consumers'. A graduate of the universities of Maastricht and Amsterdam, his doctoral research was in the area of co-creation dynamics and co-evolution between brands and consumers in the Dutch fashion industry. His research interests include brand tribalism and tribal marketing; consumer behaviour and CCT; critical marketing theory; longevity and relevance of recently established 'intermediate' luxury contexts.

Michiel Scheffer is born into a family of textile entrepreneurs. He was research fellow at the London School of Economics and completed his PhD thesis supported by Utrecht University and the University of Manchester (1992). He worked for the Dutch Fashion Industry Association from 1991 till 2000. During this period he was also a guest lecturer at the Amsterdam Fashion Institute and the Institut Français de la Mode. Between 2000 and 2015 he was consultant for international innovation in textiles and creative industries. He combined this with a professorship in textile management at Saxion Universities. He is now the regional Minister for Economy, Education and Europe of the Province of Gelderland.

Anneke Smelik is Katrien van Munster Professor of Visual Culture at the Radboud University Nijmegen, where she is coordinator of the MA programme 'Creative Industries'. Her research focuses on fashion, especially on performance and identity from the perspective of new materialism and Deleuzean thought. She has (co-)edited many books, including *Materializing Memory in Art and Popular Culture* (2017) and *Thinking Through Fashion. A Guide to Key Theorists* (2016). She published widely on issues of identity, body, memory and technology in cinema, videoclips, digital art, and fashion. Anneke Smelik is project leader of the research programme 'Crafting Wearables; Fashionable Technology' (2013–18), funded by the Netherlands Organisation for Scientific Research (see www.annekesmelik.nl).

José Teunissen is Dean of the School of Design and Technology at the London College of Fashion (UAL). She holds a Professorship in Research in the field of Fashion Theory at UAL, is Visiting Professor in Fashion Theory and Research at ArtEZ Institute of the Arts in Arnhem, and works as an independent fashion curator. She is currently a board member of the Dutch Creative Industries Council. She is also chair of the network CLICK/Next Fashion, the governmental innovation network for the creative industries in the Netherlands. In 2015 she realised the Centre of Expertise Future Makers, dedicated to new making processes in fashion and design. She has co-edited many books, including *Everything but Clothes*, 2015; *The Future of Fashion is Now*, 2014; *Fashion Odyssey*, 2013; *Couture Graphique*, 2013; *Fashion and Imagination*, 2009; and *The Art of Fashion*, 2009.

Lianne Toussaint is a PhD candidate at the Department of Cultural Studies of the Radboud University Nijmegen. The central aim of her PhD research is to critically and theoretically reflect on the socio-cultural dimensions of wearable (and in particular 'fashionable') technologies, focusing on their embodied, material, communicative, and ethical dimensions. In 2015 she received a Fulbright Grant for a visiting scholarship at Parsons, the New School for Design in New York. Toussaint holds a MA in Cultural Studies and a MA in Photographic Studies. Her PhD research is part of 'Crafting Wearables; Fashionable Technology' (2013–18), a collaborative research project funded by the Netherlands Organization for Scientific Research (see: www.craftingwearables.com).

Index

Dress cultures

Series Editors: **Reina Lewis** & **Elizabeth Wilson**

Advisory Board: Christopher Breward, Hazel Clark, Joanne Entwistle, Caroline Evans, Susan Kaiser, Angela McRobbie, Hiroshi Narumi, Peter McNeil, Özlem Sandikci, Simona Segre Reinach

Dress Cultures aims to foster innovative theoretical and methodological frameworks to understand how and why we dress, exploring the connections between clothing, commerce and creativity in global contexts.

Reina Lewis: reina.lewis@fashion.arts.ac.uk

Elizabeth Wilson: mail@elizabethwilson.net

At the publisher, **Philippa Brewster:** philippabrewster@gmail.com

www.ingramcontent.com/pod-product-compliance
Lightning Source LLC
Chambersburg PA
CBHW080414270326
41929CB00018B/3019